An Insider's Memoir

How Economics Changed to Work Against Us
From Smith to Marx to Bitcoin

Gordon Bryant Brown

The former CEO of one of Canada's "Best Managed Businesses" observes the failure of capitalism.

 FriesenPress

Suite 300 - 990 Fort St
Victoria, BC, V8V 3K2
Canada

www.friesenpress.com

Copyright © 2018 by Gordon Bryant Brown
First Edition — 2018

All rights reserved.

No part of this publication may be reproduced in any form, or by any means, electronic or mechanical, including photocopying, recording, or any information browsing, storage, or retrieval system, without permission in writing from FriesenPress.

ISBN
978-1-5255-2326-7 (Hardcover)
978-1-5255-2327-4 (Paperback)
978-1-5255-2328-1 (eBook)

1. BUSINESS & ECONOMICS, ECONOMICS

Distributed to the trade by The Ingram Book Company

Contents

Preface 9

1. A person's a person 15
   Adam Smith (1723–1790) 24
   John Maynard Keynes (1883–1946) 34
   Paul Samuelson (1915–2009) 43
   Social contracts 50
   Labour becomes a commodity 55
   Economic differences between the United States and
   Canada 56
   So, what have we learned? 61

2. Noteworthy economists 65
   Karl Marx (1818–1883) 67
      (a) Competition is self-defeating 72
      (b) Capitalism depletes resources 73
      (c) Competition exploits people 74
      (d) The rich will get richer 76
   John Kenneth Galbraith (1908–2006) 78
   John Kenneth Galbraith and the new industrial state 81
   Summary: as the economy changed 83

3. Economics lessons: marijuana, money, Kenya, and aid 87
Drug laws 88
The Cayman Islands: Swimming in money 93
The economics of illegal drugs 94
Kenya and international aid 97
The globalization of poverty 108
Following up on life's lessons? 110

4. Corporations take control 111
Changing public attitudes! 113
Think tanks 116
Global meetings for the elite 123
Privatize everything 128
Highways 130
Water 131
Auto insurance 135
Prisons 135
Health care 137
Post office 138
Profiting from education 141
Changes in law 145
Corporations are not people 146
Intellectual property laws 150
Corporate lobbying 152
Summing up the corporate takeover 154

5. A Change in government financing and the creation of debt 155
The change to government financing 163

How big is the debt? Is it logical?..................................... 167
Political naïveté or deceit? 169
Summary: Government financing created national debt.. 170

6. Money.. 173
Money in America 179
How money is created 184
The Federal Reserve 191
Gold 199
Petrodollars 201
The alchemy of interest 204
Usury and debt 209
Finance: surpassing the real economy............................... 214
Summary... 219

7. Our planet becomes their market....................... 223
Changing Our Assumptions 228
Demonizing labour 234
Changing language.. 239
Let's just say this! 246
Globalization... 248
Secrecy 255
Trade agreements 257
As work declines 262
Summary—what is the Social Contract now?................... 268

8. Voodoo Economics 270
Supply-side economics 273
The Plunge Protection Team 274

    Milton Friedman (1912 –2006) 278
    Monetarism 283
    Financialization 285
    Alan Greenspan 287
    Greg Palast, Investigative Reporter, trained by Milton
    Friedman (1952) 292
    Managing essential services 296
    Government budgets as family budgets 298
    Business in the Voodoo Era 300

9. The subservient role of governments 304
    James K. Galbraith (1952) 306
    The World Bank and the International Monetary Fund .. 310
    Shock Doctrine 314
    Blame the victim 316
    Cooking the books 318
    Derivatives 321
    Betting on food 327
    Summary 330

10. The Corporate State 334
    Executive compensation 338
    Globalization and free trade 342
    Austerity: an idea that keeps on failing 346
    How high can the Dow Jones go? 350
    Haiti, a country abused 352
    Why does poverty exist in wealthy countries? 358
    Greece, robbed in broad daylight! 359
    Lessons from Argentina 366

    Ventures and vultures 368
    Meanwhile, in the Real Economy 370
    What now? 374

11. The 2000s: the system collapses 377
    The economy: 2007–2008 383
    The bubble has burst: now what? 386
    Canadian banks were not immune 393
    What is quantitative easing? 396
    More economics events 401
    When is competitive capitalism to be buried? 407

12. What will replace capitalism? 411
    The wishful search for full employment 419
    Spain 421
    Iceland 423
    Cuba 426
    Policies that serve people 429
    Alternatives to banks and money 431
    Cyber currencies, such as Bitcoin attract speculators 433
    State-owned enterprises (SOE's) 434
    Go Green 435
    Economic democracy 439
    Three writers on economics 443
        Ellen Hodgson Brown *443*
        George Monbiot *447*
        Catherine Austin Fitts *448*
    What else can we do? 452

Appendix **459**
  Economics and the military 461
  Military policy 467
  NAT0 470
  Yugoslavia 1999—a war that paid for itself 471
  Despite the warnings of Butler, Eisenhower, and
  Galbraith 474
  Iraq: pillaging a country 475
  Libya, 2011: protecting the dollar and stealing the oil 484
  The Ukraine: stealing a country's riches 485
  Profiting from war: summary 491

Thanks to those folks who helped with this book: **495**

Bibliography **497**

Gordon Bryant Brown **505**

Some of the images in the book are less than perfect. However they are clear enough to illustrate the point they are making.

Preface

IT'S A STRANGE AFFLICTION.

While most of my friends have hobbies, like golf or motorcycles, mine has been economics.

It's always fascinated me; it determines how we live. I studied economics at university in the late fifties and fortuitously continued to be challenged by it. My early career in business in the mid-sixties was lived in conflict with the fundamentals I had studied in economics. My corporation was involved in non-competition agreements with our competitors.

At that time, I was employed as a sales representative with a major North American corporation. I competed with other sales representatives. Instead of seeing the competitive market at work, our corporation was seeking market stability as a necessity to protect its long-term investment, as the production equipment and plant that housed it were expensive, took years to conceive, plan, and build, and took more years to pay off. A stable market was essential, and the effort to control the market was self-serving.

Competition was an essential base of the bottom of the economic system, and it did exist, between me and the competing sales reps; however, our corporations were being distanced from it. There were agreements and policies that amounted to price fixing, and price fixing changes the fundamental base of the market. For two years, I studied this dichotomy. It became my hobby, and I wrote about it then, as I have again now.

Economics has many definitions, but we will use a simple one: it is the study of how the world's limited resources are shared. Capitalism is one method of sharing, and thus one form of economics, one that has simply evolved. As capitalism emerged as a social system that worked, people lived more secure and increasingly better lives. Capitalism is not simply a neutral economic term. It is a set of political assumptions, as are the assumptions of alternate systems, such as socialism, or fascism. Financialization, as I'll discuss later in the book, is the newest variation and it significantly redefines capitalism.

In 1964, I earned a trip for my prior year's sales success to the Boca Raton Resort in Florida. Thirty years later, the staff at J. P. Morgan would meet in the same hotel and create the concept of derivatives, a new type of Wall Street investment that would precipitate the 2006 financial crisis! (More on that later.)

And then I learned more about the economics of illegal drugs. 1969 was the middle of the hippie era! There was an active and extensive drug subculture in North America, and long-haired kids were at odds with the law. The drug enforcement tactics of the police were unnecessarily alienating young people in both the United States and Canada.

In 1969, the Canadian Government, under Pierre Trudeau, established The Commission of Inquiry into the Non-Medical Use of Drugs, chaired by Gerald Le Dain, a lawyer and dean of one of Canada's most prestigious law schools, Osgoode Hall. Later, Le Dain became a justice of the Supreme Court.

I started a campaign to lobby for more sensible drug laws because of the damage I could see being done to our young people, weakening their trust and belief in law. After a few years of effort, I returned to earning a living, but I had learned the economic issues of the illegal drug market.

I learned about the economics of poor nations by surprise. Because of some volunteer fundraising I had done for international causes, I was asked to go and teach a short session on small business management in Mombasa, Kenya, sponsored by the Kenyan Chamber of Commerce.[1] It was a huge learning experience for me. Our students were people of all ages: men and women, all running their own businesses. They were the brightest, keenest, most capable, hardest-working people I have ever met. The session was deemed so important that it was opened and closed by members of the Kenyan parliament. Our host, the head of the Chamber of Commerce, attended every day. When I returned to Canada, I would recall that session and wonder why we were getting richer in the West, while the bright, capable people in Mombasa were not—it never made sense.

I'll discuss these two diversions in more detail in Chapter Three.

---

1   But paid for by the Foundation for International Training and Development and the Canadian government.

Many years later, as the time neared for me to retire from industry, I began thinking about what to do next. I thought about the drug issue. Although the Le Dain Commission had recommended more sensible drug laws, decades ago, Canada never went down that road. (It seemed our southern neighbour wouldn't allow it.) Looking at the issue anew, from an economic standpoint, I knew the world of illegal drug distribution had grown so much larger: according to the United Nations it was estimated to be US$321.6 billion in 2003 about 1% of all international trade and more dangerous than it had been. The reason it's more dangerous? So much money is being made. I now understand that the purpose of the war on drugs was not to reduce drug use, but to increase its profit. It was an economic issue.

Remembering my other old interest in international development and my experience in Mombasa, I realized that unfair trade practices and the policies of international banks were the issues that kept them poor. But these were not issues I fully understood. Then my strange affliction kicked in. I realized I had not understood much of the economic dialogue for the last couple of decades. Many new terms had emerged, such as "trickle down," "supply side," "monetarism," "neoliberalism." I never understood free trade and free trade agreements—who did they benefit? I didn't understand what derivatives were.

I didn't understand money.

I didn't understand why Canada (like the US) was in so much debt, and more specifically, how we had acquired so much debt in peacetime. Prior to World War II, Canadian federal debt was about $5,000 per person. After the war, it had more than doubled to $12,500, and that made sense: money had been needed to pay for the war. In November 2012, however, debt was just over $17,200 per person. That made no sense! We had more debt per capita in 2012 than at the end of the Second World War. Why? As I looked at it, I learned that debt began to soar in the mid-1970s. And I wondered, why?

There were lots of questions. I had begun to study them decades earlier. I had read *Paper Money,* which came out in 1981. The author was Adam Smith, not the Adam Smith I'll discuss in Chapter One, but the pseudonym of George Goodman, an American journalist who studied political economy at Harvard and as a Rhodes Scholar at Oxford. He wrote for *New York Magazine* and *Esquire*, and for a couple of years had a column under his irreverent pseudonym, covering the economic topics of the day: oil pricing, inflation, and the energy crisis. I realized way back then that I was not alone with my questions about money and economics. But I feel that Goodman missed the more important stuff. In his final chapter, he wrote, "The trouble with paper money is that it rewards the minority that can manipulate money and makes fools of the generation that has worked and saved." That should have been his major point! He wrote it, but missed it! We have seen that what he called "trouble" came to pass.

Many of my friends in both Canada and the US also had ceased understanding economics. Why was debt increasing? Why were wages not increasing? Why were jobs disappearing? Why was the standard of living falling behind that of the last generation? Why was the US becoming a low-wage nation? We shared the same questions! I'd looked at issues in the sixties and seventies, and then learned more by studying the economics of illegal drugs. I had been exposed to the economic problems of poor nations, and combined all that with my experience running a small business, so my understanding had broadened. I'm Canadian and spend a lot of time in the United States, which provides me with a broad view of the strengths and weaknesses of economics in North America.

My book begins with a look at the roots of economics, and then in Chapter Two, details two economists. Chapter Three covers two topics: the economics of illegal drugs and the economics of poverty in the developing world. Chapter Four covers the 1970s, when corporations were taking control of our agenda. It was in the mid-1970s, to be specific, that a huge change occurred in economics: national financing changed, in a way that explains our huge national debt. That's the subject of Chapter Five. Chapter Six is about money and its complexities. Chapters Seven, Eight, and Nine cover changes in economics in the 1980s and 1990s, from the time when economics made sense, to the time when it no longer did. Chapter Ten describes the role of the corporate state in setting the ground for the collapse of the whole system in 2007, and that collapse is the subject of Chapter Eleven.

In Chapter Twelve, I discuss what will replace capitalism, including Spain, Iceland and Cuba, as examples. I look at options: what other models of economic organization are there, and what might come next? No solution is presented, but there are many ideas we could apply. I offer you further reading suggestions.

This book is written for those who want to understand how we got here, and what sort of world we might prefer to see next. It's written because of the things not being discussed that need to be.

Control of the global economy is beyond the reach of any one of us, but the ability to understand it is not.

1. A person's a person

DR. SEUSS SAID IT ALL:

A person's a person no matter how small![2]

Dr. Seuss' Horton is an elephant who befriends a Who, a mite of a person living on a planet the size of a speck of dust, and Horton comes to realize that "a person's a person no matter how small."

The statement is egalitarian, revolutionary, even. All persons are equal. Horton didn't say so, but it means there is no royalty, that the Pope is equal to the peasant. There is no special treatment. It's a belief many of us were raised with, and may still believe.

Assumptions like the belief in equality, are a substantial part of economics. And these assumptions, or beliefs, can vary. The belief

---

[2] Seuss Geisel, Theodor. *Horton Hears a Who*. Random House, 1954.

in private land ownership seemed natural to the North American settlers, but was alien to Indigenous tribes, who believed that land belonged to no one.

Financial equality is diminishing, despite the hopes and repeated commitments to end poverty. Wealth is concentrating at an ever-accelerating rate, and with it, freedoms are increasing for some and decreasing for more. Economic assumptions are at the heart of these issues but how has that come about? Has the self-regulating competitive market system, one that we assumed to be effective and fair, failed?

I worked in "the system," and I have included in this *Insider's Memoir* many examples of things I witnessed. Company "turn-arounds," "reverse takeovers," and "going public," became language I understood.

In the first few chapters of this book, I'll discuss some history, especially Western economic history, from the days when things used to make sense. I've included dates for persons I mention, events that are significant, or periods in history that I feel are relevant. The definition of capitalism has mutated during the last five decades, and this evolution culminated in the meltdown of 2007. I feel it's unfortunate our understanding of what capitalism is did not change as the system did, and I want to show how and when it failed!

In the late 1950s, and for a couple of decades thereafter, economics was taught from Paul Samuelson's textbook *Economics: An Introductory Analysis*, published in 1948, which has gone through nineteen different editions and been used globally. The theory it presented is referred to as neoclassical economics. Samuelson assumed that competitive enterprise without government interference was best for society. To that assumption, Samuelson added Keynesian economics.

This was the textbook I began with, and it will be our starting point.

But does economic theory matter?

To answer that, let's take a step back in history. I will be brief.

For about six hundred years, from roughly the ninth century until the fifteenth century, Europe was governed by feudal lords who owned the land. Individuals were given their own fief or fiefdom land in exchange for services to royalty. Those with fiefdoms had power over peasants, serfs, and slaves, who were not considered people, but bought or sold as part of the land. In China, Japan, and India, there were similar social arrangements. Those born poor were very much at the mercy of those born rich. That was the nature of their world and defined the social contract they lived with.

In 1215, in England, King John signed the Magna Carta to quell a rebellion by a group of barons furious about excessive taxes. The charter included the 39th Clause, which gave all "free men" the right to justice and a fair trial, and provided a new framework between the king and his subjects. Although most clauses were later repealed, the Magna Carta became a rallying cry against the arbitrary use of power.[3]

In Florence, Giovanni Villani (c1280-1348), an Italian banker, wrote *Nuova Cronica*, so rich in detail that it is regarded as the first

---

3   Magna Carta: An Introduction, British Museum. http://www.bl.uk/magna-carta/articles/magna-carta-an-introduction

book of statistics. Born into the mercantile middle class, Villani loved his city so much that he wrote:

> In the said time, our city, Florence, was in the greatest and happiest state which had ever been … great in nobility of good knights and in free populace.

He might have been more circumspect, since his "free populace" excluded the slaves in the city, who could be arbitrarily evicted, as they were in Siena during a famine. Florence at the time had 80 banks and over 300 businesses or shops involved in making cloth.

The workers had started guilds and trade associations to protect themselves. The "Ciompi," as they were called, combed wool to prepare it for spinning into yarn, working 14 to 16 hours a day, were paid little money, and had no rights. In Florence, in 1378, they revolted and took over the government. This democratic revolution, while brief, and lasting only four short years, was one of the first demonstrations of the power of the people.

New ideas were flooding the world in the fourteenth century, in a great creative explosion. A disproportionate number of these ideas came from Italy, especially from Florence. This period became known as the Renaissance. Paper had been invented by the Chinese, who then invented moveable type, making printing easier. Ideas spread even faster. The Renaissance had a huge impact on culture, education, and the arts. It was the age of Michelangelo and Leonardo Da Vinci. A scientific revolution began near the end of the Renaissance. Copernicus, Newton, and Galileo published the findings of their experiments. Reason and knowledge were starting to challenge the social norms of a society run by religion and superstition.

Modern banking practices began in the Renaissance as wealth grew. Financial wealth was becoming more significant than traditional property wealth. The Medici family founded the Medici Bank in 1397, leveraging their real estate into a bank they managed to grow. The family, now wealthier and more powerful, became the most successful family in Florence. Astute financially, politically, artistically and theologically, the family produced two popes, many cardinals, and then made money lending to the Catholic Church. Their bank became the largest and most respected bank in Europe, with branches in eight cities, including Florence, Rome, and London. It was the model of a modern bank: an independent business that lent money and kept deposits. They used the "modern" invention of double-entry bookkeeping and paid their managers with shares in the bank. They traded in gold, coins, and currencies and issued their own money. The family became a major political power, enduring about one hundred years until the death of Cosimo de Medici.

The Medici bank succeeded, despite the Catholic Church's prohibition against usury or charging interest on loans. The Church dictated it was proper to buy and sell things, to rent houses, farms, and horses, but no one should "rent money," a sin for which you would burn in hell! As early as 325, the Church had prohibited clergy from charging interest on loans. By 1311, the prohibition extended to everyone and a new prohibition was added: simply believing that charging interest was acceptable became the sin of heresy.

While the threat of being burned at the stake was an effective tool in controlling the people, it was not enough to control the bankers.

In the 1400s, to get around this prohibition, the bankers paid bribes to the Church, which called them "indulgences." There were payments to the church for all kinds of things, like buildings or art. Cosimo de Medici paid for the restoration of the San Marco religious complex in Florence, a church, a priory, and a magnificent library. Some faces in Renaissance paintings are faces of the rich, and their families, preserved in oil alongside saints and cherubs.

You could say the religious art and architecture of the Renaissance were deposits on tickets to heaven.

In 1745, Pope Benedict XIV issued an encyclical condemning usury as dishonest profit.

Why was charging interest considered dishonest? The answer is in a related question: what is money?

If money is simply a medium of exchange, a way to carry value from the market, where the farmer sells her eggs to the bakers to buy bread, there is no justification for interest. However, if money is stored value—the value of eggs stored until you need chicken feed—then that reserve value may warrant interest. Why shouldn't we pay money to the bank to keep it safe? Why should it earn interest if it just sits there? For centuries, profit had come from work—from labour—not from having money. Money never sweats; thus, money can never, despite what banks say, work for you!

I will look again at money and usury later in this book.

The Catholic Church, and the Church of England have, on regular occasions, taken a stand on economic matters. In 1891, the Catholic Church issued an encyclical on *The Rights and Duties of*

Capital and Labor, acknowledging the right to private property on one hand and the right of workers to form unions on the other. It rejected both communism and unrestricted capitalism, but made no reference to usury. It seems the Church had quietly accepted it.

Islam still prohibits it. To get around this ban, Muslims set up profit sharing, or other arrangements, to receive income without charging interest.

The Book of Ezekiel states that charging interest is among the worst sins for the Jewish people. There was an interesting theological loophole that a Jewish person could lend money to a non-Israelite, so in the nineteenth century the Catholic Church became a client of the bank owned by the Jewish Rothschild family.

In the early 1600s, Amsterdam became the wealthiest city in the world. During this era, called the Dutch Golden Age, Dutch ships dominated the world. The Dutch acquired colonies and their lawyers became experts on the laws of the sea. One trade agreement was with Japan, through its Shogunate,[4] and the Dutch became the dominant trade connection between the Japanese and the Western world. Dutch ships sailed to Japan and back to Europe, often up the Rhine River as far inland as Switzerland.

The Dutch Golden Age was golden for many reasons. The Dutch were tolerant, believed in education, and made great progress in art, astronomy, physics, mathematics, and optics. They improved clock making, microbiology, and not surprisingly, for people living below sea level, improved pumps and the windmills to drive them.

---

4   The Edo Shogunate, established in 1603, became the most powerful central government Japan had seen. It controlled the Empire, administered lands, and handled Japanese foreign affairs. https://www.britannica.com/topic/shogunate

They shipped herring, gin, and tulip bulbs abroad, and brought silk, spices, cotton, tea, and porcelain back to Europe. They sailed to India, Arabia, and Africa. Dutch ships sailed the Red Sea to Suez or Aqaba, in what is now Egypt and Israel. Later, Dutch sailors began to sail around the southern tip of Africa and then north to Europe.

The Dutch East India Company was founded in 1602, and was the world's first multinational corporation and the first company to issue shares. They were good shares to own! They paid 18% annual dividends for almost 200 years. A 21-year monopoly on the spice trade helped. At its peak, the spice trade employed almost a million people on almost five thousand ships. The company could imprison or execute convicts, establish colonies, and wage war.

The Amsterdam Stock Exchange was also started in 1602, and a few short years later, in 1609, the world's first truly central bank, the Bank of Amsterdam, was established.

A central bank is a public institution, owned by the state, which operates for the people and prints the state's money. (The Medicis' private bank, in contrast, existed to make money for the Medici family. For a time, they even issued their own currency, the Florin.)

By 1636, tulip bulbs had become the fourth-leading export of Holland after gin, herring, and cheese. Buying and selling futures on individual tulip bulbs became the rage. An individual tulip bulb could sell for as much as ten times a worker's annual wage. Fortunes were made by those playing this investment game until it imploded. This was another Dutch first: the first collapse of an economic bubble. (Perhaps the collapse of the dot.com bubble almost four hundred years later should have been anticipated.)

For about a thousand years, the Christian religion had dominated the social structure in Europe, defining the social contract of the people. Faith was in the church, not in the markets.

The Enlightenment of the seventeenth and eighteenth centuries brought that to an end, however.

From the mid-1770s, with the emergence of steam power, the structure of feudalism was replaced by the needs of manufacturing. As people moved from working on farms in the country to working in factories in towns, changes in the existing social organizations had to happen.

In towns and cities, vegetables, fruit, meat, bread, and milk had to be delivered, bought, and sold. Garbage and sewage had to be managed and paid for. Individuals were learning new and specialized skills, and some were getting wealthier as society changed.

Ideas about human rights, natural rights, equality, and inalienable rights were emerging. Political philosophy and assumptions about social contracts became topical. The philosopher John Locke (1632–1704) had written that all men have the right to the fruits of their labour. How much freedom did people have to give up, in order to have how much security?

Western Europe had become a mercantile society. Nations used tariffs on imports to increase their own exports, which was good for the merchants, so the merchants enthusiastically supported that. (If you export goods, money comes into the country, which is obviously good. If you import goods, you send money out of the country.) The mercantile system dominated for over two hundred years as governments and the business class acted together. Common people were left on their own.

The early study of markets was called Political Economy. As a subject on its own, the study of Economics would come later.

Adam Smith (1723–1790)

In the eighteenth century, the Scots were well-educated people, and they had an impact on the world far more significant than their country's small population, in such a tiny inhospitable land, would seem to justify.

Scotland, at that time, had the best universities—not just best in Britain, but best in the world. The Scots had great influence worldwide through their scientists, inventors, authors, and sailors, such as James Watt, John Paul Jones, John McAdam, and one outstanding philosopher, Adam Smith. This was the era of Scottish Enlightenment.[5]

Adam Smith was a professor of Moral Philosophy, a subject that encompassed ethics and what we might call the soft sciences: logic, philosophy, psychology, and sociology. We know him primarily for his book on economics, although probably he would have preferred to be remembered for his earlier book about the origin of human ethics, *The Theory of Moral Sentiments*. He lived in the town of Kirkcaldy on the North Sea, across the Firth of Forth from Edinburgh. As a student, he studied Moral Philosophy at the University of Glasgow and then went to Oxford, which he claimed was a waste of time, since he felt the professors had given up teaching. He returned to teach Logic at the University of Edinburgh and a year later became Chair of Moral Philosophy.

---

5   Herman, Arthur. *How the Scots Invented the Modern World*. Crown Publishing, 2001.

His first book, *The Theory of Moral Sentiments*, published in 1759, sought to explain how the human ability to make moral judgments evolved. It was the positive side of the question: are people basically good or basically evil? He believed humans were basically good. He continued making extensive revisions to this book up until his death. Smith assumed that man is compassionate, with an innate drive to do things that are decent. "That we often derive sorrow from the sorrows of others, is a matter of fact too obvious to require any instances to prove it." He also wrote, "How selfish soever [sic] man may be supposed, there are evidently some principles in his nature, which interest him in the fortune of others, and render their happiness necessary to him."

He viewed man as much more than a competitive animal. The contemporary assumptions of his work, that greed is what makes the system work, are not correct.

> The natural effort of every individual to better his own condition ... is so powerful, that it is alone, and without any assistance, not only capable of carrying on the society to wealth and prosperity, but of surmounting a hundred impertinent obstructions with which the folly of human laws too often encumbers its operations.[6]

Smith wrote that labour was the source of value in money.

---

6 Smith, Adam. *An Inquiry Into the Nature and Causes of The Wealth Of Nations*, Book IV, Chapter V, Digression on the Corn Trade, p. 540. 1776.

> Labor was the first price, the original purchase-money that was paid for all things. It was not by gold or by silver, but by labor, that all the wealth of the world was originally purchased; and its value, to those who possess it, and who want to exchange it for some new productions, is precisely equal to the quantity of labor which it can enable them to purchase or command.[7]

This sounds, to me, more like Karl Marx than the founder of capitalism.

In 1763, he got a job as a tutor and travelled to Paris, where he met Voltaire and Ben Franklin. It was in Paris where he concluded that the unrestricted market was creating reasonably fair income distribution, and although unplanned, that it was a useful benefit.

He never married and lived almost all his life with his mother. She died when he was 61. He followed her six years later.

In the West, Smith is idealized for defining (some say for creating) a perfect system of economics. But that wasn't the way he saw it. He believed he was simply observing how changes in industrialization were changing the way Scottish society functioned. In the spirit of the scientific age, he was trying to define how society was changing. Adam Smith saw that it was demand that created value. It was not a new observation. Aristotle had written about it centuries earlier.

Nor did Smith invent the science of economics. Others, including his mentor, Francis Hutcheson, who preceded Smith as Chair

---

7   Smith, Adam. *An Inquiry into the Nature and Causes of the Wealth of Nations*, Book 1. 1776.

of Moral Philosophy, had already begun exploring economics scientifically.

Nonetheless, Smith's ideas, or a neocon variation of his ideas, have since been hoisted cult-like to a near theology. His status peaked during the years of US President Ronald Reagan, when members of the Reagan administration took to wearing Adam Smith ties. Reagan's administration cut taxes for the wealthy, oblivious to Smith's view that the purpose of life was to promote not wealth, but the happiness of mankind.

In 1776, Smith published his second book, about political economy. Its full title was *An Inquiry into the Nature and Causes of the Wealth of Nations.* Published when Smith was 53, it was a time when the nation-state was just beginning to emerge. He had written a book on each of his major interests: ethics and the economy. He observed the emergence of tradesmen and craft specialization and saw the way that specialization was producing more goods, easier and faster. As more and more did that, society was prospering. The moral philosopher assumed that the purpose of the economy was to improve the quality of life for all people.

Work was changing from small, self-sufficient farms to small businesses: blacksmith shops, carpenter shops, and larger enterprises like woollen mills. Inventions were reshaping a rapidly changing world. Markets were growing more significant, and all of this was happening without planning. These changes seemed to benefit everyone as everyone pursued their own self-interest. Smith took note, writing about his observations in the spirit of the new scientific age as people were searching for order in things.

> Give me that which I want, and you shall have this which you want, is the meaning of every such offer; and it is in this manner that we obtain from one another the far greater part of those good offices which we stand in need of. It is not from the benevolence of the butcher, the brewer, or the baker that we expect our dinner, but from their regard to their own interest.

His economic analysis was in the context of the mercantilist assumptions of the day, using tariffs as trade controls to protect and improve the profits of the merchant class. Smith didn't approve. He wanted less interference from government, so wealth would be more equitably shared. Profit, in classical economics, is money earned through investment and labour, making things people need. (I feel the rich today want less interference from government, not the reduced interference that Smith supported, so they can return to the system he opposed.)

Industrialization was changing the Social Contract. The tailor in town needed the weaver, who needed the baker, who in turn had to trust the farmer to raise and sell grain. No longer did everyone need to do everything to survive. For the system to work, no one could unfairly exploit nor withhold their specialty. It was the essence of these changes that Smith summed up in *The Wealth of Nations*. Every economic student since then has learned about the benefits of specialization from the example Smith used: making pins. A dozen specialized people could make about 2,000 pins a day, while a tradesman working alone could make only 10.

Money was becoming more essential in urban life.

The idea of money was not new: Marco Polo had devoted a chapter in his book about his travels, published 400 years before Adam Smith, on the use of paper money in China. But the increasing concentration of people in cities required an easy way to trade. Money, in some form, worked. It worked for exchange and was needed to pay for long-term projects like sewers, roads, and public buildings. These early city needs were followed closely by the needs for policing, city governance, and then taxes to pay for them.

Smith noted that wealth increased as the Gross Domestic Product (GDP) increased, and that tariffs or the hoarding of precious metals distorted the natural tendencies of the market. GDP was a concept that Smith was the first to define, and although he was not the world's first economist, he is usually cited as the first.

He believed that the economic system that was emerging was inherently automatic, able to regulate itself. He used the term "invisible hand" to describe this feature of the market in relation to imports and to nothing else.

> As every individual, therefore, endeavors as much as he can both to employ his capital in the support of domestic industry, and so to direct that industry that its produce may be of the greatest value; every individual necessarily labors to render the annual revenue of the society as great as he can. He generally, indeed, neither intends to promote the public interest, nor knows how much he is promoting it. By preferring the support of domestic to that of foreign industry, he intends only his own security; and by directing that industry in such a manner as its produce may be the greatest value, he intends only his own gain, and he is in

this, as in many other causes, led by an invisible hand to promote an end which was no part of his intention. Nor is it always the worse for the society that it was no part of it. By pursuing his own interest, he frequently promotes that of the society more effectually than when he really intends to promote it.[8]

To paraphrase Smith's paragraph: it makes sense to buy local. It's self-evident—so self-evident that it happens naturally. Today, many assume that the invisible hand is mystically divine but are hard-pressed to explain why. I have to ask: why would the divinely inspired hand take jobs to China at the expense of the jobs of our neighbours?

Smith used the term "invisible hand" three times, and never implied that it was divine or a fundamental part of nature. There were no theological overtones: God didn't control this hand. It was a collection of human decisions that created the pattern. Nor did Smith attempt to develop a broad economic theory. Smith was simply observing the changing world in which he lived. He never used the term "capitalism." We will see later that it was Marx who did that.

Competition, multiple buyers, and multiple sellers, Smith observed, were making things better, or making things less expensive, and often both. No government interference was needed. Most people worked to the best of their ability and this fit with Smith's assumptions about the ethical nature of man. He did not

---

[8] Smith, Adam. *An Inquiry into the Nature and Causes of the Wealth of Nations*, Book 4, Chapter 2. *Of Restraints upon the Importation from Foreign Countries of such Goods as can be Produced at Home.* 1776.

assume that self-serving greed, which we've been taught to think of as normal, was essential. His was a far more subtle analysis: when many individuals can enter a market, some will do better than others. Open, fair competition is what Smith saw leading to improvement and is the core of his competitive market theory. It was his base, but it seems it's no longer the world we live in.

Smith was an early critic of politicians, noting three centuries ago their reputation for spending the people's money. Some things never change.

As Smith was writing *The Wealth of Nations*, the Scottish Ayr Bank failed in 1772. This failure was precipitated by a London banker fleeing to France because he couldn't make his payments. After making a small fortune early in his career, using insider information, the banker ran out when his money ran out! The Scottish bank, along with twenty others, failed, causing a depression in the Lowlands. Smith had to rewrite his chapter on money.

The first edition of *The Wealth of Nations* sold out in six months, which was a great surprise to his publisher, who felt reading the book took much thought and reflection, qualities that he claimed "… do not abound among modern readers."

Thirteen years after the publication of *The Wealth of Nations*, the social contract in France fell apart. The French Revolution began in 1789.

For years prior to that date, wealth in France had been concentrated in the hands of the king and the aristocracy. A rich example of this is King Louis XIII's construction of a hunting lodge in the village of Versailles, 14 miles west of Paris. Not a hunting lodge as we would imagine, it became a palace that required over one hundred years of construction and over 30,000 workers. The opulence that surrounds the modern visitor, in a short walk from the front gate to ticket kiosk, is so blatant that we can start to understand the French Revolution. It defies belief.

It was not just rich French aristocrats who lived such opulent lives. In London, Buckingham Palace was begun in 1705.

In much of the world at this time, the economy was changing. Cities were drawing more people, people were specializing in trades, and forming guilds (early unions), such as the Italian Ciompi had created. Democracy and economic freedom were emerging as two new ideals.

Both the US and French Revolutions were inspired by the ideals of the Enlightenment: reason replacing tradition and religion. French and American revolutionaries sought a classless society. They wanted to live in a republic, with a government in which the power resides in the people, not in a country governed by the king, the church, or the aristocracy. The desire for freedom was at the heart of both movements. So was economics.

It's interesting to note that in this same period both England and Germany had entrenched class structures, but their people didn't rebel. I'm not sure why. Did the French aristocracy choose to get too rich, or did the people of Paris have a stronger sense of justice? Napoleon Bonaparte felt that "Religion was created to keep the poor from killing the rich."

Early in the industrial era, poverty was seen as a form of depravity and dealt with by keeping debtors in work houses and debtors' prisons. A bizarrely stupid idea, it seems, jailing poor people until they paid their debts. Nonetheless, the workhouses and debtors' prisons lasted for centuries in Britain, until the last one closed in the late 1800s.

Charles Dickens wrote about debtors' prisons in the mid-1800s, after his father spent some time in Marshalsea in London for a debt to a baker. For a time, Charles' mother and sister also lived there. Eight to ten prisoners a day died of starvation. Prisons were run for profit, and the prisoners had to pay for their stays. Unpaid prison fees were added to the original debt in a hopeless and futile system.

The same system was started in America, but debtors' prisons were abolished in 1833. (It's interesting to note that in a report in 2015 on the city of Ferguson, Missouri, the second source of revenue in Ferguson was fines, especially on black citizens who, if they could not pay, would go to jail.)

In Paris, when the poor were trapped by unemployment, poverty, food shortages, soaring prices, inflation, and depression, they exploded. The people took control of a fortress in Paris that had been converted to a prison called the Bastille, and Bastille Day became the French "Independence Day." A bloody ending to years of exploitation by the rich helped the French and the rest of the world to expect fairness in the social contract.

Adam Smith had written, thirteen years before the French Revolution, about an economic system that, with little regulation, would create fairness. He believed competition in a free society would result in movement towards equality. If the blacksmiths were getting too rich, more would join their ranks. Competition, not capital, dominated. Smith defined competitive enterprise as the base for what evolved into free enterprise, then capitalism, and then the market system.

The differences become important, as I'll discuss. Karl Marx will help clarify it. Before I talk about Karl Marx, I'd like to consider two more key figures in economics.

John Maynard Keynes (1883–1946)

> The outstanding faults of the economic society in which we live are its failure to provide for full employment and its arbitrary and inequitable distribution of wealth and incomes.[9]

John Maynard Keynes was one of the first economists to study business cycles. He recognized that recessions and depressions were not part of nature but part of the economic system.

Prior to Keynes, the prevailing economic theory was that, on its own, the economy would create full employment. In spite of that assumption, unemployment existed, and Keynes wanted to know why. And then he wanted to know how to prevent these downturns.

He argued that contrary to the existing belief of that era, business cycles were *not* self-regulating and *not* self-correcting.

It was an easy case to make in the 1930s, as a worldwide Great Depression dragged on, year by year, after the US stock market crash of 1929. It confirmed what people were seeing: while the world was in a great depression, there was no end in sight. People knew something had to be done. The economy was not correcting itself, and politicians were doing nothing to remedy it.

Keynes saw what everyone in business knows: it's demand that creates business activity. Therefore, Keynes argued, the role of the state was to spend money in bad times, to create demand, and to collect taxes in good times to get the money back. The state should

---

9   Keynes, J. M. *The General Theory of Employment, Interest, and Money*. Macmillan Cambridge University Press, for Royal Economic Society, 1935.

provide stimulus money in a recession, giving people money to live on. The money spent would help the economy recover.

Keynes called his theory, and his seminal 1935 book, *The General Theory of Employment, Interest and Money*. It was a new general theory to explain the weaknesses in prevailing and failing economic theory.

He invented macroeconomics: the study of how to affect the economy as a whole. His general theory was proven right in the 1930s, and then again in 2008. For the decades in-between, he was ignored.

Keynes was tall, six foot six, and born in Cambridge, England. His father, by coincidence, had the same credentials as Adam Smith: an economist and a lecturer in moral philosophy. His mother was a social reformer. He got a degree in mathematics at Cambridge and went to work in the Civil Service. He had an abiding faith in something we have been conditioned to see as unthinkable: the ability of the civil service to do good.

He worked for the British government in the Treasury Department and during World War I, he earned a Royal Award for his work in that department. With that recognition, he got a seat at the table at the 1919 Peace Conference that set the terms to end the First World War. While having a good vantage point to view the proceedings, the seat provided no option for Keynes to have input. In the end, he vehemently opposed the agreement, the Treaty of Versailles, because of the severe economic penalties it imposed on the German people.

Keynes knew that while many German people had opposed the war, all Germans would suffer. Keynes anticipated the agreement would destabilize Germany and lead to further problems, as he wrote in his book, published in 1919, *The Economic Consequences of the Peace*. Keynes' predictions were confirmed when Germany suffered hyperinflation in 1923, followed by years of financial instability, then the rise of Fascism, and Hitler. It was a tragic lesson on why attention to economics matters.

Keynes was an economist—not a financial planner. While he predicted the hyperinflation in Germany, he bet on it by speculating against the value of the German mark. His timing was off. (Most investors today live by the rule: don't try to time the market!) The fall of the mark happened, but far later than Keynes anticipated, and he was saved from financial ruin when bailed out by his friend and publisher.

Belief in incorrect economic assumptions prolonged the Great Depression for a decade, 1930–1940: ten years of lost opportunity for millions of unemployed, idle people and businesses, as well.

The General Theory of Employment, Interest and Money was written at the bottom of the Depression, asking what caused it, and what could end it. Published in 1935, it challenged the belief that the economy functions best without government interference. Bad political/economic theory prolonged the Depression, and bad political/economic theory led directly to World War II, and the avoidable loss of millions of lives.

Today, I feel badly that economics is at the heart of the Tea Party and the neoliberals, and is damaging lives in America and Europe, especially in countries in the Eurozone.

Keynes had many interests. He was married and he was gay He was an intellectual and a member of the Bloomsbury Group, a left-leaning group of about a dozen friends who met in the Bloomsbury area of central London for regular discussions. The philosopher Bertrand Russell and writer Virginia Woolf were members.. Keynes became a successful investor, and spent money supporting the arts. But it was his advice to governments on how to deal with the great Depression and his theory that made sense and which was followed and succeeded, that earned Keynes his place in history.

The collapse of the stock market in 1929 was a fundamental failure of the economic system. The fact that the market didn't correct on its own, as had been assumed, was a second failure. Governments failing to do the right things was failure number three.

In the Depression, thousands of people lost their jobs, and lost incomes resulted in a decline in demand. Fewer people could afford to shop. Without demand, the Depression, as it did, could only continue.

Unfortunately, despite the unmistakable failure of the theory of the self-correcting free market at that time, the belief was not buried. The result was that we got to see the free market fail again in 2008, and see that incorrect theory not get buried again. But I'm jumping ahead.

The Pecora Commission, an investigation by the United States Senate into the reason for the collapse of 1929, discovered numerous banking improprieties, including one with the National City Bank, which routinely bundled bad loans into mutual funds securities and sold those to unsuspecting clients, a practice that resurfaced in 2008. The Commission's findings led to the Glass-Steagall Act, which separated commercial and investment banking to provide a more stable economy, until it was rescinded in the Financial Services Modernization Act of 1999. The Western world had yet to understand their market system was fundamentally unstable and would crash again in a few years.

It helps to take a brief step back in history to a generation prior to Keynes.

A French economist, Jean-Baptiste Say (1767–1832), made an assertion that some escalated to a theory and even an "economic law," named Say's Law. When things are produced, he argued, the money to buy those things is produced, as supply creates demand. If you make lots of widgets, you pay wages to people to make the widgets, and that money will, in turn, provide the money to buy the widgets.[10]

The problems with the theory are several, but the main problem is the arithmetic doesn't work: workers' pay is a small part of the selling price of the widgets. In the company I owned, wages were about one-third of the selling price, so we created the potential for workers to buy one-third of our production.

Say's theory, bad arithmetic and all, attracted adherents and dominated economics for about one hundred years, then waned, and resurfaced with Reaganomics to justify bad economic theories, and I will get to that, later.

Keynes challenged Say's Law when he argued that the interaction of "aggregate demand" and "aggregate supply" may lead instead to perpetual and stable unemployment. He saw the potential for high unemployment with the worse prospect of no hope of it ending. There was no economic reason that the market could or would intervene to change it.

---

10   Madrick, Jeffrey. *Seven Bad Ideas: How Mainstream Economics Have Damaged America and the World*. Vintage Books, 2015.

In such a case, he argued, contrary to the classic theory that dominated economics, the state *had* to intervene. If the state did not, the depression/recession would continue. In 1933, during the Depression, Franklin D. Roosevelt became president and promised a "New Deal" for the American people. He committed to making the social contract more humane. He embarked on multiple stimulus programs, which he summed up with this statement:

> No country, however rich, can afford the waste of its human resources. Demoralization caused by vast unemployment is our greatest extravagance. Morally, it is the greatest menace to our social order.[11]

It was Keynesian policies that ended the Great Depression. That intervention of stimulus was aided by the soaring spending on the military in anticipation of World War II.

Despite the lesson, we continue to allow unregulated corporate capitalism, and waste the energy and talent of people as the economy repeatedly cycles through booms and recessions. It is as foolish now as it was before FDR's time.

The benefits of the stimulus money from the Roosevelt era can still be seen. In the 1930s in the city of Nashville, where I live, two elegant federal buildings were constructed: a post office which is now the Frist Center for the Visual Arts, and the Davidson County Courthouse. These two art deco legacies of stimulus spending are evidence of the long-lasting usefulness of money spent for public purpose. There are thousands of similar examples across the

---

11   F. D. Roosevelt, September 30, 1934.

country, about forty thousand. In addition, water mains, roads, bridges, playgrounds, parks, hospitals, and golf courses were built.

By the time World War II ended, recovery was in full swing. National debt was at record levels because of war expenditures, but no one worried. People were excited, had lots of opportunities, and a lot to do. The years of building the machinery of war: guns, ships, airplanes, jeeps, uniforms, bullets, stretchers, bandages, and factories, had used lots of government money and left a civilian backlog in the need for houses, refrigerators, cars, radios, and so on.

As needs for these scarce items were met, rationing ended, and optimism grew.

Studies show that this level of optimism in the economy is long gone in the West. Only 13% of the people believe that their children will be better off than they are. This used to be almost 100%. However, that optimism is alive with young people in India and China. The young in emerging economies have hope, while those in the older economies, especially those in Greece and Portugal, lament.[12]

The Second World War further entrenched general assumptions about the rights of man. Prior to the war, European nations had begun giving up control of their colonies, nurturing the concept that people had the right to control their own destiny. In 1944, the United Nations was created as a global forum for the rule of law and in 1948 it adopted the Universal Declaration of Human Rights.[13] Eleanor Roosevelt, a remarkable woman, chaired the drafting committee, which took two years to create the declaration.

---

12   http://www.pewresearch.org/fact-tank/2014/09/09/the-countries-most-optimistic-and-pessimistic-about-their-economic-future/

13   http://www.un.org/en/documents/udhr/index.shtml

In thirty brief articles, the world entrenched commitment to equal rights; rights without distinction as to race, colour, sex, language, property or birth. It recognized the right to own property. It opposed slavery, torture, and arbitrary arrest, detention, or exile. Sadly, many of these rights have been clawed back in the last decade. Nonetheless, those ideals moved society, temporarily, a few more steps from feudalism.

Keynes' theories redefined unemployment. What at one time many assumed to be the idleness of workers, Keynes showed was a built-in failure of capitalism. It was prone to cycles and Keynes showed they were a manageable variable. Unemployment was not the consequence of laziness, but a failure in the system, and those made unemployed, the victims, had the right to be assisted. Serendipitously, providing aid to those made idle added stimulus to the economy: a win-win.

Consequently, in 1944, the United States drafted a "Full Employment Bill," and implicit in it was the right to a job. The bill passed a couple of years later, but the right to have a job was watered down to a soft commitment to full employment. It was during this period labour was starting to be seen as a commodity, like coal—just another factor in the business equation. The problem is when labour is "just a commodity," it's not recognized to be the purpose, the lifeblood of society.

Keynes was a free enterprise economist who sought to make free enterprise capitalism work, despite what he and Marx saw as capitalism's inbuilt contradictions.

Keynes' intent was to protect free enterprise by creating tools to overcome its inbuilt weaknesses and to enhance life for everyone, to let enjoyment replace striving. He saw "deep divergences of opinion between fellow economists"—divergence you don't see in real science.

Keynes was frustrated by his lack of success, and in 1931 published a small book, *Essays in Persuasion*, which laments his failure to influence economic events. As he said, it was the "croakings of twelve years ... of a Cassandra who could never influence the course of events." He sensed that changes in economics were obscuring what's important. "The author of these essays, for all his croakings, still hopes and believes that the day is not far off when the Economic Problem will take the back seat where it belongs, and that the arena of the heart and head will be occupied, or re-occupied, by our real problems—the problems of life and of human relations, of creation and behavior and religion."

Keynes was aware of something that Wall Street has never learned: life is more important than markets.

Science—the word comes from the Latin word for knowledge—is the systematic search and organization of various rules that describe how the world works.

Economics doesn't work that way! Many economists immerse themselves in complex mathematics to try to create scientific predictability, but fail. Many contradictory points of view on economic issues make it clear that economics is more like alchemy than science. Keynes said, a generation ago, that society and its citizens are usually slaves of some "defunct economist."

In 2012, Australian Economist John Quiggin, in his book, *Zombie Economics: How Dead Ideas Still Walk Among Us*[14] made

---

14 Quiggin, John. *Zombie Economics: How Dead Ideas Still Walk Among Us*. Princeton University Press, 2010.

the same point, by expanding on the failures of buzz terms, such as "efficient markets," "trickle-down theory," "privatization," and "austerity."

One man who did a lot to present economics as somewhat of a science was Paul Samuelson.

Paul Samuelson (1915–2009)

As mentioned in my preface, the standard textbook we used in the late 1950s was *Economics, An Introductory Analysis*, by Paul Samuelson. The ideas in this text seemed natural to me because our family dinner table discussions in the 1950s often focused on my father's career as a sales manager in a manufacturing corporation. We heard about the competition he faced and the market conditions he worked within. We knew how supply and demand affected us and how they affected and controlled prices. We did not discuss the role of banks, and money, or how they too controlled opportunities.

Samuelson's parents emigrated from Poland before the First World War and settled in Gary, Indiana, at the time a thriving steel-making town, where his father, a pharmacist, chose to practice. Unusually, there were several economists in the Samuelson family. Paul's earliest memories were of the recession of 1919–1921 and the immigrant Mexicans hired as strikebreakers in the local mills. He witnessed economic periods of boom and bust, and entered university during the Depression (1931), studying economics and obtaining a PhD from Harvard in 1941.

To him, economics was not a detached academic exercise, but a subject that had a direct impact on society. He wrote, "It is not too much to say that the widespread creation of dictatorships and

… World War II stemmed from the world's failure to meet the economic problems of the Great Depression."[15]

He saw the interrelationship of economics with politics and viewed capitalist economics as a tool to challenge communism. The so-called Cold War dominated Western foreign policy at the time. He wrote it was necessary for the US markets to perform superlatively because "… mass unemployment at home would have disastrous repercussions upon our prestige abroad, to say nothing of the internal political unrest that a slump might involve." He assumed that competitive capitalism functioned for the benefit of all.

Samuelson published his textbook in 1948, at a time when there was a well-accepted social contract called the American Dream in Western society. The dream was shared equally by those in Canada, and had been the vision of the early settlers to simply live better, in a country where anyone could be secure financially, anyone could own a house, anyone could be successful, and almost anyone could become rich: a shared optimism for freedom and opportunity.

Samuelson, and others, assumed that one of the goals of society should be full employment. He discussed this in his book, *Fiscal Policy and Full Employment Without Inflation*. In 1953, unemployment was 2.5%, but he recalled how wasteful unregulated capitalism had been during the Depression, when the energy of huge numbers of people was wasted, a sentiment carved in stone on the walls of the memorial to Franklin Delano Roosevelt in Washington:

Unemployment is our greatest extravagance.

---

15   Samuelson, Paul. *Economics: An Introductory Analysis*. 1948.

When people need things: bread, cars, clothes, etc., that need is, in economic terms, demand. Businesses emerge to supply that demand. Demand and supply are at the heart of the system.

Prices are set by the interaction between the two. If someone develops a new or better product, they prosper, and that's fair. If they provide it for less money, that's wonderful. People save money, and the efficient provider prospers. People have the maximum freedom to do things, and little government involvement is necessary. That was Samuelson's view.

It was understood that taxes were necessary to pay for sewers, defense, libraries, policing, roads, airports, ports, railway tracks, and more. Ancient Egyptians were taxed in grain; the Romans paid 2 to 5% of their income.

By the 1950s, progressive taxation was generally seen as fair: the rich were able to pay more than the poor. It was simple. In addition, the rich probably use more of the services provided by taxation: they can afford to drive more, fly more, and have more widely spaced properties to service. They could afford to pay more. Succession taxes were seen as a way to provide each generation with equal opportunity, to have a world where the class system would not re-emerge. The American Dream was based on upward mobility and succession taxes were seen as necessary to protect that.

Income tax was seen as a market stabilizer. When business was good, people earned more, and people and businesses paid more tax. Progressive taxation meant that the more you earned, the more tax you paid. By contrast, if you made less, you paid less tax but had a few more dollars left for purchases. Peaks and valleys were somewhat smoothed over. Similarly, unemployment insurance, welfare, and farm commodity stabilization programs worked the same way: collect money in good times, pay it out in bad.

The term "progressive" for taxation is one of the happy accidents of language, in which the good-sounding term works in favour of the people.

Nations have many different types of economies, which got brief mention in Samuelson's final chapter: Fascism, Socialism, Marxism and Communism. There was little discussion of a mixed economy, where state and private enterprise are mixed together; state capitalism (as in Egypt, where until recently, the army owned much of industry; or the various degrees of welfare capitalism found in Europe, especially in Scandinavia).

Teaching economics appears to have been equally bad in much of the world. Economists struggle to make their subject a science; to explain the world by creating theory and testing to see if it stands up. There are too many contradictory options about economics for it be a true science. Economic schools have been preoccupied with creating computer models of the economy, which have provided distraction but little insight.

In the 1950s in the West, our belief in the market system got good press. It was believed we won the Second World War by defeating the national socialism of the Germans, Italians, and Japanese. The Soviet system, we assumed, was threatening and scary, although we knew little about it.

We had enough to eat, could increasingly buy things, and had increasing choices: Fords, Chevys, Pontiacs, and more; multiple choices in newspapers and in radio stations. TV was on the horizon. We had lots of opportunity. "Work hard and you will get ahead. Work hard and with a good idea or a bit of luck you can get rich." Jobs were for life. Jobs had benefits. Wages increased annually, and vacations got longer the longer you stayed with one company. Some, but not all nations, made annual paid vacation a legal right. (It is a worth noting that there is almost no correlation between number of paid vacation days and the Gross Domestic Product. More national vacation days does not equate to a reduction in productivity.)

Samuelsson's book was a huge success, despite the fact it contained some major failings.

One was that it didn't differentiate between earned and unearned income, where there is an enormous difference. Earned income is the result of labour; unearned income the result of wealth: no sweat is required. Another failing was that money is not well explained. Nor is exponential growth, which is mentioned only once and in a footnote.

Now in its nineteenth printing, the book was used in Moscow in the 1990s. Samuelson earned numerous awards for it, one the Nobel Prize for Economics. He was only the third person to earn this prize, and that requires a word or two. The Nobel prizes are the result of the will of Alfred Nobel, a Swedish chemist who invented dynamite and made a fortune from it, much of it the result of making arms. The annual awards are for developments in physics, chemistry, literature, peace, and medicine—none for economics.

In 1969, a new award was created, sponsored by and named after the privately owned Bank of Sweden. The Sveriges Riksbank Prize in Economic Sciences in Memory of Alfred Nobel is awarded at the same time as the Nobel Prizes, and coattails economics on the credibility of the true sciences. The winners have a bias towards monetarist, bank-friendly economists. Samuelsson's award in 1970 was for the role of his textbook in raising economic awareness.

The world had given up on alchemy, trying to create gold from lead, but the Bank of Sweden sponsored a new contender, which makes hypothetical assumptions about how the world works that tend to not match reality.

There have been criticisms of Samuelson's economics. He assumed free markets at a time when free markets were disappearing. He assumed perfect completion: an equal balance between forces, which never happens.

Samuelsson assumed that over time, factors like prices and wages would converge. However, we now are seeing corporate profits go up and wages down. He thought free trade to be a good thing, with only a modest bow to protecting infant industries. He assumed that over time, the poor would get wealthier and the rich poorer. That has not happened.

From the 1950s until the late 1960s, an era known as the Golden Age of Capitalism, the economy thrived. Those of us living at that time did not think much about the social contract. We just felt our world seemed fair and good.

Colonial emigration to the Americas had provided thousands with hope. About 200,000 Spaniards led the way. Jobs in the colony of Brazil attracted about 600,000 Portuguese. From the mid-1600s to 1800s, North America attracted settlers from England and Ireland, including the Scots, who had been displaced from their land. Millions of people continued to emigrate for the opportunities offered in North America over the past two hundred years, including desperate Europeans, many from Germany and Italy.

What courage it must take to risk everything, to embark on an unpredictable and often dangerous sea voyage, to go to an uncivilized land—often a frozen land, with vast spaces that are such a contrast to crowded cities immigrants leave—all for better opportunities. The old class system, with its unfair distribution of wealth and power, and lack of general opportunity had become that stifling.

Thomas Jefferson (1743–1826) was the third of ten children, a grandson of people who had taken that risk. Born on a farm in Virginia and raised with knowledge of his immigrant family's values, he studied law at the College of William and Mary in Williamsburg, a classic education that included Latin and Greek, philosophy and mathematics. He read John Locke and Isaac Newton and learned to play the violin.

In 1776, the year Adam Smith's *Wealth of Nations* was published, almost two hundred years before Dr. Seuss, Jefferson contributed words at the start of the American Revolution that summed up the hopes of those in the new land: "All men are created equal ..." That was revolutionary enough, but he added more. He added the unalienable rights of "life, liberty and the pursuit of happiness." Dr. Seuss would agree.

The idea that "all men are created equal" was at odds with the class structure that existed at the time. And if all people are equal, it's only a short step to visualize that equal citizens should have equal rights, not only to life, liberty, and the pursuit of happiness but equal access to air, water, food, education, law, security, opportunity, and governing: all should be elements of the social contract.

Even in these early colonial times, there were business cycles. In 1797, the United States had a recession, called "a panic," caused in part by the Bank of England facing insolvency because of the high costs of years of fighting the French. That was followed by the recession of 1802–1804, the depression of 1807, the recession of 1812, and the depression of 1815–1821.

Adam Smith had observed European business cycles, specifically cycles in corn and textiles. These business cycles were a consequence of the laissez-faire[16] economic system, a built-in weakness, as was soon to be proven.

On November 19, 1863, during the American Civil War, Abraham Lincoln addressed the troops at Gettysburg and further clarified the concept of a social contract when he stated the soldiers had sacrificed so that future generations could have "a new birth of freedom — and that government of the people, by the people, for the people, shall not perish from the earth." This concept of government by and for the people resonated with people far beyond American borders.

The eloquence of Jefferson and Lincoln crystalized the hopes people had for the New World. There was no room in this New World for business monopolies, or restrictions on equal opportunity.

Social contracts

> It is our unfinished task to restore the basic bargain that built this country, the idea that if you work hard and meet your responsibilities, you can get ahead, no matter where

---

16   The term dates to France in the 1600s and refers to unrestricted trade.

you come from, no matter what you look like or who you love.
—President Barak Obama; Feb. 12, 2013

In his 2013 State of the Union address, Obama summarized the social contract that Western societies had depended on. What he called "the basic bargain" is a set of assumptions that had made sense and worked over several generations. At one time, before the era of rugged individualism, we shared a commitment to general prosperity. That commitment is disappearing, and despite Obama's naïve wish to restore it, I feel it may be gone totally.

It existed at one time, when most of us assumed that everyone healthy could be employed, and that everyone had the opportunity to rise from one class to another. We assumed the state would provide the infrastructure: water, sewage, national defense, and postal delivery. In the 1950s, governments and economists understood that business cycles provided more pain to its victims than was fair, and so unemployment insurance, while not enthusiastically supported, was provided.

Then, much like now, it was easier to blame the unemployed for being unemployed than to blame the system that regularly created unemployment.

However, better-informed people knew that unemployment insurance performed a twofold purpose: it provided income to those who lost work and that money, paid to the unemployed, added demand in the market when they spent it. It provided fairness and stimulus, which also served the rich, by reducing the impact of recession on stock values.

In the United States, much of this social safety net was put in place by legislation under F. D. Roosevelt when the Social Security Act was passed in 1935. The Act brought into being Old Age Security income, aid for dependent children, disability insurance, unemployment insurance, and a death benefit. These programs are sometimes now derided as "entitlement programs," but they had the positive effect of providing a steady source of demand to the economy. They reduced not only the effects of the Great Depression, but also those of every recession ever since.

Many of the programs to help people came about, not because of good will, but because of the spotlight shone on unfair labour practices after the tragic 1911 Triangle Shirtwaist fire in Manhattan. The factory was a "sweatshop" and management locked the fire doors to prevent workers from sneaking out for unauthorized breaks. During the fire, 146 people died. Legislation to improve worker safety was passed, which also enhanced the role of unions to protect workers. By 1938, The Fair Labor Standards Act was passed, creating the forty-hour week, time and one half for overtime, and a minimum wage. The Triangle Shirtwaist Company fire is sometimes referred to as the event that created the American middle class.

What most of us accept as part of our social contract are the assumptions we were raised with—things we see as "normal." I want to discuss how many of those assumptions are now under attack.

Efforts to privatize roads, privatize education, and rebrand social security as "entitlement programs" all weaken our social contract.

At one time, it was a given that universal education would improve all of society. We would educate everyone, so society could benefit from the best talent of all the people. A secondary result was that education could be an equalizer: it might help avoid the emergence of the old class system. By providing vouchers so parents can opt to send their children to private schools, we work against that.

Although many of us accepted the social contract in the North America of the 1960s as fair, we began to realize there was built-in discrimination against women and non-whites. Nonetheless, it was assumed, as Obama stated, that anyone who worked hard could get ahead. Most Americans then were not in favour of the creation of an aristocracy. Yet, as wealth has been concentrated among "the 1%," it has happened.

Of course, outside the US there are different social contracts. A business friend of mine wanted to do business in Russia in the mid-1990', at a time when Russia was going through radical change. The old Soviet society had imploded, and eventually, we learned how rampant corruption had been.

Much of this was a holdover from the Stalin era, when ordinary citizens kept a low profile and did whatever they were told, just to survive, or were executed or exiled to Siberia. Planning was done by the state and for the state. The privileged lived better; the rest were on their own and did anything to get by. Trust had been eliminated.

My friend Ross summed up his experience with exasperation, "You think you are dealing with people like ourselves … they look like us and talk like us, but act as thieves!" Russians had no social contract as we expected. Most certainly, every one of the recently created Russian billionaires stole the money. By 2013, twenty years after the collapse of the Soviet Union, 35% of Russia's wealth was concentrated amongst 110 people, according to the Credit Suisse Research Institute.

By contrast, Cuba has a society with a strong, sharing social contract. For decades, the state has provided almost everything a person needs. You wouldn't get rich in Cuba, but you wouldn't starve. The best health care is provided, and it is free. Life expectancy is about the same as in the United States. In his first 30 months as President, Fidel Castro opened more classrooms than had been created in the previous thirty years. His agrarian reform bill restricted land ownership to under a thousand acres. The 1959 Revolution provided a stark contrast to the years prior, when a rich Cuban upper-class, led by the dictator Batista, exploited the poor. Batista lasted seven years, while Castro, also a dictator, lasted 37 years, until he retired.

In Egypt, prior to the revolution of 2011, the social contract was different. The nation's military, through a host of government-owned businesses, controlled a huge portion of the economy. There were military-run janitorial services, household appliance makers, pest control services, and caterers. El Nasr Company had 7,750 employees in child care, automobile repair, and hotel administration. Military companies produced small arms, tank shells, explosives, exercise equipment, and fire engines.[17] An army career could make you rich.

Saudi Arabia provides free education to its citizens, free health care, and every citizen gets free land to build a house and an interest-free mortgage. But don't expect to vote. It is one of the few remaining absolute monarchies in the world. There are no political parties, no unions, rights for women are minimal, no alcohol is allowed, and no missionaries are permitted (which might be a plus).

---

17   *Newsweek*, February 17, 2011.

Labour becomes a commodity

In Adam Smith's time, people were leaving farms, often escaping indentured labour in the hope of finding something better in town. The industrial revolution created jobs in the mills. Towns grew. The emerging industries required capital to grow. The deck began to be stacked in favour of the rich.

Money played an increasing role, and markets appeared for almost everything: food, livestock, clothes, and slaves. Increasingly, people became the negotiable commodity of the "labour market," no longer partners in the economy. As human effort becomes a marketable commodity, it seems there's no need for compassion. People becoming unemployed is the price they pay for freedom. But that was not the idea Adam Smith, or the unemployed, had in mind.

Now, newer markets exist for drugs, cars, and guns. Everything can be made tradable. "Commoditized" is the name for it. As Wall Street and international markets increased in relevance, workers' relevance decreased.

Eventually, in 1944, the International Labour Organization, a United Nations agency, adopted a resolution that asserted that labour is not a commodity. In 1948, the Universal Declaration of Human Rights was instituted by the United Nations. Article 23 states that everyone has the right to work, to equal pay for work of equal value, to right and just remuneration, and the right to join a trade union. This declared that labour has intrinsic value.

Economic differences between the United States and Canada

In this book, I cover two perspectives, because I'm Canadian, and my wife is American, and we live and have family and friends in both countries.

The United States is financially huge, and Wall Street assumptions and US military power dominate everything, so I give more emphasis on that economy in this book.

Capitalism differs slightly between our two countries. Our American friends think of Canada as socialist. Our Canadian friends don't understand the Tea Party.

Canadians don't mythologize about "founding fathers," nor do they have an idealized faith in their constitution; in fact, many Canadians don't know what their constitution is! The Prime Minister of Canada is not seen to be near omnipotent and does not live in a shrine like the White House.

Travelling between the two countries has provided me with a better understanding of how economic issues vary between the two countries.

During the Camelot days of the Kennedy Administration (1961–1963), the influence of the Canadian-born economist John Kenneth Galbraith, by then an American, was extensive. He was close to Kennedy, and it's possible he suggested the inaugural line "ask not what your country can do for you, ask what you can do for your country," Kennedy, like Galbraith, embraced Keynesian economics.

In Canada, we had our own Camelot a few years later (1968–1979), when Pierre Trudeau's Liberal Party was elected, and

Trudeau became Prime Minister. Always with a rose in his lapel, he was a Keynesian, had studied at the London School of Economics, and had met Galbraith at Harvard.

Kennedy and Trudeau shared a gift for oratory:

> I believe that this nation should commit itself to achieving the goal, before this decade is out, of landing a man on the moon and returning him safely to the Earth.
> —John Fitzgerald Kennedy

> Living next to you [the US] is like sleeping with an elephant. No matter how friendly and even-tempered the beast is, … one is affected by every twitch and grunt.

> The state has no place in the bedrooms of the nation.
> —Pierre Eliot Trudeau

Although both countries are about the same physical size, the US has four times more arable land and about ten times more people. The border between the countries is over five thousand miles long, and almost ninety percent of Canadians live within one hundred miles of that border.

Canada's "inefficient socialist" system, as viewed by many Americans, provided health care in 2011 to everyone for 11.2% of gross domestic product. The "efficient" free market model in the United States was at 17.9% of GDP, according to the World Bank, possibly a bit higher, if the needs of the 40,000,000 uninsured were included.[18] Healthcare illustrates, despite the misconceptions, that competitive enterprise is not always the most efficient.

The competitive enterprise system of the US provides the worst health care in the world! The United States spends almost 18% of GDP on health care: the percentage for other countries is about 9%. Life expectancy in 2011 was 78.7 in the US, a bit longer than that of Mexico and Poland, but below that of 25 other countries. In the US debate about public health care, it was apparent that the debate was lost before it began. The issue "Do Americans want public health care?" became "How would we insure health care?"

I find big differences between the two countries become clear when chatting with people at cocktail parties. In the United States, at some point, discussion will focus on health care: what health provider we have, what service do we get, what doctors, what costs? Such discussions seldom occur in Canada. Canadians just assume that everyone should be covered by government health care, and though they may feel, at times, the government underfunds health care and wait times occur, they feel they get reasonable value for their tax dollars.

Discussion differs, as well, on taxation. In the US, it comes up far more often. No one likes paying taxes, but Canadians are much less hostile to it. Both countries have horror stories of government spending mismanaged, but I find there seems to be more understanding in Canada that taxes provide some value. Canadians believe that they pay more income tax than Americans but are not

---

18   Organization for Economic Cooperation and Development. http://www.marketplace.org/topics/world/comparing-us-taxes-other-countries

hostile to it. That perception is incorrect, actually: personal income tax rates are similar in both countries.

Another difference is national debt. I'll discuss the subject more in Chapter Five, but the fact is, every American owes just over $61,000 as their share of the national debt.[19]

Canadians owe about $18,000[20] for theirs. The average American is concerned about it—some are outspokenly angry, while the average Canadian seems unconcerned.

The Chinese own much of the US debt, at just over $1 trillion of the $7 trillion debt—more than any other nation by a huge amount. It's as a direct result of Americans buying so many made-in-China goods.

However, the largest piece, 67.5% of American debt, is owed to the American people themselves: $12.9 trillion owed to retirement funds, especially to the Social Security Retirement Fund, the money people depend on for their old age. When Trump talks about forcing the United States' debtors to settle for something less on the dollar, that could include the American people.[21]

Canadian debt is owed to life insurance companies, pension funds, mutual funds, and such.

Assumptions on how society works are similar, but not identical, in the two countries. There are differences of opinion on patriotism, guns, and religion. Canadians have less of all three. In 1982, almost two hundred years after the United States got its Constitution, Canada exchanged the British North America Act for its own

---

19   http://www.usdebtclock.org/
20   http://www.debtclock.ca/
21   http://money.cnn.com/2016/05/10/news/economy/us-debt-ownership/

Constitution. Whereas most Americans are familiar with "We the people ...." from their Constitution, many Canadians don't know what theirs says.

Gun laws differ, as do crime rates. Canadians have tougher gun laws, fewer guns, and lower crime rates.

Both countries are democracies, but the systems differ. Each country has its own currency, but the central banks differ.

Despite what the Tea Party says, Americans don't pay that much income tax. As a percentage of GDP, they pay 27.3%. Canadians pay 32.0%, people in France 50.2%, those in Germany 47.5%, and citizens of the United Kingdom pay 45%.[22]

US Gross Domestic product is almost $15 trillion. Canadian GDP is about one-tenth of that, in line with its smaller population.

There is a significant difference in the attitude to trade unions. While 31% of Canadian workers are unionized, only 13% are in the United States.[23] Two consequences of this are greater income equality in Canada and a less severe recession in 2007. It has not been easy for Canadian unions to grow. As everywhere, they are faced with immense corporate and cultural pressure. Because more people in Canada are in unions, the middle class remains larger than south of the border.

The largest single economic difference between our two nations is the amount spent on the military. (Because military spending is such a huge percentage of the economy, I will discuss this further in the Appendix.) According to the Stockholm International Peace

---

22 http://www.tradingeconomics.com/country-list/personal-income-tax-rate
23 http://www.nytimes.com/roomfordebate/2013/12/04/making-low-wages-liveable/canada-shows-the-power-of-union

Research Institute,[24] in 2016 the United States spent US$620 billion, 36% of the world's total 2016 arms expenditure of $1.7 trillion dollars.

Canada's US$15 billion (less than 3% of the US expenditure) seems puny by comparison. Canada has a lot less military, and for decades Canadians were proud of a tradition of peacekeeping. That is no longer warented.

So, what have we learned?

> Rats and roaches live by competition under the laws of supply and demand; it is the privilege of human beings to live under the laws of justice and mercy.
> —Wendell Berry

I have been studying economics for what amounts to four lifetimes. What have I learned?

My education began with the economics I understood in the middle-class family I was born into. The Depression was over, but we were still affected by it.

In the middle of the Depression, when Dad was in his mid-teens, his mother died. His father had died years earlier, and Dad was taken in by friends. He got his first job collecting bad debts. A successful call might get the debtor to offer a nickel a week. In time, Dad's lot improved, and he settled into a career in middle management.

---

24   https://www.sipri.org/

He confided more than once to us that he could never take the risk of going into business, that it would be too much for him. He needed security, and in that era, a job provided it. His view of how the economy worked was Samuelson's.

At that time, we believed that every generation would live a somewhat richer life than the last. The rise from the poverty of the Depression to the boom of the 1950s made that self-evident. A belief in never-ending growth was behind it, but we didn't know that it could not be sustained.

Following in Dad's footsteps, I went into business and got a job in a small company that sold systems to help reduce the capital a company required. Our major product was inventory control systems, and we taught our clients about economic order quantities (EOQ), turnover, ways to reduce inventory, and how to increase sales and profit.

This was many decades before Goldman Sachs would describe it as "helping capital to find its best use" or "doing God's work."[25]

From there, I moved to a large corporation, and it was there I started to see that corporate practices were not those my father taught, not those I expected, and not those of Samuelson. I saw corporations colluding, not competing.

Nonetheless, we accepted the way the market was working, because it seemed more or less fair. We believed that the market, plus democracy, would provide the best and fairest quality of life. The role of business cycles in providing and destroying opportunity

---

25 http://blogs.wsj.com/marketbeat/2009/11/09/goldman-sachs-blankfein-on-banking-doing-gods-work/

was not understood. Cycles we accepted as inevitable. Most of us had not heard of Keynes.

Samuelson, like Smith before him, explained the world as he saw it, and his viewpoint had dominated in North America and the West for decades. We accepted what we called a "free market economy."

Samuelson's text was probably misnamed because it was more of a free market handbook than a "study" of economics. He gave details about how the competitive market was supposed to work, and did so with the near evangelical assumption that it was at the core of the success of the Western world.

Not much attention was given to the text's weaknesses.

Other economic systems, and political/economic systems, had been tried and found wanting: state socialism had failed in Germany and Italy. The Stalinist or communist Soviet Union system had imploded; the Berlin Wall came down in 1989, and the country financially collapsed in 1991. Through the decades, the mix of democracy and free markets was working in the West. The state passed laws, as it saw necessary, to temper and protect the competitive market as it evolved, seemingly to almost everyone's benefit.

Why does economic theory matter?

It matters because the generally accepted assumptions provide the basis for our laws and those laws define opportunities: they determine if banks should be regulated or not, and if and how we need laws to protect competition. Public assumptions allow nations to print money, collect taxes, and wage wars. Good economics can preserve, protect, and develop civil society, by considering the future: our short-term future and our children's longer-term futures. The more we understand economics, the more likely we are to create a healthy future.

Adam Smith saw that it was the sum of the individual efforts that were bettering society. Good ideas would prevail; the poor ones would fail. He saw that different ideas and new concepts provided competition, and that competition was fundamental for the system. It was expected that competition would move society to an equilibrium: prices would come down to some steady level, wages would rise to some steady level, and profits would normalize at some reasonable level. For that to happen, no business could be "too big to fail"!

The purpose of this chapter has been to show how our economic assumptions began, and also to give a sense of what has changed from the world of Adam Smith. In the chapters ahead, I'll show how our understanding of economic theory has changed a little, while the world has changed a lot.

In Chapter Two, I'll examine the evolution of economic ideas as seen by two giants in economics.

2. Noteworthy economists

Of course I believe in free enterprise, but in my system of free enterprise, the democratic principle is that there never was, never has been, never will be, room for the ruthless exploitation of the many for the benefit of the few.
—President Harry S. Truman; Congressional Record; May, 1944

IN NORTH AMERICA IN THE EARLY '60S, THERE WAS HOPE AND opportunity. Young people didn't hope to find a job; it was a question of picking one. Expectations were that you would likely spend the rest of your working career at that job, or at most, two jobs. We didn't realize what a luxury we had—not all young people in the world faced the future feeling so confident and so sure that the world was fair.

My first job was in sales, like my father's, in a manufacturing company in what we call today the "real economy." I sold card filing systems that improved inventory management and the use of capital: what decades later would be called "God's work," but I will return to that. Decades later, I realized that the real economy was being overshadowed by finance, but I will come back to that, also. I was married, and our middle-class family could survive, as our parents had, on one income. We didn't realize that it was the "system" that made it possible—that same system that now makes a one-income family impossible for most couples. I picked my first job within three weeks: I say "picked" it, because it was one of three I was offered. That was the norm then. On the day I got the job, our daughter was born.

The so-called Cold War was at its height, but there was no dialogue about the competing ideologies: capitalism and communism. Both are "isms," like fascism and socialism. Capitalism and communism were not the only two ideologies, as I was to learn, but two in a wider spectrum of options. However, in the Cold War, we heard of only two: communism—the evil threat—and capitalism, the good guys. We heard about Marx, communism's evil promoter, whom Samuelson more or less dismissed as irrelevant. There was no attempt to differentiate between the horror that was the Stalinist regime, the idealism of Marx, or the reality of socialist economies. Sweden was an enigma.

Today, because of the crash of 2007–2008, there is reason to take a closer look at two economists: Marx, from almost a century ago, because he has now become relevant, and Galbraith, from a few decades ago, because he foresaw much of the economic change we've experienced. Each saw economics as integrated with governance and other life choices, the sum of which is political economy.

Karl Marx (1818–1883)

> Karl Marx … has the distinction of greatly influencing the thought of the many who have never read him.
> —John Kenneth Galbraith

Marx foresaw that with capitalism, the rich would get richer, the poor would get poorer, and that the world's natural resources would get depleted. Sound familiar? Marx predated Keynes by about a century, and his ideas weren't well-known, initially. It took him 30 years of work before his major book, *Das Kapital*, was published, and then it took over five years to sell one thousand copies. It would be another 30 years before his work was noticed enough to be mentioned in *The Economist*.

His ideas have resurfaced because of how much they apply today, and in the first year following the start of our 2007 recession, *Das Kapital* sold 1,500 copies, more than in its initial five years. In 2014, an original copy sold on AbeBooks for $40,000.

Keynes, as noted in Chapter One, wrote about how capitalism was subject to recessions and depressions, and worse, that it was the nature of the system to stay in that unproductive state. The system was not, as had been popularly accepted, self-correcting. Marx had said earlier that the system, for a number of reasons that I'll discuss, was bound to fail. Keynes tried to save it with new remedies. For most of us in the 1950s and 1960s, the work of Marx in economics was skimmed over—he was ignored, treated superficially, or demeaned—his work considered the work of a dour, bearded radical. We knew nothing of the person, the quality of his ideas, or that he is regarded as one of the founders of the social sciences. Nor did we have any idea how major his influence has been in human history. We didn't know, and most would be surprised to learn, that he was one of the first to define capitalism.

Marxism is a system for analyzing class and society, a methodology, but it's not communism. And neither Marxism nor communism is Stalinism—that was the brutal centralized police state imposed on the Russian people from 1922 to 1952, when an estimated 700,000 people died in the Stalinist purges.

Marx was born in 1818 in the town of Trier in the Kingdom of Prussia in Northern Europe. His birth dates to about the time the monarchy was abolished, and his town became part of Germany. Karl was the third of nine children of Henrietta and Herschel, upper-middle-class parents. Dad was a lawyer with a passion for reading philosophy, especially Kant and Voltaire. Mom was Dutch, the daughter of a rabbi in the prosperous family that founded the Phillips Electronics company. Before Karl was born, his dad converted from Judaism to Lutheran, probably because of a new Prussian law banning Jews from high society.

Karl studied law and philosophy at the University of Bonn. He joined the Trier Tavern Club, a drinking society, and for a while was president. After two semesters, he had run up debt, gone to prison for drunkenness, and been wounded in a duel. Dad stepped in and insisted he go to a more serious university. Karl achieved a doctorate at the University of Jena (near Leipzig) and became a journalist by the age of 23. He was fascinated by the philosophy of

Hegel and the works of Shakespeare, which he studied and quoted extensively. Later, he instilled his love of literature in his family.

Marx was 25 when he married 29-year-old Jenny von Westphalen, the daughter of a wealthy Prussian baron and a descendant of Scottish aristocracy. Jenni and Karl had been friends as children and her father, Ludwig, had been a mentor to Marx. The two men spent time together discussing everything from English literature to socialist thought. Jenny gave up her upper-class lifestyle to share her husband's revolutionary ideas. She was his partner, translating his illegible handwriting, nursing him through illness, and being his bedrock of support, even when they were broke. They had seven children. Sadly, four died before reaching adolescence. The three daughters who survived were dedicated to social reform.

In 1843, Karl and Jenny moved to Paris, at the time considered the political heart of Europe. There he met Friedrich Engels, a German thinker and writer who became a lifelong friend. The two read and wrote on widely diverse topics including philosophy, politics, and economics. (Engels developed a theory that it was men that created monogamous marriage to ensure that their children would inherit their property.)

Das Kapital, A Critique on Political Economy, was written just a few years after the French Revolution, when class struggle was well understood. In 1846, his manuscript for *Das Kapital* was overdue, and Marx wrote to his German publisher. "I shall not have it published without revising it yet again, both as regards matter and style. It goes without saying that a writer who works continuously cannot, at the end of six months, publish word for word what he wrote six months earlier." Twelve years later, still no nearer completion, he explained, "The thing is proceeding very slowly because no sooner does one set about finally disposing of subjects to which one has devoted years of study than they start revealing new aspects and demand to be thought out further." He was an obsessive perfectionist.

In 1849, Marx moved to London, where he spent the rest of his life. Engels moved to England months later. For nine years, Marx worked as the European correspondent for the *New York Daily Tribune*.

One surprising bit of Marx's writing that we hear nothing about, was his opinion that in its early stages, capitalism would be an efficient way to organize society. Few people are aware he anticipated that in the beginning, capitalism would produce wealth with fairly equal distribution, as it did. He showed great foresight in the late 1800s, when we consider the economic reality seen in America in the 1950s and 1960s, and his more dire predictions seen in this century.

In addition to his journalism, Marx published about twenty papers, but he is best known for *Das Kapital*. He believed in a classless society, where people would contribute according to their ability, and receive according to their need. In his ideal organization, all property would be owned in common by the people or by the state. Communism has many variations, but to Marx, it was the system that flowed from the Latin word *communis,* or shared: an idealized world of caring.

Our Western vision of communism has been distorted by the extreme police state that was Stalinism: a single political party, very limited personal freedom, a state-managed economy, no freedom of the press or religion, no private property. There are less rigid forms of planned or shared economy—socialist economies that have many variations, as exist in Vietnam, Russia, China, India, or the Scandinavian countries.

Marx followed Volume 1 of *Das Kapital*, in 1867, with Volume 2, in 1885. Marx and Engels published *The Communist Manifesto*, a pamphlet and guidebook on how to establish a classless society. Two years after Marx's death, Engels completed Volume 3 in 1894.

Marx's decision to entitle his major work *Das Kapital* (Capital) is significant. He had studied class struggle since his college days, and his father-in-law coached him on socialism. But he chose to write about capital, a thing and a subject not well understood. He examined the role of money and explained its role in commodity transactions. There were two types: one was the use of money in ordinary transactions, to buy and sell things. Another was to buy things in order to resell them and make a profit. That second role of money used to make a profit was Marx's definition of capital. Money used this way, he saw, would become an end in itself, and would create an unceasing search for profit. He believed that profit alone did nothing useful for society.

He elaborated on the problems he saw with free market theory. For a theory to survive, it must withstand the test of time and Marx expected capitalism to fail. By thinking intensely about the nature of transactions he concluded that competition would disappear, resources would be squandered, workers would be exploited, and the rich would get richer. His analysis was so objective and thorough that he is referred to as one of the originators of the social sciences.

After the huge failure of the markets in 2007, scholars reminded us that the absolute failure of competitive capitalism was what Marx had predicted. He never said when, where, or how it would fail, only that it would, because of its four major failings. Let's examine them.

(a) Competition is self-defeating

Marx predicted that, over time, more successful companies would triumph over the less competitive, and swallow them up. In time there would be fewer competitors, which would inevitably lead to only a few competitors (an oligopoly), or no competitors (monopoly). With that would be the end of competition. He predicted the Walmart world.

I learned one tiny example about business concentration in the 1970s, in the town of St. Thomas, Ontario, about twenty miles east of where my great-grandfather had a farm. He was a delightful, ruddy, white-haired cherub of a man, who made the best pralines and chocolates. Vair's Candy shop was in its second generation, run by one of two Vair brothers who learned candy making from their father. One stayed to run the business. His brother left and invented a caramel popcorn creation, which he called Poppycock. In 1960, he sold the rights to his invention to a Swiss company.

"My brother got rich!" I was told while I was buying pralines. The Swiss company sold it to Lincoln Snacks in 1991, which in turn was sold to Conagra Foods in 2007. Now, Poppycock is one of 40 or so brands, which include Wesson Oil, Van Camp's Beans, Chef Boyardee products, Orville Redenbacher popcorn, and the Poppycock developed by Harold Vair. Now, 26,000 employees work in this conglomerate. With every product Conagra acquires, competition diminishes. (Cracker Jack, a similar popcorn snack we all know from *Take Me Out to the Ballgame* fame, had a similar fate: created by one man, developed into a profitable business, sold to

Borden, who sold it to Frito Lay, a division of PepsiCo. The honest Quaker of Quaker Oats, and Starbucks are now PepsiCo products.)

My small business grew by becoming automated. We invested millions of dollars in automated equipment and produced more and more pieces of product, with less and less manpower. Our growth took place at the expense of another company's—one we drove out of business. As they say, we swallowed their business, and a decade later we were swallowed by our main competitor, an even bigger company.

As Marx had foreseen, fewer and fewer companies would control more and more. And with that, fewer and fewer individual people control more and more.

(b) Capitalism depletes resources

The purpose of many industries, for example, gold mining, forestry, or oil, is to extract and sell gold, trees, or oil. The faster and more they do so, the faster the owners will profit. The sooner the resource is sold, the sooner the owners maximize their profit. There is no incentive to do it right, no incentive to preserve it, and no incentive not to use it. The same is true for fish, water, coal, apples, fur, ivory—everything that can be sold. The market dynamic is to use it, use it all, and use it fast!

Environmentalists are correct when they say capitalism is the enemy of ecology.

A system that uses ever-increasing amounts of finite resources is not sustainable. We talk about managing the ecology, but it is more important for us to learn that we are part of ecology, whether or not we manage it. As corporations aren't living things, a sustainable environment doesn't matter to them.

The Canadian journalist and activist Naomi Klein explains in her book, *This Changes Everything: Capitalism vs the Climate*, that it's increasingly apparent that capitalism is doing as Marx foresaw, that it is remorselessly consuming everything as fast as it can. Klein writes we need to change our attitudes about how the economy should work if our species is to survive. Our consumption of fossil fuels illustrates what she means—the trend is exponential, a mathematical term I will often discuss in the pages ahead.

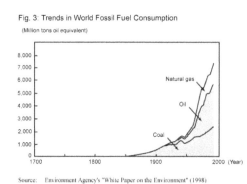

Fig. 3: Trends in World Fossil Fuel Consumption (Million tons oil equivalent)

Source: Environment Agency's "White Paper on the Environment" (1998)

Finite resources cannot last, nor will they be preserved in a market system that makes money only when things are consumed. The Green movement understands that, as do Indigenous Americans who want to protect the land. To them, land cannot be inherited but is borrowed from the next generation.

(c) Competition exploits people

Marx recognized that capitalism exploits resources, and also saw that eventually, capitalism exploits people. Why?

Businesses need to make profits, but true competition drives down prices. To stay in business, businesses need to reduce costs. The two greatest areas of expense are raw materials and wages. In many businesses, these amount to about 1/3 for materials, and 1/3 for wages. The final 1/3 covers everything else, including the need for profit. Those were the ratios in my business, in my local restaurant, and for most businesses I have known.

Material costs tend to have limited potential to be reduced. Wages, however, have more. To reduce the expense of wages, workers can be paid less, or production increased. Technological improvement is one way to increase production.

Samuelson's model of the social contract had been that competition would create productivity gains and, in his model, workers would share the benefits. Auto workers benefited more than most from this system because their efficiency suggestions earned a lot of money for their companies, and the workers got to keep a piece. Union protection insured that.

However, when opportunities for increased efficiency run out, life gets cruel. There are then two options left: one is to move production to lower-wage countries, and the other is just to pay workers less. Both options break the social contract.

When people claim it's wrong for corporations to replace local labour with cheaper labour elsewhere, they misunderstand the economic system. Businesses do not exist to serve social policy, nor to create jobs, nor to do good. They exist to make money. That trumps the social contract, and people suffer.

A significant consequence of lowering wages or moving jobs out of the country is that the wage income that is lost is money taken from the local economy, as demand for services or products decreases. These were consequences, like the poor getting poorer and capitalism reducing demand and defeating itself, that Marx foresaw.

(d) The rich will get richer

> So distribution should undo excess, and each man have enough.
> —William Shakespeare (1564–1616); *King Lear*

Marx foresaw that, as competition declined, wealth and power would be controlled by fewer and fewer people. What he anticipated, we have seen happen: increasing wealth in fewer hands, larger homes on larger lots in gated communities. Marx predicted that along with increasing wealth and increasing inequality, there could be increased violence, as well.

Most of us, including Shakespeare, expected the system to do better.

In the 1970s, those of us in business saw competitors disappearing as bigger companies swallowed smaller ones, economic growth slowed, and the income gap began to expand.

Ours is not the first period in history in which the rich have gotten rapidly richer. It happened in France prior to the Revolution, and in America in 1928, just a year before the Great Depression. In the years after the Depression, income distribution evened out for decades, until about the 1970s. Since then, wealth has again been relentlessly concentrating—squashing hopes for an egalitarian society. We've been recreating the class system the pioneers risked their lives to escape.

For the past 30 years, an ever-increasing share of economic growth has risen to the top one-hundredth of 1% of the people. In the US, this small group makes an average of $27 million per household per year, while the bottom 90% of households earn about $77,000.[26]

The Economic Policy Institute is a nonprofit, nonpartisan think tank created in 1986 to include the needs of low- and middle-income workers in economic policy discussions.[27] It released a study in 2012 of the pay of Chief Executives at America's 350 biggest companies. CEOs were paid 231 times the average private sector worker. Are these people worth 231 times the value of the average worker? How does that fit with the belief that all people are created equal? It confirms Marx's forecast that the rich will get richer.

Marxism didn't seem relevant during the boom of the sixties and seventies. However, after a few years in the workforce, I realized neither did Samuelson—because the growth of corporate power was changing basic assumptions. This concerned me enough that I spent about two years in research for a book that I've had in mind to publish since then.

In 1968, John Kenneth Galbraith published *The New Industrial State* on the same theme. He made clear from his academic perspective what I was seeing from my insider's perspective: corporations were changing the social and economic structure of the world, and an economic system that once worked for most of us now worked for a few.

---

26 http://www.motherjones.com/politics/2011/02/income-inequality-in-america-chart-graph

27 http://www.epi.org/publication/ceo-pay-231-times-greater-average-worker/

John Kenneth Galbraith (1908–2006)

> Modesty is a vastly overrated virtue!
> —John Kenneth Galbraith

Galbraith was born in Canada, and I feel some bond with him. His Scottish parents lived on a farm in the Ontario town of Iona Station, seven miles down the road from Dutton, where my grandfather McRae's family farmed. Thus, Galbraith and I share farming roots in the same rural soil.

Galbraith's father was both a farmer and a school teacher. His mother was a political activist, and they were members of an early farmers' union. They had four children. After high school, John went to the Agricultural University in Guelph, Ontario, and in 1931 earned a degree in Agricultural Economics.

Choosing to use the name Ken, he went on to Berkeley and obtained a master's and a doctorate in Agricultural Economics (1934). In 1937, he married Catherine Atwater, an educated writer who had studied at the Sorbonne, graduated from Radcliffe College with a Master of Arts, and spoke several languages. The Galbraiths had three sons, two of whom survived. For their honeymoon, they had sailed to England, so Ken could spend time at Cambridge on a yearlong scholarship to study with Keynes, but it never happened. They arrived while Keynes was on leave recovering from a heart attack.

Keynes was a towering figure, as was Galbraith: in both cases literally, as well as intellectually. Keynes was six foot four, Galbraith was six foot eight! Galbraith had almost no equal in his ability to clearly make a point. A conservative intellectual peer was William

F. Buckley, who also was an articulate, powerful debater. They were friends and debated publicly, later on the *Today* show. Galbraith had almost no humility. Perhaps it was just his well-tuned sense of his own worth.

I am fortunate to have received a letter from him, and to add a little interest to this book, I have taken a page from his book *Name-Dropping: From FDR On* [28] where he did just that. In the same fashion, I have included stories about people I've met who provided economic insight and dates to provide the context of how capitalism has changed.

During World War II, Galbraith served as Deputy Head of the Office of Price Administration. Governments needing to produce things for the war effort created large budget deficits, which raised concern that inflation might cause a runaway wage-price spiral. And so, in 1942, Roosevelt issued a General Maximum Price Regulation. Galbraith had the job of keeping prices stable. For that, he was accused of having communist tendencies.

After the war, he was hired by Henry Luce, a conservative Republican who founded many magazines including *Time, Life, Fortune Magazine*, and *Sports Illustrated*. Luce dominated American journalism. Galbraith wrote for *Fortune Magazine*, where his readers were America's business leaders, and for five years he saw his role as educating the nation and its leaders on economics and Keynesianism.

In 1948, he went to Harvard, where he stayed most of the rest of his life, with two short exceptions: one at the State Department as

---

28 Galbraith, J.K. *Name-Dropping: From FDR On*. Houghton Mifflin-Harcourt, 1999.

director of the Office of Economic Security Policy, and then during a stint as an advisor to John F. Kennedy, and as his Ambassador to India (1961 – 1963).

In 1952, he wrote *A Theory of Price Control*, referring to it as the best book he ever wrote. "The only difficulty with it," he said, was that "five people read it. Maybe 10. I made up my mind that I would never again place myself at the mercy of the technical economists who had the enormous power to ignore what I had written. I set out to involve a larger community."

The Affluent Society followed in 1958. In this, one of the top economic books of the 20'th century, his phrase "conventional wisdom," became part of our language—it refers to widely accepted, but not necessarily correct, ideas. The phrase was typically Galbraith: droll, dry, understandable, and slyly implying that not all widely accepted ideas are wise. Almost sixty years ago, he wrote about how, in the post-war period, wealth was starting to concentrate in private hands, at public expense.

It was the same era when we were hearing that the increasingly affluent United States was using the gross domestic product (GDP) to measure progress. The state of the economy was increasingly becoming news. GDP was used as a measurement, even though it failed to include useful, essential things, like improvements in education or social services. Nonetheless, we got used to it and believed that, as GDP improved, so would the lot of workers, who had learned to expect reasonable pay, the ability to buy luxury goods, and the time to enjoy them. The economy was changing from manufacturing things people needed, to manufacturing stuff they wanted. Increasingly, they were the goods corporations wanted them to buy.

In the late 1960s, the free competitive market was diminishing. Large companies were increasing their market share, and preferring stability and predictability to competition, took steps to override competition. I saw this in the corporation I worked for. Stability provided predictable profits, less risk for managers, and more bonuses. The needs of corporate leaders took precedence over competition theory, over employees' welfare, and over shareholders' rights. The intentions were not sinister, just a fact that market predictability happened to be in fundamental contradiction with the basic necessity for competition in competitive enterprise.

John Kenneth Galbraith and the new industrial state

In 1966, Galbraith gave a series of lectures on the BBC entitled *The New Industrial State*. He explored the implications of corporations controlling an ever-increasing portion of the economy. He foresaw with this development that classical economics, by then modified by Keynesian principles, was facing new challenges, defined, as his title said, as "a new industrial state."

The principal function of the free market (personified by "the invisible hand" that allowed markets to run with few rules) was being usurped by controlling hands. Businesses were managing the market to serve their needs. The traditional balance between supply and demand was being replaced with a corporate controlled market. Corporations did the planning, and planning for business usurped planning for people. A technological business class was taking control. For example, the Shell Oil Company's plans run to

2075—decades from now. The city public library board I served on could only plan for five.

The market was being changed to retain competition in image, but not in substance. The local Shell gasoline station franchisee was in competition with the Exxon station in a real struggle, while Exxon, Shell, and a diminishing handful of others managed the bigger market. Chevrolet appeared to be in competition with Cadillac, although both were owned by General Motors. It was becoming competition on the bottom, but not at the top, and it's at the top where, theory says, it's essential.

Corporate power grew as corporations learned more about how to use advertising to create demand and how to use their power, influence, and money to define culture and control politics. As Galbraith put it, "In a world of perfect competition, the control of production flows from the consumers to the organizations." In the corporate-run world, the flow is reversed. People become the servants, not the masters of the market.

About the time his book was published, not far from the farming towns of Iona Station and Dutton, there was a Mennonite community, an old-world Amish community of farming families who worked hard and lived simply. They had their own schools and their own publishing house. They didn't use electricity and depended on horses, hard work, and no doubt, the Grace of God. It was there I met David Luthy, who ran their publishing business. He was about my age, mid-thirties, bearded, dressed in blue denim, and had a traditional straw hat sitting on the edge of his desk.

We talked about the problems of trying to maintain an old-world lifestyle in the midst of the New Industrial State. He explained their biggest problem: as their families grew, they needed more land for farms, and to purchase land, the community needed dollars. In order to earn dollars, they would grow a crop in bulk. However, the purchaser might want the product—tomatoes for example—to be grown to a set of specifications that required the use of fertilizers or pesticides. They needed more dollars to buy these products. Corporate standards were being imposed on traditional farming practices.

David Luthy provided my first lesson on financialization: money increasingly being at the root of things. In the wider community, farms were getting bigger, machines replacing horses, and chemicals replacing manure. For all this, dollars were increasingly required.

Changes were visible off the farm as well. Fast-food restaurants were appearing everywhere, and bank towers increasingly dominated the core of almost every North American city. The insight from the discussion with David of the changes he and his community were trying to work around stayed with me, and I saw similar intrusions everywhere.

Galbraith has had a profound influence on my thinking. He wrote over sixty books, and each one I have read is clear and thoughtful. (One was about money, which I will examine in Chapter Six.) He was not opposed to capitalism but, like Keynes, and Marx, knew it wasn't perfect. In his view, economics should serve all the people.

Summary: as the economy changed

With the rise of corporations came the rise of corporate managers, and I was one. Our role was to make the business more profitable, and with that, we assumed, making it larger. If we did that, we had job security. Over the decades, as Galbraith noted, corporate managers moved their private needs higher on the priority list, and eventually, the list changed from serving the corporation to having the corporation serve them.

Corporate managers were engaged in long-term planning, for the benefit of the company—the interests of "the people" were not on the agenda. Perhaps the silent hand of the market would look after them; it just wasn't a corporate concern. Corporate planning slowly dwarfed public planning.

Corporate leaders benefited with this emerging arrangement as they paid themselves increasingly well. To make their salary decisions appear neutral, they established personnel committees and appointed their friends to serve on them. These friends would make appropriately generous decisions and would receive the same in return. Shareholders took second place when pay, bonuses, and dividends were decided. Management whims and greed took precedence.

As the management class got entrenched, the door between state bureaucrats and corporate technocrats began to revolve. Corporate managers would be recruited into government services, and politicians would retire into corporate ranks. While this is well-documented old news, it's important to acknowledge how it increasingly clouded decisions.

Six years prior to Galbraith's *New Industrial State* being published, we had been given a warning about an emerging dangerous influence over the economy. Dwight D. Eisenhower, a West Point graduate and career soldier, was in his final three days as president in 1961, when he addressed the nation on January 17 with a farewell address. He warned the American people they "… must guard against the acquisition of unwarranted influence … by the military industrial complex." No other president had issued such a warning, because it was a new trend. Unfortunately, it was a warning that went unheeded. (While I will look at this warning again in the Appendix, I mention it here because it raised the same principle as Galbraith's warning of corporate control in the new industrial estate.)

Both Galbraith and Eisenhower saw the uncontrolled, self-serving use of power by technocrats. Military businesses function the same way all corporations do, managed by the same self-serving technocratic class. The traffic between jobs in the military, industry, and government is extensive and well documented, and Eisenhower's warning was essentially the same as Galbraith's: beware of the power of corporations, in general!

During World War II, Galbraith's experience controlling prices and rents reinforced his awareness that unregulated capitalism could lead to disaster.

Price controls were used by the Roman Emperor Diocletian and have been used repeatedly since then. They were imposed by Nixon and Trudeau in the 1970s. Capitalism needing state control is an often-repeated cycle that should be unnecessary if the "free market" works.

The 1960s was a colourful decade. The Beatnik counter-culture of the 1950s was replaced by hippies and the peace and love movement. John F. Kennedy was president (1961–1963), and Pierre Trudeau became prime minister (1968). Each embraced the enthusiasm of the new generation and Keynesian principles. Kennedy employed Galbraith, and Trudeau had studied Galbraith's theories. As Galbraith acknowledged, Trudeau was "the only political leader ever to acknowledge openly, perhaps recklessly, a commitment to my economic views." Galbraith was right. When a news story quoted Trudeau that his economic policies were those of Galbraith, the stock market fell!

Kennedy assumed that it was the role of government to pursue full employment. It was part of the social contract in that era, and the civil rights movement became part of it. No longer was poverty expected to be the norm for African Americans. The terms of the social contract were being broadened.

From 1967, when Galbraith wrote *The New Industrial State*, until the end of the twentieth century, conventional wisdom continued to change.

> Ken Galbraith ... will be remembered, and read when most of us Nobel Laureates will be buried in footnotes down in dusty library stacks.
> —Paul Samuelson[29]

Samuelson had won the Nobel award for economics in 1970. Galbraith never did.

---

29 Samuelson, Paul, as quoted in Richard Parker's *John Kenneth Galbraith: His Life, His Politics, His Economics* (Farrar, Straus, and Giroux, 2005).

3.
Economics lessons: marijuana, money, Kenya, and aid

Life is what happens while you are making other plans!
—John Lennon; *Beautiful Boy*; 1980

I WAS EXPOSED, ALMOST ACCIDENTALLY, TO ISSUES THAT RELATE to economics. One was the market for illegal drugs. How did the drug market work? What was behind it?

Another was the complexities of poverty in what were then called "developing" nations.

These issues led me to more questions about the causes of poverty and the economics of foreign aid and the military. In this chapter, I will examine both.

Drug laws

In the late 1960s, my wife and I shared an eclectic circle of friends in the city of London, Ontario. Our friends were business colleagues, social workers, artists, university professors, hippies, and students.

I had a minor profile in our community because of activities in fundraising and local politics, and my time spent serving several years on the Library Board, for a time as Vice Chair. I was also on the art gallery board, as we built a new gallery.

The hippie era was at its peak. Pierre Trudeau personified the period and was elected prime minister in 1968.

The huge Woodstock Rock Concert occurred in rural New York State in 1969, a seminal event in counterculture history. Throughout North America, there was an active drug subculture that was at odds with the law. The enforcement tactics of the police in both the United States and Canada at the time were crude and were unnecessarily alienated young people. Police were using undercover officers to infiltrate hippie groups to search out drug use and this created paranoia. Our friends at the Addiction Research Foundation told us of the negative effect this was having on kids, who were becoming fearful of police because of police spies and entrapment. A mantra at the time was, "Don't trust anyone over thirty."

Trudeau's charisma generated, on a lesser scale, the enthusiasm that the world had for John F. Kennedy a decade earlier. Trudeau encouraged change, and this encouraged us.

In early 1969, I established the Legalize Marijuana Committee with the sole purpose of lobbying the federal government for saner laws. I became its spokesperson and co-chair with Dr. Ray Libel, a psychiatrist. We assumed that the government wanted feedback—probably even needed it—to discuss changing the law. We were right, and the government confirmed it in several ways.

First, confirmation came when we were invited to meet with the federal Minister of Health and Welfare in Ottawa. Not everyone gets that opportunity. Off we went: the co-chair, my wife, our daughter, and I. Only our immediate family knew the details.

We had booked the cheapest room in the Chateau Laurier Hotel, near where we would meet. When we checked in, nothing unusual was said, but the bellhop took us to the penthouse suite! We were in a corner turret on the top floor of the hotel, with outstanding views on two sides, four king-size beds, a living room with several sofas and a kitchen area. Someone had apparently learned our itinerary, upgraded the room, and paid the difference—feedback a second time, that the government appreciated our efforts. (When we checked out, we paid the economy rate we expected. Again, nothing was said.)

Someone had released our itinerary to the press, and shortly after we had checked in, we started receiving phone calls. Reporters were calling—the government was leaving nothing to chance to get the publicity they wanted.

The minister's office was on the top floor of a high-rise in Ottawa, a short walk from both the hotel and Parliament buildings. Ray and I arrived about ten minutes early, met the receptionist, and were asked to wait. It was a modest waiting room with about six others, who hadn't heard us introduce ourselves. As we listened, it was clear from their conversations, that they were journalists who were there because of us. "I wonder who these guys are … I see nothing wrong with it … I smoke the occasional joint … good luck to them!"

Soon, Ray and I were asked to go in, and reporters squirmed as they realized they had missed a chance to get a first interview. We were taken to a more private waiting room before John Munro, an energetic, chain-smoking Minister of Health and Welfare, welcomed us into his inner office, where sofas circled a large coffee table. On the table was a file folder about eight inches thick, too deep to close. When Munro noticed it was sitting open, he immediately closed it and put an ashtray on top.

We had sent him one letter and a small brochure, yet he had a file on us with eight inches thick. Later, as I thought about the file, our hotel upgrade, and our schedule being released, I recalled that we had a break-in in our home a few weeks earlier. The break-in was a non-event; it would have been unnoticed except someone had broken the cheap lock on the only file cabinet in the house. Nothing was taken, but in hindsight, I believe it must have been the Royal Canadian Mounted Police doing a routine report on people about to meet a government minister on a contentious topic.

We understood that it was a sensitive political issue and the meeting was for political purposes. The government was using our group to float a trial balloon alerting the world that they were thinking of changing drug laws. After a few minutes of coffee and chat, the press was invited in. About twenty journalists filled the room for about half an hour of Q and A. Then one of the journalists asked if we would agree to go to the Press Club on Parliament Hill where another thirty or so journalists were waiting. We agreed and were taken to the press media studio for TV and radio interviews by another dozen journalists.

Later the same year, the Trudeau government took a step towards changing drug laws and established a Royal Commission.

3. Economics lessons: marijuana, money, Kenya, and aid

Royal Commissions are a big deal in Canada, like a Presidential Commission in the United States. The Commission of Inquiry into the Non-Medical Use of Drugs made it clear that the government saw this as a civil rights and medical issue, not a criminal one.

The government appointed Gerald LeDain, a lawyer, and Dean of Canada's prestigious Osgoode Hall law school to head the commission., which began with a public hearing on October 26, 1969. For their opening day, they invited two organizations to appear: the Royal Canadian Mounted Police and our group, the Legalize Marijuana Committee. Each group presented briefs, and the next day's newspaper had a lead story on the hearing, including two photos: one of the Commissioner of the RCMP, and the other, me. (My mother wrote to the paper to get a copy of the photo, "… before my son goes to jail.")

The official report recommended the repeal of laws against possession of cannabis and the repeal of laws prohibiting cultivation for personal use. One of the commissionaires went further, recommending a policy of legal distribution. Now, 48 years later, we are moving to legalize marijuana in Canada.

The RCMP referred to a study they claimed showed that marijuana was a "soft drug" that led to "hard" drugs. It was a popular belief at the time, especially among North American police forces. When asked to provide copies of the study, it turned out there wasn't one, and in the Commission's final report, the RCMP were criticized for lying.

Unfortunately, the Canadian government ignored the report. We took some solace in the fact that aggressive enforcement of Canadian anti-pot laws waned, and minor issues of drug use were all but ignored. We can only speculate why the Canadian

Government failed to act, but suspect it was probably because the government to our south opposed it.

Looked at as a business, illegal drug distribution serves the market well. Distribution by pyramid selling is one of the most efficient methods of distribution. People decide they want to make a few dollars and get some grass and sell it to their friends. Some of those friends become sub-dealers.

One of the most recognized models of legal pyramid selling is Mary Kay Inc., a hugely successful company. Pyramid selling is cheap, effective, understandable, and low risk. Whether to sell cosmetics or illegal drugs, anyone can be hired, and then hire any number of sub-dealers. Everyone gets a cut, and the profit margins are high enough in cosmetic sales to award the occasional pink Cadillac. Profit margins for drugs are higher because they are illegal—the market more dangerous. The vehicles tend to be bigger, and black, usually with tinted windows.

Thirty-three years after the LeDain Commission, I was a member of a Social Action Committee (2003) that was studying the "War On Drugs," and supported a progressive resolution on alternatives. I was invited to attend a national conference, and to prepare for it I updated myself on some 30 years of changes. I learned how huge and dangerous the illegal drug market had become.

At the conference, I met Judge Jim Gray from the Superior Court in Southern California, who told me about how teenagers in his California town could get crack cocaine easier than beer, because beer was legal. Privately, he told me how much he respected Judge Le Dain and the work he had done with the Commission.

How big is the illegal drug market? One answer can be found in the Caribbean.

The Cayman Islands: Swimming in money

Grand Cayman Island is the largest of three Cayman Islands, about two hundred miles south of Cuba in the Caribbean Sea. It's a tropical paradise, where you can swim with stingrays in North Sound or take a submarine ride along the coral reef cliff on the south.

Grand Cayman is about an hour or so by plane south of Miami, about two hours north of Columbia, and two hours east of Mexico—therefore, central to two drug-producing nations and the huge drug-consuming American market. Politically, the islands are British Overseas Territories. They are not independent, not a country, and not truly British. They occupy a small area, one-quarter the size of New York City (102 vs. 468 sq. miles) with a small population of 57,000 people.

About 30,000 of those people live in George Town, on Grand Cayman, and this tiny town is the fifth-largest banking centre[30] in the world. There are 279 banks, and 260 of them do no banking in the Caymans. With the Caymans' unusual political structure, laws get strange and enforcement stranger. Drug lords can take a day trip to the Caymans, do some banking, avoid all taxes, and be home for dinner. Money laundering and tax avoidance are reasons the Caymans have become one of the world's largest banking centres.

Tax avoidance is the increasingly popular trend for corporations and the rich to avoid tax. The chart below is Canadian. A chart for the US would be similar. In 2015, Canadian corporations funnelled $13 billion to the Caymans, resulting in a loss to Canada of, at least, a billion dollars in tax revenue.

---

30   *The Economist,* February 2007. http://www.economist.com/node/8695139?story_id=8695139

Some people say that the war on drugs has been a failure, but they have misunderstood its purpose. It has made billions of dollars for those in the market; it has fueled a private prison industry in the US, made money for the banks, and has been used to politically control nations. Was it intended to control drugs, or to make them more profitable? From my perspective, over thirty years, it has been enormously successful at making drugs more profitable, and a dismal failure at control.

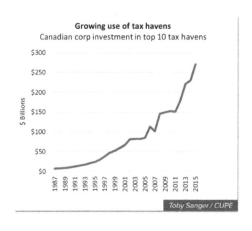

The economics of illegal drugs

> How do you make a pile of weeds worth a million dollars? Make them illegal!

Those words were spoken by an Indigenous speaker at a conference I attended on alternatives to the war on drugs. He asked and answered his own question.

Back in the seventies, when I was involved in the politics of marijuana, I had an acquaintance. A shy accountant type, he flew once a week to New York from Toronto dressed as a banker: white shirt, conservative tie, dark suit, and a briefcase in hand. One way his briefcase contained drugs, the other way it was money. The border was easier to cross then and the profits big enough to pay for the trip.

Charles Bowden, an American journalist who lives in Las Cruces, New Mexico, wrote *Down by the River*, about the death of a young man who was killed in 1995. Bruno Jordan was the young brother of a Drug Enforcement Agency (DEA) officer. While researching the death, Bowden learned a lot about the Mexican/US drug war.[31] The river in the book's title is the Rio Grande, which runs through El Paso, Texas on the border with Mexico. While doing his research, Bowden learned of a US Customs officer who made $1,000,000 one night for simply not "seeing" a single truck cross the border.

The export of drugs from Mexico to the US had started to boom decades earlier, after alcohol prohibition was repealed in the US and a new trade—drugs—emerged. No one is certain as to the extent of the drug market. A low estimate is $20 billion a year. Tragically, about 20,000 Mexican people are killed every year as a result of the drug trade.

Mexico, Colombia, and Panama have all had major roles in the drug trade. Panama had its government overthrown, because of its leader, Noriega's, role with cocaine in 1989. In order to be able to return to normal lives, the people of Colombia have pleaded to have foreign drug enforcement squads leave their country. The problems for Colombians began in the 1960s with a government war against communists, which morphed into a war against drugs. With ever-increasing US aid, large areas of hillsides were defoliated, possibly

---

31   Bowden, Charles. *Down by the River: Drugs, Money, Murder, and Family*. Simon and Schuster, 2004.

by carcinogenic sprays. (Colombia has oil reserves, but that is another, probably related part of the story.)

Afghanistan regained its status as a narco-state after 9/11. Prior to 2001, the Taliban had ended opium poppy growing, and farmers reverted to food crops. After the Western invasion and occupation, opium poppy crops resumed.

Costa Rica, a nation without an army, with more teachers than police officers, allowed hundreds of US DEA officers to be stationed there in 2013. A nation that in 2009 was rated first on the New Economic Foundation's Happy Planet Index is probably on its way to drug wars like those in Mexico, Colombia, and Afghanistan. There is money to be made in the drug trade.

Nixon declared the war on drugs in 1971. This raised several questions. How do you declare a war on things? Wars used to be declared on countries who were enemies—on people with an army that could fight back. What are the economic effects of a war on drugs likely to be? A standard practice in analyzing questions like these is "*cui bono*," a Latin phrase used in police work and forensic accounting, meaning "to whose benefit?" It's a handy question to keep in mind.

Now, 40 years since the War on Drugs was declared, the United States Drug Enforcement Administration has spent billions of dollars, charged millions of people, and drug use in the United States is higher than ever. In 2012, there was a marijuana-related arrest in the United States every 48 seconds. The DEA confiscates millions of dollars of illegal drugs a year, which simply drives up the price.

If the war on drugs was intended to end drug use, it's a failed program.

If the war on drugs was intended to preserve the illegal drug market and increase illegal drug profits, then it has been a most successful program.

We should have known better. We had the experience of Prohibition (1917–1933), when prohibiting the use of alcohol made alcohol sales increase. By making alcohol illegal, the risk of selling it went up, so did the profit, and so did the number of speakeasies. That's economics. Someone summed up the argument for drug legalization, this way: "It would take the profit away from the bad guys."

The war on drugs ruins lives and communities, who are considered just "collateral damage."

In economic terms, the war on drugs has been an enormous success. It has increased the profit of drug dealers and banks, and made corporate prisons more profitable. It has been used to support neoconservative governments and to defeat people-focused ones.

Kenya and international aid

> A world without poverty is a world where all voices are heard and all human beings are treated equally. Poverty is more than a lack of food, shelter or health insurance. Emerging from poverty means being a full member of a community and able to participate in decision-making processes.
> —From the Oxfam International Annual Report; 2013–2014

When I was in my late twenties, a local fundraising walk for Oxfam was planned, and I volunteered to help. So began years of involvement, first in walks as an organizer, then as an advisor to the Canadian Miles for Millions organization and as a volunteer for Oxfam. In time, I was elected as a director of Oxfam Canada and became vice chair.

Oxfam, an international organization headquartered in Oxford, England, is dedicated to reducing poverty and injustice. Originally called the Oxford Committee for Famine Relief, the organization was formed by a group of Quakers in 1942, to provide food for starving people during the German occupation of Greece.

The Quakers, like the Scots, have had a disproportionate influence on our world: so few have accomplished so much. Quakers founded Barclays Bank, Lloyds Bank, Clarks shoes. Chocolate lovers are indebted to them for Cadbury, and Fry's chocolates. (All three companies are now part of larger multinationals.)

Quakers were a major force in ending slavery, in starting both Amnesty International and Greenpeace, and in founding Cornell and Johns Hopkins Universities. Quite a list of accomplishments for under half a million of them worldwide. The Religious Society of Friends believes in personal responsibility, equality, nonviolence, and passive resistance.

In 1974, I was part of a Canadian delegation that attended an international meeting of all the Oxfams, which at the time were five: England, Canada, Quebec, the United States, and Belgium. Today, there are about a dozen. The meeting was held in a thirteenth-century manor house, in the town of Charney, just southwest of Oxford. Charney Manor is still owned by the Quakers.

Michael Rowntree was head of Oxfam UK, and the meeting ran on Quaker principles: there was an agenda but no votes. After a period of discussion, whenever the chair felt it appropriate, he would comment. If he sensed agreement, he would say something like, "I think we agree we would like to …" And if he heard no objection, we would move on. If he sensed conflict (as on more than one occasion), he interjected with "I do believe it's time for tea …" Tea usually came with side conversations, but if there was still not agreement when we reconvened, the item would be deferred. On occasion, it was deferred to the pub.

At the meeting were people worth mentioning. Brian Walker, the newly appointed executive director of Oxfam International, was a Quaker and his name on two "death" lists for his role in trying to negotiate peace in Northern Ireland. Two of our Canadian delegations were later awarded the United Nations Pearson Peace prize for Canada: Dr. Hugh Keenleyside in 1982 and Meyer Brownstone in 1986. Hugh Keenleyside was our Canadian chair, I was vice chair, and honoured to be in his shadow.

A partial list of Dr. Keenleyside's achievements explains why I was in awe. Healthy, active, and busy at seventy-six years of age after a long, distinguished career as an academic, diplomat, and civil servant, he had served with the 2nd Canadian Tank Battalion in the First World War, served in Japan, became ambassador to Mexico, and was commissioner in the Northwest Territories. From 1950 to 1958, he had served as director-general of the UN Technical Assistance Administration, then became chairman of the British Columbia Power Commission. (He has a dam on the Columbia River named after him.) He'd played a unique part in the Second World War, smuggling American fighter aircraft across the frozen St. Lawrence River into Canada. He was awarded the Order of Canada, Canada's equivalent of a knighthood.

Jacques Jobin, our executive director went on to a lifetime of activism in international affairs. For years he was director of the City of Montreal's Bureau of International Affairs. Professor Immanuel Wallerstein, an American teaching at McGill University in Montreal, was a delegate from Oxfam Quebec. Born in 1930, he earned over a dozen awards and continues working as a senior research scientist in sociology at Yale University on problems with capitalist theory. In 2013, he was one of several authors of the book *Does Capitalism Have a Future?*[32]

In Charney, we discussed how to help Ethiopian people who were starving because of a civil war; we discussed South African racism, and the boycott that was succeeding against it. We heard reports from our field directors, who returned from around the world to update us. All the Oxfams agreed that education was a growing responsibility: people in the wealthy world did not comprehend the realities of poverty. (They still don't.)

To enhance this understanding, Oxfam and Christian Aid founded *The New Internationalist Magazine* in 1973, and it continues forty years later, focused on ideas and actions for social justice. We realized that any amount we would raise to help the needy was close to useless in the face of a political/economic system that created and sustained inequality. Working with Oxfam was an enriching experience.

It prompted me to write to Galbraith and ask if he was thinking about writing a book on the causes of poverty. He was kind enough to write back. "Alas, I'm not working on one. I did deal with the subject, however, in *ECONOMICS, PEACE AND LAUGHTER*,

---

32   https://www.youtube.com/watch?v=EPcryvhSOco

which I assume is still available, and may be in the paperback stores. Indeed, some of the essays were originally prepared for the Massey Lectures for the CBC."

A few years later, in 1979, he published *The Nature of Mass Poverty*, and followed that with *The Voice of the Poor*, in 1983.

The Foundation for International Training and Development surprised me one day by asking me to put on a short course on small business management in East Africa, in 1978. They were funded by the Canadian government, and a friend had submitted my name. The Kenyan government and the Kenyan Chamber of Commerce promoted and supported this small course, for about 35 people. Branch Grieves, another Canadian, and I taught it. This was a rich experience for me, and although it's a cliché to say, I learned more than I taught.

The course was to be taught in Mombasa, Kenya, which I soon learned was on the Indian Ocean just south of the Equator. At the time it was home to about 300,000 people. Now it's grown to over a million.

As a teen, I had learned a little about Kenya because Saturday afternoon movie matinees always included a 15-minute newsreel, and almost weekly we saw news about Kenya's Mau Mau uprising. From 1952 to 1960, native Kenyans were calling for independence from Britain, and the Mau Mau were fighting for it. The British had "claimed" the country in 1895, and the people were claiming it back. Over those eight years, 2,000 people were killed—32 were European, the rest were black, but the tone of the newsreels was that it was whites that were being slaughtered.

Then, when I studied at York University in Toronto, my roommate with Samuel Mungai, a student from Kenya, and a Kikuyu.

He came from a large family. His father had several wives and many children, and Sam was raised during the Mau Mau period. The Mau Mau were primarily Kikuyu. He gave my parents a goatskin as a gift and encouraged me to attend my first lecture on Foreign Aid, which I did in November 1961. Living with Sam had raised my awareness of the unfairness of colonialism and exploitation.

Mombasa is on an island on the shore of the Indian Ocean, with a sheltered deep-water port and a history that goes back to ancient Swahili and Muslim eras. The Portuguese built Fort Jesus there in 1591, and it changed hands nine times over the centuries. For a period, it was part of the Sultanate of Oman and for seventy years was British.

The harbour was filled with dozens of dhows, small single-mast sailboats about 30 or 40 feet long, a type of ship used for hundreds, if not thousands of years. They sailed the Red Sea and Indian Ocean with traditional cargoes of gold, spices, ivory, dates; anything that would make money. I expect when I was there, newer cargoes of drugs, currencies, guns, and people were being carried.

Bau Bau Kamau, the head of the Kenyan Chamber of Commerce, was our very obliging host. He was so keen he attended every day. He was about 70 years of age, head of the nation's Chamber of Commerce, and lots of fun. In the 1950s, he was jailed by the British for his part in the Mau Mau uprising, as was Jomo Kenyatta, who later became prime minister; both were Kikuyu.

One night after class, Bau Bau told me about his experiences with Kenyatta and their fight for freedom. He explained, with a wonderful Kenyan lilt, that one man's terrorist is another man's freedom fighter. "Bryant," he said with passion, "a terrorist is a person with a cause but without an army. They are freedom fighters!"

That prompted me, back in the 1970s, to read more about the causes of terrorist behaviour. Even then, decades ago, there was lots of good academic work, and it all backed what my personal tutor on terrorism had said: the root cause of terrorist behaviour was unfairness. The Mau Mau wanted freedom. They wanted an end to white British rule. It was the same fight the North American Indians had a century before and that those who live in oil-rich countries are fighting today.

As you can imagine, when NATO and the West embarked on a war on terror, I saw it differently. It made as little sense to me to declare war on an emotion, as it had been decades earlier to declare war on drugs. Both "wars" were propaganda and a part of a bigger economic agenda. To me, it was an example of the excellent marketing the military does: declaring a war without an identifiable enemy and thus it can in no way be won or ended. But I will return to this issue later.

East Africa has some of the world's best beaches. North and South of Mombasa are miles of beautiful, wide, white clean sand, and, like the Caribbean islands for Americans, are an easy escape from winter for Europeans. At the time, the Kenyan government was trying to get African women to wear shirts, while vacationing Europeans were going topless on the beach.

Kenya has a population slightly larger than Canada's, about 40 million people, in a far smaller country. Canada averages 8.3 people per square mile, Kenya 174!

We saw people walking everywhere, even in remote savanna that could possibly be lion habitat. It's a poor country but not the poorest in the world.

56% of Kenyans live below the poverty line. Agriculture employs about 75% of the workers, producing coffee and tea mainly for export. Tourism is the largest contributor to GDP. There is an oil refinery in the country, but reserves are limited. [33]

There are seven major tribes, with Kikuyu the largest at 22%, and there are many religions; Christian, Islam, Baha'i, Hinduism, Jainism, and a few traditional African religions. What we would refer to as the middle class—storekeepers, small business owners, and professional people—lived modestly comfortable lives. Many had what seemed to be an extravagance, live-in help! But it was seen as a duty to hire those less fortunate, just as the shopkeepers showed similar care with their nightly practice of putting a few flattened cardboard cartons into their covered storefronts to serve as beds for the homeless. They were also free security guards.

East African English has a delightful lilt. I remember "I will be with you now" meant "I am leaving but should be back." Just as the Inuit have multiple words for snow, the Kenyans had about a dozen words for skin colour: tan, dark, brown, mahogany, black, ebony, coal, and occasionally white. "A rich person" defined someone overweight.

Our students for the business management course were middle-aged men and women who were running their own businesses. This group was the brightest, keenest group I have ever known. Classes started at eight in the morning; all were present by seven thirty. This small session that I thought might be modestly useful was seen to have such importance that it was opened by a member of

---

33   https://www.britannica.com/place/Kenya/Agriculture-forestry-and-fishing#toc259733

the Kenyan parliament. Another MP attended the last day to close it, and his unique speech has never left me. "I am here to close the session, not to open it but to close it, someone else opened it. My job is to close it, to send you home, to wish you on your way, to wish you well," and twenty minutes more of the same. Bau Bau was there, as he was for all of the sessions.

Several members of the Akamba Wood Carvers' Association took the course, as did storekeepers, the manager of Hotel Splendid, small business people, and one very interesting student who owned a small local pub.

The pub was a part-time job for him—he was a full-time customs agent at the harbour. We visited each of our students' businesses to learn and give hands-on advice. When we drove a dusty road into the suburbs to get to the pub, children saw us and ran laughing beside our car and shouting "white people" in their language. In the pub, they made their own beer: three types. Staff gathered coconut milk, tree sap gathered in gourds from the top of palm trees, and corn for mash. Each type was fermented at least 24 hours in open 50-gallon barrels like old oil drums, before serving. A staple part of the local diet was inexpensive Billy Beef canned stew, and the empty stew cans were reused as drinking glasses in the pub.

The pub owner was making so much money he was lending it to his neighbours and wanted to know how to open a bank. He understood the role of money in society, and especially the profit in lending, better than most of us. He did not understand that he was not allowed to do it.

The Akamba Wood Carvers[34] ran a business in which about 100 people made carvings of elephants, giraffes, crouching Masai warriors, and hippos, which we see in gift shops worldwide. The cooperative is still in business, and their website shows that they have grown to some thousands of workers, still located on the same dusty road. They had done a very good job, as many Kenyans we met seemed to do, of absorbing lessons completely. They learned Adam Smith's lesson about pin makers and took it to heart. They had their wood carvers specialize: one would gather wood, another rough shape it, another carve it, another sand and polish, and finally, someone would paint it. They did an excellent job of following the Adam Smith vision of job specialization, but unfortunately, it matched their business only slightly. As there was no automated machinery to master, no capital investment on which to maximize return, and only marginal improvement in labour efficiency, they were not the first group to misapply the lessons of Adam Smith.

Old Town Mombasa is the oldest part of the city, with streets only three or four feet wide. One evening, while walking, I experienced the generosity of the poor.

A group of young men were hanging about in a small storefront football club and were keen to talk to the white guy wandering by. In minutes, a cold Coke appeared for me. No one else had one. It was just the generosity of the poor. It happened again as our class ended; the students pooled their Kenyan shillings and presented me with a delightful silver mug. It's been my experience that the poor go out of their way to share, and do so with more grace than the rich.

---

34 http://www.akambahandicraftcoop.com/

In hindsight, our program was unfair. We taught basic accounting and other bits of running a business that work in the West, but by teaching business as we did, we implied that if you do the same—work hard and smart—you will get as rich. Implicit was the belief that capitalism works and would help "emerging" nations to become as rich as the West.

We had not yet learned that belief in a free market that would cure all ills was a myth. We did not understand the economic imbalances these people faced. Later in life, I realized that Kenyans were not poor because of lack of ability or lack of money, but poor because of more basic things: lack of resources, rain, arable land, health care, and safe drinking water. And colonialism had taken away tribal self-reliance.

After I returned to Canada, I thought about Africa and wondered why we in the West were getting richer, while my friends in Mombasa stayed poor. It was not because we have more talent. It was not because of laziness of the Kenyans! Was it just a resource difference? I disregarded the question for another twenty years.

In the late nineties, I was invited to a conference in Winnipeg on Canada's role in International Development, a business-oriented conference with people attending from around the world. There was a workshop and a choice of round tables. I chose one with a few Canadians, four or five women from a woman's cooperative craft business in Thailand, and a member of the World Bank. I picked it in order to learn more about the World Bank, but as it happened, the craft workers were far more interesting. The women showed the same care and keenness for their enterprise as I had seen in Kenya and were a vibrant contrast to the uncaring banality of the World Bank rep.

Most poor countries have been victims of international finance. The end of colonialization did not end exploitation. That continues. In 1970, the fifteen nations the World Bank classed as "heavily indebted" owed almost $18 billion, 9.8% of their GNP. By 1987, this debt had increased to $402 billion, 47% of their GDP. That is not only wrong, but it is also unjustifiably stupid.

The result is that ever-increasing amounts of money go from the poor to the rich. For every one dollar sent for aid to the poor nations in 2000, the poor were paying thirteen dollars of interest to the rich world.

In 2010, 388 people owned as much as the bottom one-half of all the people on earth. In 2015, that number had been reduced to 62 individuals owning as much as 3.6 billion people.[35] The report shows that poverty is getting worse, women suffer more than men, corporations increasingly avoid taxes, and the system fails the vast majority.

Oxfam released a report in 2016 entitled *An Economy for the 1%: How privilege and power in the economy drive extreme inequality and how this can be stopped*, which showed that the 1% had increased their share of the world's riches.

The globalization of poverty

In the early 2000s, I read *The Globalization of Poverty*, by Michel Chossudovsky, an economist from the University of Ottawa. Chossudovsky was raised in Geneva, graduated from the University of Manchester, then obtained a PhD from the University of North

---

35   Oxfam International. https://www.oxfam.org/en/research/economy-1

Carolina. His Russian father worked for the United Nations; his mother was Irish. He is Professor Emeritus at the University of Ottawa, and by coincidence, I knew Michel's publisher before I met Michel. I mentioned to the publisher that I was reading *The Globalization of Poverty* and was impressed with Michel's research and Ian responded that it was being well received and they were going for a second printing. I asked if they were going to fix the typos.

"Typos?"

"Yes!"

"Many?"

"Yes, and scattered throughout!" I offered to show him, and consequently helped edit the next edition of the book.

I was amazed at the scope of the research. There was so much detail from so many countries that, about two thirds through the manuscript, when I was emailing my recent edits, I asked, "Where does all this research come from? Is Michel exploiting grad students?" (As I said, I had not yet met Michel.)

Within minutes, my office phone rang with a voice laughing on the other end.

"Bryant, this is Michel Chossudovsky. You may not be aware, but every email you send to Ian is automatically copied to me. And to answer your question, no, I don't exploit grad students. That book is 15 years of my life. I have been in every one of those countries, and I have seen everything I have written about."

That was over ten years ago. Michel and I remain friends. His book is filled with examples, chapter after chapter, about how the World Bank and/or The International Monetary Fund have gone into country after country and made the countries poorer. There are examples from Ethiopia, Somalia, Bangladesh, Vietnam, Brazil and Peru; the same issues Oxfam was dealing with. (I will discuss the IMF and World Bank more in Chapter Nine.)

Following up on life's lessons?

As I was thinking about retiring, with energy to spare, I wondered about getting re-involved in raising awareness about drug laws, or in international aid once again.

Drug laws were wasting money and lives, and destroying communities. I knew that drug laws had not failed, but had made huge amounts of money for some, and were used to control people and nations.

Failed Third World economic policies, and the plight of the poor, had grown steadily worse since the 1970s. The deck seemed to be stacked against them. Thinking about these issues led to write this book. Economics is behind both issues.

Now I want to return to the 1970s and 1980s, when economics stopped making sense. I'll examine what was changing, and why.

4.
Corporations take control

> Our country is now geared to an arms economy bred in an artificially induced psychosis of war hysteria and an incessant propaganda of fear.
> —Douglas MacArthur; May 15, 1952

BY THE 1970S, THE MEMORY OF EISENHOWER'S WARNING ABOUT the military-industrial complex had faded. Many had heard of J. K. Galbraith, but few were troubled by his similar warning of corporations taking over the public agenda. We believed, as we had since the Second World War and Korean War, that we were on the side of right and that our way of life—capitalist democracy—was best. Our attitudes had not just developed by chance, but were nurtured.

North America had a large middle class that could afford to buy things, lots of things. Jobs were plentiful and usually long-lasting. Benefits were improving, and paid vacations became the norm. The market was healthy because there was a lot of demand. We assumed that growth could be endless and that all these good things were because of the free market.

Workers wearing their union jackets with pride, knew that unions had forced business to share the wealth. It was the unions that created and entrenched the middle class, and without union successes in the sixties and seventies, there would not be forty-hour weeks, overtime pay, vacations, sick days, paid holidays, benefits, or safe working conditions. As the power of unions has waned, so have those benefits.

I was employed by a corporation, and saw and helped corporations increase their role in the economy. They were, we were, improving our ability to look after ourselves—to manage markets and insure continuous profit. As unions, governments, and public attitudes could easily derail corporate plans, corporations felt unions, governments, and attitudes needed to be managed. Assumptions that people had the right to clean air and clean water were assumptions that could cost companies money. People were told that ...*the smell of smog is the smell of money*! They were told to choose between clean air and jobs.

Corporate leaders worried about the growth of unions and about the growing distrust of corporate power. In order to regenerate that trust, public opinion had to be changed.

Before I look at how corporations set out to do that, I'll take a brief look at one major economic assumption that was a fundamental belief in the 1970s. So fundamental, that corporations felt it essential to change public opinion.

We believed that businesses could be "too big to survive." The US government assumed it a duty to preserve competition and "*too big to fail*" was inconceivable. Trust in completion was shared by the government and public alike. Everyone was convinced that competition provided better value for all; competition brings down prices, increases value, and stimulates innovation. A majority of people no doubt still believe it. These were the years when capitalism depended on competition but it was becoming the era when monopolies were taking control.

For example, in 1974, the US Department of Justice filed an anti-trust suit against AT&T, the parent company of about thirty Bell Telephone businesses. At the time, the AT&T monopoly had the warm fuzzy nickname of Ma Bell. The Department of Justice proceedings were to break up the monopoly and eight years later, Bell was broken into what were called "mini Bells." This created many opportunities and I joined an emerging Telco.

Although the breakup of Bell was popular with the people, it was not welcomed by business. Corporate managers thought it was their right, their obligation even, to make their businesses bigger. To be able to accomplish this, they knew attitudes needed to be changed. The question was how to do so. More corporate breakups were not what they wanted.

Changing public attitudes!

> It's so easy for propaganda to work, and dissent to be mocked.
> —Harold Pinter, British poet, playwright; Nobel Prize in Literature

In 1947, the ad council (a US pro-corporate lobby) launched a national campaign to sell the free enterprise system to Americans. Opinion polls showed the public generally did not support it and many still believed that the Depression was evidence of a failed economic system and believed government oversight of markets to be essential.

$100 million was raised in cash and free media from the major corporations. The book, *The Free Market Missionaries*,[36] expains; "what followed was 'the most intensive "sales" campaign in the history of the industry' according to Daniel Bell, then editor of Fortune Magazine who added. 'What was being sold was free market dogma, and the full weight of business resources was poured into it.' Bell listed the resources: 1,600 business periodicals, 577 commercial and financial digests, 2,500 advertising agencies, 500 public relations counsellors, 4,000 corporate public relations departments, and more than 6,500 "house organs" with a combined circulation of more than 70 million.

---

36 Beder, Sharon. *Free Market Missionaries: The Corporate Manipulation of Community Values*. Earthscan, 2006. She is a professor at the University of Wollongong in Australia.

4. Corporations take control

In the seventies, the corporations felt it was time to act again. Big business needed to offset the liberalism of the hippies, who "didn't trust anyone over 30," or trust corporations. Again, big business organized, and its leaders were encouraged to find opportunities to speak in support of capitalism. They hired public relations professionals and funded "research" through a variety of organizations to create supportive arguments. I had been vice president of the Whitby Chamber of Commerce in Canada in the sixties, and we did our part to promote the role of business in our community.

The campaign in 1976 was so well endorsed that organizers boasted their supporters read like a "who's who in American business." Supporters even included the US Government Department of Commerce that used taxpayer money to support a propaganda campaign! It was "the most elaborate and costly public-relations project in American history" and, the council added, it was the most successful.

This campaign was like the 1947 campaign, but with a larger budget. The organizers issued media advertisements, newsletters, films, teaching materials, training kits, booklets, point of sale displays, messages on envelopes, and free inserts to include in bank statements, utility bills, and insurance premium notices. The media contributed $40 million of free time and space to the campaign in the first two years. The objective was to reprogram us to believe and trust corporate power. It was propaganda.

There was no counter-campaign. No apparent effort was made to discuss economic theory or the weaknesses in capitalism, nor worker rights, nor the danger of secret corporate planning, nor the demise of public planning. The unions didn't have the money to compete, and the government opted to be in bed with corporations.

Galbraith had forewarned us of corporate encroachment and we not only watched silently as it happened, but because corporations employed many of us, we assisted. Few of us recognized that this growth of corporate power was an inevitable consequence of the system, nor did we realize that it was changing the balance of power.

Think tanks

Think tanks blossomed. Today, we are accustomed to news commentary from "experts" who present "research" that can modify how we see the world. Much of this research is from think tanks, and while all have bias, it's important to see the correlation between the bias and who supports the think tanks. The better-funded usually encourage a so-called "conventional wisdom," as Galbraith would have described it. This has become an ever-friendlier corporate view.

Susan George is an American-born political economist who lives in Paris and is president of the Transnational Institute, an Amsterdam-based alternate policy group that supports social justice and ecological sustainability. Their work is commendable. Her first book, *How the Other Half Dies: The Real Reasons for World Hunger* was published in 1976. She wrote a few books on national debt, and in 2008 published *Hijacking America: How the Secular and Religious Right Changed What Americans Think*. In it, she showed the way attitudes changed from a people-focused "normal" to a corporate "normal." Using the five M's: money, media, marketing, management, with a sense of mission, the pro-business think tanks used the religious right to successfully manufacture a new common sense.

In her analysis of think tanks, Susan George shows how those on the right have attacked funding of those on the left, how they have sought to dominate the process of appointing Supreme Court Judges, and worked to roll back decades of progressive and environmental laws. And, that think tanks support ongoing wars not just for the money that's made from them.

During a war, presidential decrees can override the Constitution. David Addington, who was Chaney's chief of staff from 2005 to 2009, used this power so effectively that *U.S. News and World* magazine called him "the most powerful man you have never heard of." He is now a vice president of the Heritage Foundation.

In 1997, George wrote of the impact of changes nurtured by think tanks:[37]

---

37 http://www.globallabour.info/en/Dissent%20Summer%201997%20-%20George.pdf

> Recent history, if we are attentive, might still teach us that a society can go from law based on the equality of persons to the laws of the market; from relative social justice to deep and chronic inequalities within a few short years. The neo-liberals' onslaught continues ...

Friedrich Hayek[38] and Milton Friedman were both from the University of Chicago. Hayek, 13 years older than Friedman, was Friedman's mentor, and he established one of the first neoliberal think tanks, the Mont Pelerin Society. Its first meeting was in 1947, and it's named after the Swiss town in which they met. The think tank still exists. The members are dedicated to protecting private property and the competitive market.

Many economists belong to the Mont Pelerin Society: eight members have received the Bank of Sweden version of a Nobel Prize in Economics. The ideas of the Society were credited for Margaret Thatcher's victory in 1979.

The London-based think tank, the Institute of Economic Affairs, was founded in the 1950s, and in 1973, the Heritage Foundation in the US. Both are designed to enhance corporate freedom at the expense of human welfare. Joseph Coors, grandson of the German brewer Adolph Coors, was a founder of the Heritage Foundation.

Think tanks in Canada have been studied by Professor Donald Gutstein of Simon Fraser University. Gutstein teaches in the School of Communications and Media Studies and has conducted over two decades of research on business propaganda. In 2000,

---

38   Hayek, born 1899, an economist, became a Professor of Social Thought at the University of Chicago.

he published *Not a Conspiracy Theory: How Business Propaganda Hijacks Democracy*, and his title tells the story. In 2014, he published a book on Canada's prime minister: *Harperism: How Stephen Harper and His Think Tank Colleagues Have Transformed Canada.* In his book he, documents some of the steps think tanks facilitated to weaken labour unions, restrict scientists from speaking, and reduce aboriginal rights—even managing to rename Alberta's "dirty oil" as "ethical oil."

Reports from the Heritage Foundation or the Fraser Institute leave the impression that they are studies from learned organizations, when actually these reports are propaganda. Research into how often think tank stories made the news and by whom showed that, in 2003, left-wing think tanks were covered 13% of the time, right-wing think tanks 87%.

I've listed below a few think tanks, their year founded, annual revenue, and affiliations.

United States: Think Tanks (6 from a *Wikipedia* list of about 190) and their annual revenue.

RAND Corporation	1948	Created by Douglas Aircraft Revenue in 2014, $269 million.
Brookings Institute	1916	$90 million in 2010 from diverse sources
Council on Foreign Relations	1923	$54 million in 2011

American Enterprise Institute	1938	$32 million in 2012
Heritage Foundation	1973	$80 million in 2011, founded by Joseph Coors
Kato Institute	1974	$21 million in 2011, founded by Koch brothers
National Endowment for Democracy	1983	$135 million in 2009, funded by Congress.

Canada: Think Tanks (4 from a *Wikipedia* list of 30)

Canadian Centre for Policy Alternatives	1980	$4.2 million in 2011 from individual members
CD Howe Institute, Toronto	1973	$3.7 million in 2011 – corporate board[39]
Fraser Institute, Vancouver	1974	$10.8 million – primarily from corporations
Business Council of Canada	1976	Budget not published

Have you heard of Tax Freedom Day? It's a creation of these two groups: the Tax Foundation in the US and the Fraser Institute in Canada. The Tax Foundation was established in 1937 by four

---

39   A lecture delivered by the C.D. Howe institute in 2004 was sponsored by NM Rothschild & Sons Canada, Limited.

senior executives, two from General Motors, one from Standard Oil, and one from Johns-Manville. It gets its funding from corporate sources and, no surprise, it has a pro-business, conservative bias. The Fraser Institute gets over eighty percent of its money from corporations, including Exxon and the American billionaire Koch brothers.

These two groups issue press releases in the spring announcing Tax Freedom Day as the day that individuals stop paying tax to the government and start paying themselves. It's great marketing! The release of the story creates the illusion that it's news, and implies that taxes are wasteful, unfair, and unnecessary.

Both these "think tanks" want to lower, or better yet, eliminate taxes—a move that favours the wealthy more than the rest of us. Tax Freedom Day could more rightly be called "I've got this covered day"—the day when I've paid my fair share to cover many of life's basics needs: roads, police, water, old age security, airports, harbours, national defense and if Canadian, health care. It's the day of the year when I've paid my fair share towards sustaining a decent society. They fail to acknowledge that 100% of the money the government collects is intended to benefit its citizens. *Forbes* and *The New York Times* both describe Tax Freedom Day as a libertarian, or Tea Party idea!

The Business Council of Canada, (formerly the Canadian Council of Chief Executives) is another think tank, and at one time, when I was a chief executive, I thought I should listen to them. I was wrong. I managed a company with sales of $30 million dollars, considered a small company, as most CEOs have sales under $100 million. The men (few women are CEOs in North America) who make up Business Council of Canada run companies with average revenues of five billion dollars—a number so big that they couldn't possibly speak for the average CEO. The Council makes regular announcements on Canadian policy. If they were honest, they would clarify that they are saying what's best for their corporations. Never have I seen a journalist clarify that, when reporting on the Council's announcements.

A recent report from the London-based Institute for Economic Affairs stated that retirement is not good for people: it causes a major decline in physical and mental health. This "report" states that people should work more years and, to make that happen, that the government should drop support for pensions and unemployment insurance. The group defines itself as a free-market think tank. It's been around since 1955, and does not disclose its sources of funding. However, a report has leaked that shows that tobacco companies are big sponsors. The goal of this report, which is rife with bad science, is to reduce unemployment insurance and pensions, thus reducing government spending and opening the door to more corporate taxes cuts.[40]

Peter Munk, a Canadian, founded Barrick Gold, which became the world's largest gold mining corporation. An articulate, bright, energetic man, he's not a billionaire, but at last count, he's close to becoming one. He gave $35 million in 2009 to the University of Toronto, and the School of Global Affairs was named the Monk School of Global Affairs in his honour. For that donation, he got a $16-million tax reduction. The university paid about $70 million of

---

40 The IEA's mission is "to improve understanding of the fundamental institutions of a free society by analyzing and expounding the role of markets in solving economic and social problems." https://iea.org.uk/about-us

the total $100 million cost of the building. I don't mean to belittle Monk's net donation of $19 million, but he got his name on a $100 million-dollar school and the rest of us, who paid 81%, got no credit. Two years after the gift, the president of the university retired, and was appointed to Munk's Board of Directors.

Monk has also given millions to the pro-business Fraser, and C. D. Howe Institutes,[41] and for these donations, he gets tax deductions as well.

Over time, with the concentration of wealth, the rich have accumulated more money.

Global meetings for the elite

It's a cliché to say that modern communication, the internet, and easier travel have changed the world. Those changes alone haven't made the world one international marketplace, but they help, and global banks and global corporations are pleased to make more money in a bigger market.

The term globalization has a soft and innocuous ring to it, as does "free trade." Both imply neutrality or fairness, which is far from the fact. Noam Chomsky is a well-known MIT Professor Emeritus. He's a respected, articulate, soft-spoken linguist and philosopher and he describes the current use of the word globalization as propaganda. Propaganda for economic integration that favours investors and lenders; a bias he believes is vulgar and idiotic![42]

---

41 http://donaldgutstein.com/follow-the-money-part-2-barrick-golds-peter-munk/#sthash.Uy1oeNE1.dpuf
42 Chomsky, Noam. *Profit over People: Neoliberalism and Global Order.* Seven Stories Press, 1999.

The program to make one world market seem inevitable to us has been helped by private, exclusive meetings for those who qualify. You qualify by being influential or simply rich. They meet secretly. Attendance is by invitation only. The press is excluded. Those attending are a who's who of global corporate and political leadership. Their private gatherings reinforce their insular beliefs about themselves. They are the people who "know," and they are the people who "understand." Their worldview is reinforced in plush, protected settings and the process has been very effective!

Here is a list of some major meetings of the very rich and influential, the year they began to meet, and a bit of detail:

The Bilderberg Group	1954	Annual meeting for about 150 of the world's powerful. Co-founded by Prince Bernhard of the Netherlands and named after the Bilderberg Hotel in Holland where they first met.
World Economic Forum (Davos)	1971	Davos, Switzerland. Annual meeting for about 2500 people funded by 1000 corporations. Comedian John Stewart refers to them as the "money Oscars."
The G7 (later the G8)	1975	The International Monetary Fund
The G20	1999	International Monetary Fund

The problem with elite groups having secret meetings is simple: the needs of ordinary people are not on the agenda. John Kennedy explained this in 1961:

> The very word "secrecy" is repugnant in a free and open society; and we are as a people inherently and historically opposed to secret societies, to secret oaths, and to secret proceedings.[43]

A few years before Kennedy made this comment, the Bilderberg group had its fifth meeting, (in secret, as always) on St. Simons Island, in Georgia, in February of 1957. Coincidently, St. Simons Island is on the coast south of Jekyll Island where, forty years earlier, another secret meeting created the Federal Reserve. (I will cover that in Chapter Six.)

These gatherings have no input from the poor. Nor do attendees hear of the problems with capitalist economics. Nothing challenges their existing beliefs. Clichés are reinforced about the need for less government, less government spending, and lower taxes! The media air a few snippets provided by the organizers; they provide a bit of credibility. But the very rich own and thereby control the media. So, they dine in elegance while the rest of us are fed selected scraps of sound bites.

In addition to think tanks and private meetings, two corporate-friendly organizations need to be noted: the Council on Foreign Relations, and the Trilateral Commission.

---

43 Kennedy, John F. *Secret meetings cannot produce results good for all.* Speech, Waldorf-Astoria Hotel, April 27, 1961.

The Council on Foreign Relations was founded in 1921 and has a board of directors of 36 people, a number so unwieldy it suggests a token board much like the 80-person board of the Ad Council. (The Wharton School of Business recommends five or six people for an effective leadership group.)

The Council employs about seventy scholars in their "think tank" and has been referred to as "the real state department." Hilary Clinton, as Secretary of State, said as much in a speech in 2009. "We get a lot of advice from the Council … {we are told] what we should be doing and how we should think about the future."

In 2014, the president of the Council on Foreign Relations, Richard Haass, was appointed as a top foreign policy adviser to the Obama administration.

The second group, The Trilateral Commission, was founded by David Rockefeller in 1974, following a Bilderberg meeting, to develop closer ties between North America, Western Europe and Japan. Closer ties meant closer business ties. It's probable that it was, and is, funded by the Rockefellers, but since the Commission publishes no annual report, we don't know.

One of the Trilateral Commission's unspoken purposes was to offset the damage done to the reputation of the United States by unilaterally ending the gold standard. Membership is by invitation only, and has included business people and the politicians they support: Condoleezza Rice is a member, Bill Clinton was, and 11 members of the Obama administration were. About sixty people sit on its executive committee—another unwieldy, obviously token, committee.

Bland stories on the meetings of these groups are produced by the media with the sound bites they are given. Protesters, increasing in numbers and age, are dismissed as radicals.

The media miss three significant points. First, the obvious: secret meetings are anti-democratic. Second, they miss the increasing size of public protests as people raise those issues that the press used to raise. Finally, they miss the demographics: it's often grey-haired people, not young radicals, who are protesting. That is the important message. More and more seniors know that these meetings are not innocuous, that they do not serve the people. However, it seems most journalists, or their bosses, are afraid of biting the hand that feeds them.

The meetings of the G7 and G20 need special comment. These meetings are now accepted practice and leaders of a few nations meet and privately and make deals. I don't believe they have the mandate to do so! In Chapter Five, I'll discuss in more detail a 1944 meeting in New Hampshire to deal with international finance after World War II. Seven hundred and thirty people from forty-four nations met to hammer out an agreement. About 100 journalists attended. Because of its large numbers, and press coverage, it had credibility, and a deal was obtained. Since then, any pretext at democracy has been dropped. Seven, or sometimes twenty, leaders meet in secret to "decide" whatever they want.

In December 2013, the G20 met in Brisbane, Australia, and made a decision to rank interbank loans above obligations to depositors. While that may sound bland, the outcome was that if your bank were to have a crisis, other banks, such as Goldman Sachs, will get paid before (and possibly instead of) you. Your life savings on deposit could disappear. The decision bypasses national laws with a new banking protocol.

In September 2016, the G20 met in China. Serious problems continued in the world: hunger, wars, the amount of arms sales, the causes of the refugee crises, and unequal income distribution. The final communiques showed what they discussed: tax evasion, more open trade, fiscal stimulus, supporting refugees (not questioning why refugees were occurring), and how to combat attacks against globalization.

I doubt that Marx's prediction that competition would lead to the end of competition was discussed. I doubt if they wonder why we have fewer airlines, fewer newspapers, and fewer soft drink companies. They certainly wouldn't worry about the concentration of wealth.

However, at elite conferences, the worry about the concentration of businesses leaving them with fewer companies to invest in is a problem that required a solution.

Privatize everything

> Sell a country? Why not sell the air, the great sea, as well as the Earth? Did not the Great Spirit make them all for the use of his children?
> —Chief Tecumseh (1768– 1813)

After World War II, as I noted earlier, there was a backlog of demand for things. People needed basic items, and after that need was met, they wanted better radios, telephones, appliances and then television. In the years now referred to as "the golden years of capitalism," new products begat new businesses. People no longer were making bombs and stretchers but things like refrigerators, radios, television sets, and cars. New businesses created new jobs and new companies to invest in.

However, there's a finite number of things that we need: groceries, clothes, electronics, transportation, and medicine. It's a limited number of things: more than one hundred, but less than a million.

To illustrate: grocery stores as we now know them, didn't exist until 1916, when Clarence Saunders founded Piggly Wiggly Stores in Memphis. Up till then, store clerks stood behind the counter and took a grocery list from the customer to fill it. Saunders moved "the back" into the front, so you could pick your own groceries, and he patented the idea. He advertised his store as having a "maze" of 605 items. As the number of items expanded, larger stores replaced smaller stores, and grocery chains replaced thousands of small businesses. The average American supermarket now carries over 45,000 items.

Interestingly, over time, with more and more "choices" of goods, the goods have been made by fewer and fewer companies, and sold by fewer and fewer chains. Wikipedia lists 480 brands of breakfast cereal made by about a dozen companies. General Mills alone makes 28. Our local grocery store has over 1,000 types of shampoo, 1,500 types of hair products (colours, styling, etc.) and 300 types of deodorant. Lots of apparent choice, little difference. This week our drug store had a display for an "eye nutrient," which seems bizarre.

David Harvey, an English-born professor of anthropology at the City University of New York, published *Seventeen Contradictions and the End of Capitalism* in 2014. Contradiction number fifteen explains that a consequence of compound growth is that investors with capital need more and more places to invest. (In Chapter Six, I'll examine compound growth, and in Chapter Ten, I'll review Harvey's wonderful summary on the economics of neoliberalism.)

As businesses get bigger by merging, there are fewer businesses, leaving investors with fewer companies in which to invest. Technology provides new places to invest, as does privatization of what was once public. By convincing the public that the free market is the efficient way to deliver a service, the case to "privatize" what used to be public becomes easy. Drinking water, prisons, electricity, social security, firefighting, and schools can be privatized. The argument that competition is more efficient is aggressively made, with little substance to back that claim up.

There are some things that should never be privatized: the military, or prisons, for example. National, state, or city planning should never be privatized. There are very few things the free market does better. While rhetoric claims otherwise, the data doesn't back it up. Let's look at the details.

Highways

One example is found in Toronto, Canada, where people commuting to work pay tolls to use Highway 407. The profits from this highway go to private investors in Spain.

Over many decades, Canada built a national infrastructure of roads; publicly built and publicly owned. However, an ultra-conservative government in the Province of Ontario decided to sell a newly completed Highway 407 for short-term cash. At the time the sale of the highway was announced, the province had already spent $1.6 billion to build it, and the new government sold the rights to the highway for ninety-nine years for $3.1 billion dollars. The government announced that the public had doubled its money!

It is possible that the Ontario premier believed it. He had been elected on a "Common Sense Revolution" slogan, with a pro-business agenda. What was not said, and possibly not understood, was that for the $3.1 billion dollars of short-term cash, the public lost revenue forever. So much for Common Sense!

The sale had been negotiated in secret, and shortly after the announcement of the sale, outside investors valued the highway at over twice the selling price. There is no logic to selling public assets for short-term gain. Money that Torontonians now pay to commute daily could be reducing their own taxes rather than enriching Spanish investors.

Privatization is the process of selling public assets to private buyers. These sales should be identified as property grabs! Unfortunate nations have had privatization forced on them by international banks. I'll discuss how these deals weaken the social contract—but first, another example of privatization of public assets.

Water

Peter Brabeck is a big fan of privatization. He's the Chairman of Nestlé, a huge Swiss company that dates back to 1866, when Henri Nestlé developed and sold milk-based baby food.

Nestlé is the world's largest food company, with over 300,000 employees and over 8,000 brands, including Gerber, Purina, Carnation, Lean Cuisine, Stouffers, and many types of chocolate. Chairman Brabeck has piously taken it upon himself to ask (on behalf of all of us, it appears) "… should we privatize the normal water supply for the population?" He explains that he has examined two options: one extreme and one rational.

The extreme position, Brabeck explains, is believing water is a right. "That means that as a human being you should have a right to water." That's what he views as an "extreme" position. The other view, the logical one as he sees it, is that water is not special and should have a market value. He doesn't seem to understand that water is special because, unlike chocolate, it's essential for life. Nor does he mention his conflict of interest: his company makes millions of dollars each year selling water. He seems unaware that the United Nations Water Conference in 1977 declared water is a right,[44] and in 2010 reaffirmed their commitment:

> Clean, accessible water for all is an essential part of the world we want to live in. There is sufficient fresh water on the planet to achieve this. But due to bad economics or poor infrastructure, every year millions of people, most of them children, die from diseases associated with inadequate water supply, sanitation and hygiene.[45]

Should we trust Brabeck, who lives isolated from the real world? He attends the annual World Economic Forum in Davos. His hobby is Formula One Racing. He lives in a rarified atmosphere and seems to have a limited understanding of economics.

44　http://www.un.org/waterforlifedecade/pdf/human_right_to_water_and_sanitation_milestones.pdf

45　http://www.un.org/sustainabledevelopment/water-and-sanitation/

If everything has a market value, what is the value of child rearing, safe water, or of Bach?

Should we trust Nestlé, "the healthy hydration company," which sells water under 64 brand names? (Eight of those brands are in North America.)

Moreover, should we trust Nestlé, the company that promoted its baby formula in the 1970s as a better food than breast milk, resulting in over a million baby deaths each year according to the World Health Organization? A world boycott against Nestlé formula caught the company's attention but did not alter its behaviour.

In 1999, three decades after the worldwide boycott, a Nestlé salesperson, Syed Asmir Raza, quit the company and wrote *Milking Profits: How Nestlé Puts Sales Ahead of Infant Health*. Despite the global ban to stop companies from providing perks and free samples to doctors who promoted baby formula, Nestlé was still doing so. The movie *Tigers* is Raza's story about his years employed by Nestlé in Pakistan and his whistleblower activities since.

Bottling water can create problems. In the small community of Bhati Dilwan[46] in Pakistan, children are being sickened by filthy water because Nestlé drilled a well so deep that it lowered the water table. Formerly, water had been accessible at about 100 feet, but that traditional level dropped to between 300 and 400 feet, too deep for the existing local wells and too deep for ordinary budgets. That was because Nestlé could afford to drill deeper. Whoever owns the land can extract as much as they want; all the water there is, and they get it for free.

---

46   http://www.bottledlifefilm.com/index.php/home-en.html

In California, during a drought, Nestlé has been bottling water it takes from deep wells in Cabazon, a town on the old stagecoach route from Phoenix to Los Angeles.

In February 2015, the *Vancouver Sun* reported that Nestlé had negotiated a deal with the British Columbia government to pay $2.25 per million litres of water. That's 0.000,000,225 cents per litre, and they sell this at about a dollar a bottle. Generally, retail markups are two or three times cost: buy it for $30 wholesale and sell it between $60 and $100. Nestlé prefers a markup closer to a million times the cost.

Any decision on whether or not to privatize water was pre-empted by the United Nations reaffirmation, in 2010, that people have a right to water and sanitation. That has not stopped Brabeck's corporate zeal to privatize. Giving water a market value to preserve it, as he proclaims, does not match his company's action, which is to sell all the water they can bottle.

In mid-2015, the people of Oregon took on Nestlé, who wanted to build a bottling plant and buy mountain water from the Columbia River as it tumbled over the cascade locks. The plan was to pay a couple of bucks per 1000 gallons and sell it for hundreds of times that amount.

A group called Some of Us runs a website that allows people to organize petitions, which helped those protesting the Nestlé plan to get over 250,000 signatures. The group, Food and Water Watch, has been providing lawyers to fight the proposal. Together they have won the right to have it publicly reviewed. The fight's not over yet, but at least whatever is decided will be decided openly.

Nestlé promotes itself as a global problem solver with a mission to create shared values. This is a delusion. No corporation exists to solve problems. Corporations exist to make money. At one time, the profit was for the shareholders. And now, it seems, the officers and directors take the first cuts.

Auto insurance

Ontario in the mid-1980s had an election that showed how wrong the "efficient free market" argument is. The government at the time was socialist and promised that, if re-elected, it would set up a state-run automobile insurance company to compete with private companies, with the aim of driving down prices. Private insurance companies panicked and ran a counter campaign proclaiming two things: firstly, that free enterprise was the most efficient system, and secondly that they could not compete with government-run insurance.

What did they mean? The difference in cost between state-run insurance and a private business would be profit, which is usually 5 to 10% of sales. The insurance companies were stating, if you looked closely, that they were "much more efficient" on the one hand, but that this was less than 10% on the other.

Prisons

Privatizing prisons is one of the worst ideas in the move to privatization.

Europeans do a better job, they jail fewer people, don't jail them as long, and their society stays safe. They see prisoners as citizens and believe a person should be sent to prison primarily for rehabilitation, possibly for punishment or social deterrence. Rehabilitation is aimed at preventing the reoccurrence of the behaviour; it's good economics—improve the person, and if that's properly done, it will save money in the long run.

A prison run for profit, one that rents rooms by the night, has no incentive to rehabilitate. Why shorten the stay when repeat sleepovers create profits and management bonuses?

The Corrections Corporation of America (CCA) was founded in 1983, ten years after DEA was created, and it now runs over 65 facilities in the US. They claim to have started a new "industry." It's a private company and promotes public/private partnerships. The CCA view of partnership was outlined in a 2011 letter they sent to dozens of state prison administrations, offering to buy their prisons in exchange for 20-year contracts. The states could get a one-time infusion of cash. All they had to do was agree to keep the prisons 90% full. This public/private partnership was to provide short-term cash for the state and guaranteed long-term profit for the corporation.

Not only have American prisons become a source of corporate profit, but the prisoners have become a source of cheap labour. UNICOR, also known as Federal Prison Industries. is a company that advertises that it runs *Factories with Fences,* 110 factories in 79 penitentiaries. Their website[47] lists their services: apparel, telephone call centres, electronics, and fifteen more. Prison labour is neither protected by any labour laws nor any union. Wages are less than those in Third World nations—as low as 23 cents an hour. Using prison labour takes work out of communities, destroys unions, and with it the middle class.

In 1998, the journal *Prison Legal News* reported:

---

47 http://www.unicor.gov/index.aspx

The phenomenon of people outside prison walls being thrown out of their jobs by companies employing convicts is not confined to Wisconsin. A replay ... occurred in Texas, where U.S. Technologies sold its—electronics plant in Austin and laid off 150 workers; 45 days later, the company's owners opened a facility using convict labor in a Texas prison.

Nationwide, more than 100 private firms have reached convict-for-hire agreements with 29 states. Microsoft, IBM, Victoria's Secret and TWA are among the companies that have exploited prisoner labor.[48]

In September 2015, *The Atlantic* magazine carried a story on American prisons, "American Slavery, Reinvented," about the forced use of America's large numbers of prisoners as a source of workers cheaper than slavery. Companies don't have to worry about health care for workers; the state pays that. Incarcerated workers are expressly excluded from the Fair Labor Standards Act and so often must choose between solitary confinement or making garments for Victoria's Secret for pennies an hour.

Health care

Privatization was at the heart of national debate on Medicare during Obama's first term, and health care corporations quickly won when their lobbyists rigged the question.

---

48   https://www.prisonlegalnews.org/news/1998/may/15/prison-jobs-and-free-world-unemployment/

The logic for Medicare is simple. It is based on the facts that anyone can get sick—rich or poor; that everyone deserves care; and, that a single-payer system is the most efficient.

Most nations pay for health care by collecting money through taxes. Canada does so at 11.2% of GDP and covers everyone. The United States spends 17.9% of GDP, one and one-half times as much as Canada.

The last thing those in the US health care industry wanted was to see their share of the GDP go down.

If the American system became as efficient as the Canadian system, health care cost per person would drop from over $9,000 per person per year to about $4,500. People could still have their choice of doctors and hospitals. But corporations would lose about $800 billion a year.

Corporations rigged the debate by changing the question. Instead of asking "Do we want to provide health care?", the debate was about "How to insure health care." With that move, the business of health care remained open.

Post office

The post office too, is a target for privatization. Historically, it has facilitated communication between families and businesses throughout the nation so that everyone, no matter how remote, is included in society. Many mail routes, especially remote ones, for example, can never be "profitable." The system was designed to work for other reasons than profitability.

As the United States Post Office slogan says so poetically, "Neither snow nor rain nor heat nor gloom of night stays these couriers from the swift completion of their appointed rounds."

(This motto is a translation from the Greek historian Herodotus, who wrote about the mounted couriers of the ancient Persian Empire of about 550 B.C.)

The United States Post Office has existed for over 200 years and is the nation's second-largest employer. Walmart is the largest.

The Post Office has been self-funded (i.e., profitable), despite what the media have been saying. Talk of the Post Office being insolvent began after Congress passed a bill in 2006 requiring the Post Office to pre-fund health care for its workers for the next 75 years. No other organization, public or private, has been forced to do that. How devious. The purpose of that legislation was to make the Post Office a target for privatization.

Corporate America was following a pattern started years earlier in the European Union, when the EU was pushing member states to privatize their post offices. "Sell the service and reduce your debt" was their mantra; short-term cash for long-term loss of income was the deal.

In the Netherlands, the post office was privatized in 1989 with the announcement that they had created 22,000 new jobs. What an amazing story of job creation! The 22,000 new jobs were part-time jobs created by terminating 34,000 primarily full-time jobs, and closing 90% of their post offices. The same story was repeated in Spain, Sweden, and Germany, along with job cuts, fewer offices, fewer deliveries per week, and higher rates for sending mail for all but corporate customers![49]

---

49   http://www.globalresearch.ca/deregulating-and-privatizing-postal-services-in-europe/5363277

Those who want to privatize public institutions are not the "job creators" they claim to be. At best, as you can see by the post office examples, privatizers create a bunch of poorly paid new jobs by displacing well-paid old jobs. The rich use the trashy argument to say they are job creators by referring to the jobs they create for hired help in their McMansions. Those job numbers are minuscule, the pay poor, and the job security and benefits are rare. The self-deception of the nouveau riche is reminiscent of the delusions of Marie Antoinette and Peter Brabeck.

Public/Private Partnerships (P3s) have been such a rage in both the US and Canada that there are now organizations to promote them: the National Council for Public-Private Partnerships in the US, and a government-run agency in Canada. Both encourage arrangements that sound fair but serve corporations more than people—the "partnerships" tend to lock-in profit for corporations, and leave the risk for the public. In December 2014, the Auditor General for the Province of Ontario released a report on 74 P3s in the Province: Ontario had spent $8 billion dollars *more* than if the Province was to manage the services alone.

Jobs are important to people, but it is not the purpose of capitalism to create them. It is demand that creates jobs; capital and capitalism simply react. Jobs can be created as they were in the New Deal, or in the 2009 Recovery Act, with new projects to build roads and bridges, or clean up waste. When people have money to spend, demand follows; demand for things, for teachers, for police, for health care. Demand is generated by spending, and when there was a large middle class, there was great demand. If there were any truth to the myth that it's the rich who create jobs, then with an increasingly rich 1%, we should have no unemployment!

By privatizing functions that used to be public, the 1% concentrate their control.

Profiting from education

Efforts to privatize schools continue. Documented in her 1996 book *The Manufactured Crisis: Myths, Fraud, And the Attack on America's Public Schools*,[50] Diane Bavitch debunks the myths that test scores in schools have been falling, and more recently in her 2014 book, *Reign of Error: The Hoax of the Privatization Movement and the Danger to America's Public Schools,* she warns that major foundations, individual billionaires, and Wall Street hedge fund managers are encouraging the privatization of education, some for idealistic reasons, and others simply for profit. Many equity funds are eyeing public education as an emerging market for investors. Ravitch is a professor of education and was Assistant Secretary of Education during the first Bush administration.

Overlooked in the drive to make education a profit centre are two fundamental points: that education creates a better trained upcoming generation from which everyone will benefit; and that equal access to education serves to avoid the re-creation of a class system when all children, not just the children of the rich get an education.

George Roberts, Director of the Oshawa Board of Education and Past President of the Canadian Teachers Federation, wrote, "The role of public education is to be an equalizer, an agent for equal opportunity!" (He was my uncle.)

---

50   Berliner, David C. *The Manufactured Crisis: Myths, Fraud, And The Attack On America's Public Schools*. Bruce J. Biddle: 1996.

With a rush to privatize everything, it's sometimes hard to remember that not all things need to make money, like libraries or schools. And, some things are natural monopolies, like fire protection, sewers, and airports. Privatizing schools or prisons is to misunderstand their reason for being.

The United Nations Declaration of Human Rights in 1948 stated that education is a right, which should be free and serve to develop people to their fullest, and to promote understanding and tolerance. Education was assumed to be a tool in reducing poverty and the simplest way to insure the greatest development of everyone.

In Canada, in 1968, the Hall Dennis Report on Education, *Living and Learning*, prepared for the Ontario Government, stated:

> The society whose educational system gives priority to the economic over the spiritual and emotional needs of man defines its citizens in terms of economic units and in so doing debases them. There is a dignity and nobility of man that has nothing to do with economic considerations. The development of this dignity and nobility is one of education's tasks.

The Hall Dennis Committee supported free, student-focused, general education, with the same goal as the United Nations Declaration: the full development of the human personality. It recommended one education system that supports curiosity and understanding. One common system would serve as a social equalizer. Education for everyone was an investment in our collective future and not the elitist education of a class system.

This view is at odds with corporations and Wall Street. Corporations prefer job training to education, and Wall Street prefers schools run for profit, not as a social investment; they prefer profit from student debt to the wisdom of human development.

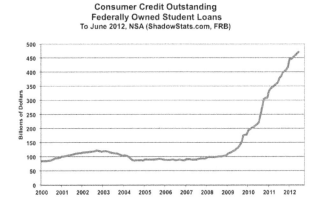

The chart above from Shadow Statistics shows the growth of student debt from 2000 that soared after 2009. In the seventies, it was closer to zero.

To pave the way to more privatized education, public funding has been reduced or frozen. Paying for schools has gone from public responsibility to an individual responsibility, resulting in massive student debt. With the reduction in public funding, incomes for those employed in education started to decline, and part-time teachers in American universities are now among the working poor.

In 1975, a year's advanced education in North America cost less than $1,000. By 2013 that had increased to over $6,000 in Canada, and higher in the United States. Tuition at the University of California, Berkley, grew from about $700 in the 1870s to around

$15,000/year in 2011. Graduates leaving school with large debt is socially outrageous but good for bank profits.

In the 1960s and 1970s, when we had much more affordable tuition, we had a more volatile student population. The need now for college and university graduates to get jobs to pay off their enormous debts seems to temper idealism and makes them more compliant.

David Bond, one-time Chief Economist of the Hong Kong Bank in Canada, explained how the government could, at no cost, make education free. All a student would have to do for a free education was agree to pay two or three more percent points of additional income tax for life. Then, that student could graduate debt-free. Some graduates would move into low-paid professions, and wouldn't pay much tax; others would pay more. It would balance out across all participants and the nation would get a better-educated workforce. It was a great example of a creative economic solution to a problem we still live with—a solution that would the benefit everyone, except the bank Bond worked for.

In the United States, "for-profit" education institutes have blossomed, and student debts have grown to over $1 trillion. For-profit schools have generated one-third of national student debt. Their school recruiters teach student customers how to borrow money. These schools spend a higher percentage of their budget on marketing than on teachers and most belong to APSCU, the Association of Private Sector Colleges and Universities, the trade association, or union, for their businesses.

Student debt is debt the banks, especially US banks, love because it is the most collectable debt of all. It doesn't disappear in a bankruptcy. Planning ahead for an increase in student debt, the Bankruptcy Abuse Prevention and Consumer Protection Act passed by Congress in 2005 changed a law that had worked since the 1970s, and made it more difficult for individuals to declare bankruptcy. There seemed to be no apparent reason for the change. The major cause of bankruptcy at the time was medical expenses. However, an increase in student debt did two things, made money for the banks and made graduating students more compliant.

> People in debt are slaves to their employers!
> —Tony Benn, British Labour Politician[51]

The law did not change bankruptcy abuse by the rich. For example, in 2014, when Atlantic City's Trump Plaza folded, Trump was on Twitter praising his wise timing in getting out of his investment, which left 1,000 people without jobs, and someone else to cover his losses.

Changes in law

Joint stock companies were becoming more common in 1844, when Britain passed the Joint Stock Companies Act, followed eleven years later by the Limited Liability Act that clarified the definition of companies as legal identities. Liabilities of the business were limited to what the corporation owned. Neither employees nor shareholders were personally liable (as long as their actions were legal!) for things done in the company's name.

It was practical to allow these legally defined "things" to borrow money, buy, sell and own things, sue and be sued. They were

---

51   2005. https://www.youtube.com/watch?v=qX-P4mx1FLU

corporate things, not people and the change was an enormous boost to business and to the welfare of everyone. However, as time passed, that definition was not good enough for corporations.

Corporations are not people

In 1989, the oil tanker *Exxon Valdez* ran aground in Prince William Sound in Alaska on its way to California. Its owner, Exxon Mobile Corp., a US multinational, was sued.

The tanker struck Bligh Reef on the southern Alaska coast, a reef named after Royal Navy Captain Bligh (remembered because his crew mutinied on his ship, the *Bounty*), who had been in Alaska in the 1770s on an expedition with Captain Cook. The reef was the centre of halibut and shrimp fishing. The oil spill, some believe, was the worst man-made disaster, ever, and journalist Greg Palast was hired by the Chugach people as a spill investigator. (I will mention him again in Chapter Eight.) He went to Alaska to see for himself. Twenty years later he went back again and summed up his experience in his book, *Exxon is immortal—but Natives die!*

Despite court fines levied in 1994, 2002, 2006, 2007, and 2008, Exxon stalled on settling, as they warned they would.

The ruling in 1994 was for $287 million, plus $5 billion damages. An appeal in 2002 reduced payment for damages to $4 billion. Another appeal in 2006 cut damages to $2.5 billion. An appeal in 2007 was denied, but Exxon appealed in 2008, and the case was sent back to a lower court for review. The Supreme Court, on June

26, 2008, cut Exxon's liability by 90% to half a billion. It's so cheap, it's like a permit to spill.[52]

In 2009, twenty years after the oil spill, Exxon made its first payments to those who were still alive.

Individuals die, but corporations don't. Consequently, it is to corporations' advantage to stall, forever if possible. Exxon got to pocket about one billion dollars in interest earned on money that the corporation should have paid out.

In 2011, twenty-two years after the spill, spilt oil was still there. The $5 billion award by a jury for damages was reduced to one-tenth; or $0.5 billion. By that time, one-third of the people in the suit Palast had known had died.

By late 2012, a $90 million fine from the government remained unpaid.[53]

Corporations can easily cross borders. People cannot—they need passports. With every new trade treaty, corporations seem to get more power. This allows them to more easily do what they did in Alaska, leaving the living in their wake. (I'll discuss this further in Chapter Nine.)

If we view corporations as "people," what sort of people are they?

Joel Bakan, a Law Professor at the University of British Columbia, wrote *The Corporation; the Pathological Pursuit of Profit and Power*, which examines the behaviour of modern corporations.[54]

---

52 http://www.gregpalast.com/court-rewards-exxon-for-valdez-oil-spill/
53 http://www.huffingtonpost.com/richard-steiner/exxon-valdez-oil-spill_b_1377011.html
54 The Canadian film documentary, T*he Corporation*, which is based on this book, won the Sundance Film Festival Award in 2004.

It's a fascinating subject to a behaviourist. For example, companies don't hire people; they rent their behaviour. Behaviour's not what you say, it's what you do. Actions speak louder than words. That is behaviour. If we judge a corporation simply by its behaviour, what type of behaviour is it exhibiting?

Bakan's answer: psychopathic!

Psychopathy is a personality disorder characterized by lack of empathy, antisocial behaviour, cold-heartedness, amorality, criminality and lack of remorse. Psychopathic individuals are described as the most charming people you will ever meet; they set out to be trusted by you in order to use you.

The serial killer Ted Bundy was an educated, handsome, and charming young man. Before he was executed for killing thirty women, 42-year-old Bundy's last words were, "I'd like you to give my love to my family and friends."

Corporations have no emotion. They don't have human characteristics. They cannot show compassion, decency, love, or caring. People managing companies can have those qualities, but in the workplace, we find corporate needs regularly trump human needs. Capital and corporations share the same traits.

It's a given that people can be cruel. As an example, the transAtlantic slave trade kidnapped and sold an estimated 12 million people. Slave traders' behaviour was immoral, and there were an estimated 300,000 of them. Money and profit motivated the trade.

Corporations don't mate, bond, or procreate; they don't eat or drink or breathe. They can easily exist with no concern for the preservation of whales, rainforests, or clean water or air. Corporations don't care if we consume all the fish in the sea. It is not their concern if people go hungry. They do not understand "unfair."

They don't worry about the effects of genetic modification. Climate change won't affect them. Businesses function to make money. Any behaviour that serves that end dictates is what they do.

Eric Kierans, Canadian economist, businessman, and politician raised this issue in 2003, a few years before the movie *The Corporation* was released, and before the US Supreme Court decision to allow corporations to be "persons" in law (2010).

Kierans had a distinguished career. He was a director at McGill University, president of the Montreal Stock Exchange, Member of Provincial Cabinet in Quebec, and then a Federal Cabinet Member in the Trudeau government. When he left politics in the 1980s, he became a popular radio commentator on a cross-Canada morning show, *Morningside,* and I listened often. (The CBC is a publicly owned national radio and TV network that 40% of Canadians listen to, which has nurtured a national identity, a role "for profit" radio stations can't play.)

In 2001, Kierans wrote his memoirs, *Remembering*. His daughter-in-law, a friend of mine, gave me a copy of this interesting book, which includes more than a bit of economics;

> Markets cannot fix the problems of our schools and universities, nor provide all our people with the health care and employment that they need. Governments have had to broaden their activities to provide housing, help for the poor, and money to clean the environment. We organize ourselves and our land and people to meet the needs of all members of the community. An economy is a social organization.

He wrote about meeting Ronald Reagan, a man he described "of stunning simplicity." About two-thirds of the way through his book, he included a few paragraphs on capital. I wrote to him and asked if, when he wrote the words "capital has no conscience," he was writing something profound. He wrote back and said that I understood exactly why he wrote the book! Capital's self-interest would bury all community and human interests.

With changes in American law that recognize corporations as people, thirty million or so psychopathic corporations have rights and powers that now exceed our own.

Intellectual property laws

> A disproportionate number of innovations are developed by entrepreneurs, as opposed to big firms.
> —Robert Litan, Economist; PhD, Yale

The idea of being able to patent or protect an idea was recognized by the ancient Greeks, and also in Venice and Florence at about the time of the Medicis, where the patent system was useful to protect ideas in glass making. Patents exist so an inventor can reap the rewards of the invention, but for how long, or until how much is earned? Libertarians argue that all patents are unfair because they limit freedom. The current trend is to try to extend them forever.

"Ideas" are regarded as property-based on several assumptions: one is that people develop new ideas to make money. However, if profit were the only reason for new ideas, people wouldn't improve medicine because they care, or invent new tools because they are helpful, or write songs because they are in love. Some ideas may be developed with making money in mind, but not all. However, all ideas can now be copyrighted or patented.

Adam Smith, it is safe to say, never envisioned anyone making the money Bill Gates has made because of his patents. Those patents occurred because of his ideas, which were government-funded for his college sophomore research project.

On the other hand, a research group called The Structural Genomics Consortium makes its research available to anyone with "no strings attached." They do, as researchers once did, share their new ideas to serve all of humanity. It's the opposite of Monsanto and drug corporations, which survive on patents, copyrights, and litigation.

The pharmaceutical industry says that it needs laws to protect the investment they make in developing new drugs. The fact is, much of what is developed comes from research by dedicated scientists at universities. They are the ones who discovered the drugs for smallpox, polio, and diabetes.

Research, not profit, has been the motivator. A new Ebola vaccine was recently developed in a Canadian Government laboratory, despite the right-wing government's preference at that time to close it. Developed over 15 years by the National Microbiology Laboratory in Manitoba, the vaccine was sold to an Iowa tech company for $205,000, which then licensed world rights to manufacture to Merck & Co., of New Jersey, for $50 million. An inexplicable move; the rights should have stayed with the publicly owned company.

Now, it is not uncommon for universities to sell patents and cash in. If it's to a drug company, the company will use copyright law in several ways to protect profits. Companies use international agreements to extend the life of patents by "evergreening" them, extending patent life by simply changing one inactive ingredient for another, or by adding new language about uses for the product.

The question is, how long should a patent last? Until the cost of developing the drug is covered? Until they make a reasonable return on investment? Or forever? New pharmaceuticals are given twenty-year patent protections, no matter what the research cost. Often, at the end of 20 years, drugs are "reconfigured," modified ever so slightly and patented anew to extend the patent life. It seems that better skills in semantics or law, keep the profit high.

Should Monsanto be allowed to patent seeds for foods? They do so, and have sued over 150 farmers for doing what farmers have always done—saving some of this year's crop for next year's planting. If Monsanto has its way, this eons-old, sensible, ecologically sound practice will be a quaint tradition from the past.

Competitive economic theory depends on competition. Patents eliminate competition, for at least 20 years, and copyright protection for up to 70 years, after the death of the copyright holder.

Intellectual property law has nothing to do with public welfare. Corporations attempting to control all the crop seeds are another example of the sort of thing Galbraith foresaw and his son, as we will see in Chapter Nine, writes about—how governments have become subservient to corporations.

Corporate lobbying

In the last century, corporations began circling the wagons for their own protection, and we have witnessed the steps they took to deliberately change public opinion. Corporate-funded lobbying has been used to attack governments in order to eliminate spending that is not in support of business. Not surprisingly, they lobbied to have government funds increased for corporate welfare.

Noam Chomsky, whom I mentioned earlier, co-wrote *Manufacturing Consent: The Political Economy of the Mass Media*, published in 1984 (updated in 2011). As the title suggests, he found that instead of the media being left-leaning agents for social change, as they once were, the media have become guardians of the economic agenda serving the corporate state and the rich. The North American press, which at one time was the freest press in the world, is now pro-corporate and pro-military. At the age of 88, Chomsky still speaks about the dangers the corporate worldview has for humanity. (I will examine press freedom more in Chapter Seven.)

In addition to Chomsky and Gutstein, others have written about manipulating the public. Alex Carey, an Australian psychologist and specialist in corporate propaganda, wrote in 1996, *Taking the Risk out of Democracy; Corporate Propaganda versus Freedom and Liberty*.

In *Selling Free Enterprise: The Business Assault on Labor and Liberalism; 1945–60* (1994), history Professor Dr. Elizabeth Fones-Wolf looked at how the views of people in the United States changed from belief and trust in government and unions to uncritical support for corporations.

There was the more subtle effort to rename capitalism itself. Galbraith wrote in 1999:

> Let's begin with capitalism, a word that has gone largely out of fashion. The approved reference now is to the market system. This shift minimizes — indeed, deletes — the role of wealth in the economic and social system. And it sheds the adverse connotation going back to Marx. Instead of the

owners of capital or their attendants in control, we have the admirably impersonal role of market forces. It would be hard to think of a change in terminology more in the interest of those to whom money accords power. They have now a functional anonymity. [55]

Summing up the corporate takeover

Corporate think tanks grew to fight the fight and established their own union to coordinate their efforts. The Philanthropy Roundtable was established in 1987 to coordinate the endeavors of hundreds of corporate foundations, so they get the best-coordinated bang for their conservative agenda bucks. As the Roundtable states, they exist to "help philanthropists connect with like-minded peers in their field of interest to share ideas, leverage resources, and strategically collaborate to create significant change."

Belief in unregulated capitalism is not part of the natural order, but was introduced, nurtured, and reinforced with corporate money into this century, when it acquired almost reverential status.

In the late 1970s, the incomes of the rich began to soar, economic inequality began to grow, and the middle class began to decline, as ordinary incomes stagnated. It was in the mid-1970s that Canada and the United States changed the way they financed new projects. How that happened and what it meant are the subjects of the next chapter. This change in finance is of huge significance. I think it's the most important issue in this book.

---

55   Galbraith, John Kenneth. "Free Market Fraud," *Progressive Magazine*, January 1999.

5. A Change in government financing and the creation of debt

Let me issue and control a nation's money and I care not who writes the laws.
—Mayer Amschel Rothschild, c 1790[56]

DEBT CAN BE A GOOD THING. WHEN A YOUNG FAMILY IS GETTING started, it's best if they can get a down payment, get a mortgage loan, buy a house, and pay for it during the years they need and use it.

---

56 http://www.themoneymasters.com/the-money-masters/famous-quotations-on-banking/

The same is true for nations. As the United States Capitol building has been in use for 206 years, paying for it over time has made sense. Too much debt, however, can be an issue. And the motive for banks to encourage too much debt is enormous.

In the mid-1970s, the governments of Canada and the United States changed the way they paid for things. Unfortunately, the change occurred almost unnoticed, because the change was so significant that it started the relentless escalation of national debt that continues to this day.

What happened in the mid-1970s is the biggest economic issue of our age, and the most important subject in this book. Debt is behind the events that would implode in 2007, and the effects continue to reverberate.

What happened in the 1970s to cause so much national debt? I don't have a precise answer.

I can't tell you exactly how this change came about, nor who was behind it. I have looked for answers, literally for years, hoping to uncover a person or event, a smoking gun. But I can't. I can describe the economic culture at the time and the change that occurred but can't say definitively why, or how, or by whom.

It is probable that the change came about because of three international meetings: one that took place decades earlier in the 1940s in Bretton Woods, New Hampshire; a second that occurred in the early 1970s at the Smithsonian Museum in Washington, after the US abandoned the gold standard. A third meeting was held in Basel, Switzerland in 1974.

In 1944, people were hoping World War II would soon end, and some started planning how to deal with the issues that peace would bring. Churchill and Roosevelt had had a secret meeting in

1941 and developed The Atlantic Charter, which aimed to create "… the fullest collaboration between all nations in the economic field with the object of securing, for all, improved labor standards, economic advancement and social security."

In July 1944, three years after Churchill and Roosevelt's meeting, a month after D-Day, the United Nations called a Monetary and Financial Conference in the small town of Bretton Woods, in the White Mountain National Forest in New Hampshire. It was one of the first acts of the newly emerging international organization.

The exclusive Mount Washington Hotel was chosen—large enough and posh enough for such a prestigious meeting. Seven hundred and thirty delegates from forty-four nations met for three weeks in the shadow of Mount Washington, the tallest mountain in the eastern states. Only seven of those invited were bankers! The press was there.

The mission of the delegates was to prepare for the financial issues that would arise when peace arrived. The meeting was historic: the first attempt in history to develop a global financial system. (Up until then, the financial system was the result of ad hoc developments.)

The result of this meeting was the first fully negotiated international financial agreement and, unknown to us, the work of those seven hundred and thirty people was to directly affect our lives for decades to come. (It had the unintended consequence of elevating finance—especially money, banks, banking, and investment banking, above the real economy, but I'll discuss more about that later.)

In addition, this meeting led to the creation of the International Monetary Fund (IMF), the World Bank, and the International Bank for Reconstruction and Development (IBRD).

It laid the groundwork for the General Agreement on Tariffs and Trade (GATT), which was signed three years later in 1947, when 23 nations agreed to reduce tariffs and other trade barriers. It was the forerunner of the multitude of trade agreements that would follow.

The Bretton Woods Agreement required member nations to adopt monetary policies that tied their currencies to gold, and named the US dollar as the world's reserve currency. At that time, the US dollar was the world's most-used currency and was tied to gold at $35.00 per ounce. (Today, gold is worth about $1,100 an ounce; thus, the dollar is worth a lot less.) At the time, the US population equalled the total sum of the populations of Japan, France, and Germany, and it was believed that the currency of a population so large would provide enough stability to be the global reserve currency.

A "reserve" currency is a currency that is widely accepted, making it easy to pay bills between countries—easier than paying in gold, and smoother than having to negotiate currency details with every transaction. During the Dutch Golden Age, the guilder was the reserve currency.

No matter what currency is issued, once it is agreed upon, every nation needs to keep some "reserve currency" to pay its international bills. This creates demand—the greater the demand, the higher the price—simple, competitive Economics 101. Having the status of reserve currency inflated the value of the US currency, which favoured Wall Street, but worked against exports and American jobs. As the United States imported more goods than it exported, more money was needed to be sent abroad to pay for them. The money sent abroad would come back to buy US bonds. In this way, other nations financed the booming American economy.

At one time, the British pound was the world's reserve currency. It's now used about 4% of the time. The Swiss franc, Japanese yen, and even the Canadian dollar, also have minor roles. In November 2015, the Chinese yuan was designated by the International Monetary Fund as an official world reserve currency, even as the Chinese were advocating for the creation of a new reserve currency to replace what they refer to as "debt currencies." In October 2016, the yuan got another boost when the International Monetary Fund announced it would be included in their basket of International Currencies along with the US dollar, the British pound, the yen, and the €uro.

Tariffs have historically been useful for protecting fledgeling industries. Often, they outlive that purpose and remain to prevent competition. In the late 1800s, Britain led the way to "free trade" by ending its tariffs while, at that time, the United States had tariffs as high as 45%.

John Maynard Keynes was at the 1944 Bretton Woods conference, but he was unhappy with the outcome. He predicted that the Bretton Woods Agreement would cause debt to grow relentlessly. That's exactly what happened. The United States negotiators, led by Henry Dexter White, were opposed to Keynes' ideas and overrode him on almost every point, although history would prove Keynes right.

The meeting achieved the ends the American negotiators wanted—created the IMF and the World Bank, and located them in Washington—moving the centre for world banking from London to America.

The Bretton Woods agreement guided the world economy for the next 26 years, until the early 1970s.

The late 1960s and early 1970s were volatile years. American involvement in the Vietnam War continued, and increasing war debt was making Americans apprehensive of inflation. Because of this fear, those who could were exchanging cash for gold, while they could. The US dollar was seen as less stable, and the US gold reserves were diminishing.

On August 12, 1971, in the midst of the run on gold, Britain asked the US for a $3 billion "cover" for Britain's US dollar assets. In preparation for a response, fourteen presidential advisors and a speechwriter were told to each pack a bag, not to tell their wives or secretaries where they were going, and to catch a helicopter ride to Camp David. There would be no external communication allowed.

Over that weekend in August 1971, with secrecy reminiscent of the meeting to create the Federal Reserve bank, President Nixon met with his advisors.

Camp David is a 142-acre mountain retreat in Maryland, about a half-hour helicopter ride from the White House. Selected as a retreat during the early 1940s because it was ten degrees cooler than Washington in summer, it's run by the US Navy. (Years later, President Obama opened seven of its cabins to the public for one weekend a month. You could spend a weekend for $1,200, presidential meals included!)

On Sunday, August 15, 1971, the president announced the end of the gold standard: the US would no longer buy gold at $35 an ounce. Nixon, and a handful of people, had ended the system agreed upon by 730 delegates from 44 nations, twenty-seven years earlier.

With the dollar having no "real" value, turmoil was created in international financial markets. With the United States dollar no longer backed by gold, the value of the dollar started slipping, and fixed contracts for things like oil became more expensive.

This precipitated the oil crisis of 1973. OPEC nations embargoed oil bound for the United States, Canada, Japan, and the UK. In 1974, Henry Kissinger negotiated a new agreement with the Saudis (which soon expanded to include most OPEC countries) to have oil sold in US dollars. This provided a new prop for the American dollar—any nation needing oil first had to have US dollars.

The Bank for International Settlements (BIS) had been established in 1930 to deal with war payments—the fines imposed on Germany, after WW I. As I noted in Chapter Two, Keynes had thought these reparations too onerous. They were too onerous, and they did, as he had predicted, lead to WW II.

(It's interesting to note the Greeks were recently forced, primarily by Germany, to cut their standard of living to pay debt of about 175% of their GDP. After WW II, Germany was forgiven debt of 280% of GDP.)

The top ten central banks had been meeting since they had established the G8 in 1962. There is no problem with the heads of private banks meeting, but when they deal with public policies, as they always do, it seems fundamentally wrong. It's collusion, and they have a huge conflict of interest. In October 1974, three years after the end of the gold standard, the central bank governors of the G10 nations established the Basel Committee on Banking

Supervision, named after Basel, the city in Switzerland which was the home of the BIS.

Often referred to as "the bankers' bank," the BIS exists to serve the banks, especially central banks, and is used to settle international accounts. It has one exceptional feature: it is an extraterritorial organization and abides by no national laws. (In Switzerland, Swiss police have no right to enter its premises.) It hosts a secret meeting every two months for the world's central bankers—people like Alan Greenspan, Ben Bernanke, and Janet Yellen from the US, or the head of the Bank of Canada (always less well known), now Stephen Poloz, or formerly, Mark Carney (now head of the Bank of England).

We can only speculate on what influence the Bank for International Settlements has in banking, since the members meet in secret and keep no minutes. The bank is owned by its 140 customers, the world's central banks, and reportedly has a marvellous dining room with an exceptional wine list there on the twenty-fourth penthouse floor of the BIS building, nicknamed the Tower of Basel.

In 1974, two major banks failed: the Bankhaus Herstatt in Germany, and the Franklin National Bank of Long Island, which was the biggest American Bank ever to fail. (Apparently, the Franklin had had some dealings with the Mafia.) The two failures, plus the rapid growth of international trade and finance, the quadrupling of the price of oil, and the shift of money that it created, fueled concern about inadequate banking supervision, leading to some important meetings.

The heads of state of the G6 (France, Germany, Japan, the UK, Italy, and the US) met at the Banque de France on Sept 6, 1974.

That meeting was followed on Sept 7 and 8 by the ministers of finance and the heads of their national banks at Champs sur Marne in the west of Paris. Finally, on September 9 and 10, the G10 governors met. According to the Bank for International Settlements, the Group of Ten is made up of *eleven* industrial countries: the G6, plus Belgium, Canada, the Netherlands, Sweden, and Switzerland. The richest nations and their central bankers created the Basel Committee on Banking Supervision.

The goal of the Basel Committee sounded innocuous enough: to provide a "forum for regular cooperation between member countries on banking and supervisory matters." The original ten members has grown to almost thirty.

Since their first meeting in February 1975, they have met three or four times a year. They release no minutes, so we don't know what they do, nor do we know what they did in 1974, and that's a concern.

Something changed in international finance in the early 1970s that probably changed national financing, but it's not clear what. It could be the coming off the gold standard in 1971 or the creation of the Basel Committee on Banking Supervision in 1974. Let's look at what changed and what the effects were of those changes.

The change to government financing

> Once a nation parts with the control of its currency and credit, it matters not who makes the nation's laws. Usury, once in control, will wreck any nation.
> —William Lyon Mackenzie King, Prime Minister of Canada, 1935

When a government needs money, it has choices. More choices than families do.

Nations rely on taxes—the people pay all the bills. For long-term projects, a nation has choices. For example, a government can print money, or print bonds and sell them. At one time, savings bonds were a great source of money for governments. Bonds were sold to the people and repaid to the people, with interest. The government could also print bonds, then sell them to a publicly owned national bank, with the interest repaid to the people through the national bank. The worst option for governments is to print bonds, and sell them to the private banks, with banks getting the interest.

Prior to the 1970s, if the US or Canadian governments had significant projects to fund, they paid for it from their own resources. If they wanted a new battleship or new bridge, they simply paid for it. The money could be raised from money on hand, or from newly printed money, or borrowed from the federal bank, then repaid with interest to the government. After the mid-1970s, money for new projects was obtained by selling bonds to banks, which would be repaid with interest. The change was that simple.

The charts below show the result of that change: the United States chart is on the left[57] and Canada on the right[58]. The obvious features are the similarity of the start dates and the similarity of the steep rise in debt.

---

57 http://www.brillig.com/debt_clock/faq.html
58 http://sceo.archives.math.ca/edu/edu04/edu04_0171d-eng.htm

5. A Change in government financing and the creation of debt   165

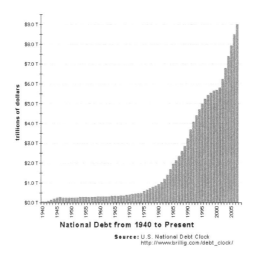

National Debt from 1940 to Present

Source: U.S. National Debt Clock
http://www.brillig.com/debt_clock/

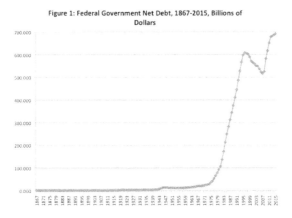

Figure 1: Federal Government Net Debt, 1867-2015, Billions of Dollars

In both charts, national debt from about 1900 is all but flat through the 1940s, 1950s, 1960s, and stays more or less flat until the mid-1970s. Flat for thirty years, then it soars. The decades when debt did not increase include the 1930s stimulus spending to end the depression, the huge expenses of the Second World War in the 1940s, and the Korean War in the 1950s.

Between the years 1954–1960, Canada and the United States built the St. Lawrence Seaway, an expensive undertaking that allowed ships from the Atlantic Ocean to sail inland through the Great Lakes to Chicago and Minnesota. To accomplish this, fifteen locks had to be built to lift ocean ships almost six hundred feet above sea level. Bridges had to be raised, canals deepened, and one town moved. When it was completed, prairie grain, coal, and iron could be shipped directly to Europe. Hydroelectric power was a spin-off that added another $600 million to the cost and rapidly paid for itself.

The total cost was huge for the time: C$470 million (C$336.2 million from Canada), which was eventually to be paid for by tolls. By 1978, the Canadian portion had been paid, and in 1986 the US eliminated tolls on their portion. The Canadian government lent the seaway corporation the money repaid as shares (equity). There was no surge in national debt.

In 1969, the US embarked on a program to put a man on the moon, which cost about $25 billion. The US also had the costs of its involvement in the Vietnam War, which cost the US about $111 billion. Both occurred without a spike in debt. But in the mid-1970s, with no similar huge expenses, for no apparent reason, debt began to soar.

None of these costly items created debt to compare with whatever occurred in the 1970s.

A standard rule in finance is to pay for things over the useful life of the project. As I mentioned earlier, paying for a house over twenty or thirty years makes sense for young people. If a business buys a machine to use for ten years, paying for it over more than ten years would be foolish. For projects that will last decades, like harbours or museums or bridges, interest can be amortized over those longer periods, but cost because of interest soars enormously. Soaring debt in the mid-1970s was a direct result of governments financing everything by borrowing and paying interest to the banks.

Governments *did no*t have to do that then, and *do not* have to do that now. Governments are assumed to be the source of money: the US Constitution gives the government the right to "coin" money. It can lend money and can charge interest, but if it lends it to itself, the interest is to be paid to itself.

In the US, the escalating national debt has increasingly put pressure on the social contract. For example, social security has moved from being something natural, decent, and fair that we once could afford, to an "entitlement" program we cannot now afford. The national debt is used to threaten health care, Old Age Security, education, and all social programs, which have all been redefined as "expensive and unaffordable" in our wealthier modern world. It makes no sense to me.

How big is the debt? Is it logical?

The United States debt is larger than the sum of all the United States dollars in existence: it is four times larger than all the US dollars in the world, which total $1.43 trillion. According to the Federal Reserve in 2016, the US debt was $19.9 trillion. In contrast, Third World debt, the total debt of all the poorest countries on earth, is $4 trillion. America, with almost five times the debt of the world's poorest nations, somehow remains a rich country, while that less-in-debt are labelled poor!

There is no chance that either American or Third World debt ever will be repaid. It doesn't take a rocket scientist, or an economist, to know that. The sums are just too large. These debts are the result of building the global financial system on debt, a fact which Keynes warned about, long ago. And I don't believe building the global financial system on debt was done accidentally.

There is a case before the Canadian courts, as I am writing this, demanding that the Canadian government return to the practice of using the Bank of Canada for what it was originally intended: to finance government projects. This case has been brought by a group of people who believe that the federal bank should serve the people. In the US, several American researchers are making similar arguments for a real American national bank to serve the nation. As well, activist economists and writers are arguing for a return to the original purpose of a national bank—to finance government projects. (I'll discuss this further in my final chapter.)

Why did nations allow the counter-intuitive practice of paying interest to banks, rather than to themselves? There are a few possible answers. One is simple: to give a handout to the banks. It wouldn't be the first, or the last time. Another reason would be to cater to politicians so fundamentally opposed to government involvement that they would starve the government to end its programs. Better for them if the government were broke. However, as I said, I've found no reason why the change in government financing happened, so I don't have an answer.

The economic issue of the mid-1970s was fear of inflation. That fear created an atmosphere for some to argue that the state shouldn't print money. Printing money is always assumed to be inflationary. Sometimes it is. Fear of inflation dominated the economic discussion in the 1970s, and there was some discussion about possibly creating an international currency, an idea Keynes had recommended with the Bancor as an international currency back in 1944.

The recession of 1973–1975 in the US meant unemployment went up, and some banks failed. Germany and Britain suffered the same fate. But none of that explains the change in national financing.

Nixon, a Republican, became President of the US in January 1969, until he was forced to leave office in August 1974, and was followed by fellow conservative Gerald Ford. In Canada, a Liberal, Pierre Trudeau, was prime minister for the period between 1968 and 1984. A Republican government in the United States, and a Liberal one in Canada—different political stripes—still, debt began to soar during both their tenures. So, no clue there to why there was a change. Neither do the histories of the respective finance ministers provide any clues.

Still, debt began to soar, and the banks prospered.

In Chapters Eleven and Twelve, I'll discuss the subject of national debt and its role in causing the collapse of the system in 2007 further, when I look at alternative banking choices.

Political naïveté or deceit?

National debt has grown exponentially since the financing change, and political rhetoric about insupportable debt has risen almost as fast. Not an election goes by when it is not a major topic. And no elected tenure ends with anything being done about it!

Are these politicians naïve, uninformed, or out to deceive us?

The United States' national debt has been paid off only once—in 1835, when Andrew Jackson was president. The economy was booming, he arranged for the debt to be paid off, and a recession followed. Not fond of paper money, Jackson did not trust any bank, much less an early attempt to create a Federal Reserve, and so vetoed a bill to create one.

Three more times in history American politicians sought to reduce debt: in 1869, 1980, and in 2000. Each time debt was reduced, a recession followed. Despite that, during every election, we hear politicians harping about national debt. Perhaps they get away with it because politicians, journalists, and the general public lack understanding about the cause of the debt.

Whether people are naïve, or politically devious, the argument that a national budget is like a family budget comes up repeatedly, and that argument, although convincing, is wrong. (I'll examine why it's wrong in Chapter Eight.)

All a nation needs to do to reduce debt is to go back to financing projects the way governments used to: pay for them or finance them through a government bank. As interest begins to be paid to the nation, we can watch the debt decrease.

This also explains why a national budget is not like a family budget: families can't create money to lend to themselves, but nations can.

Summary: Government financing created national debt

> Of all the many ways of organizing banking, the worst is the one we have today.
> —Mervyn King[59]

---

59   Economist, ex-governor of the Bank of England, 2003–2013.

With the creation of the Basel Committee on Banking Supervision in 1974, it appears that we gave up the power to be masters in our own house! Both in the United States and in Canada. The debt for both nations began to soar. We were tied into the international financial community and its civil protocols. This change seems to have happened with no public meetings, no press releases, and no discussion: national finance simply changed. It was followed by more changes from secret meetings of the G7 (now the G20) and others. A handful of people are changing the rules for the entire globe.

From my experience, it's highly probable that most, if not all, the politicians who made these changes didn't understand what they were doing. As we were coerced into believing we should trust free markets, it became accepted practice for elected leaders to go and make decisions on international finance at global meetings behind closed doors. The electors were never consulted. In the background of the meetings, teams of corporate planners work with big budgets and their corporate agendas. At one time, elected leaders reported to the people. Now many decisions on banking and trade sneak in under the radar.

To sum up, national debt could be eliminated by reverting to the practice of using a nation's power to create money. A government should not borrow from banks. In a couple of decades, the debt would steadily be paid down. It's that easy: finance new government projects as they used to be financed.

Adam Smith wrote about industrialization as he saw it emerging in the late 1700s. Now, we have lived through much de-industrialization while most economists stood silently by. The media tell us that the changes are the result of capital (money) seeking the highest return, which could be true, but should people and nations give up sovereignty to capital? When we had the middle class, the economic system worked, and we had less inequality.

In the chapters ahead, I'll discuss the myth and manipulation of "free markets," the decline of the real economy, and the decline of the middle class: all signs of the decline of competitive capitalism.

6.
Money

It is well enough that people of the nation do not understand our banking and monetary system, for if they did, I believe there would be a revolution before tomorrow morning.
—Henry Ford

HENRY FORD WAS RIGHT ABOUT THAT. HENRY FORD AND THOMAS Edison were opposed to the government borrowing money from private banks. They were interviewed by *The New York Times* on Dec. 6, 1921, about funding $40 million for a power plant on the Tennessee River. The choice for the government was either to print bonds and sell them to the banks and then repay about $80 million, or simply print the $40 million. Ford and Edison said it was absurd "to say that our country can issue $40 million in bonds and not $40 million in currency."

Ford was a visionary who paid his employees $5.00 a day in 1914 (well above the average pay rate), so that his employees could afford to buy his cars. That move, and his decision to create the forty-hour week, effectively established the American middle class. He had great foresight about the economy and understood the money system.

Chapter Fourteen of Samuelson's 1948 textbook was entitled *Prices and Money*. He gave the impression that money is a somewhat benign topic. He failed to give money the significance that the Medici or Rothschild or Ford families understood. But to his credit, Samuelson went to some length explaining the way banks create money out of thin air, because the idea was, and remains, alien to what most of us believe.

People created money for good reasons, and different people at different times have defined it differently. Today, most money is actually fiat money (fiat: from Latin roots, an arbitrary order), not the substance that it once was. A $100 bill is made of a fraction of a cent of paper, but the state says it's worth more and we believe it.

Money can be complicated. Possibly, it's less understood now than before, but money doesn't need to be as complicated as it seems to have become. We don't teach our children about the fundamentals of money, even though it's essential to their lives. It should be part of their basic education. At best, we teach a bit about bank accounts and budgeting. Seldom do we teach about the sources of money, or the wisdom of alternate sources of money, or the consequences of exponential interest growth. Most of us assume we know what money is, and we assume that everyone else shares the same understanding. That includes many economists. However, in the majority, those assumptions are wrong. Samuelson noted in his textbook that many bankers didn't understand then, just as many don't understand now, that they create money.

Instead, most people assume that governments produce money. But that hasn't been true for decades: governments today create only about 3% of our money. In the US, most people believe the United States government produces their money, but it does not. It creates none! Not even the token 3%. Instead, an independent organization called the Federal Reserve prints an alternate to what once was US government money. The last United States government dollar issued was in January 1971. Since then, Federal Reserve Notes became the only currency, and those words are printed on every bill, a secret in plain sight.

To illustrate; below are two bills. They just happen to be $1.00 bills, but the same is true for all bills. The top one is from 1928, the bottom one from 2009. They look identical, but there is one profound difference. The bottom one is a United States Bank note. The top one is a Federal Reserve Bank note: it says so in white letters over the head of Thomas Jefferson, and in the very fine print around the letter B. The fact that the notes are almost identical suggests someone may not have wanted the public to notice that they had changed. The new bill was supported by the Federal Reserve of New York, and not by the nation.

We seldom wonder how much money there is in the world, but most of us would find it hard to believe that there is more debt in the world than there is money. How can that be?

Paper money was first used in China in about 800 AD. At the time, money primarily was copper coins used for exchange, which is economic language for "to buy and sell things." But copper can get heavy. The Chinese had invented paper and printing with woodblocks. When they realized paper would be easier to work with than coins, paper money was born. It made life easier, and over the centuries, money morphed into its current role, along with assumptions about what it is, and how it fits into our social agreements. We live with assumptions about who has the right to print money. At one time, anyone could. Today, that option is limited. As our world has become more financialized, money and our assumptions about it have increasingly controlled our lives.

The value of money is always changing. Understanding that is how the Medicis and Rothschilds flourished. In the Medicis' Florence, centuries after Jesus chased the money changers from the synagogue, money-changing was done across a "*banka*," or bench. The Medicis' original business of storing and exchanging money expanded to include lending and grew from there.

Amschel Moses Rothschild (1710–1755) was a merchant in the Jewish ghetto of Frankfurt. He traded in silk, supplied coins, and operated a money-changing service from his home. He died at 45, in a smallpox epidemic. His fourth child, nineteen-year-old Mayer Amschel Rothschild, took over and expanded the family's business into an enormous enterprise. In 2005, *Forbes* magazine ranked Mayer Amschel as the seventh most influential businessmen of all time. The family has been ranked as the wealthiest in all of history.

When he was 13, Mayer served as an apprentice in a banking firm in Hamburg, where he learned currency exchange. With this training, he returned to run the family business in rare coins for a growing list of wealthy patrons and then provided them with more banking services. Meyer had eight children, and all his five boys (but none of the three girls) were invited to join the family business.

The sons extended the business into France, Austria, and Naples. In 1789, he sent his third son to England to open a branch in London. The British were fighting Napoleon in France, and this was an opportunity for the Rothschild family to lend money—to both sides. Over the centuries, banking served the family well, and the Rothschild family is said to have a net worth today of $400 billion. (Bill Gates has a mere $66 billion.) In early America, the Rothschilds financed Standard Oil, the Carnegie Steel Empire, the Vanderbilts, and J. P. Morgan.

The Rothschilds developed a business that went beyond simply storing money or gold or other assets in their vaults. Lending money (paper money that they printed, backed by the gold in their vaults), was very lucrative.

Bankers realized that all depositors never come to withdraw their gold at the same time. Thus, bankers need to keep only a portion of deposited gold available for withdrawal. That way, it was possible to lend more than the value of gold they had on hand, and the idea of fractional reserve banking was born. Banks lend up to ten times the amount they have on deposit and collect interest on ten times the money they hold.

By the end of the 1600s, after 50 years of war with France, Britain was financially ruined and needed to beg money from the moneychangers. With British bulldog tenacity, they wanted to rebuild the British navy and carry on the war. The banks agreed the king could have the money, but to get it, the government would need to establish a national bank: a government-sanctioned, *private* bank, and they would have to tax the people to pay back the loan.

The Bank of England was established in 1694, and, thirteen years later, taxes were being collected. The first tax rate was based on the number of windows people had in their homes—a progressive tax—the more windows, the more tax. The private bank had the right to print money—when the government wanted money, the printing press was turned on. The government printed bonds. The bank printed money, and the private bank bought the bonds. For merely the cost of paper and ink, money began to appear

So, the government got the money for their war, and the bonds had to be repaid with interest. To the bank, it was a pretty safe loan, backed by the Government of England and paid through new taxes. (It was the same practice I discussed in Chapter Five, when nations in the mid-1970s started printing bonds, rather than money.)

Just after WWII, in 1946, the Labour Government nationalized the private Bank of England.

Money in America

> The study of money, above all other fields in economics, is one in which complexity is used to disguise truth or to evade truth, not to reveal it … With something so important, a deeper mystery seems only decent.
> —John Kenneth Galbraith; *Money: Whence It Came; Where It Went*; 1975

The titles of Galbraith's books tell us everything about them. In *Money: Whence It Came; Where It Went*, he examined issues that are still with us. Because of the way money is created (whence it came), there is less money than debt (where it went).

How can that be? Where did the money go? First, let's look at how it's created.

In the 1700s, Benjamin Franklin made four trips to Europe: once as the agent of the Pennsylvania assembly. When he was in Britain, he was asked why the colonies were growing so wealthy.

"That is simple," he is said to have replied, "… in the colonies we issue our own money." When the bankers heard that, the British Government passed the Currency Act in 1751, banning the colonies from issuing money, and demanding that the colonies use the gold and silver currency provided by English bankers. "In one year," Franklin later reported, "the conditions were so reversed that the era of prosperity ended and a depression set in ... the streets of the colonies were filled with unemployed."

Predictably, this led to war.

The British Stamp Act of 1765, also known as the Duties in American Colonies Act, imposed taxes on many things (paper, glass, paint, etc.). As well, the tax had to be paid in British currency. A few years later (1773), the British passed the Tea Act to help the privately owned, politically powerful East India Company get rid of overstocked tea. If this had gone according to plan, surplus tea would have been shipped to the colony, sold and taxed, and British currency sent back. Several shiploads were sent to the colony, and on Dec. 16, 1773, three of the ships were raided by colonists; 342 chests of tea were thrown into the Boston Harbor.

Two years later, the War of Independence (or Revolutionary War) began—an unintended consequence of self-serving British economic policies.

The people drafting the American Constitution were aware of the impact money had on the new colony and included in the Constitution the clause that "Congress shall have the power to coin money and to regulate the value thereof."[60] That right and power for the nation to print and control its money, a right earned in battle, as I'll discuss, has been long forgotten and unused.

Alexander Hamilton created the nation's first central bank in 1790,[61] a private bank known appropriately as the First Bank of the United States. The nation owned 20% of the shares, while others

---

60　American Constitution, Article 1, Section 8, paragraph 5, 1787.
61　http://eh.net/encyclopedia/article/cowen.banking.first_bank.us

held the rest. The British Rothschilds were lenders. The First Bank of the United States had a 20-year charter and the right to print money. When, in 1809, the charter was not renewed, Nathan Rothschild warned that either the US would renew the bank charter or it would "find itself in a most disastrous war." In 1812, Britain indeed declared war that, reportedly Rothschild warned, would "teach those impudent Americans a lesson. Bring them back to a colonial status."

The war of 1812 lasted just under three years. In April 1813, American forces captured the City of York (now Toronto), burned many of the buildings, and left. Discussions for peace began in August 1814, the same month in which the British, in retaliation for the sacking of York, attacked Washington. (Dinner had been prepared for the president, but his party fled the White House, and dinner was left for the invaders. With full stomachs, they torched the White House and much of the city.)

The war was ended with the signing of the Treaty of Ghent. (Ghent, in Belgium, was then part of the United Kingdom.) The treaty was ratified by the US Congress in February 1815. An unusual part of the settlement was that Britain agreed to reimburse American slave owners more than $1 million, in compensation for slaves who had fled the plantations. War and money always overlap.

Three years after the Treaty of Ghent, the charter of the Second Bank of the United States was granted: another privately owned national bank. The war had killed about 4,000, and wounded about 8,000, but it appears, as Nathan Rothschild had put it, that the war, indeed, had "brought the rebellious colony to its senses" and a private national bank was back.

Like the First Bank of the United States, the Second Bank was a private corporation. The nation owned 20% of the shares. It, too, had a twenty-year charter. When Andrew Jackson became president in 1829, he believed that the federal private bank was an "engine of corruption" and refused to renew its charter. He wrote "… controlling our currency, receiving our public moneys … would be more formidable and dangerous than military power of the enemy."

Jackson changed the law, so the people had to use gold and silver, rather than bank currency, for land payments. The new nation had a debt of $58 million, and he paid it off. As I noted in the last chapter, he was the first and only president to do so, and a recession followed; about one-half of the nation's banks failed, and the market collapsed. The recession that followed lasted about five years, national debt returned and has remained with us ever since.

Among the first to see recession as opportunity were the Rothschilds. In 1837, they dispatched August Belmont to America to see what opportunities the recession panic was creating. The Rothschilds were innovative in using disaster to their advantage and did so, 140 years before Naomi Klein would write about the rise of "disaster capitalism" and explain how corporations prosper from crises. (I'll discuss her work further in Chapter Nine.)

August Belmont was born in Germany, where he'd started as an apprentice with the Rothschilds, then worked his way up. Eventually, he travelled to Naples, Paris, and Rome for them. Prior to his trip to America, the Rothschilds had lent money to the Bank of the United States and to many individual states. Belmont organized new loans that enabled the United States to fight the Mexican War of 1847, in which thousands were killed. The United States paid $15 million to Mexico for new territory and created the

Mexico/US border as it now exists. (Belmont made enough money to set up his own investment business, acquire horses, and take up horseracing. He built the Belmont Park racetrack and ran the first Belmont Stakes in 1867.)

The Rothschilds' banks grew to become the largest in the world. They lent money, as I noted earlier, to royalty and nations—often to both sides in a war—as they did with England and France, and with Austria and France. Known as "Money's Prophets," the Rothschilds were building a financial empire as the British were building forts in the New World, in Quebec, Halifax, Kingston, and Niagara. Log palisades, with moats and drawbridges for fighting wars as they used to be fought before gunpowder was invented, the forts were obsolete before they were built, and now are tourist attractions. The Rothschilds made better use of their time.

The American Civil War began in April 1861. In 1863, the National Banking Act was passed to allow the government to borrow money to fund it. Lincoln had gone to the bankers in New York, who offered to lend him the money, but at interest rates of between 24% and 36%. Lincoln refused and instead, as allowed in the Constitution, printed $450 million in debt-free "Greenbacks." The bankers fought back and had the act rescinded. When Lincoln was re-elected in 1864, he said; "I have two great enemies. The Southern Army in front of me and bankers in the rear. And of the two, the bankers are my greatest foe." Lincoln understood more about money than most contemporary politicians.

So did William Jennings Bryan, who explained in 1896, "The issue of money is a function of Government, and the banks ought to get out of the Government business … When we have restored the money of the Constitution, all other necessary reforms will be possible, but until this is done, there is no other reform that can be accomplished."[62]

From the 1870s to the end of that century, the US economy grew rapidly because of industrialization and railroad building. Wages grew quickly, but unevenly. Mark Twain co-authored a history of the period in a satirical novel entitled *The Gilded Age: a Tale of Today*, which satirized the greed and political corruption of the era and was a best seller. The term "Gilded Age" stuck from the 1870s to about the end of the century, despite two major depressions in 1873 and 1893.

In 1893, a panicky run on gold was followed by a run on money. Unemployment soared at 43% in Michigan, and 35% in New York. The United States Federal Treasury was almost out of gold when President Grover Cleveland accepted an offer from J. P. Morgan who, with the Rothschilds, supplied 3.5 million ounces of gold. The rescue came after over 500 banks had failed, crop prices dropped, bankrupt farmers left their farms, and over 15,000 businesses closed. It took five years for the economy to begin to recover.

Our look at money in America will continue after a look at how money is created.

How money is created

> The process by which banks create money is so simple that the mind is repelled.
> —John Kenneth Galbraith; *Money: Whence It Came, Where It Went*; 1975

---

[62] Bryant, W.J. *Speech to the Democratic National Convention.* July 1896. http://historymatters.gmu.edu/d/5354/

The next few paragraphs are about how money, as we understand it—dollars, yuan, or pounds—is created. It's not about how wealth is created, or value, but simply how money is created.

It is not what most of us expect. I circulated a draft of this section of my book to experienced business and professional people, and asked for their input, in order to ensure this topic would be clearly understood. I think getting this help has improved what I'm including here. You will be the judge of that.

Most of us aren't aware that banks actually create money, because most people understand that banks can lend more money than they have on hand. As I noted above, this is "fractional reserve lending." But we don't wonder where the extra money comes from. This I will try to explain

We create money daily. Most of us don't grasp this.

When you use a credit card, for example, to buy gasoline, you slide your card, pump the gas, and drive away. No dollars change hands. But dollars have been created: credited to the gas station and charged to you. Your new debt is added to the money supply. In 2013, that amounted to an $850 billion credit card debt in the United States. That money appeared out of nowhere.

Similarly, if you have received a bank loan, your bank created money. The bank accepts your loan application, and with a computer entry puts the loan amount into your bank account. That number represents money that you can spend, but no "money" changed hands. The bank added more dollars to their loan account, which shows as a bank asset and adds to the total number of dollars in existence. Money, out of nowhere, has again been created.

> Each and every time a bank makes a loan, new bank credit is created, new deposits, brand new money.
> —Graham F. Towers, Governor, Bank of Canada, 1934

There are laws that banks need to abide by, but those laws don't seem to be too onerous, given the towering buildings they have afforded. About three hundred years ago, Amschel Rothschild reportedly said, "Give me control of a nation's money and I care not who writes the laws." The Rothschilds have managed to control lots of the world's money. While most people believe that nations control money, the Rothschilds have understood that the power to manage money could be usurped, and, once usurped, would trump (pardon the expression) national policy.

On March 5, 1997, Scottish Parliamentarian Malcolm Sinclair declared, in the British House of Lords, "… our whole monetary system is dishonest, as it is debt-based … We did not vote for it. It grew upon us gradually but markedly since 1971." (It's worth noting his reference to 1971 in Scotland, which coincides with the 1970s change in national financing in America, discussed in my previous chapter.)

In case you are not yet convinced that the banks create money, the footnote below is from a Bank of England Quarterly for Q1, 2014[i].[63] In that issue, it's explained, "… how the majority of money in the modern economy is created by commercial banks making loans."

---

63   http://www.bankofengland.co.uk/publications/Documents/quarterlybulletin/2014/qb14q1.pdf

The US Federal Reserve produces two regular updates on the amount of money in circulation, which also confirm the point. They report on M1, what we all consider to be money, and on M2, which is M1 plus money created by the banks.

- M1   Oct 2016 $ 3,348 billion
- M2   Oct 2016 $ 13,137 billion

To illustrate; the chart below is from the St. Louis Federal Reserve and shows M2, it's the top increasing line and M1, the lower steadier line. The chart covers from 1991 on the left to 2011 on the right. M2 growth accelerated in the mid 90's.

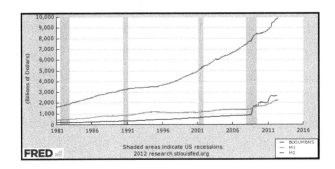

Now, if you understand how money is created out of thin air, it's time to consider how money disappears. It's simply the reverse process.

Just as you create money when you buy on credit or take out a loan, you destroy money when you pay off your credit card or pay off your loan. Paying down debt ends the debt, and the money that was issued when the debt was created, vanishes.

The practice has evolved so that nations do not just allow the banks to create money; nations need banks to do so. As a population expands, the economy expands, and more money is needed. The number of dollars in existence in the 1800s would not fill the need today. For the economy to grow, someone has to create the extra money required.

It would be sensible to think that the state would print more money at about the same rate as the increase in the population, or at the rate of the increase in the economy, or possibly at the same rate as the growth of the Gross Domestic Product. However, we let the banks lend money into existence as they wish. Money created this way is debt. It's not the only way money can be created, but it's how it's done now.

One problem with this practice is the arithmetic.

To explain: when new money is created by making loans, not quite enough money is created! If you borrow $100,000 to buy a house, the bank creates $100,000 by making an entry into your bank account and theirs. You need to pay back the bank, but not just the $100,000—you must pay $100,000, plus interest.

If interest is 5% and the term is 25 years, you will repay $175,377.01—and that's the problem. Where do the extra $75,377.01 dollars come from? Those dollars were never created. The money system avoids this problem with never-ending growth. As long as more loans are being made than are being paid off, there will be enough money.

Exponential is the term for never-ending growth. It occurs in bacteria, cancer, debt, population, and atomic explosions. Exponential growth always has significant consequences.

Exponential is a math function and clearly illustrated in the legendary story of rice and a chess game.

In about 1100 BC in Persia (now Iran), the king enjoyed chess, so he challenged a visitor to a game. To make it interesting, he suggested they bet. The visitor agreed, with the condition that if he won he would be paid the sum of one grain of rice on the first square, two on the second, four on the third square, and so on. The visitor won and was owed 18,446,744,073,709,551,615 grains of rice; rice that would fill over 100,000 trains now! That's exponential growth.

Exponential growth seems to have been better understood in Persia about three thousand years ago than by most of us today. That may have been because exponential growth and interest were better taught then than they are today. The Persians also understood that exponential growth becomes impossible to maintain, as the numbers get too large.

With our current system, in which the banks create money, if a time comes when people are afraid to take out new loans and, instead, pay off their loans and mortgages, not only will no new money be created but money will disappear. In such a down-turn, the banks could run out of money. (In Chapter Eleven, I'll look at what happened in 2008, when the banks did run out of money.) For the moment, though, back to my story about how money is created and the problems that come with it.

While the situation in America is strange, with a private federal bank controlling the money, the situation in Europe is even stranger. Their new money, the €uro, has been created by the European Central Bank, which is a private bank owned by other European private central banks, with no accountability to any nation or people. Thus, the European currency is controlled beyond the reach of European nations and European governments. To bankers, that's progress!

Canadian notes are issued by the Bank of Canada, which is 100% owned by the Queen, on behalf of the nation. Originally created as a private bank, it was made public in 1938. You might think that would be a good thing, but it was only good for a short time. Now it functions the same way a private bank does.

To illustrate the significance of controlling money creation, I'm going to give you an interesting example from Portugal.

Alves dos Reis was born into a poor family in Lisbon in 1898. He studied engineering but never finished his degree. He emigrated to the Portuguese colony of Angola in southern Africa in search of work, but he knew that his prospects for employment would be better if he had a degree. So, he forged one in engineering from a school that doesn't teach engineers. No one bothered to check.

He started in the sewers department and later moved to the Angolan state-run railway. There, he forged another document, this time a contract in the name of the Bank of Portugal (a private company) to have Portuguese banknotes printed. He explained they were to develop the economy in Angola. The company that printed Portugal's escudos was Waterlow and Sons, in England. They received his order, and in 1924 printed 100 million escudos, two hundred thousand 500-escudo notes. The order was for about the same number of escudos as were already in existence.

Reis then had to decide what to do with them. He returned to Portugal, opened a bank and began to lend them. The bank grew so fast that branches emerged throughout the country. He and a few partners became instantly rich. They created a boom in the Portuguese economy—money can do that. In 1925, quite by accident, a clerk discovered a duplicate serial number on one of the forged bills. The game was up. Reis was arrested, the government fell, democracy ended, and the dictator Salazar came to power and ruled for the next 36 years. Ries had understood that it was better to own a bank than to rob one.

He understood how money mattered. I doubt if he was aware that he would create an economic boom—but we can learn from that lesson how important it is for the people, not the banks, and not the few, to control the money.

The Federal Reserve

> The worst policy is one made in secrecy by the experts.
> —John Kenneth Galbraith

The American Panic of 1907, known as "The Bankers' Panic," was precipitated by attempts to manipulate the stock of the United Copper Company during a recession. This led to a run on banks and many went bankrupt. The New York Stock Exchange dropped 50% and the City of New York was on the verge of bankruptcy.

Once again, as he had done fourteen years earlier, J. P. Morgan intervened. For more than a week, his home on 36th St. was a hive of activity. He called one meeting at 3:00 a.m. and about 120 presidents of banks and trust companies duly assembled as he requested.

The crisis was resolved by back-door emergency negotiations. One historian reported, "J. Pierpont Morgan decided which firms would fail and which survive. Through a nonstop flurry of meetings, he organized rescues of banks and trust companies, averted a shutdown of the New York Stock Exchange, and engineered a financial bailout of New York City."[64] One outcome of the crisis was the understanding among bankers that something had to be done to avoid a reoccurrence. Some believed a central bank was the answer. At the time, the United States didn't have one.

Three years later, on a cold November night in 1910, five of the major financiers in the United States boarded a train on a New Jersey siding to travel in secret to the Jekyll Island Club.[65] Jekyll Island today is home to a luxury resort hotel on the coast of Georgia. Then, it was a private retreat for the wealthy. The financiers had received explicit instructions: come to the private car under the pretext of going on a duck hunt, arrive alone, do not meet for dinner, use only first names. and speak to no reporters.

On the train for the two-day ride were: Henry Davison, a senior partner of J. P. Morgan; Charles Norton, president of the First National Bank of New York; Frank Vanderlip, president of National City Bank of New York (one of the most powerful banks at the time, and a Rockefeller bank); Benjamin Strong, the head of J.P. Morgan Trust; and finally, Paul Warburg, one of the partners of Kohn, Loeb, an investment bank. (Paul Warburg, a naturalized American came from a very wealthy German banking family and was reportedly the inspiration for the bald Daddy Warbucks character in Little Orphan Annie.)

---

64 Chernow, Ronald. *The Death of the Banker: The Decline and Fall of the Great Financial Dynasties and the Triumph of the Small Investor*. Vintage Books, 1997.

65 The Club was described in the February 1904, issue of *Munsey's Magazine* as "the richest, the most exclusive, the most inaccessible club in the world." Its members included J.P. Morgan, William Rockefeller, Vincent Astor, Joseph Pulitzer, William K. Vanderbilt.

J. P. Morgan had so much power he seemed a giant, compared to the puny American government. A son and grandson of rich bankers, he had power both in his own right, and as an agent for the Rothschilds. His father, Junius Morgan had established J. S. Morgan & Co., a merchant bank, in 1854. He sent his son to learn French in the Alps and then to learn German at the University of Göttingen. In 1857, when J. P. was twenty, Junius got him a job in merchant banking in London, where he spent a year before he returned to work in New York. Banks have never been fond of competitors: J. P. always referred to other banks as "ruinous competition."

J. P. Morgan was not on that train, but two of his men were. Also on board were US Senator Nelson Aldrich (it was his train car), and the Assistant Secretary of the Treasury, Abram Piatt Andrew, Jr. They met for ten days in luxurious seclusion to come up with a plan for a central bank or, as it later became known, the Federal Reserve. Not surprisingly, it was a plan that met their needs, a banker-controlled central bank.

> Picture a party of the nation's greatest bankers stealing out of New York on a private railroad car under cover of darkness, stealthily riding hundred[s] of miles South, embarking on a mysterious launch, sneaking onto an island deserted by all but a few servants, living there a full week under such rigid secrecy that the names of not one of them was once mentioned, lest the servants learn the identity and disclose to the world this strangest, most secret expedition in the history of American finance.
> —Bertie Charles Forbes, founder, *Forbes* magazine[66]

66   *Leslies Weekly,* October 19, 1916.

This meeting embraced all the dangers that arise when economic decisions are made in secret.

Those attending knew it, thus their elaborate precautions for secrecy. So they were unlikely to be recognized, the lodge was far from Wall Street and far from reporters. They hid away as The First Name Club. They understood that if the general public got wind of their planning, their project would be dead in the water, and they took an oath of secrecy. Together they represented one-fourth of the financial wealth in the world.

Three years later, on December 23, 1913, the Federal Reserve Act was passed. It's interesting to note the centennial of the founding of the Fed, unlike most 100-year anniversaries, was all but ignored. Possibly, like at the meeting on Jekyll Island, the members of the Federal Reserve do not wish to draw attention to themselves. Attention could lead to questions.[67]

There was also a plan to control public perception of national finance. However, on February 9, 1917, Congressman Oscar Calloway, a Democrat from Texas, in his third term, read a statement into the Congressional Record. He must have viewed the information as important, because he wanted it captured in the official record. At the time, the house was debating whether or not to increase the budget of the US Navy, a "war matter," as they called it. *The New York Times* carried the story five days later, on February 14, 1917.

"The Chairman will recognize the gentleman from Texas."

---

67   http://www.webofdebt.com/articles/time_to_buy_the_fed.php

Mr. CALLOWAY: "Mr. Chairman: It will be a little, short statement not over 2 ½ inches in length in the Record."

The Chairman: "Is there any objection?"

There was no objection.

Mr. CALLOWAY: "Mr. Chairman, under unanimous consent, I insert into the Record at this point a statement showing the newspaper combination [sic], which explains their activity in the war matter, just discussed by the gentleman from Pennsylvania [Mr. MOORE].

In March 1915, the J.P. Morgan interests, the steel, ship building and powder interests and their subsidiary organizations, got together 12 men high up in the newspaper world and employed them to select the most influential newspapers in the United States and sufficient number of them to control generally the policy of the daily press in the United States.

These 12 men worked the problems out by selecting 179 newspapers, and then began, by an elimination process, to retain only those necessary for the purpose of controlling the general policy of the daily press throughout the country. They found it was only necessary to purchase the control of 25 of the greatest papers. The 25 papers were agreed upon; emissaries were sent to purchase the policy, national and international, of these papers; an agreement was reached;

the policy of the papers was bought, to be paid for by the month; an editor was furnished for each paper to properly supervise and edit information regarding the questions of preparedness, militarism, financial policies and other things of national and international nature considered vital to the interests of the purchasers ...

This policy also included the suppression of everything in opposition to the wishes of the interests served. The effectiveness of this scheme has been conclusively demonstrated by the character of the stuff carried in the daily press throughout the country since March, 1915. They have resorted to anything necessary to commercialize public sentiment and sandbag the National Congress ... They are playing on every prejudice and passion of the American people."[68]

2013 was also the 100th anniversary of the Sixteenth Amendment to the United States Constitution. It, too, went almost unnoticed. Introduced by the Senator for Rhode Island, Nelson Aldrich, and passed in 1909, it took four years to be ratified. (Yes, this was the same Nelson Aldrich who owned the train car that ferried the few to Jekyll Island.) This amendment created income tax in the United States, which provided the money that in due course would go to the banks.

If you retain any doubt that the Fed is NOT a government agency, let's hear it from the horse's mouth. In 2007, Jim Lehrer of

---

68   *U.S. Congressional Record*, February 9, 1917, page 2947.

the PBS program *News Hour* asked Allan Greenspan a question, a year after Greenspan had retired from his job as Chairman of the Fed.

> Jim Lehrer: "What is the proper relationship between a Chairman of the Fed and a President of the United States?"
>
> Alan Greenspan: "Well, first of all, the Federal Reserve is an independent agency, and that means, basically, that there is no other agency of government which can overrule actions that we take. So long as that is in place and there is no evidence that the administration or the Congress or anybody else is requesting that we do things other than what we think is the appropriate thing, then what the relationships are don't frankly matter."

It was one of Greenspan's clearer statements: the Fed does not serve the nation; thus, it doesn't matter what the government thinks. Unsaid was that Greenspan served the Fed shareholders, and the United States government is not a shareholder.[69]

Reportedly, at that time, the top eight shareholders of the Fed were: the Rothschild Banks of London and Berlin; Lazard Brothers Banks of Paris; Israel Moses Seif Banks of Italy; Warburg Bank of Hamburg and Amsterdam; Lehman Brothers of New York; Kuhn, Loeb Bank of New York; Chase Manhattan; and Goldman, Sachs of New York.

---

69 Who Owns The Federal Reserve? http://www.globalresearch.ca/who-owns-the-federal-reserve/10489

By law, the seven members of the board of governors of the Federal Reserve are appointed by the president and must be confirmed by the Senate. They serve for 14 years. The chair and vice chair are chosen by the president from among the governors and serve for four-year terms. The chair must, by law, report twice a year to Congress, but the reporting has no teeth: Congress can neither tell the chair what to do, nor replace the governors. Government control of the Fed is an illusion, and when the chair of the Fed speaks, the chair is not reporting to the public, but to the shareholders.

Very effective for the shareholders, wealth has been concentrated in the hands of the few since the Fed was created.

While the Medicis were seen to run the "state" of Florence, the Rothschilds and modern bankers have preferred to keep a lower profile: to control the money of the world, but do so quietly.

The creation of the Federal Reserve must have pleased the Rothschilds. They had their representative, Paul Warburg, at the Jekyll Island meeting. And this time, no war was required to keep control of the money.

To further create the illusion that the Fed is a state agency, any profit it makes, and it makes lots, is returned to the government. Profit is primarily the interest on government-issued bonds, and thus the profit comes from the American government and is returned to it. The purpose of the Fed is not to make money but to control money.

Evelyn de Rothschild (sixth generation, and born in 1931) dropped out of Cambridge to go and play: he preferred racing fast cars and playing polo to study. When he reached 26, he went to work in the family business at its London branch.

This private company office sets the price of gold for the world, twice each day. For almost 20 years, Evelyn was chairman of the *Economist Magazine*, and is said to have a net worth of about $20 billion today. He married a few times, and spent a night on his third honeymoon, on the 30th of November 2000, at the White House.

Gold

For thousands of years, long before money came into being, gold had been used as money. As trade increased, paying for things became an increasing problem, especially between nations. Gold was awkward. Paper money made it easy. Many silver and goldsmiths became moneychangers.

Sir Isaac Newton was Master of the Royal Mint from 1699 until his death in 1727. His office was in the Tower of London. (We know him better for his work in physics, mathematics, calculus, and the invention of telescopes. He was the second Lucasion Professor of Mathematics at Cambridge University, a position recently held by Stephen Hawking.) Newton established a silver/gold ratio that effectively put England onto a gold standard. The British pound (£), sometimes known as the pound sterling, has at various times been backed by silver, gold, or as now, by nothing.

Fiat currencies, those not backed by gold or silver, have risk. To illustrate, on Black Wednesday, September 16, 1992, the British people took a huge loss, and George Soros earned an estimated £1.1 billion, when Britain tried to prop up its dollar against European currencies. Soros had felt they didn't have the resources to do so and bet against the Bank of England. And Soros was right. His gain was Britain's loss, and the loss was blamed on the

Conservative Government. They were thrown out of office at the next election.

Five years later, the British government did it to themselves—lost billions without outside help! Gordon Brown, a Scot with a PhD in History from the University of Edinburgh, and Leader of the Labour Party, was then Prime Minister. (As I've mentioned, this was an era when, in my experience, things weren't making sense.) It was inconceivable that Gordon Brown could be a Labour Member of Parliament, because he never acted for Labour. He followed Tony Blair, the first Labour leader who acted like a conservative, like Thatcher or Bush. The party of Labour had ceased to exist.)

From 1999 to 2002, under Brown's direction, the UK sold about 60% of the nation's gold reserves at a time when the price of gold was low. Why would he sell then? After the sale, the price skyrocketed. The price the British people received was just under $300 an ounce, or $3.5 billion dollars. Only a short time later, that gold was worth about $19 billion. Why would he make that decision to sell? And who made the gains?

The story is that Brown was told he faced a global collapse in the UK banking system, and so he took the decision to bailout the banks by selling Britain's gold. There was so much gold on the market that Britain selling it forced the price lower. The banks bought it, held it for a short time till the price went up, and pocketed the profit.

That multi-billion-pound gift to the banks was the first bank bailout of this century. The second bailout of British banks began in 2008, and six years later (2014) was ongoing. (I will return to that.)

Petrodollars

Oil, like gold, warrants more attention. Both are forms of money.

OPEC (the Organization of Petroleum Exporting Countries) is an international union to fix oil prices. Formed in the 1960s in response to oil companies arbitrarily reducing prices, the group has grown to have fourteen countries, including Iran, Iraq, Kuwait, and Venezuela, and to produce about 40% of world crude.

In 1973, two years after going off the gold standard, Nixon sent Henry Kissinger to Saudi Arabia to negotiate a deal for the Saudis to sell their oil in United States dollars: *only* in US dollars. In exchange, the US promised weapons and protection for the Saudis from Israel. (It's intriguing: we never heard about any Israeli threat to attack Saudi Arabia.) Kissinger got the agreement, and the dollar was then nicknamed the "petrodollar," because it was backed by demand for oil. From that date if, for example, North Korea wanted Saudi oil, they needed first to get US dollars.

The agreement soon included all the OPEC nations, which immensely increased demand for US currency. There were two sides to the deal. On one hand was the United States, its currency, and its banks. On the other hand, the mediaeval, monarchist, Saudi family. The deal was to have profound effects on currency, Western banks, oil companies, the military, and mid-east stability. Not all nations that produce oil are members. Listed below are the top ten oil-producing nations:

	Oil Producing Nations	Barrels per day, 2014
1	United States	13,973,000
2	Saudi Arabia *	11,624,000
3	Russia	10,853,000
4	China	4,383,000
5	Canada	4,001,000
6	United Arab Emirates *	3,471,000
7	Iran	3,375,000
8	Iraq	3,371,000
9	Brazil	2,950,000
10	Mexico	2,812,000

*OPEC members

The agreement has served the United States well. For decades, it has been a currency prop that allowed people in the United States to have a standard of living well above their means, and it happens with no visible hint as to why. They can import billions of dollars of goods, and their currency doesn't depreciate. It was oil, the petro-dollar, not gold, that then backed the dollar.

We have seen how seriously the US takes this policy. In 2001, Saddam Hussein announced that Iraq intended to sell its oil in €uros.[70] Two years later, war was declared, Iraq was invaded by the

---

70 http://www.time.com/time/magazine/article/0,9171,998512,00.html

US and Hussein killed. In 2009, Muammar Gaddafi said he was thinking about selling Libya's oil in a new currency, a gold African dinar. Two years later, his country was invaded by the US and other NATO countries, and he was murdered. Iraq remains in chaos, and Libya, a country with a population the size of Denmark's, has been left in in chaos. It's now called a "failed state."

While Arab nations have sold their oil in US dollars for the past decades, it appears they have priced it in a steadier currency: gold. The chart below shows the price of a barrel of oil in US dollars (the top line), in €uros (the middle line), and in ounces of gold (the flat line).

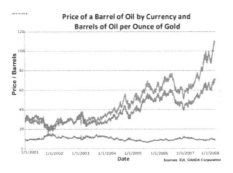

Most of us believe that gasoline has been going up in price. The chart below shows that the price of oil in gold has been very stable, while the value of the dollar and €uro have varied.

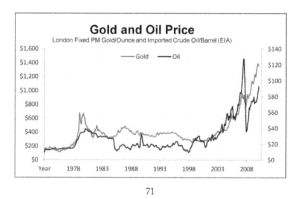

71

The alchemy of interest

> The only function of economic forecasting is to make astrology look respectable.
> —John Kenneth Galbraith

In Chapter One, I looked at the ethics of interest, and the early Christian aversion to it, an aversion that continues in Islam.

Now I'll look at how interest works: the arithmetic of it. Ethical or not, it's an integral part of our world, not very well understood, and with enormous consequences.

Professor Margrit Kennedy was a German architect and ecologist. She died, aged 74, in 2013. In about 1982, she ran into a problem funding ecologically sound building projects. She wondered why. While the projects she created were sensible and best for the environment, they were declared too expensive, and she became aware it was due to interest on the loans required to build

---

71   http://goldratefortoday.org/gold-oil-relationship-3-theories/

them. This prompted her to study the nature of interest, and she became an expert. In 1987 she published a book with the lengthy title, *Interest and Inflation Free Money: Creating an Exchange Medium that Works for Everybody and Protects the Earth*. It's easily readable, and available free in English on the internet.[72]

What she found was, it is "virtually impossible to carry out sound ecological concepts on the scale required today, without fundamentally altering the present money system." She recognized that, because of exponential growth, compound interest was the problem. As I discussed in the last chapter, exponential growth is physically impossible to sustain. The issue in financing projects was not their economic soundness, but the financing. Projects like building subways, which cut down on pollution by displacing automobiles, will exist for decades, but financing over that long period of time more than doubles the price.

Investors know that invested money will double at regular intervals. At 3% interest, it doubles in 24 years. At 12% interest, it doubles in six years. In the 1970s, when I started investing, people assumed that investments would double every seven years. That assumed a return of 10% per year. Good news if you have money—but not good if you are borrowing money. It's not good, because compound interest creates such huge numbers. If Jesus had taken a moment from evicting the money lenders from the temple and invested one shekel (let's say a shekel was worth one dollar), his investment at 3% interest would have increased in value today to:

---

72 http://www.margritkennedy.de/books.html

$173,809,134,400,000,000,000,000,000 [73]

That is 173 trillion, trillion, trillion, trillion dollars. That is more than all the money on earth! All the money on earth is a mere $70 trillion.

A trillion is a large number to visualize. One trick to comprehending big numbers is to consider them as time. Start with a million: a million dollars is a lot of money. In the year 2000, my company received our first check for just over a million dollars; the person who mailed the check added a yellow Post-It note with a single word on it: WOW! A million seconds is 11.6 days, (1,000,000/365/24/60 = 11.6). A billion seconds is 32 years (1,000,000,000/365/24/60 = 31.7)!

A trillion seconds is almost two million years (1,902,587 years).

The calculation of potential interest on Jesus' investment is not as silly as it appears. It's easy to dismiss, because no one lives that long, or perhaps no investment can last that long. However, families can endure for centuries, and investments like Roman roads, or modern railroads exist for centuries.

The Catholic Church has survived that long, and its net worth has grown so large that it's impossible to calculate. Its annual expenses are as large as those of Apple, or General Motors, and the Vatican is so wealthy that it owns its own bank, with assets of over five billion €uros. If the Rothschild family had invested only $66

---

[73] If the interest is compounded continuously, the formula is $B=Pe^{rt}$ where B = balance, or accumulated value, r = rate = .03, t = time in years, and e is a non-ending decimal 2.71428. (Thanks, to Dr. Richard Harville.)

dollars when they began to prosper in the late 1700s, that would explain their $400 billion wealth today.

Nations and corporations borrow money, and since their chances of enduring for long periods are excellent, they can secure financing over long periods. And, on occasion, they should. Greek and Roman buildings, still standing, predated the birth of Jesus, and parts of Roman roads are still in use. The Kongo Gumi construction company in Japan lasted 1,400 years, until it merged in 2006.

The point I'm making is that the problems created by compound interest over lengthy periods of time can be significant. A lending system based on exponential growth captures so much interest that it makes the religious prohibitions against usury logical. It explains why Canadian philosophy professor John McMurtry titled his 1999 book, *The Cancer Stage of Capitalism*. Cancer cells grow exponentially, and in his view, capitalism has matured to a stage where it is eating its base. (Later, John McMurtry and I were both patrons of a Toronto forum on the research behind the 9-11 attack.)

Other writers have used cancer-like terms to describe today's capitalism. The economist Michael Hudson, an ex-Wall Street analyst, now a professor at the University of Missouri, was the first economist to predict the real estate collapse of 2008. He did so in a 2006 *Harpers'* article, "The New Road to Serfdom—an Illustrated Guide to the Coming Real Estate Collapse." In 2015 Hudson published *Killing the Host—How Financial Parasites and Debt Destroy the Global Economy*. And another ex-Wall Streeter, Catherine Austin Fitts (whose ideas I'll discuss in Chapter Twelve), describes our economy as "the tapeworm economy."

It's exponential growth that makes the rich richer and exponential interest that makes government debt impossibly large. From

Adam Smith's time until recently, the usual solution to impossibly large debt has been bankruptcy. The United States' debt, so large that it will probably never be paid, is 20% larger per person than the debt of impoverished Greece.

Professor Kennedy learned that the average German in the mid-1980s spent 45% of his/her total expenditure on interest. That seems like a lot! Most of us are aware that we pay interest—interest on mortgages and car loans—but it turns out those payments are the tip of the iceberg.

We don't think of the interest that is built into the price of everything we buy. Farmers borrow to buy seed, the miller borrows to buy trucks, the baker borrows to buy ovens, and the grocer borrows to buy stores. Even if an individual has no debt, he or she is paying a significant amount of interest, because it's built into the price of everything.

To check her analysis, I reviewed the costs built into the $50 million of sales of my company, Lofthouse Brass, about 2005. We paid interest on $3 million of loans and $5 million of equipment leases, which came to just under $1 million a year. We were also paying interest that our suppliers included in their prices. That was $2 million to $3 million in interest passed through our company. In total, our prices on goods we sold included about 5% interest. We sold parts to a shower valve manufacturer, who assembled and packaged the valves and sold them to the retailer, with more interest built into the price. The retailer then added interest of its own. All this quickly added up to about the percentage Professor Kennedy had noted.

Interest charges are built invisibly into the fabric of everything! It happens quietly and routinely, and when you realize how high it is, it's stunning. In addition to revealing the amount of interest built into our economy, Kennedy studied who pays interest and who receives it.

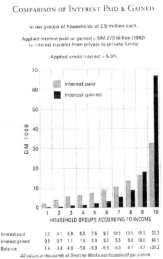

The chart, even though small, shows it's the poor that pay interest and the rich that collect it. It groups people in terms of income from lowest group on the left to highest on the right. The grey bars show interest paid, and the black bars show interest received. (I use the word received, not 'earned' because no-one works to earn it. It is unearned income.)

The chart reveals the role of interest as an effective method to transfer wealth from everyone to the rich. It's an innocuous, silently effective wealth transfer system.

Usury and debt

> Once a nation parts with the control of its currency and credit, it matters not who makes that nation's laws. Usury, once in control, will wreck any nation. Until the control of the issue of currency and credit is restored to government and recognized as its most conspicuous and sacred responsibility, all talk of the sovereignty of Parliament and of democracy is idle and futile.
>
> —Mackenzie King, Prime Minister of Canada, 1935

The Oxford dictionary defines usury as the practice of lending money at unreasonably high rates of interest. One of the earliest references to interest was in 1772 BC. Hammurabi, the sixth Babylonian King, enacted a code of laws that were, literally, "carved in stone." The stone, or stele, is about ten feet high and on display in the Louvre.

We still use one of his laws, called scaled justice: the law should be fair, and the penalty should match the crime. Another of the 282 laws established the right to be presumed innocent until proven guilty. There were laws that dealt with commerce, fraud, theft and interest rates.

The practice of general debt forgiveness had existed for as long as six centuries before Hammurabi. His code explained that if a farmer had a year of drought, he need not pay back a loan because the lender and borrower shared the risk. Oh, I can hear today's farmers saying, "Those were the days!"

Four thousand years ago, it appears, people were aware of the perils of compound interest. The Babylonians developed algebra and number theory, and measured time by designating sixty seconds to a minute and sixty minutes to an hour. To be a scribe, you had to study mathematics. One clay tablet that has survived shows the calculation of compound interest. They were aware that debt could grow faster than, for example, the growth in the size of cattle herds, and therefore believed that it was unjust for debt to grow faster than the farming economy.

A thousand years after Hammurabi, in about 630 BC, Solon of Athens, one of two sons of a privileged family, was a leader and social reformer. In the style of the day, he wrote poems:

> Some wicked men are rich, some good are poor;
> We will not change our virtue for their store:
> Virtue's a thing that none can take away,
> But money changes owners all the day.

Solon was chosen to be Chief Magistrate and passed a law forgiving all debts, including those owed to him. Although people owned land,[74] land could not be sold or mortgaged. The term mortgage itself comes from Latin: death (*mort*), plus pledge (*gage*).

The Greek economy was simple. Most people lived off the land, barely producing enough to survive. If a farmer needed money, he couldn't borrow against his land; all he could put up for security were the bodies of his family members. Consequently, the number of slaves in Athens had increased. Solon introduced the Seisachtheia, a law which cancelled all debts, including freeing those in debt slavery.

Solon also encouraged farmers to plant olive trees, for which we remain grateful. Olive trees live for eons and olives from the trees he encouraged continue to be harvested.

About one hundred years after Solon, the Book of Leviticus was written and became part of the Hebrew and Christian Bibles. It instructed the people to "take no interest or increase" and advised that God instructed Moses to forgive debts about every 49 years. That practice became the norm, although, as the 49th year got closer, credit started to dry up.

The book of Deuteronomy has similar advice;

---

74 It's interesting to note that aboriginal people don't accept the concept of land ownership. They believe that we are born with nothing and die with nothing and only the land survives.

> This is how it is to be done: Every creditor shall cancel the loan he has made to his fellow Israelite. He shall not require payment from his fellow Israelite or brother, because the LORD's time for canceling debts has been proclaimed.

And Matthew wrote in the Gospel in about 80 or 90 A.D.:

> Give us this day our daily bread, and forgive us our debts, as we forgive our debtors.

Matthew, prior to becoming an apostle, had been a tax collector. The translation from Greek to the English, which I've used above, was done by a team of scholars commissioned by the British King James to create a Bible to unite Britain. Written in English, it took seven years and was completed in 1611. Eventually, common usage changed the section above from "forgive our debts" to "forgive our trespasses." The bankers must have cheered.

The advice of Solon, Leviticus, Deuteronomy, and Matthew was to forgive debts. Some understood that by doing so, it would end credit bubbles. It was good economics, and the reasons for doing so seem to have been better understood then.

In 2000, when the G8 were meeting, one issue was debt forgiveness for poorer nations. George Monbiot, a *Guardian* journalist, wrote about the debt and suggested that the gold and silver stolen earlier from North America should be included in the discussion. Venezuelan writer Luis Britto García wrote much the same way in an essay in 1990 titled "Guaicaipuro Cuatemoc." Guaicaipuro was a Venezuelan tribal chief who was famous for fighting the Spanish who were stealing their land and gold. Garcia put words into the chief's mouth:

> Those 185,000 kilograms of gold and 16 million kilograms of silver must be considered as the first of many friendly loans from America, destined for the development of Europe.
>
> To say otherwise would be to assume the existence of warcrimes, which would give us the right not simply to demand their immediate return, but also indemnification for damages.[75]

Monbiot concluded in a similar fashion that the G8 idea to "forgive" the Third World's debts is laughable. "Rather, the G8 leaders must beg the forgiveness of the Third World for the dreadful and deliberate mess they have made of the global economy."

If the money used to bailout the Western banks in 2007/8 had been used to bailout homeowners or students, the economy would have recovered far faster, and the payments would be within the Christian, Islamic, and Jewish traditions. Using money for the people would have been sensible economics and decent ethics. In January 2014, Pope Francis called usury "a dramatic social ill," and that the practice was not Christian and not human.

---

75 http://onkwehonwerising.wordpress.com/2013/08/27/luis-britto-garcia-guaicaipuro-cuauhtemoc-charges-europe-for-debt/

The simple arithmetic of compound interest seems so benign, when actually it is not. George Meany, the US labour leader in the seventies, summed it up: "It's like Robin Hood in revoise!"

Finance: surpassing the real economy

A few generations ago, people lived in ways that didn't require the money people need today. Cities were designed for walking; houses were closer together, shops and parks were close by. Home vegetable gardens were common, so people saved money, and got exercise and fresh food. People lived together in extended families, somewhat more crowded, but less dependent on spending. People owned less stuff, and most could make ends meet, often with one income. Seniors lived with family, not in isolated villas. Kids played in the creek or sandlot, not the video arcade, and street sports were common. People entertained themselves: they played cards and picnicked in parks. Most gatherings involved live music, spontaneous singalongs around the piano. Life was not designed around the car. Driving a car was a novelty, with the Sunday drive a treat. People didn't have credit card debt. Mortgages would be paid off.

The world of finance grew, slowly at first, and then like a weed. In the 1940s, the finance "industry" amounted to about 2% of United States Gross Domestic Product. By 2005, it had reached 8.3%. An additional 6.3% doesn't sound like much, but 6.3% of $17 trillion dollars does: it comes to $1,070,000,000,000! What extra value do we get from the added expense?

The Gross Domestic Product is the total dollar value of all things made, and includes everything grown or produced, plus all services, minus the value of imports. It requires a bit of imagination to include financial services as a national product, but we do. The whole economy normally grows as population grows, but the financial services share has grown faster. Why? Why do we need three times more from the financial sector? What additional benefit does it provide?

The "real economy," as described by *The Financial Times*, is the part of the economy that is concerned with actually producing goods and services, as opposed to what we could call the "unreal economy," which is buying and selling in financial markets. My business was in the real economy: plumbing parts created by the labour of factory workers, just as farmers, fishermen, service workers, doctors, teachers, social workers, and city planners are part of the real economy. The financial community produces nothing and is not.

The increase in the financial industry's slice of the GDP pie began with a small step in the 1950s, with the introduction of the credit card. The Diners Club® card was the first, and the most unique feature of it, and of all the credit cards that followed, is that it created money out of thin air. The money it created was debt. Both of these factors—money created out of thin air, and money as debt—are important to understand about today's economy.

The Diners Club® card started an explosion in credit cards: they were practical, easy to use, and made a bundle of money for companies. American Express started shortly thereafter, with the same type of card. At that time, it had to be paid off monthly. New cards were created by banks which provided revolving credit: "Pay off what you can, and we will charge interest on the balance." Soon, oil companies, retail stores, grocery stores, and car companies had their own credit cards.

General Electric, the company that began with Edison's light bulb, grew to provide lots of other real stuff: stoves, aircraft engines, and medical equipment. GE eventually created a Capital Division and credit cards, which now employs over 60,000 people, about 20% of GE's workforce. GE defines the Capital Division as "building the world by providing capital, expertise and infrastructure for a global economy."

Credit card and banking divisions were once secondary to corporations' real economy activities, such as making new cars. These grew into businesses unto themselves: big businesses! General Motors Acceptance Corporation, now called Ally Financial, is a bank holding company with 15 million customers. In addition to automobile loans. it provides mortgages, insurance. and online banking. The US supermarket chain, The Kroger Company, has its own credit card. Canada's Loblaws grocery stores has opened its own bank. Sears and Macy's have cards. Wal-Mart has "Money Centers," which offer several types of accounts and two types of credit cards. In the 1970s, the baby food company Gerber started selling college investment plans and life insurance to families, making it a near-finance business. (In 2007, Gerber was sold to Nestlé.)

Hidden in all of this is the true cost of credit cards. The retailer pays about 2% when the cards are used. It can be more. American Express has been as high as 5%. To cover this cost, retailers increase their prices for everyone by adding at least 2% to the price of everything we buy. As I mentioned earlier, it's part of the hidden interest costs of about 45% of our budget. Even with no personal debt, you pay interest—because it's built into the price of everything we buy.

With this evolution in finance, many businesses changed from making stuff to simply making money. The share of the finance industry grew. We had been through it before. The chart following shows the growth of the financial industry: the first spike peaked in 1929 in the Depression, then dropped to almost its old normal. Since the late seventies, it has grown steadily.

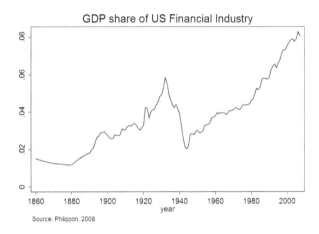

Source: Philippon, 2008

With every increase in the share of Gross Domestic Product going to finance, more eager young business graduates line up to go to work on Wall Street (or Bay Street in Canada). Bright young people, hired to invent new financial products and new ways to make money, none of which will help the welfare of ordinary people. They create products like derivatives to be sold among themselves, and for those sales, they get paid commissions. The commissions get built into the prices of real things. Commissions paid to a Wall Street salesperson for arranging a corn futures contract are paid for in the price of our corn flakes. These are the new entrepreneurs!

One old-world entrepreneur I liked was Paul Helliwell. He was about seventy-five, twenty years older than me, when he came to my office one summer day. His parents had been missionaries, and Paul was born in China. He owned a successful parts-making business similar to mine. As we walked across the parking lot, there was a brand new, top-down, forest green Morgan convertible, a classic British sports car with a distinctive leather strap across the engine compartment. "Paul, that's got to be yours!" "Yes," he said, "and it goes far too fast!!!" I didn't know they were still making them, but he explained that they made a few a year. The waiting list was about five years. This meant that when he was about seventy, he ordered a new sports car, not expecting delivery for at least five years into the future. That was the nature of the old entrepreneur: honest, visionary, and willing to risk. He was not a "dealmaker," but worked in a business to earn money. He was not in it for a quick buck but worked for decades to create a real-world metal parts casting company. He had no children and left his money to a foundation that supports higher education and health care.

As the economy changed from rewarding people for doing useful work in the real economy, to financialized deal-making, a new type of businessperson was required: dealmakers, and I've met a few of those.

While working in printing, I saw my first leverage buyout and reverse takeover. I was on the fringe of that "deal" and learned some of the terms. My manager and those above his rank participated, and for an investment of about a half-million dollars plus a few years of work, each made a $1 million or more. I was close enough to watch, but I was a bystander. That was in early days of deal-making. Later, as they became more common, I saw more, two from inside, but I'll come to that later.

Summary

> Banking was conceived in iniquity and was born in sin. The bankers own the earth. Take it away from them, but leave them the power to create money, and with the flick of the pen they will create enough deposits to buy it back again. However, take away from them the power to create money and all the great fortunes like mine will disappear and they ought to disappear, for this would be a happier and better world to live in. But, if you wish to remain the slaves of bankers and pay the cost of your own slavery, let them continue to create money.
> —Josiah Stamp[76]

Money has grown to dominate everything. Through the recent decade, business has changed to become less about making things and more about making money. One symptom was the ever-increasing number of businesses that were becoming banks. Competitive enterprise was becoming financialized capitalism.

---

76 Baron Stamp (1880-1941) was an economist with a PhD from the London School of Economics and wrote a dozen books on economics. He became one the wealthiest men in Britain and a director of the Bank of England. His comments in debate with Keynes are quoted in a 2012 lecture by the current governor of the Bank of England. http://www.bankofengland.co.uk/publications/Documents/speeches/2012/speech606.pdf

Ford Motor Company, in addition to making cars, makes about $2 billion a year from Ford Credit.

Even the Vatican opened its own bank in 1942. The Institute for the Works of Religion doesn't sound like a bank, but it is, located within Vatican City. That has curious implications. Vatican City, not governed by Italian law, is an independent city/state, and fewer than a thousand people live there. (It's like the "City" of London, a square-mile block in central London where the banks are located and where the laws differ. If the Queen wishes to visit "the City," she stops at the edge and waits for the Lord Major to invite her in! The laws of England don't apply.)

The Vatican bank has had more than its share of scandal, rumoured links to the Mafia, and the "suicide" of Roberto Calvi, known as "God's Banker" because of his contacts within the Vatican Bank. He was found hanging under Blackfriars Bridge, which crosses the Thames River into "the City," in London, June 20, 2007, with five bricks and about $14,000 in his pockets. The murder is unsolved.

The trend towards every business becoming a bank is evolution to a purer form of capitalism and away from what should be the prime function of the economy: to improve the lot of people. The change is seen in the decline of manufacturing in America and the changing architecture in Western cities.

Every era has left its architectural mark: the Greeks left theatres and temples; the Romans, arenas; the Middle Ages, fortresses and castles; the Renaissance, cathedrals and chateaus; the Enlightenment, universities; and the Industrial Revolution, factories and rust belts. The temples in our era are banks! Every major city has banks dominating their skylines. In Toronto, the Royal

Bank Plaza flaunts its wealth in its two glistening gold towers with over $3 million of gold fused in its windows!

Professor Margrit Kennedy made us aware that up to 45% of everything we spend is spent on interest: money going from the public to bankers and financiers, from Main Street to Wall Street, from the average to the rich, all built into the system.

> I sincerely believe that banking establishments are more dangerous than standing armies, and that the principle of spending money to be paid by posterity under the name of funding is but swindling futurity on a large scale.
> —Thomas Jefferson to John Taylor, May 28, 1816

Since 2008, the privately owned Federal Reserve Bank of the United States has been buying overvalued assets from the banks by creating money out of thin air at the rate of about $30 billion dollars a month. This eventually will lead to devaluation of the US currency. Since the United States imports much of what it consumes, when the currency devalues, the US will experience significant inflation. Future prospects are unsettling. (I'll elaborate on this in my final chapters.)

Money also includes non-financial currencies: frequent-flyer miles or reward points that can be exchanged for value.

There are alternate currencies, alternate to the bank-created money. The island of Guernsey has had their own currency since about 1813,[77] when they had no money to build a seawall to protect their land. So they, as they had the right to do, printed some money

---

77   https://ccc4mr.wordpress.com/guernsey-island/

and used it to pay labourers and suppliers. The wall got built with no inflation and no debt. And today, others in the world try to escape being controlled by dominant currencies by creating their own. The small community of ten thousand people on Salt Spring Island, off the shore of Vancouver, has its own dollar, as does the community in the Berkshires in the United States.

With some understanding of how national debt has come about, and how money is created out of thin air, we can return to the subject of how our beliefs about what capitalism is are used to control our lives.

The fact that there is more debt in the world than money is bizarre. There is simply not enough money to pay off the debt. Financiers will say that it doesn't matter, because debt is paid back over time. That is how the situation has been allowed to continue. The accounting reality is that debt on one side must equal assets on the other, and if it doesn't, the system is insolvent.

Our assumptions about how the free market is supposed to work increasingly don't match what is happening, and our assumptions about how governments got into debt don't match what actually occurred. Our assumptions about how money is created are simply wrong.

It is fundamental for us to change our understanding of these things if we are to get back to an economy that serves the people.

7.
Our planet becomes their market

How can it be that it is not a news item when an elderly homeless person dies of exposure, but it is news when the stock market loses two points?
—Pope Francis[78]

MARX FORESAW THAT SUCCESSFUL COMPANIES WOULD INEVITABLY eliminate their competition or, as we say today, "Eat the weak!" The media industry is no exception.

Six corporate giants now control 90% of the media in the United States. A few decades ago there were thousands.

---

78   From the November 2013, statement of Pope Francis outlining his core beliefs.

Worldwide, as of May 2016, the top ten are[79]: Alphabet (it owns Google); Walt Disney; Comcast; Twenty-First Century Fox[80]; Facebook; Bertelsmann (German based); Viacom; CBS; Baidu (the Chinese search giant); and News Corporation (the current form of the Australian Murdoch family business we know as Fox News).

When a few firms dominate a market, it's called an oligopoly. As competitors disappear, competition fades away. In 1990, 17.3% of daily newspapers in Canada were independently owned. By 2005, it was down to 1%. The views of fewer and fewer people increasingly control what the rest of us get to hear, read and eventually believe.

It was, as I noted earlier, a phenomenon Marx had predicted.

At one time, every small town had its own newspaper, and often they were the local printing house. In the 1970s, I dealt with most of the printers in southern Ontario. I knew their journalists, and many became friends. I joined the London Press Club. Three of the members were City Editors.

These were the unflappable guys who sat in the middle of the newsroom both in reality and in old movies shouting orders.

Get to the fire!" "See the Mayor!" "Stop the presses!"

City Desk was the hub of the paper. Our local paper was the *London Free Press,* and one editor had a serious drinking problem. A high school class was taking a tour of the paper. They stopped at City Desk to have it explained to them.

---

79   http://www.businessinsider.com/the-30-biggest-media-owners-in-the-world-2016-5/#11-advance-publications--642-billion-20

80   Fox News and News Corporation are Rupert Murdoch's, including about 20 TV stations and 20 newspapers, publisher Harper Collins and their dozens of brands, and 21st Century Fox.

"Any questions?" "Yes," said one student, pointing to a guy curled up under one of the desks. "What's he doing?" "Making a decision!" the City Editor responded.

Another of the city editors was Isaac Turner, a dour Scot labour organizer who had been awarded a scholarship to study at Nuffield College in Oxford. (This small college was funded by Lord Nuffield, a.k.a. William Morris, a bicycle repairman who developed the Morris Automobile and Car Company.) Later in life, Turner became the Washington correspondent for the *Free Press* and attended the annual White House Press Corps reception hosted by Lyndon Johnson. While Turner was talking with the president, a white-gloved waiter offered them flutes of champagne. Isaac declined, and the president asked if he drank. "I'm a beer drinker," Isaac replied. The president asked the waiter to bring a Canadian beer "… and bring me branch water and bourbon." They then got drunk together. Next morning, the wire services carried Isaac's exclusive story announcing that Johnson would not run for re-election.

Now, with media concentration and fewer reporters, chances for such reporting are slim.

There are two noteworthy exceptions to the perils of media concentration: *The Guardian* newspaper (mentioned in Chapter Five) and *Reuters*. *The Guardian*, at one time known as the *Manchester Guardian*, was established by a group of liberals in Manchester in 1821. In 1872, C. P. Scott became editor and remained for 57 years. When he became owner, he continued his modest salary. In 1936 the ownership passed to a trust, set up to protect the newspaper's independence, with more than £1 million in reserves. It continues to produce a weekly newspaper, read in 173 countries. In 2014, it was awarded the Pulitzer Prize for public service.

Reuters began in London as a family business using carrier pigeons to send stories. Later, it was one of the first to use the telegraph. It's had a reputation for high standards in objectivity and integrity. (*Reuters* won't use the term "terrorist," because it's a prejudicial political term, not a proper description of an enemy.) *Reuters* was purchased in 2008 by the Canadian Thompson newspapers, which is likely to change things: their CEO started to attend the Bilderberg meetings.

Keeping alive the myth that all journalists are left-wing is a major accomplishment of corporate media. There were left-wing journalists—my friend Isaac Turner was one. He organized workers for a meatpackers' union before he got into journalism. When there were lots of newspapers, there were lots of journalists and a broad range of opinions. Journalists were often better educated than their readers, and many had opinions corporations didn't like. But with the concentration of media today, that no longer applies. Many people, especially in America today, don't read anything that approaches left-wing opinion.

Media concentration was not simply the inevitable result of competitive economics. On occasion, it had explicit help, like that of J. P. Morgan and the twelve others in 1917, as I discussed in the previous chapter.

"We are smothered in the business-oriented, neo-liberal 'consensus' instructing us to reconcile ourselves to 'the new reality'— rollbacks in social welfare and universal publicly funded programs; huge tax cuts to business and the rich, driving up public debt and enriching finance capitalism; an end to secure employment and guaranteed benefits; surrendering our dreams of home ownership unless we are prepared to accept a lifetime of debt enslavement; a future of uncertainty and endless personal struggle to sustain ourselves and our children," as Professor J. F. Conway, a political sociologist at the University of Regina sums it up.[81]

Increasing media concentration distorts our understanding of how the world works.

To reinforce the importance of a free press, the United Nations, probably in reaction to this trend, created World Press Freedom Day in 1991. Reporters Without Borders, a group started in France in 1985, published a global index of Press Freedom in 2002, and Finland had the highest rating. Korea, at #139 was the lowest. Canada was #5, and the United States, #17. By 2015, Canada and the U.S dropped to #8 and #49 respectively. Media concentration and less freedom in reporting go hand in hand.

Journalist restrictions also happen explicitly. Carl Bernstein, one of the journalists who broke the 1972 story of the illegal Watergate break-in, also revealed that more than 400 journalists had, by 1977, worked for the CIA. Reported in *Rolling Stone* magazine, his story included details on the secrecy agreements journalists signed, and on the payments, money, trips, or whatever, they received. Government-funded bribery was controlling what the public got to read.

In 2014, another journalist, Dr. Udo Ulfkotte, a German who also became a whistleblower, revealed that he had been CIA-sponsored and he'd written articles that later made him ashamed. He published *Gekaufte Journalisten* (*Purchased Journalists*), revealing

---

81   http://www.socialistproject.ca/bullet/1295.php#continue

how high-finance controls Germany's mass media and listed the gifts he received for abetting: travel, stays in five-star hotels and gold watches. All he had to do was write pro-NATO, anti-Russian articles. He decided to speak out because he could see propaganda being used to set the stage for the next war, a war against Russia to be fought in Europe. Sadly, he died too young, in January 2017, at the age of 58.

Robert Parry, the journalist who broke the Iran/Contra scandal in the 1980s,[82] established an independent news service in 1995, explaining, "I was distressed by the silliness and propaganda that had come to pervade American journalism. I feared, too, that the decline of the US press corps foreshadowed disasters that would come when journalists failed to alert the public about impending dangers ... fewer and fewer media outlets interested in that history, ... as the memories of Ronald Reagan and George H.W. Bush were enveloped in warm-and-fuzzy myths that represented another kind of danger: false history that could lead to mistaken political judgments in the future."

Changing Our Assumptions

> Propaganda normalizes the unthinkable!
> —John Pilger, veteran Australian journalist

---

82 A United States program in which government officials sold arms to Iran, despite a law forbidding it, and used the profits, in another illegal act, to sponsor a rebel group, the Contra, fighting the government of Nicaragua.

Generally held assumptions about economics were changed significantly by Margaret Thatcher (elected in 1979) and by Ronald Reagan (elected in 1981). Though this was several decades ago, the effects are still with us. They were pro-business, and monetarists and both had influence far beyond their own borders. Both were anti-union, which in Reagan's case was odd, since he had been president of the Screen Actors Guild for seven terms. Thatcher trashed the National Union of Coal Miners. Reagan trashed the air traffic controllers, firing 11,345 of their 13,000 members and banning them from federal service for life, a strange, punitive act for a freedom-loving trade unionist.

This was class warfare and accomplished with almost no backlash. Few spoke out for the right to organize, nor did they remind us that it was unions that had created the middle class, a factor that had been crucial to creating decades of prosperity. There was little backlash because the rich had the power, the money, controlled the media, ran the government, and didn't want unions.

The attack on workers succeeded, also, because of the general decline in understanding about the nature of unions. I think a brief lesson is appropriate here. Workers have few ways to improve their lot: they can lobby, they can coerce, they can argue. But if all that fails, they are left with three choices: get another job (if there is one), quit, or withhold their labour. By "workers," I refer to teachers, clerks, air traffic controllers, coal miners, doctors—anyone who works for wages.

If and when workers feel that they need to withhold their labour, it's not an easy decision. Wages are lost from the moment a strike begins, and most workers have minimal, if any savings. Some unions collect money from workers for a strike fund to provide income if they need to strike, but payments workers receive from the strike fund are never as much as they lose. To strike is the toughest decision, and people on a picket line should be respected for exercising one of our most basic liberties.

Businesses also lose money during a strike. For a few decades, companies avoided strikes by sharing the wealth with the workers: the logic was simple—the workers were creating it. In those years, many remembered fascist European governments banning unions in the thirties and forties, and unions in the West were evidence of a free society. It was commonly believed that big corporations needed to be balanced by big unions. As John F. Kennedy said, "Our labor unions are not narrow, self-seeking groups. They have raised wages, shortened hours and provided supplemental benefits. Through collective bargaining and grievance procedures, they have brought justice and democracy to the shop floor."[83] They also, to say it again, created and kept the middle class alive.

Thatcher, elected two years before Reagan, was a libertarian. One of her more famous comments, "There is no such thing as society …" was a paraphrase of Ayn Rand's self-interest philosophy, that our world is run by individuals pursuing their own, and only their own, self-interest; that no one does things for the common good. (I'll discuss Rand again in a later chapter.) It said more about Thatcher's ethics, than reality, because there was and still is, a society.

The current British Prime Minister, Theresa May, also a Conservative, said something equally stupid when she said in

---

83   Kennedy, J.F. *Inaugural Address*. January 20, 1961.

late 2016 at a party conference that there is no such concept as global citizenship.

Thatcher and Reagan both believed in tax cuts. It was shared faith, not good economics.

Reagan repeatedly said that government was "the problem" and said it so often that it became gospel. Thatcher and Reagan sought to reduce the size of government, usually without thought as to consequences. Thatcher stopped milk programs for school children. Reagan cut food stamps and welfare for the poor. Political doctrine trumped decency.

The death of Thatcher in 2013 reminded me how much she had rebranded Britain. Famous for saying there is "no alternative" to unregulated capitalism, she revealed her lack of knowledge of economics, or her lack of compassion. Probably both. The rebranding was so pervasive that even now, more than two decades later, the left-wing parties have not re-emerged. The economics known as Thatcherism continues within the Euro banks and, despite the fact that her policies failed, these economics are still being followed. Both Thatcher and Reagan did one thing magnificently well: they each gave their people hope. They lifted spirits and restored faith using a crock of economic jargon. Thatcher and Reagan were friends and held joint cabinet meetings, reinforcing their insular worldview and embedding it in their cabinets.

At that time, Canada was led by the Liberal, Pierre Trudeau, a millionaire intellectual and Keynesian. Yet Canada, too, was affected by neo-con attitudes coming without criticism across the border from our English-speaking allies. His party was replaced by the pro-corporate, pro-global business party led by Brian Mulroney, prime minister from 1984 to 1993, who shared many of the values of Thatcher and Reagan. (He's remembered for a meeting on St. Patrick's Day in 1985 in Quebec City, when the two Irish leaders, Reagan and Mulroney, and their wives sang *When Irish Eyes are Smiling*.) Five years later, Mulroney and Reagan signed the North American Free Trade Agreement (NAFTA). I did not understand NAFTA, and I will come back to that later. It had seemed to me Canada had been doing fine without it.

Many Canadians opposed NAFTA, fearing it would destroy Canadian sovereignty, making it essentially the 51st state. As it turns out that vision was too narrow: NAFTA turned out to be just the first pact, diminishing the independence of not just Canada, but of both nations. A corporate-dominated world was emerging.

The minute-by-minute news reports on changes in the stock market that we get today reinforce the illusion that stock values matter. Implicit in their message is that financialization is innocuous and in our best interests. The reality is that the value of the Dow Jones or any stock exchange has almost no relevance to most people, since 5% of the people own over one half of the wealth.

In my business, the value of the stock markets had no bearing: not on my business, not in my life, not on the decisions of any business owner I have met. Our decisions were affected by demand, totally by demand! What concerned us was, "Are we selling our products?" And, "What profit can we make on those sales?" The hourly changes of stock exchange indexes affect only day traders, a portion of the population. However, providing hourly stock reports leads us to thinking they must be important, while they obscure real issues.

For example, stock markets are touted as places where wealth is created. Not so! They are places where wealth is shifted around, from losers to winners. No value is generated.

It's the real economy that matters to ordinary people. For example, what percentage of people are working? The higher the employment rate is, the more money is available to buy things. We seldom hear of the "employment rate" but instead get the unemployment rate.

What's the inflation rate? If it's going up, we are getting poorer. The unemployment rate and inflation rate can be tampered with. On occasion, we hear news of the minimum wage, but seldom do we hear of the living wage. Real wages and the percentage of people employed can affect the value of stocks, but seldom does it work the other way around.

Reports on hiring, job creation, job conditions, benefits, job quality trends, training opportunities, youth employment, and union rights are newsworthy. So, too, are national comparators, such as the trends in how workers fare between countries. These are underreported. If American workers knew that their incomes were going down while workers' incomes in most of the rest of the world were going up, there would be outrage.

Reporting on changes in banking regulations has also been atrocious. Fundamentally wrong changes have been made, yet reported on with bland naïveté.

I recall no journalist questioning Reagan's endlessly repeated "The government is the problem!" The expression is meaningless. "The Problem!" What problem? To fix any problem, you have to be a lot more specific. Most journalists parroted the phrase as if

Reagan was right and seemed to assume that we all knew what he meant. We didn't, but he got away with it.

The Thatcher and Reagan theology of small government and lower taxes became so engrained that it lives on. Abetted by think tanks and, in the US, by the religious right that supported this libertarian creed, this new theology was changing the social contract and replacing traditional competitive market theory.

Demonizing labour

> No business which depends for its existence on paying less than living wages to its workers has any right to continue in this country. By living wages, I mean more that a bare subsistence level- I mean the wages of decent living.
> —Franklin Delano Roosevelt, June 16, 1933

Manufacturing has two major areas of cost: raw materials and wages. The lower those costs, the higher the potential profit. Raw material prices tend to be controlled by global supply, which economists call inelastic. Wages, on the other hand, are elastic, set locally, and, if a union is involved, the union has a say. But have no illusions, unions are the less powerful party. The company can move its business to new locations. Families of the workers cannot. Companies are immortal, people die. Companies have deep pockets; workers' pockets are shallow. The single power, the only power the worker has, is to provide or withhold labour.

It's the cultural norm for business folks to dislike unions. It's like a kneejerk reaction. That's understandable for true entrepreneurs, because true entrepreneurs are very independent, and unions impose on their independence. But only a few managers are entrepreneurs, and managers have learned it's better for their careers to toe the same line as the company.

Less than a century ago, the workers were seen as the lifeblood of the enterprise. It was the skills, energy, and dedication of "our people," the managers proclaimed, that made it happen. The sweat of the worker created value on the farm and in the factory. There is still poetry in that image. That spirit continues in Northern Europe where labour is treated as a partner. The head of IG Metal Labor Union is Chairman of the Volkswagen Board of Directors, and perhaps that is why European car companies prospered while Detroit became a ghost town.

The problem most business leaders face when dealing with unions is their ignorance of labour law. Union leaders are better trained. Managing people in a union or non-union facility is the same: treat everyone fairly. But that's not as simple as it sounds.

In my company, we set up courses to teach our managers labour law, the rights of workers, and the responsibilities of managing, and we made the courses available to everyone. The people who worked for us lived nearby, and we chose to be as tied to the factory locations as the workers were to their homes. We did not consider a global business strategy. Nor did we consider trying to break the unions. Larger enterprises use those choices.

We've all heard companies issue statements like, "We regret this decision, but market conditions make it necessary." Their regret is usually less than their commitment to larger bonuses.

As businesses became global, they increasingly viewed labour as a commodity. Like wheat, oil, or pork bellies, labour was just another business input to be bought and sold on the open market.

The acceptance of labour becoming a commodity sneaked up on us because we assumed that the market was fair, and thus we accepted corporations doing whatever they wanted with people. Workers were just an input.

The view of labour was further changed by the neo-liberals, who successfully used the concept of individualism to separate workers from their right to organize. We were told that rugged individualism, like the Marlboro Man, meaning tough self-reliance, was who we are! That's what humanity is! In fact, we live in families, and in groups, we depend on and need one another.

The nearly sinister development of the "right to work" campaign manipulates the self-reliance belief. Who can argue, especially as jobs disappear, that everyone has the right to work? At one time, it meant the right to a job. The term implies the right to a job, but in some black irony, the term now means the right to work without a union. The National Right to Work Legal Defense Foundation is a Virginia-based nonprofit that employs 15 lawyers and publishes no annual report. Perhaps the annual report doesn't exist because if we knew of the Foundation's source of funds, it would jeopardize their innocent-sounding purpose. Recently the state of Indiana passed right-to-work legislation that cut off union funding. The powers of the state had been usurped to serve employers and not the people.

It's ironic to realize that corporations regularly do what they abhor: they act like unions. Companies unite as members of trade associations, Chambers of Commerce, and other union-like organizations. They go beyond the mandate of doing their own business to fund pro-business think tanks, political parties, and politicians. They generate profit and spend it to get their way. They know the power of working as a group. The Pacific Maritime Association was founded in 1949 as the bargaining agent for the 72 member shipping companies on the US West Coast. Corporations know that by working united, you have more power than working alone. It's why they organize and why they oppose workers organizing!

During the golden years of capitalism, from the mid-1940s to the 1970s, workers shared in productivity gains. Eventually, this came back to haunt the auto workers: the auto industry got increasingly profitable, and so did the auto workers. Other workers were not making the same gains. Eventually, auto workers were paid so much above the norm that people started to accuse them of being greedy. Part of the argument was jealousy and part was misdirected. Other industries had either not improved as much, or had not shared as fairly. While the auto workers were accused of being greedy, the auto companies. which were pocketing the larger share of the gain, escaped those charges.

The practice of sharing productivity gains with workers is gone, as the chart below shows:

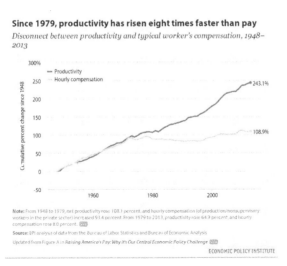

The Washington-based Economic Policy Institute (EPI) studied employer behaviour in relation to unions and found that during union-organizing campaigns, 57% of companies threatened closing plants, 63% insisted that employees have one-on-one meetings with supervisors, 34% fired employees, and 47% threatened to reduce wages.[84] This behaviour has been consistent for over 20 years. A high percentage of employers deliberately create punitive, coercive environments. Any government regulation that we once had to protect worker rights has lost its teeth.[85]

The EPI regularly releases data showing what a worker *should* be earning, if wages keep pace with productivity gains: a worker who earns $40,000 a year would be making about $61,055, simply by getting his/her share of productivity gain.[86] We would still have a middle class, and there would be less income inequality, more demand for goods, less family debt, and more social stability, if wages had kept pace with productivity gains.

The chart below[87] shows one reason why this didn't happen: the decline in union membership. The bottom line shows the growth, and then the decline, of union membership. The top line shows the increased share of wealth going to the top 10%.

---

84 Economic Policy Institute Briefing Paper #235, May 2009.
85 http://www.epi.org/publication/attack-on-american-labor-standards/
86 http://www.epi.org/publication/the-top-charts-of-2016-13-charts-that-show-the-difference-between-the-economy-we-have-now-and-the-economy-we-could-have/ Chart number 1.
87 Mishel, Lawrence, and Kimball, Will. *Unions' Decline and the Rise of the Top 10 Percent's Share of Income*. Economic Policy Institute, February 3, 2015.

One of the keys to changing our perception of economics, and corporations, and unions was to change the language. We should have seen it coming!

Changing language

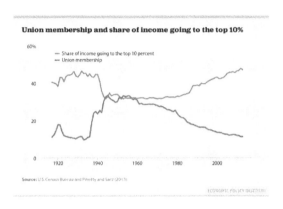

Eric Arthur Blair was born in India in 1903, to a British father who worked in the Opium Department of the Indian Civil Service, and a French mother. The British government managed the production and sale of chests of opium to China. The Blairs eventually left the colony, returned to England, and Eric was sent to study at Eton, an elite live-in high school that served mutton and potatoes for lunch and dinner 365 days a year. Charles Dickens wrote that poorhouse prisoners ate better. He spent four years there as a King's Scholar. At 19, Arthur finished high school, could not afford university, so went back to the East and served five years as a policeman in Burma (now known as Myanmar, home to fifty million or so people between Thailand and Bangladesh).

After five years, he returned to write and lived in London and Paris (1927–1929). His first major work was *Down and Out in Paris and London,* recounting his destitute days and he changed his name so his book wouldn't embarrass his parents. We know him as George Orwell.

Paris in the late twenties was the culture capital of the Western world because, as Hemingway wrote, "Paris ... was one long binge, all the more delightful because it was so inexpensive."

Orwell volunteered in 1936 to fight in the Spanish Civil War on the side of the democratic socialists against the Nationalists, led by Francisco Franco and supported by Mussolini and Hitler. Fighting for socialist democracy in Spain became an international cause as people became increasingly opposed to the rising tide of European fascism. Fascism won in Spain. Franco won, and remained dictator for the next 36 years. Idealistic fighters like Orwell, Hemingway, Picasso, and Norman Bethune[88] were horrified as Spanish democratic socialism was shattered. A street in Barcelona is named after George Orwell.

Orwell's sixth novel, *Nineteen Eighty-Four*, published in 1949, anticipated what the world would be like 35 years in the future. (When I studied this book in the 1950s, I didn't respect the book as much as I should have. I was not aware of the depth of character of the author and 1984 seemed inconceivably far in the future.) In the future, Orwell predicted, society would be run by a psychopathic Big Brother. There would be endless wars and language would be sinister. The Ministry of Truth, using "Newspeak," would manage state propaganda. Slogans would dominate. "War is peace." "Freedom is slavery." "Big Brother is watching you!"

If alive today, Orwell wouldn't be surprised to hear of "humanitarian bombing" or "pre-emptive wars." Back in 1949, Orwell was

---

88 Bethune, a Canadian physician, developed a mobile blood service in Spain. He went to China to aid the communists, where he modernized their medical system, became a hero, and Mao Zedong wrote his eulogy.

warning of omnipresent government surveillance and mind control. "Doublethink," Orwell's term, was political language designed "to make lies sound truthful and murder respectable." He predicted the use of a term like "collateral damage," which the military now uses to make murder sound respectable.

Nineteen Eighty-Four predicted that totalitarianism and technology would control society by oppressing the people. Language control by the state would be the key: words would define the parameters of thought. The repetition of ideas would limit the things people were capable of thinking, as Fox News now effectively does.

When I was a teen, wanting to understand propaganda, I subscribed to *Pravda*, the Soviet Union's Communist party magazine, and to the newsletter of the American Nazi Party. The Soviet Union has since collapsed, but the American Nazi Party continues, from Arlington, Virginia. Reading their propaganda for a few years increased my sensitivity to Orwellian Newspeak and how much of it we live with today.

In a somewhat Orwellian way, the terms "market economy" and "free markets" have replaced the disappearing term "competitive market." New terms displace the word capitalism and thus suppress the image of class, power and capitalists. The term "open market" is more acceptable than "managed markets," and 'free trade" has replaced the more accurate "unregulated trade." In the popular press, democracy and capitalism, although unrelated practices, are regularly equated.

Business language has changed too. "Rightsizing" now means terminating people. A large Canadian general insurance corporation got caught up in "rightsizing" some years ago. Senior management were enthusiastic. I can almost hear them explaining it to their board: they would get "leaner and meaner," terminate staff, close offices, and pocket the savings. They were right in one respect, costs would drop, or would, once they finished paying severances. But with no plan how to get the same amount of work done by fewer employees, the service to customers plummeted, and morale among the remaining frustrated and overworked employees hit bottom.

In the 1950s, we experienced a bit of Newspeak with the repeated stories of the political "domino theory." The West was fighting the North Koreans and the reason, we were told, was because if the North Koreans were to invade South Korea, it would become communist. If we allowed that to happen, then next would be Vietnam, Laos, Thailand, Cambodia, Indochina, and Australia: tumbling like dominos. The theory was simple, visual, effective, and unquestioned. It was also nonsense.

The war in Korea was called, in Orwellian terms, a United Nations "police action." It lasted three years, ended in a draw, and killed (using the traditional term) over a million people. This we were told was a preventive war so other dominos would not fall: a war to prevent war. Orwell could not have said it better!

Changes in language have been used to eliminate many social security programs that once had dual reasons for being: fairness, and to offset market swings. Now, Old Age Security, food stamps, Medicare, Medicaid, and unemployment insurance are referred to as "entitlement programs." No longer are they defined as necessary, caring, and decent, but are described as unnecessary or unaffordable. Somehow, what we once could easily afford, we cannot afford now. Changed language has torn away sensitivity. Job loss is reported as "negative employment growth."

The Texas State Board of Education in March 2010, voted to accelerate language change:

> The Texas Board of Education on Friday approved a social studies curriculum that will put a conservative stamp on history and economics textbooks, stressing the superiority of American capitalism, questioning the Founding Fathers' commitment to a purely secular government and presenting Republican political philosophies in a more positive light ... "Let's face it, capitalism does have a negative connotation", said one conservative member, Terri Leo. "You know, 'capitalist pig!' " [89]

So, the votes of ten people at the Board of Education changed how all Texas kids would be exposed to the world.

People like Bill Gates, Warren Buffet, or the offspring of Sam Walton are no longer called capitalists, but are now called entrepreneurs, investors, or just billionaires. The word "capitalist" is out of favour.

Western governments claim they are too poor to help the poor, but they have poured money into the banks. Since 2007, government aid poured into the banks' accounts, but somehow that public aid was never called welfare. I'll discuss more about that in Chapter Eleven when I examine quantitative easing.

---

89 http://www.nytimes.com/2010/03/13/education/13texas.html?_r=0

The Citizens United organization is one of the worst at misusing language, beginning with their name. Their website claims that it stands for restoring the United States Government to citizen control, but Citizens United has no members, no "citizens"! So, who are Citizens United? Primarily, it's the Koch brothers, the fourth and fifth wealthiest men in America. Their father, Fred Koch, founded an oil business—Koch Industries—and was a founding member of the ultra-right John Birch Society. His sons seem to provide the money to Citizens United. (With no annual report, it's hard to prove, and with no memberships, they have no requirement for accountability.) Secrecy, as we repeatedly see, is never good for the people. Citizens United sued the United States Federal Election commission and won the right for corporations to be treated as people. With this decision, all real, living, breathing American people lost rights!

The Koch Foundation invites judges and others to spend time on the Matador Cattle Company Ranch, one of three ranches the Koch family owns. Their guests listen to speakers from the Foundation for Research on Economics and the Environment while being served fine food and vintage wines. The Foundation (FREE is its acronym), believes in something they call "free market environmentalism." It fits with the Koch brothers' fight against environmental legislation. That fight may be motivated because of the multiple times they have been sued, often for bad environmental practices. There were over 90 suits before 2000, with a potential $350 million penalty. They got out of paying many fines with a half-million-dollar political donation.

Michael Copps was Chairman of the Federal Communications Commission for ten years: it's the US government agency that oversees the media to ensure fair and reliable coverage. Since retirement, he has been campaigning about the threat media concentration poses for democracy. In North Carolina in 2013, he spoke about media concentration and its racist bias. Although the US population is one-third black (minority, as Americans call it, and the ratio was growing), minorities owned only 2.2% of the media.

The new "corporations are people" ruling allows almost unlimited advertising sponsored by anonymous groups, and it now overwhelms political campaigns. Copps explains that it violates Section 317 of the 1934 Communications act that declared that people are "entitled to know by whom they are being persuaded." He reminded his audience that the American Legislative Exchange Council has existed since 1973 as a "bill mill" to draft and market state legislation for its corporate sponsors. The Council's work is so biased that corporate sponsors have started walking away. One study of the reporting on the 2014 election campaign found that Philadelphia stations gave 45 times more airtime to political ads than they gave to their own news coverage of the election. That, to Copps, is a biased misuse of the public airways.

With changing language, we have declared war on stuff, status, and emotions: first was the war on poverty, then the war on drugs, and now a war on terror. At one time, we required an enemy to have a war. Military Newspeak about terrorists is easy to see as propaganda. Consider the many people who were once labelled terrorists, and now seen as statesmen: Menachem Begin in Israel, Nelson Mandela in South Africa, Jomo Kenyatta in Kenya, José Mujica of Uruguay, and my friend Bao Kamau at the Kenyan Chamber of Commerce.

President Pohamba, the outgoing President of Namibia, was awarded The Ibrahim Prize for Achievement in African Leadership in 2014, including its $5 million award for raising living standards for his people and then resigning from the presidency. The prize is given to leaders who retire, to buck the trend of leaders of poor countries becoming dictators. Before becoming a politician, he was active in the South West Africa People's Organization, a liberation movement. He had been arrested, publicly flogged, and jailed for objecting to South African rule of Namibia. Was he a terrorist? He would be called one today.

While academic research on the subject of terrorism is extensive, we just don't hear about it. The research continues to reveal just what I read back in the 1970s, that the root cause of terrorism is injustice. The solution lies in dealing with the injustice. As Bao Kamau said, "A terrorist is a person with a cause but not an army."

Language is used to change how we think of domestic issues, as well. The Canada Pension Plan collects money throughout the working years of Canadians, to pay back to them when they retire. It protects them from the risks inherent in banks and private investment firms, and provides the government with the extra returns that come from large collective investments. Today, neocon politicians call that a "tax grab."

Let's just say this!

Time for a step back for a few words on another economist.

Say's Law, sometimes known as "the law of market," is an assertion named after the French businessman, journalist and economist Jean-Baptiste Say (1767–1832). He was born in France in the same era as Adam Smith, to a family of textile merchants. He supported the French Revolution and was appointed by Napoleon as a member of the Tribunate that ruled France, until Napoleon fired him. He was a writer and edited a pro-revolution publication advocating Adam Smith's views. In 1804, he published *A Treatise on Political Economy,* his principal work, with over two hundred pages, and the subtitle, *The production, distribution, and consumption of wealth.* He was in favour of competition, free trade, and removing constraints on business. He wrote that in a free market economy, there could not be a surplus of labour. In 1819, he helped to found the world's first business school and was later appointed a professor of political economy at the Collège de France.

His believed that "products are paid for with products," an idea that can also be stated as "supply creates its own demand." He felt that the very act of making something created the money to buy it. The problem is the arithmetic doesn't work. Assuming that 30% of the selling price of goods goes to the workers (that's typical, it was our number), the rest of the cost is material and overhead. Thus, the 30% that the workers get paid could never buy 100% of the goods produced.

Somehow, his assertion acquired the title, "Say's Law," with the unfortunate implication it was a fact, not a theory! Even the Theory of Gravity sounds weak by comparison. He stated that depressions or recessions would self-correct—another wrong assumption, as the Great Depression, the writings of Keynes, and our recent great recession have made clear.

Wrong as it was, Say's Law became generally accepted throughout the nineteenth century and was modified a bit to incorporate the "boom and bust" cycles of business. During the first half of the twentieth century, following Keynes' lead, economists increasingly disputed Say's conclusions.

The reason I'm mentioning Say is because of the effect his ideas have had behind the political jargon called "supply-side economics." It's jargon, because supply side arguments are political, not economic theory.

The belief that by creating a product you create a demand for it faced a sad unravelling when the Ford Motor Company developed the Edsel in 1957. It was introduced to great fanfare during a recession. Although there was loads of hype leading to a much-advertised television special, *The Edsel Show*, the car never reached one-half of its break-even point. Although it was created, it did not create the money to buy it, nor did it create its own demand. As always, supply follows to meet demand, not the other way around. Say's Law and supply-side economics were simply nonsense.

Adam Smith saw competitive enterprise as a balancing act between supply and demand, but it's not an equation that goes either way. Demand without supply results in shortages, and creates the need for supply. Supply without demand creates waste. Economists equate it to pushing on a rope. Unfortunately, mislabelling Say's assumptions as a "law" gave it unwarranted credibility that could grammatically overpower "theories" like those of Keynes. Supply-side assumptions dominated economics for decades, and in some corners, still persist. They clouded out established economic principles that made sense.

Globalization

Marco Polo, one of the earliest global traders, made his 24-year voyage from Italy to China in the mid-1200s. And, for centuries, sailors traded from Mombasa and around the Indian Ocean. The New World offered great riches to European traders. Following the Second World War, international trade soared, due to huge improvements in both ships and aircraft. In the 1950s, the invention of shipping containers provided a huge boost. This simple innovation was a dream: a large, reusable, secure, stackable box that was easily loaded onto a ship, train, or a truck, reducing both labour and time.

With trade increasing, changes in banking followed. International payments for those trades were needed that would be as easy as the containers made shipping the goods. Money needed to move around the world fast—as fast, or faster than goods. At Bretton Woods, the agreement had been reached to have currencies tied to gold and to use the US dollar as the international reserve currency. Three years later (1947), the General Agreement on Tariffs and Trade, known as GATT, had been signed to further eliminate tariffs and other barriers to trade.

By the 1970s, more and more people were travelling by air. The world seemed to shrink. Larger airplanes increased air shipment of goods as well. In 2004 and 2006, I made a couple of trips to China and flew Toronto/Hong Kong. Our plane needed to refuel at Anchorage: land, refuel, take off. On the ground in this small town, I saw literally dozens of windowless 747 aircraft: cargo carriers. In 2008, Anchorage would be handling almost eight hundred aircraft a day!

Globalization and global trade are different things. Global trade is trade between nations. Globalization is the process of changing the rules to suit the corporations. In the 1960s, globalization was not even in our vocabulary, but by the 1990s, it was considered to be inevitable. As steps were taken to make trade easier, the term globalization was captured by the neoliberals and corporations. Changing the rules could better be described as world-wide financialization. Competitive enterprise was changing to financialized capitalism. With better air travel and the internet, the world seems smaller, but that did not necessitate the push we have experienced towards unregulated and unrestricted global finance.

Trade deals, and we've been subject to an unending series of them, are making the world into a giant corporate playground. The Auto Pact between the United States and Canada in 1965 was one of the first, modified some decades later by the extended Free Trade Agreement (1987), then the North American Free Trade Agreement (1994), which included Mexico. Several new agreements are in negotiation as I write this, and controversy increasingly surrounds them. These deals are presented as they have always been: for free trade as a good thing. In fact, they are about controlling trade. Let's look at why!

The Transatlantic Trade and Investment Partnership (TTIP or TAFTA) between the United States and Europe is being negotiated. In the language of the new world, the nature of the "partnership" is corporations partnering for their mutual benefit. New agreements enshrine corporate rights and routinely ignore national, human, and worker rights. The agreements take precedence over the historic rights enshrined in national constitutions, over state or provincial laws, and over international laws. These agreements become new laws, judged in private business courts of their own making.

Critics of the TTIP agreement point out that it's not about trade: there are almost no remaining impediments to trade between the United States and Europe. It is about patent law and regulations, specifically those relating to medicines and seeds. Europeans pay far less for their drugs and TTIP is intended to slip through a stealth price increase on European drugs. The proposed agreement would also define French laws that ban genetically modified seeds as a "restraint on trade," thus illegal. The agreement may fail because of the French passion for food and the reluctance of the French people to tamper with the food chain. The passion for good taste may defeat Monsanto.

In February 2016, the twelfth round of negotiations on the agreement took place, and 248 pages of documents were leaked and published by Greenpeace. Corporations knew the details. The public had been kept in the dark. The details revealed that corporations would be given unprecedented powers over any new public health and safety standards or changes in social policy or the environment. The agreement is intended to accelerate the shift in power from the people and their governments to the economic sphere in which banks and corporations dominate. Nations and national laws will become more of an anachronism.

In an effort to sell TTIP as a good thing, computer models were created, projecting expected results. Critics pointed out that the projections included none of the obvious negative consequences. There are so few trade barriers remaining that agreements now aim to eliminate non-trade barriers like health and safety regulations, paint on children's toys, milk safety standards, and environmental protection.

For the TTIP talks, corporations created new lobby groups. "FoodDrinkEurope" represents Nestlé, Heinz, Coca-Cola, Kellogg's, and a few others, to promote the interests of their seventeen companies. They produced a very pretty annual report that provides no details on who pays their bills. It has glossy pictures of the seventeen directors and names the companies. However, the directors for FoodDrinkEurope include no farmers, no dieticians, nor members of the general public. They have a staff of 23 people based in Geneva to lobby. If their organization were properly identified it would be called a corporate union!

TTIP is not to be confused with the Trans Pacific Partnership Agreement (TPP), which has been in negotiations since 2009 and, if approved, would cover about 40% of world trade. That's 790 million people in 12 nations around the Pacific Ocean, from the west coast of the Americas to the east coast of Asia. The intent is to get agreement on a corporate wish list from the dozen nations. The White House, for no explicable reason, fast-tracked the act in January 2014. Obama was given "enhanced power" to negotiate on behalf of corporations, and the details kept secret.

More than 600 corporations have been lobbying for over four years on TPP, and some folks are leaking details. The "partnership" would be between 600 corporations, not between the millions of people around the Pacific who would be subject to it. WikiLeaks published the Environmental Chapter, which proposes ending environmental protection. How's that for an oxymoron? The Intellectual Property Chapter proposes allowing patents on everything imaginable, including plants and animals, in effect turning everything into a commodity. It proposes increasing the length of patents beyond 20 years and making safety warnings on food packages illegal. Governments have kept the TPP negotiations classified. If approved, it will be the first trade agreement not just negotiated in secret, but kept a secret. The lead negotiator from Chile resigned because he was concerned that the emerging agreement would restrict Chile's ability to control its financial institutions and national policies in health, education, and development.

The concept of allowing an international trade deal to be "fast-tracked" began in the US with the Trade Act of 1974, sometimes referred to as the Trade Promotion Authority (an innocent-sounding title). The bill allows the president to negotiate a deal and, when completed, requires it be returned to Congress for approval. Then come the conditions! Congress cannot change the bill, cannot amend it, and has only 90 days to discuss it. According to research done by the Centre for Responsive Politics,[90] over $200,000,000 was given to members of Congress to pass the 2014 version of the bill, most of that money coming from banks and financial companies. About $23,000,000 was spent for votes against it: about one-tenth the budget for the "yes" side. Most of the "no" money came from unions. Even with the huge bribe, the bill passed by only one vote.

Increasingly, people are seeing through these corporate ploys. In Australia and New Zealand people have been demonstrating in the streets. The New Zealand Nurses Association was concerned that private tobacco companies were being given the right to sue the government for loss of profit from anti-smoking legislation. In Japan, 4,000 farmers protested in Tokyo because of concerns about foreign workers, about their health care being threatened, and generally wanting to prevent Wall Street's ethics from dominating

---

90 Their annual report lists their donors. https://www.opensecrets.org/about/

Japanese business. Malaysians in Kuala Lumpur protested the probable rise in the price of drugs.

Leaked documents say that Canadian Crown corporations, such the post office and the CBC, would have to function entirely for profit. The end to a public broadcaster would end any semblance of objectivity remaining in the news. The province of Newfoundland has withdrawn from both the Trans Pacific Partnership (TPP) and the Comprehensive Economic and Trade Agreement (CETA) with Europe, because neither benefits its people.

The Sierra Club issued a report that said that the TPP deal is "Rife with polluter giveaways that would undermine decades of environmental progress, threaten our climate, and fail to adequately protect wildlife because big polluters helped write the deal." The attorney for the organization Popular Resistance says it's "a global coup d'état. Corporations will become more powerful than countries. Corporations will force democratic systems to serve their interests. Civil courts around the world will be replaced with corporate courts or so-called trade tribunals."

If TPP is passed, it will, along with the other trade agreements, become global law, and prior agreements, like those made through the United Nations, will effectively become null and void.

The CETA was approved by Canada in 2016 between Canada and Europe. Controversy in Europe about this 1634-page-long massive free trade agreement continues. Some regions have described themselves as CETA-free zones. The head of the Newfoundland Federation of Labour has written about it.

> European corporations want to sell Canadians the services we now receive publicly, services such as health care,

education, water and mail delivery, and CETA will give these private companies the right to bid on government tenders for goods and services including schools, hospitals, airports, public transit, ports, and hydro projects to name just a few. Any rules or practices that favor local economic development, support local food production or promote local or Canadian goods and services will be challenged as unfair barriers to trade. As well, these corporations will have the right to challenge any local laws that promote fair trade or reflect the environmental concerns of the community, such as bottled-water bans.[91]

These agreements put corporate power above national law. Who gave corporations the power to do that? Who gave our national leaders the right to bargain away our rights to the corporations?

Secrecy

We have accepted that global trade agreements are negotiated in secret. But why the secrecy?

I've discussed how secrecy has no place in an open society, but for the moment let's give trade agreements the benefit of the doubt. Is secrecy truly necessary or have they got something to hide?

International agreements historically have been done in secret, for peace, security, and diplomacy. At a later time, tariffs and trade have been discussed, also in secret, since that had been the accepted practice. That tradition has been maintained, while the subject

---

91 http://theindependent.ca/2014/10/03/the-threat-of-ceta-trade-investment-and-workers-rights/

matter has changed to be exclusively about corporate benefit. When hundreds of corporations attend meetings at which there's no one representing the people, things get dicey.

The meeting to establish the FED in 1912 was held in secret. In 1961, Kennedy warned that secrecy is "repugnant," just as Galbraith later warned, "The worst policy is one made in secrecy by experts!"

The Bank for International Settlements (BIS) operates in secret, as it has the right to do—it's a private corporation. However, we should never allow a private corporation to control public international finance. International banking secrecy has allowed private corporations to manage the money supply for their own needs and set the stage for multiple secret banking schemes like tax evasion in offshore banking accounts.

(For what it's worth, I don't have an offshore account nor do any of my business owner friends. We are not wealthy enough. Offshore accounts are for corporations and the ultra-rich, who use them to avoid taxes, leaving the poorer rest of us to pay the governments' bills. Even the language of offshore accounts is deceiving, conjuring up images of palm trees and beaches when the motivation fits better in Alcatraz!)

Secrecy is used to launder profit—moving profit from company to company, and from country to country, to avoid taxes. Once profit is out of the country, paying taxes that are morally due is avoided. Profit at one time was money, somewhat tangible. Now, with digital money, it takes a few keystrokes to move it to Grand Cayman or wherever, instantly. According to Merrill Lynch and the Boston Consulting Group, in 2003 there was about $36.2 trillion held in offshore accounts. If the taxes were paid on the income of those accounts, national debt would be eliminated.

The Google search engine was created by National Science Foundation money provided to two Stanford students, Larry Page and Sergey Brin. Their new business followed. Now, like most large enterprises, Google plans to avoid taxes, in one case through a scheme called the Double Irish. They shift earnings around: some goes to their subsidiary Google Irish Holdings, which, strangely, is headquartered in Bermuda, beyond the taxman.

In 2013, a Washington-based nonprofit journalism group[92] released the details on 130,000 offshore accounts. People know these practices are wrong; nonetheless, the accounts stay secure and, more importantly, untaxed. Because offshore accounts are wrong, people like Julien Assange, founder of WikiLeaks, feel duty bound to provide details. Many whistleblowers are quoted in this book because they are truth tellers. The severe reaction they elicit is because of the implications for the 1%.

Trade agreements

> This land is your land,
> This land is my land,
> From California to the New York island;
> From the redwood forest to the Gulf Stream waters
> This land was made for you and me.
> —Woody Guthrie, 1945

---

92 The International Consortium of Investigative Journalists. http://www.icij.org/

The 1948 General Agreement on Tariffs and Trade (GATT), with the purpose of eliminating tariffs, was replaced seven years later by the World Trade Organization.

Tariffs are charges that nations pass that increase the price of imported products. Tariffs violate all the basics of "free markets" and were one of Adam Smith's concerns with the Scottish mercantilists, who used them to protect their profits. On the other hand, tariffs are a historic tool used to strengthen national economies, especially emerging economies. Import tariffs were used in the founding years of the United States and sped the creation of an economically successful nation. By making imports more expensive, local industries grew to provide what was needed. In the modern era, tariffs have become so universally unwelcome they are discouraged in poor nations that would benefit from them.

Tariffs between Canada and the United States were significantly eliminated with the Auto Pact of 1965, which allowed cars and car parts to cross the border duty free. It's debatable whether it was good for the workers of either county, and whether it was good for either government. What is not in dispute is that it was good for the auto industry. Auto companies' centralized production had longer runs, pitted workers in one country against those in another, and in the end, made more money. There is nothing inherently wrong with that, but it illustrates that free trade serves corporations, not people.

The United States and Canada negotiated a new free trade agreement in 1987, which was expanded to include Mexico in 1994. This agreement has strange terms—strange if you expect things to make sense. The act states that if a commodity is sold once to another country, the government can never stop further sales!

Ever! So, if one bottle of Canadian water is sold to someone in the US, all the water in the country is up for sale! If water in Canada was to become scarce, export sales of water would be assured, but domestic sales would not.

Wikipedia lists 15 international trade agreements, starting with the Auto Pact, up to the newest Trans Pacific Strategic Economic Partnership. We're told these agreements promote better trade and more opportunities, and that is true. They do create better trade and more opportunities. But these partnerships are between companies, not people, and they create opportunities for corporations, not people. The result? People get poorer, nations lose control over their economies, the environment declines, and corporate power expands. People still expect their governments to protect them, but that role is all but gone.

AbitibiBowater Company (now Resolute Forest Products) is a Canadian firm that closed its pulp and paper mill in Newfoundland in 2008. The company wanted to sell its remaining assets, including certain timber-harvesting licenses and water-use permits. Those permits were granted by the government, contingent on the mill being in business. Under Canada's constitution, forests and water are a trust owned by the province. So, the Newfoundland government moved to re-appropriate them. AbitibiBowater sued and won under the terms of the North American Free Trade Agreement. The Canadian Government paid $130 million dollars to settle the claim on something not illegal in Canada that was done in the interest of the Canadian people. $130 million!

This is the reality of trade deals: corporate profit dominates civil law. Corporate rights take precedence over all other rights: human, civil, or national.

Monsanto, the company that brought us Agent Orange, is enthusiastic about trade agreements. Monsanto is the world's leading producer of genetically engineered seed, and the company describes itself as committed to sustainable agriculture. Their mission appears to be to control the world's food supply by controlling the world's seeds. To them, sustainable agriculture is one in which Monsanto is sustained by profit from providing all the seeds on earth. They employ over 20,000 people, a much larger enterprise than Adam Smith ever could have imagined, especially for a farm seed business. In 2009, 75 of their employees were lawyers. Monsanto even has lawyers in China.[93] Monsanto uses international trade agreements to prevent labelling food "genetically modified," as if they're not proud of it.

They run a "feel good" farm web site (americasfarmers.com) showing folksy concern for "our families," listing about a dozen of them, including "amazing farm moms." In one ad campaign, Monsanto pictures those honest farm people who "grow America," suggesting they care about farms and farmers, while, actually, Monsanto sues farmers, because their desire for profit is far greater than their concern about farm families.

In Saskatchewan, in 1998, Monsanto sued Percy Schmeiser and his wife for growing a Monsanto-trademarked seed. The family were not using Monsanto seeds but were using their own seed, grown on their own land. However, Monsanto seed had blown onto their land and taken over their crop. The Schmeisers were victims, but copyright law doesn't view it that way. It took six years

---

93   http://www.superlawyers.com/missouri/article/Defending-Monsanto/e290bf37-cafc-42da-9c99-a6f2f562a982.html

and about $400,000 in legal fees to fight the case. Monsanto spent an estimated $2,000,000, and at one time had nineteen lawyers in court. Monsanto won, but no penalty was imposed on the Schmeisers. The 2009 documentary *David versus Monsanto* documents the story, including how Monsanto spied on the family and tried to intimidate neighbours.

According to their website, Monsanto has sued 145 farmers in the United States. Their 2013 annual report states, "Intellectual property rights are crucial to our business, moratoria on testing, planting or use of biotechnology traits; and particularly our Seeds and Genomics segment."

In the talks for a Trans Pacific Partnership, one of the United States negotiators on agricultural issues was Islam Siddique. In Washington, there are 100 senators and 435 congressmen: 535 people elected to protect the interests of the people. Washington also has between twelve and fifteen thousand lobbyists: that is about 25 people on corporate payrolls for each elected person. Each lobbyist has a budget for wining, dining, and campaign contributions to grease the way for their employers. As if that ratio is not enough, the incestuous revolving door between corporations and elected representatives worsens it. Siddique, the US negotiator on agriculture, was previously a Monsanto lobbyist

While corporations lobby, people around the world are increasingly protesting global economic conferences and pending trade agreements. The sizes of the protests have grown, and the age of the protestors has grown as well. Decades ago, protesters were mainly young idealists. Protestors these days are often the elders, grey-haired and concerned about fairness and the next generation.

Also, a number of fair trade (not free trade!) organizations have emerged. The Fair Trade Federation works to unite North American and international fair trade groups. Ten Thousand Villages is the oldest fair trade organization in North America, started by the Mennonite Central Committee in the 1940s. Oxfam, which began selling fair trade crafts in the 1950s, continues to lobby for international fair trade and warn of the dangers of free trade.

Corporations are not content to risk their profits on national laws or public courts, so they set up their own. They agree to binding arbitration by a court that uses only the law in the trade agreement. Since the creation of NAFTA, Canada has been sued 35 times and is now the most sued developed country in the world, paying damages of C$172 million. The awards cover issues such as not letting foreign companies export Canadian water, or restraining drug company profiteering. As I'm writing this, there are eight claims by corporations against the Canadian government. In 1996, the Ethyl Corporation sued the Canadian government for banning the fuel additive MMT, which appeared to be a carcinogen. The private tribunal forced Canada to pay $13 million dollars and make the product available because, under the agreement, profit trumps medical safety and the laws of the nation.

The chorus for the song "This land is your land" embraces what most of us still believe: "… this land was made for you and me." Corporations want it for themselves.

As work declines

> Where there is no work, there is no dignity.
> —Pope Francis

Since time began, people have been trying to live well, while doing as little work as possible.

All but the rich need to work: we need to earn money to buy food, housing, and basic necessities of life. Thousands of innovations have made work easier. In developed nations, we don't have to work as hard as our ancestors. Normal work days have been reduced to eight hours and a work week to five days. As we reduced the hours worked, we created jobs for others, sharing work with them.

In Sweden, Toyota switched to a six-hour workday and reported improved productivity and better staff wellbeing. At the same time, people in much of the rest of the world have been pressured into working more hours. In the UK, the percentage of people working over 48 hours a week has increased by 15% in the last six years. [94]

Some researchers refer to our current era as the "fourth industrial revolution." The original Industrial Revolution occurred around Adam Smith's time, when steam power and factories changed almost everything in daily life. The second revolution followed in about 1870, when electricity was introduced, and mass production became common. The third was the information technology and automation revolution of the 1960s and 1970s, and finally, the fourth is the digitalization of the economy, which we are living through: instant communications and change at exponential speed. The long-term trend of these changes is the reduction of the hours of work necessary and thus, the reduction of jobs. This creates two problems: one economic, and one of justice. Economically, if we employ fewer people, fewer people will have money to buy what's

---

94 http://www.neweconomics.org/blog/entry/how-a-shorter-working-week-is-becoming-a-reality

produced. And with less demand, businesses will fail. The justice problem is: how are people who are not needed, to survive?

In 1536, King Henry VIII was concerned about beggars, and instructed Cromwell to come up with a job creation scheme for London. In 1848, in France, the provisional government adopted a resolution to "… engage themselves to guarantee labor to every citizen." Full employment has regularly been a public goal. At one time, it was the bedrock of economics: the basis for shared prosperity and essential for a civil society. Full employment has been steadily pushed into the background. Federal legislation in the US, in 1978, directed the Fed to pursue maximum employment. The bill was ignored. The control of inflation took precedence, and in recent years, it's the deficit that has trumped employment.

In 1995, Jeremy Rifkin, an economist and social theorist, published *The End of Work: the Decline of the Global Labor Force and the Dawn of the Post-Market Era*, and he predicted that worldwide unemployment would increase because automation and information technology would eliminate jobs. As machines replace people, just as tractors replaced horses a generation ago, we will run out of work. How do we treat those we don't need? Rifkin foresaw the decline in the American middle class with the benefits of the change going to a small elite of corporate managers. The term "the 1%" had not yet evolved. One of his recommendations was to provide a "social wage" to displaced workers.

The inevitable cyclical of ups and downs of capitalism have been managed with layoffs—the involuntary contributions of people at the bottom to make free enterprise work for those at top. People get hired in boom times and laid off in bad. Central bankers exploit workers when they deliberately create unemployment to control the value of money. History is filled with examples: in the mid-1970s, Paul Volker, as head of the Fed, raised the interest rate to over 20% to stop inflation, resulting in recession and over 10% unemployment. The unemployed were protecting the value of the currency. As unfair as that system has been, we are approaching a more significant problem: not enough work to go around.

When the troops returned after WW II, thousands of retiring soldiers needed jobs. Those jobs didn't exist, so the veterans were offered programs to go to back school. This had two beneficial effects: it kept bodies out of the workforce and improved the nation's skills.

Eliminating work is a truly wonderful development. The specialization of labour, new tools, new technology, and progress has made possible shorter work days, shorter weeks, more vacation time, and a higher standard of living. As work became less essential, the workday shortened, people entered the workforce later (with more years of education), and ended their working lives sooner, with earlier retirement.

It was in the 1920s in North America that the work week shortened to five days. Vacation time and holidays improved life for workers and made work available for others. Keynes expected the work week to shorten even more and faster than it has. These steps to work less and share work postponed the issue of what to do when that is not enough.

Today we hear of a "jobless recovery"—the economy improves, but no one goes back to work. As strange as a jobless recovery sounds, it shouts out that we don't need everyone to produce everything that we need. But a jobless recovery will leave increasing numbers of people who cannot buy things, and recession or depression will continue.

After WWII, the huge, pent-up demand for consumer products created lots of work, and with it innovation and efficiency gains. Then computers decreased the manpower required to do things. All in all, more was being produced by fewer. In 1950, the United States had 5.38 million farms. In 2000, this had dropped to 2.17 million, and with only one-half the number of farms, the farmers are producing surpluses.

How are people to survive when the system assumes almost everyone has to work, but there are not enough jobs? How can we reconcile a sound economy and a high percentage of unemployed? How are the people not needed to survive?

France cut back on weekly hours in 2000 and adopted a 35-hour work week to add jobs. Adding more vacation days and more holidays can also create jobs. Canada and the US could do a lot by increasing their 10 to 15 vacation days to the global norm of 20 to 30 days. In this way, the available work is shared, and the income spread around. However, it won't deal with the bigger issue that the French, too, will have to face: how will we provide income for the people who are not needed to produce what we need?

It's more than a social problem: business needs to sell everything produced and to do so requires almost all the population to have the money to buy it.

> NEW YORK Jan. 13, 2013— Five years after the start of the Great Recession, the toll is terrifyingly clear: Millions of middle-class jobs have been lost in developed countries the world over.

And the situation is even worse than it appears.

Most of the jobs will never return, and millions more are likely to vanish as well, say experts who study the labor market. What's more, these jobs aren't just being lost to China and other developing countries, and they aren't just factory work. Increasingly, jobs are disappearing in the service sector, home to two-thirds of all workers.

They're being obliterated by technology.[95]

The working world I entered is long gone: the one where finding a job was easy, the job was meaningful, had a future, and was for life. It's depressing when bright young people can't find work and optimistically apply their energy and hope to "starting a new venture," such as a fast food truck.

Professor Wassily Leontief, a Harvard/New York University economist, predicted in the 1980s that automation would displace labour as surely as the tractor had displaced the horse. With numbers of the unemployed in the United States now at about Great Depression levels, it seems he had a point. At some point, technological change will make a guaranteed basic income a necessity: a necessity simply for people to survive and a necessity to protect business by creating demand.

---

95 http://www.huffingtonpost.com/2013/01/23/middle-class-jobs-machines_n_2532639.html

Summary—what is the Social Contract now?

So what do we do? Marx believed that the inevitably increased use of machines to replace human labour would prove self-defeating. Eliminating labour from the production process would create a "reserve army of unemployed workers," as he called them. The effect would be to drive wages lower, and that is just what we are witnessing. This is digging the grave for capitalism because workers have less money, so there is less money to buy things. Businesses fail. Recessions follow, then depressions, and the depressions will stay.

Faith in capitalism won't survive the failure of the basics, despite all the money spent in the advertising campaigns of the 1940s and 1970s. The decline of the middle class, and the decline in faith in capitalism, are going hand in hand.

A new social contract is required.

This new contract will have to address many things, like the dichotomy between how much a person is paid, and how much a person is worth. People essential to society, such as the people who prevent plague by cleaning sewers and collecting garbage, should be paid at the high end of the pay scale.

Instead, people doing non-essential things, like football coaches or professional athletes, earn the most. Recently, the Seattle Mariners reached an agreement that is expected to make Felix

Hernandez the highest-paid pitcher in baseball. Hernandez's deal is expected to pay $175 million over seven years. [96]

In January of 2014, the progressive mayor of Seattle increased the pay for city workers, which includes garbage and sewer workers, to no less than $15 per hour, backed by a campaign of union and civil rights groups. Now Seattle has one of the highest minimum wages in the country, at $15.37 an hour for hotel workers. However, they have some distance to go to match Hernandez, with his $12,500 per hour.

Providing financial assistance such as pensions, in addition to being a stimulus, has a wonderful benefit. It's population control! Without pensions or income security, the poor globally have, and continue to have, too many children, in an attempt to protect their future.

I've looked here at the way media concentration has allowed a corporate agenda to displace a human agenda. A lot of bad economics has become accepted, and poorly educated journalists report things like "recoveries" that have not happened. Their misinformation clouds our understanding, and doesn't address the right issues. I'll talk more about the wrong ideas we've come to accept, in my next chapter.

---

96 http://www.capitalgazette.com/sports/pro_sports/baseball-roundup-mariners-finalize-deal-with-hernandez/article_16c5fed6-835f-5340-97d5-4942812f7edd.html hernandez/article_16c5fed6-835f-5340-97d5-4942812f7edd.html

8.
Voodoo Economics

> By the time I was forty, I could see our country was changing fast, and that these changes were causing us to live differently.
> —Plenty Coups, Chief, Crow Indians, 1898

I TURNED FORTY IN 1980, AND MY WORLD WAS ALSO CHANGING. Not as cruelly as the world of the Crow but it was changing almost as profoundly. Chief Plenty Coups and his people in Montana had experienced the invasion of settlers and troops. Custer fought the battle of Little Big Horn the same year Plenty Coups became Chief. He and his people fought for the right to keep their land and were more successful than many tribes. Most native people were blindsided by the Western legal tradition, which assumed that land was a commodity, not a shared natural asset.

8. Voodoo Economics

As my world changed, the forces were not as visible as cavalry and guns. All I knew was things were increasingly making less sense to me. Prior to Reagan's election in 1981, supply-side economics was considered weird—even moderates in the Republican Party thought so. George H. Bush, debating with Reagan for the presidential nomination, referred to Reagan's economics as "voodoo economics."

As it happened, Reagan won and chose Bush as his vice president and "voodoo economics," or "Reaganomics," became policy from 1981 to 1990. There were four key points, or "pillars," as they were dubbed, to their policy: reduce government spending, reduce federal income tax, reduce capital gains tax, and reduce government regulation. They embraced monetarist economics to control the economy. (Monetarist economics uses the money supply to control inflation.) Reagan's economics came from the University of Chicago's School of Economics, specifically via Milton Freedman. Reagan's eight years were followed immediately by four more with George H. Bush as president, resulting in twelve unbroken years of voodoo economics.

As cutting taxes was a major pillar, let's take a closer look. There are different types of taxes, and no matter what type of tax, no one likes taxes. But we need a way to pay for things that benefit us all. Usually, nations tax the money people earn. Milton Friedman had helped develop the tax system where American employers would withhold taxes from employees' wages and submit the money to the government. It's a logical, efficient system.

In addition to taxing wages, there are taxes on capital gains, which are taxes on the increase in value of things, such as a house or investments. When income tax was first introduced in 1913, both wages and capital gains were taxed at the same rate. Was that fair? A logical argument could be made that the money people have "earned" with their time, and skills, and possibly sweat, should be taxed less than money earned without effort. The issue is the difference between earned and unearned income. However, any effort to challenge the unfairness of taxing earned income and unearned income at the same rate, was unsuccessful.

Then, in 1942, capital gains taxes were cut in half: a gift to those with capital. In the 1980s, Reagan reduced taxes on capital gains again. Presently, in the United States, the maximum tax rate on money people work for is 39.6%, while the maximum rate on money they don't work for is 25%. Fairness would suggest those rates should be reversed. Reagan believed in a balanced budget and proposed a constitutional amendment that would require the president to balance the budget or be impeached. As it was contrary to everything the world had learned about economics, the Democrats refused to pass the amendment. If they had passed it, Reagan would have been the first president impeached for not balancing the budget!

His promise to downsize government and lower taxes is out of sync with what he actually did. He raised taxes more often than he lowered them, and in the process, he moved a huge amount of the tax burden from the rich to working people. Instead of reducing government spending, he turned the US into the largest debtor nation on earth: debt rose from $900 billion to $2.8 trillion. His policies also squeezed out the middle class, but the reality of his record seems forgotten.

Despite Reagan's opposition to Keynes' ideas, he used them, and his increased military spending provided stimulus and led to a booming economy. The world worked just as Keynes, not Friedman, had taught us.

Supply-side economics

> The modern conservative is engaged in one of man's oldest exercises in moral philosophy; that is, the search for a superior moral justification for selfishness.
> —John Kenneth Galbraith

Supply-side economics is an outgrowth of Say's law, discussed in Chapter Seven. Sometimes it's called "neoclassical economics," a school of macroeconomics that argues that lowering barriers to trade is the best way to create growth. By reducing regulation and taxes (a pillar of Reagonomics), people are supposed to invest more and create more. Consumers are supposed to benefit from a greater supply of goods and services at lower prices.

Microeconomics is essentially the economics I have been discussing: day-to-day experience in the real world of supply and demand. Macroeconomics deals with the bigger picture: attempts to control the larger economy, to control the inevitable peaks and valleys in capitalism. Efforts to stimulate the economy of a nation, or to offset the tendency of the economy to go into and stay in recession are macroeconomic, as are efforts to affect unemployment, inflation, savings, and the money supply.

Supply-side economics were sometimes called "trickle-down economics," with the hope that if you improve the general economy, it will trickle down so that everyone benefits. It was more poetically expressed as "a rising tide lifts all boats!" A rising tide can also flood Miami and drown Indonesia. Less poetic writers called it "the horse-and-sparrow" theory: if you feed the horse enough oats, some will trickle down to the road for the sparrows.

During this period, fear was generated that if you tax the wealthy too much, they'll take their money and go, and jobs will disappear. Nonsense on multiple counts! First, no one was talking about increasing taxes, and the wealthy had not yet left. And if they did leave, where would they go? People can't easily leave their country. What would they do with their money?

On the other hand, there were positive arguments for tax reductions: if you cut taxes, people will have more money, to spend and invest, and thus create jobs. But here again, having more money does not ensure it will be invested, nor do investments, such as mutual funds, for example, necessarily create jobs. Both arguments were nonsense. Nonetheless, Reagan cut the top tax rate from 70%, gradually, to 20% during in his two terms in office. None of the boom he promised followed.

Practical experience in the real economy confirms that it is demand that drives the economy. People, both ordinary citizens, and businesspeople, buy stuff when they need it. Businesses will make stuff when they can sell it, and will borrow or invest when they can see a use for the money. It is demand that drives the economy.

The Plunge Protection Team

In March 1988, President Reagan signed Executive Order #12631, a strange thing for a free-market president to do. The Order created The President's Working Group on Financial Markets. Informally this group is known as the Plunge Protection Team, and their "official" role is to prevent another "Black Monday," when, on October

19, 1987, stock markets around the world crashed. The Dow Jones went from a record of 2,722 in mid-August to under 1,800 in late October! The group appointed to prevent a re-occurrence consisted of four people, all insiders: Secretary of the Treasury, Chair of the Federal Reserve, Chair of the Securities and Exchange Commission, and Chair of the Commodity Futures Trading Commission. This group still exists and functions without any input from outsiders.

The existence of such a committee raises questions—are free markets free? Can they be, if there is a group that manipulates them? Why does it operate in secret? The Committee could have real use in preventing another Black Monday market collapse if there were some agreement on what caused the collapse—which there isn't. Nonetheless, a Market Manipulation Committee was established, and it continues to exist, and act.

It was Reagan, the penultimate free marketer, who introduced top-level market manipulation, yet we continue to live with the myth that markets are "free." The Working Group has the entire US Treasury at its disposal and can manipulate several things: general stock prices, prices of commodities, the price of gold, and prices of currencies. To illustrate, twenty-five years after it was created, on September 29, 2008, the Dow Jones lost 777 points in one day, the largest one-day decline ever. Days later, the US began bank bailouts, and on October 16, for no definable reason, gold dropped $45 an ounce in minutes. Gold dropping means the dollar goes up. In a couple of days, despite a decline in US industrial production, the Dow Jones shot up 130 points. A strategist for the Bank of Montreal reported that this was "… the most massive intervention of government into the capital markets or the financial system since Roosevelt closed the banks back in 1933!"[97]

Other analysts have pointed out that after the collapse of Bear Stearns (a global investment bank that failed in March 2008), and, in order to avoid more collapses, the central banks colluded to sell the yen and €uros and to buy US dollars, thus inflating the value of US currency. They were successful, and the Dow and the value of the dollar both rose: once again, market manipulation was on a global scale.

In about 1995, I discovered the newsletter of a retired Wall Street insider, Bob Chapman, who wrote about market manipulation. As a young man, he'd spent three years in the Army in counterintelligence, and then went to work on Wall Street, where he eventually ran his own gold and silver brokerage firm. He did this for 18 years and produced a rambling, insightful newsletter for his clients. When he retired, his clients, 6,000 of them, pleaded with him to continue the newsletter because he had been providing investment advice and forecasts that proved to be correct. He restarted it in 1991.

(He provided me with personal investment advice: "Buy gold.") For decades, he wrote that the status of the US dollar as the world's major currency was coming to an end. Repeatedly, he wrote to not trust anyone on Wall Street. "I know," he would add, "I worked there!" He spent his last twenty years repeatedly issuing the same warning not to trust Wall Street, and regularly added not to trust the mass media either, because it simply parroted Wall Street tales. His early speculations regularly turned out to be accurate. He

---

[97] Brown, Ellen. *The Not So Invisible Hand.* http://www.webofdebt.com

looked beyond the headlines: in one newsletter, after a body of a corporate financial manager was found face down in Tampa Bay, he wrote, "I wonder what he was up to?" Often, he speculated that certain shares were being manipulated, and later, the facts confirming his suspicions would surface. Sadly, he died in 2012, when he was 76.

What I had learned from Chapman was reinforced by a local friend who had taken early retirement and, to make some extra dollars, took up day trading. Every morning he would go to his computer, look at the handful of stocks he was following and, on most days, buy a few thousand dollars' worth. He planned to sell them in the afternoon before the market closed, and his pub opened. His intent was to make a couple of hundred dollars a day, and he'd done so for a few years. Some days he would sell early. Those were the days that he explained "… when the big boys came in!" These market manipulators were too big for him to mess with. Peter had learned that, some days, parts of the market were free enough to trust, but on other days there were "pump and dump" schemes and other manipulations that cost naïve investors their money.

Still, however, the media keep up the myth of "free markets," reinforced by the almost minute by minute reports of market averages. After the September 2001 attack, just when the Wall Street stock market was set to reopen, the British newspaper, *The Guardian* (discussed earlier) ran the headline, "Fed to Prop up Wall St.," and outlined the plans to spend billions "to support the U.S. stock market":

> A secretive committee—the Working Group on Financial Markets, dubbed 'the plunge protection team'—includes

bankers as well as representatives of the New York Stock Exchange, NASDAQ and the US Treasury. It is ready to co-ordinate intervention by the Federal Reserve on an unprecedented scale.[98]

On October 6, 2008, the Plunge Protection Team intervened again and issued a press release[99] explaining that they were embarking on multiple actions in the economy, such as buying assets, directly strengthening balance sheets, and providing people and institutions with guarantees.

In 2014, the Editorial Board of *The New York Times* released a study that showed that one-quarter of Wall Street deals involve insider trading: they are rigged against the general public. Seldom (or is it never?), do insiders go to jail.

In no system of free markets is there room for secret manipulation, nor room for insider trading. In 2008, as had happened in the crashes of 1929 and 1988, the competitive free market system failed—died even! The system has died three times, but has yet to be buried.

Milton Friedman (1912 –2006)

> Milton Friedman's misfortune is that his economic policies have been tried.
> —John Kenneth Galbraith

---

[98] http://www.theguardian.com/business/2001/sep/16/useconomy.september11, 2001

[99] http://www.treasury.gov/press-center/press-releases/Pages/hp1177.aspx

If ever there was a high priest for voodoo economics, it was Milton Friedman. Born in Brooklyn, Friedman got his undergraduate degree in mathematics from Rutgers University, then went to the University of Chicago to do graduate work in economics with the idealistic goal of putting an end to the Depression. At the time, Friedrich Hayek, a libertarian professor of politics and economics, taught there and had a huge influence on Friedman. (Hayek was also a big influence on Margaret Thatcher. On one occasion she pulled Hayek's book, *The Constitution of Liberty*, out of her purse and said, "This is what we believe!"*)*. Her belief confirms what Keynes had written years earlier:

> The ideas of economists and political philosophers, both when they are right and when they are wrong, are more powerful than is commonly understood. Indeed, the world is ruled by little else. Practical men, who believe themselves to be quite exempt from any intellectual influences, are usually slaves of some defunct economist.[100]

After graduation, Friedman spent 1941–43 working on wartime tax policy for the Federal Government and advised senior officials of the Treasury. He advocated Keynesian policy and helped to create the payroll tax withholding system. Income tax was necessary to provide money to fight the war and withholding money at the source insured it. He later said, "I have no apologies for it, but I

---

100 Keynes, J.M. *The General Theory of Employment, Interest and Money*. 1936.

really wish we hadn't found it necessary and I wish there were some way of abolishing withholding now."

In 1946, Friedman accepted an offer to teach economics at the University of Chicago and stayed for the next 30 years. More Nobel Prize winners in economics came from the University of Chicago than from any other university. (As I mentioned earlier, a Nobel Prize in economics is not a real Nobel Prize and seldom do the winners get economics right. Milton Friedman got one in 1976 for theories disproved within the decade.)

In 1962, Friedman published *Capitalism and Freedom*, modelled somewhat on his mentor's book, *The Constitution of Liberty*, which linked economics and politics. It was 186 years after Adam Smith's *Wealth of Nations*, and Friedman was suggesting that capitalism and political freedom were synonymous. His assumptions were to become so much a part of Western culture that many today consider capitalism and a free society mutually dependent.

At one time, Friedman supported a negative income tax. That's a progressive way to deal with the decline of work and ensure that everyone has money to live on. Everyone reports their income to the government: if you earn a lot you pay a lot of tax, and, as income goes down, so do taxes. At the bottom, the government pays money out. The poor receive money as a right, because it's considered the decent thing to do, and, because it stimulates the economy. Friedman sounded more caring in his early years than the image he acquired.

In the mid-1950s, the US State Department, with support from the Ford and the Rockefeller foundations, established the Chile Project to train young Chileans in economics. The University of Chicago set up the program. One hundred graduates went back to South America, especially to Santiago. Not much happened until the 1970s, when the graduates acquired the nickname of "the Chicago boys." Chile was the first nation to embrace and the first to fail because of neoliberal economics.

In 1970, Salvador Allende was elected President of Chile. He was a socialist. The country had significant problems: unemployment, inflation, and malnourishment. The government planned to nationalize both the copper mines and the banks. With the clandestine help of the CIA, Allende and his elected government were overthrown on September 11, 1973. Henry Kissinger, not a big fan of democracy, said at the time, "I don't see why we need to stand idly by and let a country go communist due to the irresponsibility of its own people …"

General Augusto Pinochet was put into power and ruled for the next 26 years. Up to 3,000 people became "the disappeared" during his regime. When Pinochet took power, unemployment was down to 4.3%, about 20% of the people still lived in poverty. The Chicago boys were invited to help "fix" the county and by 1980 Milton Friedman was referring to their results as the "Chilean Miracle." Over nine years, his trainees had abolished the minimum wage, outlawed trade union bargaining, privatized the pension system, privatized 212 state industries, and abolished taxes on wealth and business profits. These changes were supposed to create a wealthier country within months. When it didn't, they urged more of the same. Twenty-seven years later, when Pinochet left office, unemployment was up to 22%, poverty had increased from 20% to 36%, and real wages had dropped by 40%. Some "miracle."

The economic transformation of the country from socialism was led by "the Chicago boys": Chile became the experimental lab for Friedman's theories. With Ford and Rockefeller foundations' funding, Friedman travelled to Chile with missionary zeal to teach the new dictator his unproven creed. The Chilean think tank Centro de Estudios Publicos was established, and Friedman's mentor Hayek was invited to join. Hayek had written in a letter to *The Times of London* expressing his support for the new Chilean dictator Pinochet and his policies: policies in which wages were cut, family allowances were cut by 75%, national assets were privatized, and foreign corporations were welcomed. (Pinochet was not totally stupid: the state held onto the copper company and a bank.)

The free market policies of Friedman gathered more momentum during the 1970s, when Friedman found he had fans in Margaret Thatcher and Ronald Reagan.

Thatcher, elected in 1979, was the first elected leader to use his theories. The British inflation rate dropped, but the rate of unemployment doubled, and three million people were unemployed. Prior to Friedman, keeping unemployment low was regarded as the key role of government. He disagreed. He coined the phrase "the natural rate of unemployment," which implied that full employment was impossible, and unemployment just had to be lived with.

One problem with Friedman's assumption was that it overlooked the fact that employed people buy things and unemployed people don't. It's employed people who make the economy function. Along with the acceptance of the idea that some unemployment was natural came the end to the belief that people had a right, as they once did, to a job.

In 2002, the Cato Institute initiated the Milton Friedman Prize for Advancing Liberty. The Cato Institute was originally called the Charles Koch Foundation, started in 1974 by the father of the

Koch brothers. It's a libertarian think tank that changed its name in 1976 to Cato to emphasize its republican roots. Cato was the Roman politician who believed in republican government: government where the people hold the power. Cato was used in the early 1700s as the title for a series of essays, published in London, supporting republican government and the essays were popular in the New World.

Despite the award for "advancing liberty," Milton Friedman admitted only a year later, in 2003, that he had erred: "The use of quantity of money as a target has not been a success." He added, "I'm not sure I would, as of today, push it as hard as I once did."[101] That, to an economist, equates to a type of religious conversion, possibly even to repentance. In any case, it was too late! Enormous damage had been done.

Monetarism

Friedman became an anti-Keynesian and developed a very different theory, called monetarism, using the money supply instead of supply and demand, to control the economy. Controlling the money supply, so monetarists believe, is done by increasing and decreasing the interest rate. (Money is created by borrowing, not by the mint!) Monetarists believe that the market is always right, and the government is always wrong.

The issue of money supply is important, so let's examine it.

The bigger a nation gets, or the bigger an economy gets, the more money it needs. There just have to be more dollars today

---

101   http://www.guardian.co.uk/business/2003/jun/22/comment.economicpolicy

than at the time of Ben Franklin. Thus, as an economy grows, more dollars should be created. If you don't, then money becomes scarce, and people and businesses suffer. Properly managing the nation's money is a delicate process.

The belief that managing the economy could be done by managing the money supply became immensely popular and was accepted by politicians, bankers, and journalists alike. Alan Greenspan and the Fed followed monetarist principles, and almost everyone assumed that changes in the interest rate are fundamentally important. Bernanke, and his successor Yellen, are no different.

Monetarism has many problems: the major one being that it doesn't relate to the real economy. Ordinary businesses don't borrow money because the interest rate is down. They borrow money when they can use it. The need for loans is demand-driven, not price-stimulated. New ideas, new products, and more customers cause us to borrow, not low rates.

It was a surprise to hear from Friedman in his later years, when he almost apologized (as noted above). It was not a surprise to learn he was wrong: monetarism assumes businesses will borrow if money is cheap, invest it, and new investments will create a boom! For twenty years we have had low interest rates and no boom! The monetarist arguments are nonsense. And worse, the decades of low-interest violate one of the norms of the old social contract: retired people are not getting the interest on savings that they rely on for their security.

Financialization

> The financial sector has succeeded in depicting itself as part of the productive economy, yet for centuries banking was recognized as being parasitic.
> —Michael Hudson, Professor, Economics, University of Missouri (Kansas)

Years of monetarist economics gave money and its managers (in other words, Wall Street), more power. That came at a cost to the rest of us. In older cultures, where tradition or religion are more dominant, such as India, China, and tribal cultures, they benefited by lagging behind. If you are interested in reading more on financialization than I will cover here, the Trans National Institute has a booklet available free on their website.[102]

In the mid-1940s, the US financial industry accounted for 2% of the Gross Domestic Product. It grew to 4.9% by 1980, and to almost 8.4% by 2010. The financial world has quadrupled—but for what? The finance industry creates nothing, so why did It need to grow? Now we are paying for a bigger banking world—at least four times bigger—and the financial "industries" take a bigger share of our economic pie. The share that was left for people, industry, farming, natural resources, and public services shrank.

An extra 6% sounds small. However, 6% of $17 trillion amounts to just over $1 trillion, and $1 trillion pays a lot of bonuses. Financialization seeks to change every activity into a financial transaction. Take out a mortgage, and it is no longer just a loan,

---

102   https://www.tni.org/en/publication/financialisation-a-primer

but a financial asset that others can buy and sell. Every product, every activity that's marketable, is configured into an asset that can be traded, speculated on, or speculated against, and profits on trades make money. But all this activity provides no value to the real economy.

Financial services industries have been a strong proponent of globalization—one huge world market can pay more commissions than multiple small ones. To paraphrase Lloyd Blankfein, CEO and Chair of Goldman Sachs, the folks at Goldman Sachs were "… doing God's work," helping money find its best use.[103] The better use of money trumps the better use of people. This is the amorality of capital, summed up with less theology in a memo credited to Michael Eisner, CEO, Disney Corporation, 1984–2005:

> We have no obligation to make history. We have no obligation to make art. We have no obligation to make a statement. To make money is our only objective.

Sadly, he was right. Eisner understood. Anyone who says that corporations "should" be responsible, or act ethically and respect the environment, misunderstands the free market system.

Thomas Palley, (MA, International Relations, and Ph.D., Economics, Yale), lives in Washington, DC. His career as a post-Keynesian economist has included working for the AFL-CIO, and for George Soros's Open Society Foundation. He has recently started a project to stimulate public discussion about what kind of economics is needed to promote democracy and an open society, a

---

103   *Reuters News*, November 8, 2009.

discussion that is essential, as I will discuss in my final chapter. He recently summed up the effects of financialization:

> All three dimensions: ideas, politics and the economy—financialization captures them all on behalf of the rich.[104]

Financialization reduces people to one use: to consume. Labour is just a commodity, and finance is more important than the real economy. Doing the deal becomes more profitable than doing the work. Real issues like happiness or public safety are ignored. Faux industries that make nothing, like the "private equity industry," emerge.

One day, I expect, historians will speculate about financialization and ask why the people didn't rebel. Their jobs were shipped offshore—where were the economists? Where were the protests? Where was the government? Why was financialization allowed to create the disaster of 2007 and 2008? What was done to avoid it happening again?

In the last chapter, I will look at the relationship between the increase of financialization and the decrease of happiness.

Alan Greenspan

> If I turn out to be particularly clear, you've probably misunderstood what I've said.
>
> —Alan Greenspan

---

[104] Pauley, Thomas. TV interview, January 2014 https://www.youtube.com/watch?v=BsBn3jNHlJw He is the author of *Financialization: The Economics of Finance Capital Domination*.

Alan Greenspan was appointed Chair of the Federal Reserve by Ronald Reagan in 1987. A Wall Street insider, he was a director of the investment bank, Brown Brothers Harriman, and other companies. He was a director of the Council on Foreign Relations, an American think tank often referred to as "the real state department." During his tenure, he acquired near rock star status as the "maestro" of the economy, and he served for almost twenty years (to 2006). He was appointed and reappointed by Republicans and Democrats alike. During his tenure, the seeds were planted for the massive bank failures, the subprime mortgage scandal, and the Great Recession that were to follow.

Born in New York City, his dad was a stockbroker, and his mom a homemaker. Five-year-old Allan had a talent for doing math in his head and a memory for reciting baseball batting averages. In high school, he learned to play jazz saxophone and with his schoolmate, Stan Getz, they studied at the Julliard School of Music, along with Woody Herman. He earned an MA in Economics at New York University.

Greenspan's dissertation is not available at the university because he had it pulled from the archives in 1987. Apparently, it dealt with soaring housing prices, the possibility of creating a housing bubble, and the effect that would have on consumer spending. How ironic. Because, while he was head of the Federal Reserve (1987–2006} he was a cheerleader for the housing boom. He knew, as he said in October 2004 at a bankers meeting in Washington, that "there is no perpetual motion machine which generates an ever rising path for the price of homes." But throughout the early 2000s, he denied the existence of a housing bubble. In his 2013 memoir, *The Map and the Territory: Risk, Human Nature, and the Future of Forecasting*, he denies all accountability that he fueled the housing bubble by driving interest rates to all-time low levels and by also turning his back on illegal new types of mortgages.

In 1952, he had met Ayn Rand and become a convert to her philosophy of objectivism—a simplistic, libertarian, passionate form of capitalism. (I first heard of Rand in the late 1950s, when I had a summer job as a park ranger. Many campers were academics, and one of them taught me about objectivism while we sat around a campfire.)

Greenspan, Rand, and a few others used to meet weekly in Rand's New York apartment and discuss philosophy for hours. Greenspan contributed a chapter to her book, *Capitalism, the Unknown Ideal* (1966), about the wisdom of a nation using the gold standard, a principal he later ignored. She was famous for two earlier books, which have become gospel to libertarians: *The Fountainhead* (1943), which spells out her neocon philosophy in 752 pages, more succinctly than the 1168 pages of her second, and better-selling, *Atlas Shrugged* (1957), one of the longest novels ever written. Her heroes enthusiastically personify capitalist individualism. There is no need to read both books; the philosophic content is the same. It is common to find her books on the bookshelves of Washington Republicans.

Howard Roark, the main character in the *Fountainhead*, is an architect modelled on Frank Lloyd Wright: a man of high standards, a big ego, with unquestioned confidence in his own ideas. The movie starred Gary Cooper. Roark was a male Margaret Thatcher. He was the Marlboro Man, the rugged individualist. Roark speaks of the nature of man as fundamentally selfish. This worldview from the 1950s–1960s fuels the Tea Party today.

Certainly, humans are capable of being selfish, as Rand's characters show, but we are also capable of loving and doing good. I see human nature as not as fundamentally competitive, as Rand and the neoconservatives would have us believe: our biology demands cooperation simply to survive. Research in the social sciences is showing that we are biologically wired to care. Look at our offspring: without adult care, our children would not survive. Rand is less remembered for her advocacy of free love. I suspect if her Tea Party followers were aware of that, they might have a problem.

Before Greenspan retired, he visited Adam Smith's hometown of Kirkcaldy, in eastern Scotland, to deliver the Adam Smith Memorial Lecture, on February 6, 2005.[105] The speech is remarkably articulate, given that Greenspan prided himself on being incomprehensible. He acknowledged Smith's work in ethics, which recognized that our human capacity for sympathy was a major reason why society worked. Greenspan mentioned Say's Law and its prediction of a self-stabilizing economy: a bizarre comment, because it was wrong. Nonetheless, his pro-free-market speech, supporting a system where the banks exist without constraint, was right on target.

Greenspan was revered as a near saint for steering the US economy through the dullness of the 1980s–1990s, to the boom of the 2000s. Like Teflon, no criticism stuck to him. His motives were never questioned. In 2006, he announced that the Fed would end the long-established practice of reporting on the M3, a measure of the amount of money in the economy. Why did he do that? When

---

105   http://www.federalreserve.gov/boarddocs/speeches/2005/20050206/

the Fed no longer produced the M3, others picked up the ball to emulate it and reported that there was a huge drop in the money supply in the two years that followed. It was as if Greenspan knew the drop in the amount of money was coming.

It was Greenspan who created the increase in housing prices, the housing bubble, by making cheap loans available. Bubbles by nature are unstable, unsustainable, and bubbles pop.

After he was replaced by Bernanke, Greenspan almost apologized for the massive failure he set up. I say *almost* apologized because, while it was clear that the housing bubble and subprime loan crisis were his fault, in Greenspan's mind, he was not responsible. Instead, as he explained at a hearing in Washington in October 2008, where the participants were trying to uncover the causes of the world's second greatest depression, the meltdown was not a result of his decisions, but his "models were at fault!" He took no personal responsibility. Millions had lost their wealth and savings. He came somewhat closer to a confession later, when he said that, despite the fact the world thought he walked on water, "… I was wrong 30% of the time."

Ben Bernanke, his successor, had been a member of the Federal Reserve Board following six years as a professor of economics. He has a Bachelor of Arts from Harvard and a Doctorate in Economics from MIT. He was known for the Bernanke Doctrine, which claimed that business cycles were a thing of the past. How foolish was that? His theory didn't survive 2008, and Bernanke lasted only until 2014, when he was replaced by Janet Yellen, another insider.

Greg Palast, Investigative Reporter, trained by Milton Friedman (1952)

Greg Palast calls himself a reporting investigator and forensic economist. In Chapter Five, I discussed his work on the Exxon Valdez shipwreck. He lives in New York, but his writing is seldom seen in North American media—it's too controversial. He can frequently be heard in England on the BBC or read in *The Guardian* newspaper. Occasionally, he's been published in *Rolling Stone*.

At the early age of 13, Greg was already attending civil rights demonstrations. And in 1970, when he was 18, he was arrested at a Vietnam War protest.

"Before I finished high school, I talked my way into college. Before I finished college, I talked my way into graduate school." After a brief stint at San Fernando Valley State College, Palast transferred to the University of California and then UC–Berkeley.

At Berkeley, Palast met a member of the radical political group called the Weathermen, who encouraged him to familiarize himself with right-wing politics and learn about the "ruling elite" from the inside. So he applied to the University of Chicago, where he studied economics and earned a BA in 1974 and an MBA in 1976.[106]

One of his professors was Milton Friedman, and there Palast learned of the Chicago School economics and the "Chicago boys." As Galbraith had gone into the sheep's pen (so to speak) to study under Keynes in Cambridge, Palast had gone into the lion's den to study under Friedman in Chicago.

---

106 http://www.gregpalast.com/wp-content/uploads/GregPalast-Bio.pdf

After graduation, instead of following the path to corporate economics, he instead went to work for the United Steelworkers. From there, he went to the Enron Workers Coalition and then to environmental groups. He also started writing for Britain's *Observer* and *Guardian* newspapers. As his reputation grew, so too, did the number of "confidential" documents that seemed to get dropped on his desk. He's published a couple of books and won six Project Censored Awards.[107]

More recently, Palast has written about Venezuela, where the socialist Hugo Chávez, elected in 1999, led the country until his death in 2013.

> First, US operatives would monkey with voter registrations—and if that didn't steal the election from Chávez' party, the next step was to provoke riots against Chávez' elections "theft". The riots would lead to deaths—the deaths would be the excuse for the US to back another coup d'état to "restore order" and "democracy" in Venezuela— and restore Venezuela's oil to Exxon. (Chávez had seized majority control of the oil fields and Exxon was furious.)[108]

Chavez died of natural causes and was replaced by a socialist, ex-union president Nicolas Maduro. In February 2015, Venezuelan

---

107 In 1976, Dr. Carl Jensen founded Project Censored at Sonoma State University as a media research program with a focus on student development of media literacy and critical thinking skills as applied to the news media censorship in the US.

108 Palast, Greg. *Did Chavez' Pick Steal the Election in Venezuela?* April 23, 2013.

television reported a failed coup to overthrow him, and in March, the US declared his Venezuelan government a threat to US security. Low oil prices, which are dire for the Venezuelan and for the Russian economies, were probably a managed event, and Venezuela became possibly the most chaotic economy in the world. War by other means.

Palast explained that corporations don't die but have the ability to stall issues forever, pocketing immense savings in doing so.

In 2013, he wrote that "… a little birdie dropped the End Game memo through my window, its content was so explosive, so sick and plain evil, I just couldn't believe it." The original memo, dated November 24, 1997, was sent by Tim Geithner, assistant secretary for International Affairs, Larry Summers,[109] a senior Treasury Department official during Bill Clinton's tenure as president. It advised him to contact the heads of the five major financial firms on the "end game" of discussions on banking regulation at the World Trade Organization. The "end game" was to have an addendum added to the WTO financial service agreement to eliminate control of banking, globally! Every nation except Brazil went along. For that act of defiance, Brazil thrived during the years 2007–2009, when the Western world crashed. It was the End Game memo that led to the 1999 repeal of the Glass Steagall act, which in turn led to the 2007 crash.

Early in 2014, Palast had quadruple by-pass surgery and, as he recovered, he took on a new assignment, writing for *Al Jazeera*, a news source that has steadily gained world attention.

---

109   At one time, Obama's Chief Economic Advisor and nephew of Paul Samuelson.

Launched in 1996 with a loan from the Emir of Qatar, *Al Jazeera* has earned multiple awards for fairness in journalism, though it's been demonized in the West. It's rumoured that George Bush wanted to bomb their offices, but Hillary Clinton was quoted in March 2011, that "… viewership of Al Jazeera is going up in the United States because it is real news … you feel like you're getting real news around the clock instead of a million commercials." The not-for-profit *Guardian* newspaper, and the state-owned *Al Jazeera*, have filled the void traditional media left in America.

Al Jazeera won two Peabody Awards for excellence and relevance in 2013, for two of their TV documentaries aired on a program called *Fault Lines*. The first was on the outbreak of cholera in Haiti after the 2010 earthquake, reporting that it was a near certainty that UN rescue workers were the source of the cholera. The other story revealed that businesses in Bangladesh regularly turned a blind eye to dangers that put workers at risk. Both documentaries were praised as "aggressive journalism."

Al Jazeera is headquartered in Doha, the capital of Qatar, a small country that sticks out like a small thumb on the east side of Saudi Arabia, in the Persian Gulf. Part of the British Empire until 1971, now there are two million people living there, ruled by Sheikh Tamim bin Hamad bin Khalifa Al Thani, who succeeded his father in 2013. There are no political parties, no democracy.

This tiny country has the world's third-largest natural gas reserves, plus billions of barrels of oil, and consequently is, per capita, the world's richest country. The oil company is owned by the state. *Al Jazeera* is funded by the state!

Managing essential services

In 2003, Greg Palast co-authored *Democracy and Regulation: How the Public Can Govern Essential Services*, with Theo MacGregor and Jerrold Oppenheim, for the International Labour Office of the United Nations, in Geneva. Their mission was to explain how the provision of water, electricity, gas, telephone, and sewers can be controlled. The world is filled with horror stories about how privatization of these services has failed.

Essential services are those a society must have: water and sewers, and fire and police protection. Included could be electricity, hospitals, telephones, pensions, air traffic controllers, border agents, and more, and these are often mentioned as areas for possible privatization by the World Bank and the neocons.

Their study pointed out some little-recognized facts!

> America has the toughest, strictest, most elaborate system for regulating private utility corporations found anywhere in the world (with the possible exception of Canada). This may come as a surprise. America, after all has sent out an army of consultants to every corner of the Earth to extol the virtues of deregulation, free markets and less government ...

> In the land of free enterprise, a century of practical experience has led Americans to adopt as faith the idea that public services—especially those owned by stockholder corporations—are unique monopolies which the government and public, not markets, must tightly control ...

> In America there are no secret meetings, no secret documents. Any and all citizens and groups are invited to take part … It is an extraordinary exercise in democracy—and it works.

And consequently, "Americans pay astonishingly little for high-quality public services, yet low prices do not suppress wages. American utility workers are the nation's industrial elite, with a higher concentration of union membership than in any other private industry."

Their study looked in detail at a few failures: the California experiment with open pricing, and the experience with Enron and the brown-outs that followed.

The study also examines policies in other nations. They looked at the 1997 sale by the Brazilian government of Rio de Janiero-based Light SA to foreign investors. The new owners cut staff by 40%, resulting in almost daily blackouts. They increased prices by 400%, and while service plummeted, share price and dividends soared. Privatization in Peru was followed by 3,000% price increases. Privatization of water in Britain led to a 58% increase in water prices.

The three authors' research revealed that unregulated free enterprise is neither more efficient than publicly owned utilities, nor does it serve the public interest. What conservative economists have opposed and called "overregulated industries" abroad are heavily regulated in the US, and deliver better value than unregulated private companies everywhere else in the world. Regulation works, not the free market crapshoot.

Obviously, some businesses do not lend themselves to the competitive model. It's not practical to have two electrical grids, nor two water or two sewage systems. Capital investment is high. Properly done, the investment lasts longer than a lifetime. Electricity can't be stored, and when it's needed, price is a low barrier to sales. Utilities serve local markets with fixed local infrastructure and monopoly is the natural consequence. With appropriate regulation, monopoly can work effectively. The same could be argued for the banks.

Government budgets as family budgets

> Living within our means: Like any Australian family or business, the Government is focused on keeping expenses down to balance the Budget and pay down debt.
> —Australian Government Budget; 2016–2017

We have all heard the refrain the Australian budget quotation above reinforces, that "a government is like a family and just like the rest of us, it needs to balance its budget," but there's one problem—it's not true. Technically, it's a fallacy of composition, because it assumes that a government and a family are identical. "Hokum" is what the *Guardian* calls it. The *Guardian* also explains the reason so many believe it is because of our financial ignorance. Let's look at how the two budgets differ and differ enormously:

1. People die – governments don't
2. People cannot print money – governments can
3. People (or families) have no responsibility for the economic health of the nation – governments do

Individuals are born with no debt. With the purchase of a house, car, furniture, and/or the expenses of family, that changes. By contrast, nations can be in debt for lifetimes: the US has been in debt since 1776.

The game plan for most individuals is to build wealth and decrease debt to, hopefully, have enough assets for comfortable retirement, and possibly even leave some inheritances for families. Debt remaining when the person dies expires. Government debt lives on until it's paid.

The reality is that we should pay for our homes in the decades we live in them. Governments are able to pay for museums and bridges over much longer periods. Time horizons are enormously different.

Families don't have any responsibility for the nation's money. Nations need to ensure that money is printed at a rate necessary to keep the economy working. Nations can even print money to pay off debt. Homeowners can only dream of doing so! Even if a nation has debt so huge it can never be repaid, a nation's money can still have value. (That's somewhat illogical, but true.)

When a recession comes, the biggest danger to a family is that someone will be laid off. If that happens, family income will drop, and the family will have to cut back on expenses. When recession comes, it is inevitable that expenses will go up! Recessions bring layoffs, and with them, unemployment insurance payouts go up. In addition, income tax revenue goes down. Any attempt to stop unemployment payments during the recession will make the situation worse, as will any attempt to increase taxes. So how does a nation pay out increased unemployment insurance payments with less tax revenue?

Keynes would compare it to writing an IOU to yourself—borrowing money from the savings jar and replacing it with an IOU when times are bad, and money is needed, and paying it back when times get good. Because a family is not like a nation, they have different responsibilities. When families need to tighten their belts, nations need to loosen theirs.

The better parallel for a government budget is not to a family, but to a business. In a family, you hope to build worth, decrease debt, and have net worth towards the end of life, but a business is structured to survive forever. It has no end game, no need to retire and, just as the government, can outlast mortals.

If the nation had not borrowed to build schools, bridges, sewage plants, stop Hitler, and build highways, how could we have coped? How would we know what was on the moon? When properly done, a nation can borrow and spend to create a richer nation. A family never has that duty.

What is often behind using the family/government budget analogy is the simple desire to have government spend less. To confuse family budgeting with national budgeting is simply wrong—as wrong as confusing family and business budgeting. Business leverages itself to grow—to take on ever-increasing debt as the enterprise produces ever-increasing profit. Business, even a family-owned business, has vastly different budget priorities.

Business in the Voodoo Era

> Annual income twenty pounds, annual expenditure nineteen [pounds] nineteen [shillings] and six [pence], result

happiness. Annual income twenty pounds, annual expenditure twenty pounds ought and six, result misery."
—Charles Dickens; *David Copperfield*

As I noted in Chapter Four, the breakup of AT&T created opportunities. One was for me. In 1987, I was recruited to join a new telecommunications firm owned by a friend of mine, Don Fergusson. He was my age, and I saw him as an entrepreneur. Later, I would learn, he had been lucky!

While at university in the late 1950s, he'd gotten the job of selling blotters for the student council. (Blotters, for those too young to remember, were desk-sized pads of absorbent paper for "blotting" wet ink from fountain pens. Most office workers used them. Blotters often had advertising around their edges.) The student council needed to sell the advertising around the edge, then sell the blotters. Banks, beer, cigarette, and car companies wanted to market to students and new graduates, so sales were easy. Don volunteered. He soon realized that, with the same effort, he could sell the advertising for all the blotters at universities across Canada. So he did.

And then he did the same with university football programs: first across Canada, and then across the United States. As his business grew, his younger brother came to help. Eventually, they sold the company for millions. Although Don never told me who he sold his business to, he did tell me about one offer. A guy with a dark suit, a raspy voice, and a briefcase came to his office. He opened the briefcase, pulled out a bottle of whiskey and two glasses, "Mister Foigusson," he rasped, "we need to talk!" He wanted to buy the business; price was not a concern. Don's business took in lots of money in an afternoon and legally put it in the bank. Profits from crime could top up the deposit—it was perfect for money laundering.

Don and his brother/partner used the money from selling that business to invest in a small telecommunications venture in Calgary. Telephone deregulation was opening up opportunities, and they saw them. Don was a delightfully honest, cheerleader investor willing to work. His brother wanted to make deals. It was my first exposure to that mentality. It soon became apparent that the brother viewed us newly-hired operational managers with near contempt. "You've never done a deal!" That attitude became a fatal problem when they couldn't fix operational problems.

They had purchased a pay phone manufacturing business in Alabama, and half a dozen smaller companies across the United States when I was joining the business. My job quickly became trouble-shooting, and one of the troubles was accounting. We thought we were making money, a lot of it, but we had no cash. I discovered that our inventory was overstated by $10 million, which was about the value of the business. Obviously, the implications were huge.

To get more cash, a bank loan of millions was needed. Don asked if I would shepherd various bankers around and I met about a dozen of them. Half a dozen banks were out for the deal: a loan, especially one in the millions, is a banker's "big deal." Not one banker asked a sensible question! One bank provided the loan, and within a couple of years, the money was gone, forever. The winning bank lost. Years later, I met one of the winning bankers in an airport, and we were sharing stories. He hadn't learned much! He blamed the client, not his process, for their loss.

8. Voodoo Economics

I was to meet more deal makers as years passed. One was a very young student at a local high school I met at a "meet a business guy" program for the kids, where I had volunteered. I asked the students what they would like to learn. Predictable requests followed. However, one cocky young guy piped up, "I want to learn how to make a billion dollars! Not a million but a billion!" He was a dealmaker in training.

I couldn't help him, but I asked if he knew how big a million is and how much larger a billion? I explained, "Think of money as time: a million dollars as a million seconds, which is about 12 days, 11.57 days to be precise. A billion seconds is 32 years!"

In the next chapter, I'll look at the way the role of government has changed and in Chapter Ten, I'll talk about corporate control of the state, and the consequences that come with it.

9.
The subservient role of governments

> There is no question that this is a time when corporations have taken over the basic process of governing.
> —John Kenneth Galbraith[110]

WHEN ELECTED WORLD LEADERS MEET TO DISCUSS TRADE, patents, banking, and other items from the corporate agenda, it's because corporations have overridden the role of government. Important social issues such as peace, security, survival, the environment, and culture are ignored. That is the subject of this chapter, and it begins with thoughts from my favourite economist.

As decades passed, John Kenneth Galbraith's writing ability never left him, but he became more forgiving. Perhaps it was his

---

110 Galbraith, J.K. (2006) quoted by Richard Parker, Galbraith's biographer, in PBS NewsHour interview. 2006.

comfortable, tenured life as a Harvard professor, or perhaps it was just time that made him mellow. He published his last book, *The Economics of Innocent Fraud* in 2004, when he was 96. The *Economist* newspaper proclaimed, "Galbraith returns to the battle lines." He returned, to the extent he was as aware as ever as to how the economy was changing; however, he didn't, as he once did, point a finger.

Corporate fraud today is commonplace, and Galbraith had warned us, decades ago, to be wary. The older and gentler Galbraith now called corporate fraud "innocent"! With what we have learned about Wall Street, he was too kind. Financial corruption has been self-serving, planned, devious, and vicious.

Galbraith noted that the way the term "capitalism" had been replaced with the more innocuous-sounding "market system" was fraudulent, weakening the image that it was capitalists/the wealthy who controlled the market. He claimed it was fraud to rely on the Gross National Product as a measure of progress, since it failed to account for education, health, literature, and many other important parts of life. He believed it was fraud to retain the myth that shareholders controlled corporations when corporate bureaucracies had long since taken control. The justifications for huge corporate salaries he saw as fraud because no one is worth the money corporate leaders were paying themselves. And it was fraud the way the Federal Reserve pretended to manage the economy through interest rates. It's easy to see that much of the fraud he mentions was, and remains, too self-serving to be innocent.

He died in 2006 at age 97. Fortunately, he had a son who picked up where dad left off.

James K. Galbraith (1952)

> American capitalism is neither benign competition, nor class struggle, nor an inclusive middle-class utopia. Instead, predation has become the dominant feature — a system wherein the rich have come to feast on decaying systems built for the middle class.[111]

James Galbraith is John Kenneth and Catherine's youngest son, an economist at the University of Texas. The quote above is from his 2008 book, *The Predator State*. Like his father, he chooses his titles well. His father's book, *The New Industrial State*, summarized in the title how industry was changing economics to put corporate needs ahead of the people's. James warns in his title that it's government, "the State," that's become a predator we need to fear. He explains that the state is now the servant of corporations. As a consequence, the corporate-controlled state has become, "… a system wherein the rich have come to feast on decaying systems built for the middle class."

One feature of capitalism, he explains, is how periods of economic stability create instability! The logic is simple. In good times, banks and others feel confident and lend (or borrow) money. As good times continue, they take on projects of steadily increasing risk. With every increase in risk, the collapse gets closer. Instability is an inescapable component of uncontrolled free markets.

---

111   Galbraith, James. http://www.motherjones.com/politics/2006/05/predator-state

James got a bachelor's degree at Harvard and then went to Yale for both a masters and PhD in economics. In the mid-1970s, he chose to then go to Cambridge in England, as his father had done, to do a year of postgrad work. After that, again as his father had done, he spent several years working in government as executive director of Congress' Joint Economic Committee. One of his tasks was to prepare hearings on monetary policy. From there, he went to teach at the University of Texas, where he remains.

In 1979, the Federal Reserve tried to manage the economy with short-term monetary targets, and the result was, as James called it, "a cascading disaster," with interest rates soaring to 20%, and 11% unemployment, recession and many industry closures. The Fed policy also threw much of the Developing World into crisis and Mexico faced default. (I recall not being able to afford a mortgage at the time; those high rates spread to Canada as well, so did the recession!) That period is referred to as the Monetarist Recession of 1981–82. It illustrates how much the subject of economics matters; how wrong people can be and how wrong assumptions can affect everyone.

In March 2008, James Galbraith was invited to give the Milton Friedman Distinguished Lecture at Marietta College in Ohio. He began by stating he was there to "… bury Friedman, not to praise him,"[112] and this he proceeded to do. His lecture focused on the collapse of monetarism, which occurred in August 1982, when the Fed dumped the Friedman policy of monetary targeting.

---

112 http://utip.gov.utexas.edu/papers/CollapseofMonetarism delivered.pdf

It took twenty-two years for Friedman to admit that he had been wrong. In 2003, in the *Financial Times*, in an apology as vague as Greenspan's had been, Friedman explained, "… the use of the quantity of money as a target has not been a success. I'm not sure I would, as of today, push it as hard as I once did." The word "sorry" didn't come up.

Monetarism may be dead, but it is not buried. When news of small changes in the bank lending rate are reported, it implies that it's important: that's a monetarist assumption. We hear much about "staying the course" and "being disciplined" in the fight against inflation, although inflation has not been an issue for decades. There have been hundreds of anguished reports about the "struggling manufacturing sector," but almost no reports explaining why this sector is struggling.

James Galbraith writes about the relationship between economic instability and the decline of the working class. The decline of the working class is the direct result of actions such as moving jobs offshore, which serve to concentrate wealth at the top. James Galbraith points out it doesn't have to be that way. Countries, such as Sweden, have freedom and prosperity, combined with greater equality and more economic stability.

Instead, in America, the state became increasingly pitted against the people, with cutbacks in social services, pensions, job security, and union rights.

One of the first campaigns against the people was Nixon's "War On Drugs," in 1971. That was an attack that produced multiple effects. It disproportionately targeted blacks, resulting in the loss of their right to vote (usually Democratic). It also led to an explosive growth of prisons, and expanded the role of the police. When the "war" was declared, there were about 400,000 people in American jails, which was about 100 per 100,000 people. The chart below shows the effect.

Forty years later, in 2011, there were 2.2 million people in jail, or 743 per 100,000 of population: five times the world average of about 150 per 100,000. Not only were there more prisoners per capita, but people were also kept in jail longer than in any other nation on earth. In the US, there are now more prisoners than farmers!

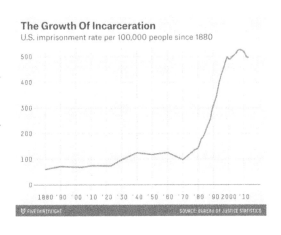

About 10 percent of those prisoners are housed in institutions run for profit. These for-profit institutions have no incentive to rehabilitate—worse, they have incentive *not* to rehabilitate—keeping prisoners longer maximizes revenue. To insure and expand their profits, the Corrections Corporation of America spends about $1 million dollars a year on lobbying Congress.

James Galbraith's more recent book, *The End of Normal*,[113] is not an optimistic book. He writes that so many of the essential assumptions of economics have been altered that the system has no direction. Any sense of what we believe to be normal, is gone! Nothing is normal. Changes have occurred to protect corporate-finance

---

113 Galbraith, James. T*he End of Normal: The Great Crisis and the Future of Growth*. Simon & Schuster, 2014.

capitalism and military capitalism, while the people have become unprotected. His ideas are being ignored in America, while, at the same time, he has been asked for advice from abroad: the government of Greece asked for ways to recover from nearly a decade of bad policies which stole hope from the young and pensions from the old. (I'll talk more about Greece in the next chapter.)

He anticipates, at best, slower growth, and sees that we are living through the end of the American Era. He sees it as underway both financially and militarily, but this can lead to less military spending and more social spending.

The World Bank and the International Monetary Fund

In Chapter Five, I discussed The World Bank, and the International Monetary Fund, together with the agreement from Bretton Woods, signed in July 1944, when the whole of the Western world agreed to monetary and economic rules to govern the world's financial affairs. That meeting, shortly before the end of WW II, set the stage for economic assumptions that would be made for decades to come.

There were other steps taken that we need to think about.

The International Bank for Reconstruction and Development (which became the World Bank) was created with the mission to reduce poverty—at which they failed. As well, the International Monetary Fund (IMF), with the mission to facilitate the international flow of money, was created. That worked. Three years later, the General Agreement on Tariffs and Trade, known as GATT, was agreed to and in 1995 it became the World Trade Organization.

9. The subservient role of governments

By agreement, the president of the World Bank would be appointed by the president of the United States and serve for five years, as the United States was the largest shareholder of the bank with 16% of the shares. (The twelve World Bank presidents have been male and American citizens.) The head of the IMF is called the managing director, and by agreement comes from Europe. Both organizations are headquartered in Washington, a hint as to whom they serve.

The expressed intent for these institutions was to protect and grow trade, banking, and the global capitalist system. At the 1944 Bretton Woods meeting, which stretched over three weeks, John Maynard Keynes was actively involved. He represented the United Kingdom but unfortunately, he was not listened to. He and the British delegation argued for a new world bank and a new global currency, to be called the Bancor, that would be used to balance national trade accounts as fairly as possible. The American delegation was opposed to them. Instead of this new currency, the American dollar was adopted as the International Reserve currency, with the major purpose of serving American needs. Keynes' suggestions would have provided currency stability and economic growth everywhere. Instead, with the new agreement, the poor got poorer, the wealthy got wealthier, and the stage was set for the 2008 collapse. At the time, the editor of the *Economist Magazine* stated, "… the world will bitterly regret the fact that … [Keynes'] … arguments were not followed."

(I have to digress here … *The Economist* is a weekly business publication that's standard reading in executive offices. More accurately, it's standard coffee table display in executive offices because the issues come too often and are too numbingly long to be read—especially too long to read if you have work to do. The magazine's name suggests academic neutrality but that's misleading. It sells about a million and a half copies every week, mainly in America, although it's London-based. The writers and editors keep their biases just below the radar. One critic describes their writing as a genteel version of Ayn Randism. When you've read a few issues, you begin to see the pro-global, pro-corporate, and pro free trade bias. There's a reason for that: the Rothschilds are major shareholders and Evelyn Rothschild was chair of the magazine for seventeen years, from 1972–1989. Lady Lynn Forester de Rothschild, who married Sir Evelyn and is chief executive of a Rothschild holding company, is now on the board. She was introduced to Sir Evelyn by Henry Kissinger at a Bilderberg meeting in 1998.)

The World Bank and the International Monetary Fund employ a lot of people: 9,000 in the World Bank and 2,500 at the IMF, and increasing numbers of them have become whistleblowers, insiders speaking out against the policies of their employers. Increasingly, too, when these organizations meet, there are protestors—no longer just the young idealists of a few decades ago, but increasingly white-haired.

One of the first to blow the whistle on the International Monetary Fund was Davison Budhoo,[114] a senior economist who, in May 1988, after twelve years with the organization, wrote an angry open letter of resignation. The Grenadian graduate of the London School of Economics wrote, "… there is not enough soap in the world to cleanse me from the things that I did." In fourteen pages (and a second, equally long note filled with details), he

---

114   http://www.naomiklein.org/files/resources/pdfs/budhoo.pdf

relates things that were done, especially in or to Trinidad-Tobago, an island country next to Grenada. Things he felt were wrong. He disapproved of the perks provided to those like himself, supposedly on a mission to help the poor: first class travel, allowances for maids and for nightclub entertainment. He felt he was guilty because he accepted pay "from five to ten times the budgeted salary of almost every Third World head of state." He disapproved of the internal secrecy and censorship, at the manipulation of data to fit preconceived assumptions, and to the lies that the organization told. In an interview he said, the IMF policies are "… geared to benefit the elite and to punish the poor."

Joseph Stiglitz, another economist, became a whistleblower. Born in Gary, Indiana (Paul Samuelson's hometown), he studied economics at the University of Chicago just prior to "the Chicago boys," and then at MIT, where he got a doctorate. He served as chief economist of the World Bank from 1997 to 2000, and, to his credit, was fired for speaking out against their policies. He wrote *Globalization and Its Discontents* (2001), examining the policies of the World Bank, the IMF, and the World Trade Organization and what they did to, not for, the poor. He criticized the World Bank policy assumptions, such as how low wages help the people, how money would trickle down, and other bits of failed free market thinking.

More recently, in 2013, Karen Hudes joined the whistleblowers. She's a lawyer, a graduate of Yale and an economist who left Wall Street in 1986 to work in the Legal Department of the World Bank. She did post-graduate studies in Economics at the University of Amsterdam. After twenty-one years at the World Bank, she was promoted, and part of her job as Senior Counsel was to report corruption if she found it. She found that the bank failed to follow standard auditing procedure in the corrupt takeover of the second largest bank in the Philippines. Included were securities fraud and the improper termination of staff lawyers.

In 2007, following the bank's internal procedure, she was attempting to move her report on corruption up the corporate ladder, but no one wanted to know. As per their policy, she escalated her complaints to the president of the bank, and was fired. The issue then was no longer just the corruption she uncovered, but the bigger issue of the cover up.

The World Bank and the IMF were creatures of the Bretton Woods agreement that, as I mentioned, Keynes did not agree with it because he felt we were giving too much to the Western world and its banks. We did, and the banks cashed in.

Shock Doctrine

Winston Churchill is rumoured to be the first person to declare that you should never let a crisis go to waste! Friedman himself wrote, "Only a crisis — actual or perceived — produces real change." More recently, in 2010, Rahm Emanuel, Obama's chief of staff, said the same thing. "You never let a serious crisis go to waste. And what I mean by that is it's an opportunity to do things you think you could not do before."

In her book, *The Shock Doctrine: The Rise of Disaster Capitalism* (2007), Canadian journalist Naomi Klein argues that many globalization practices are easier to introduce in times of disaster.

Klein, whose work appears in *The Guardian*, documents the way corporations use the social trauma of disaster and the distraction that accompanies critical events, to their advantage. Apparently, tsunamis create cheap beachfront property for corporate hotels. Natural disasters, economic meltdowns, social disturbance, and questionable elections all create opportunity for someone to get their way. Klein quotes Republican Congressman Richard Baker, telling lobbyists after the 2005 hurricane, "We finally cleaned up public housing in New Orleans. We couldn't do it but God did."

Klein was 37 when she published *Shock Doctrine*. She's the Montreal-born daughter of two war-resisting hippies who moved to Canada during the Vietnam War. She astonished me with her ability to get insider information and interviews that seemed so improbable. I later learned that her father-in-law is Stephen Lewis, the former leader of the socialist New Democratic Party in Ontario for some years. He served as Canada's Ambassador to the United Nations, followed by five years as the United Nations Special Envoy for HIV/AIDS in Africa. He has a wonderful international reputation, is well respected, well connected, and one of the world's most eloquent speakers. He may have been some help! Klein writes about the way tsunami victims in Sri Lanka and hurricane victims in New Orleans lost their homes and their land to the economic shock treatment of corporate makeovers.

One of the gurus of using shock to change society was Milton Friedman. When he was 93, long after he had acknowledged the failure of his economics but still had still not learned enough to be humble, he wrote an article for *The New York Times*. He saw that the tragedy of the hurricane that destroyed New Orleans schools could be used as an opportunity to also destroy the school system. Within two years, it was gone, most of the teachers gone, their union gone, replaced by private schools and more poorly paid teachers. New Orleans did to itself what Friedman's students had done to Chile.

Economic disaster occurred when the Russian Federation imploded in 1991. Just prior to that, Professor Stanislav Menshikov, possibly Russia's top economist, and John Kenneth Galbraith, had gotten together to study the Russian economy. Neither of them saw the implosion coming. Two years later, Russia had 17 billionaires. There had been none before. Almost forty years after Stalin, the Russian system imploded and without rules or regulation, a new market economy emerged. Global corporations happily jumped into the Russian feeding frenzy.

The earthquake in Nepal in 2015 might have prompted the world to offer debt relief, since the poor country owed about $3.8 billion to foreign lenders. With a population of 26 million, smaller than Canada yet Nepal must send $220 million dollars a year out of the country to foreign lenders. Rather than do the decent thing and provide debt relief because of the earthquake, the IMF, as I predicted, lent them another $50 million.

Blame the victim

In 1971, the year busing was approved in the US, sociologist William Ryan wrote *Blaming the Victim* which became one of the bestselling academic books of all time. His phrase, "blame the victim," stuck. He defined the phenomenon as "justifying inequality by finding defects in the victims of inequality." Black poverty was being wrongly blamed on black culture when the actual problem was in the discriminatory social system. Blaming the victim is an old tactic.

> ... unemployment is regularly blamed on the workers. A standard response to higher unemployment figures is the call for better worker training. This is the politically respectable remedy. Education, training ... is not relevant to the cyclical downturns that are here discussed. When depression or recession comes, both the trained and the untrained, the educated and the ignorant are affected. Of this there should be no doubt. A call for better-prepared workers as the remedy for recession-induced unemployment is the last resort of the vacant liberal mind.
> —John Kenneth Galbraith [115]

Herman Cain, a Tea Party activist, was hoping to be the Republican Candidate in the 2012 presidential election. He was an entertaining orator whom I heard in Texas a few years before his campaign. A successful business guy, he was incredibly uninformed on economics. He told the Occupy Wall Streeters, "Don't blame the big banks if you don't have a job and you're not rich, blame yourself." He explained there were 3.1 million job openings in the nation, so if they were not working, it was their own fault. The 14 million people looking for work were not impressed.

Cain, like so many rich people, was unaware that capitalism creates cycles, which create unemployment. He, like so many others, wrongly and unkindly characterized victims of that cycle as lazy. He didn't know that it's the forced unemployment of workers at the bottom that allows the system to work for those at the top.

---

115   Galbraith, J.K. *The Good Society: The Humane Agenda*. Houghton Mifflin, 1996.

Cain's campaign for president withered when enough women came forward to charge him with sexual impropriety.

Cain, like Brabeck at Nestlé, and most of the Tea Partiers, share the self-assurance that they are the chosen ones, the exceptional few, on the side of right! They shame and filibuster and cheer with their own radio networks, with hosts like Rush Limbaugh, lauding themselves, totally without economic understanding, humility, or justification.

Cooking the books

> Capitalism is the legitimate racket of the ruling class.
> —Al Capone

Data about the economy, from time to time, seems strange. That's because, as you'll see, some of the numbers are skewed. For example, how can we be having a "recovery" when there are no jobs returning? Let's look closer.

After getting his master's degree in economics in 1972, Walter J. (John) Williams began working as a consulting economist. He had a client that manufactured airplanes. To do good manufacturing planning, they developed an econometric model for predicting revenue per passenger mile with formulas that were heavily dependent on the Gross National Product figures produced by the US government. It worked like a dream for years and then, for some reason, his formula stopped working! Without the formula, he would be out of business. Williams needed to know why his formula failed, so he could fix it. He identified that the government's GNP calculation had been altered and so he went back to the way they used to do it, and his formula worked again.

That changed his career! Since 2004, he has provided government statistics as they once were. He calls his new venture Shadow Government Statistics (Shadowstats.com). Why the government would change its parameters is best understood when you see that the government has a bias for certain results. Inflation is one: old age security payments are tied to inflation, so if inflation is understated, old age security payments will be less. If unemployment is understated, then government action to create jobs can be less.

Here are a few examples, as of February 2016:

	US Gov't Figure	Shadow Statistic
Inflation	0.1 %	8%
Unemployment	5%	23%
GDP	2%	-1%

The way unemployment statistics have been skewed is revealing. Decades ago, anyone who didn't have a job was considered unemployed. Now it's only those who have been unemployed for less than a year are counted as unemployed! When that change occurred in 1994, it took almost five million people off the officially unemployed US totals. The rate of inflation is skewed by changing, every two years, the "basket of goods" on which it is based. Today it excludes the price of oil and gasoline. They were dropped as those prices were going up, but the inflation rate, we were told, didn't.

Another skewed number, this one reported by Truth in Accounting, an American nonprofit organization that runs the national debt clock, is that while the US government reports the national debt at $18 trillion, Truth in Accounting reports it about five times larger.

Because their dollars don't go as far today as they used to, Williams says average people have a better sense of the state of the economy than the professionals. We know inflation is more than the "under 2%" as we are told. Ron Cooper, a retired data executive in England who keeps his own data, sent a note to me in January 2015. "I can vouch that living expenses are increasing by 10% per annum, not the inflation of 1.6% that our government states."

Similarly, average people have a better sense of the rate of employment. We can tell whether our neighbours are employed or not, and we know how hard jobs are to find, especially good jobs. We know things are bad when we see more people selling homeless newspapers or sleeping on the street. At the peak of the Depression in 1933, the unemployment rate was just over 20%. In 2014 in the United States, with 2.4 million fewer full-time jobs than before 2007, the real unemployment rate was about 23%, and there had been no real recovery.

Active use of the Gross Domestic Product to define the state of the economy is not new. It was a measure originally defined by Adam Smith. But it became actively used in about the 1930s. Some economists say it's a fuzzy number because it's neither simple to define, nor easy to measure and that most significantly, it doesn't include a significant amount of human output, raising the question of what a product is. Prior to the use of GDP, there was little concept of "the economy"—it was all just business. But as the term became accepted, so did the idea of an "economy," followed by the thought that we could manage it. Russian economist Simon

Kuznets developed the term GDP in a paper for the United States government in 1934, which came with a warning:

> Economic welfare cannot be adequately measured unless the personal distribution of income is known. And no income measurement undertakes to estimate the reverse side of income, that is, the intensity and unpleasantness of effort going into the earning of income. The welfare of a nation can, therefore, scarcely be inferred from a measurement of national income as defined above.[116]

GDP is now well-accepted, yet there is no sense of its limitations. It confuses and sometimes deceives us about the wellbeing of people—ours and others. *The Happy Planet Index* is a more useful measure because it takes the emphasis off the economy and onto more important things. Unfortunately, we seldom hear of it.

We don't expect the government to rig the numbers, nor do we expect misdirection on what's important, but both happen. And there's an even stranger development, as well!

Derivatives

> Derivatives are financial instruments whose value is derived from the value of something else. They generally take the form of contracts under which the parties agree to payments between them based upon the value of an underlying asset

---

116   Kuznets, Simon. *Uses and Abuses of National Income Measurements.* Report to US Congress. 1934.

or other data at a particular point in time. The main types of derivatives are futures, forwards, options and swaps.[117]

The word derivative, prior to its use in financial markets, was used in calculus in relation to calculating rates of change: knowing the velocity and direction, you can derive the time. It is interesting to note in this economics context, that calculus was developed by Isaac Newton, the same Isaac Newton who worked in the Tower of London as Master of the Royal Mint and developed the gold/silver standard.

Before I had ever first heard of derivatives, which was back in the 1990s, the economy was already making less sense to me. What little I understood came to a full stop when we entered the 2000s. I had no understanding of derivatives, credit default swaps, sub-investment grade bonds, hedge funds, or bundled assets! What was neoliberalism? What was neoconservatism? They seemed to be the same thing, but the words appeared opposite!

In June 1994, the J. P. Morgan bank had a retreat at the Boca Raton Resort in Florida. (It was the same hotel mentioned in the introduction where I'd attended a conference decades earlier, but my meeting didn't change the economic world.) The J. P. Morgan people spent part of their time discussing how to make loans less risky. The idea they developed was to separate the risk from the loan. Not just separate the risk, but separate it and sell the "risk of default" in something that would soon be called a "credit default swap." It is enough to make your head spin!

---

117 http://www.hedgefund-index.com/d_derivatives.asp

Separating risk from the loan and selling that risk was an entirely new idea. Bundling risks so they would seem more secure and then selling bundles of them was Step Two. This securitized risk was the basis of financial derivatives and fed a worldwide credit boom.

Swaps were not a new idea. The first had occurred in 1981, when IBM swapped European currencies for US dollars. Nothing changed hands, only the values.

With these new swaps of risk, the potential sales were huge, because there is lots of risk around. The sky seemed to be the limit.

Separating risk from loans is an understandable idea to a lender: for example, if you were making a loan to Exxon for a $4.8 billion credit line, in preparation for the billion-dollar penalties they were expecting from the Exxon Valdes oil spill. As the lender, you want to profit from the loan but prefer not to pay any of the risk, so why not sell that part?

To repeat, a derivative derives its value from something else: something else could be the value of risk, or stocks, bonds, commodities, or currencies. It is a contract between two or more parties, sometimes used to hedge bets against price changes in things.

One of the earliest uses was in farming, when a farmer might agree to sell his crop before it was harvested in order to fix the price. If, when the crop was ready the market price was higher, the farmer lost. But if it were lower, the farmer profited. Financial contracts can be as short as a season or as long as years. Many ordinary people now take out hedging contracts: by signing a contract in the fall for heating oil or gas for the winter, you have hedged your cost.

Hedging risk is not a bad idea, but when the sum of bets that hedge risk is greater than the global economy, something is wrong.

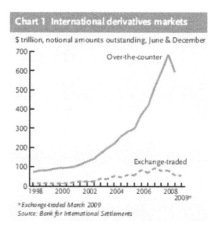

Globally, we produced about $75 trillion US dollars of goods in 2012. In September 2013, according to several news services, the value of the derivative market was over $1 quadrillion! Below, you can see the two numbers:

- $1,000,000,000,000,000. Derivatives
- $ 75,000,000,000,000. Global GDP

The derivative market is almost completely unregulated. US laws actually prohibit its regulation.

One quadrillion dollars is more than fourteen times the value of all things made in the world in a year. It is about 14 times larger than all the money on the earth. Many people make commissions buying or selling these virtual things, things that have no substance. It makes no sense.

The derivatives market does raise lots of questions. For example: how does a market determine the value of arbitrary things? How can a market in arbitrary things be 10 or possibly 20 times larger than the real market? No one has answers. Because the market is unregulated, the market makes it riskier. Warren Buffet's successful investment strategy has been based on the real economy: understandable things that have real value that he calls bricks and mortar. On the other hand, he says:

> Derivatives are financial weapons of mass destruction, carrying dangers that, while now latent, are potentially lethal.
> —Warren Buffet; Annual Report; 2002[118]

Compare Buffet's wariness of derivatives with Alan Greenspan's enthusiasm. Buffet was concerned with protecting his own money, while Greenspan, as chair of the Fed, was promoting bank profits. In the same Boca Raton Hotel where derivatives had been conceived in 1994, Greenspan said, in 1999, "By far the most significant invention in finance during the past decade has been the extraordinary development and expansion of financial derivatives."

London became a major player in the emerging over-the-counter derivative trade. Over-the-counter means done without regulation, and in 2007 it peaked in London at just over $2 trillion a day!

Stocks on the stock market are shares in companies that have the assets of the company behind them. Bonds have the assets of the bond issuer behind them. Derivatives have other derivatives behind them, and the dollar value of all of them is between 7 to 20 times the value of the global economy, which means there is not much behind them.

---

118   http://www.businessinsider.com/warren-buffett-quotes-2011-11?op=1

The German Deutsche Bank reported their exposure to derivatives in their 2012 Annual Report. On the left hand chart below, Bloomberg compared the bank's derivative exposure to the Gross Domestic Product of Germany. German GDP. is the short left-hand column. The total of Deutsche Bank derivatives owned is the enormously tall column. And the chart called Towering Folly shows the global scale of derivatives as compared to the world's gross domestic product; almost twenty times more stuff is traded than is produced.

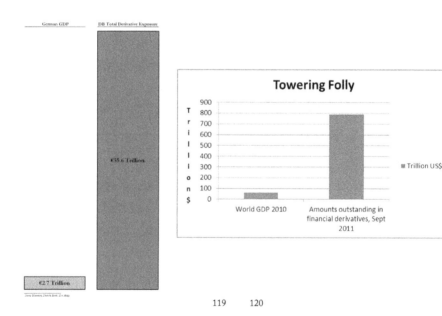

119   120

---

119 http://www.zerohedge.com/news/2013-04-29/728-trillion-presenting-bank-biggest-derivative-exposure-world-hint-not-jpmorgan

120 http://ecopoliticstoday.wordpress.com/2012/02/28/tottering-tower-of-financial-derivatives-dwarfs-world-gdp/

Since the 2007–2008 crisis, derivative trading has gone up by about 20%, despite warnings from many people. Warnings from Warren Buffet, Ellen Brown, Paul Craig Roberts, Bob Chapman, and others, have gone unheeded and the derivative casino balloon keeps inflating. It has even affected the price of food.

Betting on food

> People don't go hungry because there isn't enough food; they go hungry because they can't afford to eat.
> —Amartya Sen, Nobel Prize in Economics, 1998

At the 1996 United Nations World Food Summit the nations of the world agreed that people have the right to food. That was profound. They also took the immense step and committed themselves to cutting in half the number of hungry and malnourished in the world by the year 2015, almost twenty years later. The results were puny. They achieved a 5% reduction, one-tenth of their goal.

The financialization of food has been profitable for businesses. Businesses, as we have learned, don't care if people starve.[121]

A study conducted by Lehman Brothers just before its bankruptcy revealed that the volume of index fund speculation increased by 1,900% between 2003 and March 2008. Morgan Stanley estimated that the number of outstanding contracts in maize futures increased from 500,000 in 2003 to almost 2.5 million in 2008.

---

121 http://www.globalresearch.ca/the-derivative-bubble-speculating-on-food-prices-banking-on-famine/5320379

Holdings in commodity index funds ballooned from US$13 billion in 2003, to US$317 billion by 2008.[122]

Back in 1991, the folks at Goldman Sachs defined food as a commodity and created a new product: a food fund. They bundled a lot of foodstuffs and, pardon the pun, felt they could make a great deal of bread! They began to sell shares in the Goldman Sachs Commodity Index Fund, which included eighteen items like wheat, cattle, corn, coffee, and hogs. As more shares were sold, two things happened: the price of food went up, and more investment firms created their own food indexes.

North America is the major wheat source for the world. For more than a century prior to this one, the price of wheat had steadily declined, but by 2005 that reversed, and the price of wheat began to rise. So too, did the prices of rice, corn, soy, and oats. By 2008, *The Economist* magazine said that food prices were at their highest level ever. Prices had risen 80% since 2005, despite a record harvest in 2008. Cargill Incorporated, the largest US private company in the grain distribution business, had an 86% jump in annual profits.

The reason can be seen in the producer price index chart below.

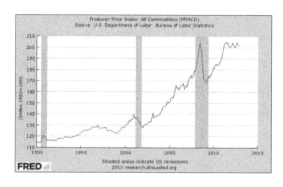

---

122 http://www.motherjones.com/tom-philpott/2011/09/un-wall-street-speculation-fuels-global-hunger

Creating food funds introduced another level of profit between farmers and people, feeding Wall Street at the expense of and before the people. No value was created. The jump in food index profits was matched with the jump in the number of people who could not afford to eat. In one year, that number grew by 250 million. It was a tragedy that we in the West didn't see.

Goldman Sachs made about $400 million betting on food prices in 2012, and that $400 million came from consumers. Estimates are that there are twelve times as many dollars invested in food than there are dollars' worth of seeds in the ground.

The organization Foodwatch published a report in 2011 called *The Hunger Makers: How Deutsche Bank, Goldman Sachs and Other Financial Institutions Are Speculating With Food At the Expense of the Poorest*. It's a good source if you want more information.

Executive bonuses top the menus of the food funds. However, Barclay's bank became an exception! In January 2013, it announced that, for ethical reasons, it would stop speculating in global food.

Food, like water and labour, is different from other marketable commodities. Frederick Kaufman of *Harper's Magazine* is a food journalist and has studied the role of financialization of food. His book *Bet the Farm* explains that we grow enough to feed everyone, yet one billion people are hungry. He explains the role of speculation in driving up the price for wheat to record highs. Speculation changed the laws of supply and demand in setting prices. Because of speculation, we had the anomaly of the highest prices at the same time as the largest crops in history.

The needs of markets differ from the needs of people: markets need profits, people need food. Also, market-driven distribution changes everything. Bigger farms are employing fewer people. This means fewer people who can afford to buy things. Bigger farms require more capital: more dollars to buy more acres and bigger machines, which is good for the banks, but adds more interest to the cost of food. Big farms require gasoline and chemicals. Small farms provide more employment and are more ecologically sustainable. Economist Ted Schmidt, at SUNY University in Buffalo, writes in *The Political Economy of Food and Finance* about the way food has been changed from a life necessity to simply another type of asset.[123]

One final word: government subsidies also distort markets. Many nations provide agricultural subsidies. The United States pays about $20 billion a year to farmers who grow corn, cotton, wheat, rice, and even tobacco. In the US, corn is the most subsidized crop, and most of it's not for food: by law, billions of dollars of corn ethanol must be blended into vehicle fuel, which creates extra demand for corn. These American subsidies resulted in agribusiness driving down the price of Mexican corn and have bankrupted up to 3,000,000 Mexican farmers.

Summary

Corporate dealmakers have learned to use the state to enhance their power. Their successes with global trade agreements, legislation to reduce worker protections, and legislation to reduce taxes for themselves and their owners—the wealthy—are among the dealmakers' achievements.

---

123 Schmidt, Ted. *The Political Economy of Food and Finance*. Routledge: 2015.

To make it easier to pass bills that work against the people, the process has become devious. "Omnibus Legislation" is often used to hide legislation. Bills are presented disguised as one thing, and hidden within these bills are often major changes in other things. Both the US and Canada do it. For example: a United States budget bill for a tax decrease included anti-abortion text. If a representative voted for the tax decrease, he/she was also voting for anti-abortion laws.

When the Canadian Government passed the Omnibus budget bill C45 in 2013, it was about 450 pages long, longer that the traditional 75-page budget bill. In addition to the budget, the bill ended environmental protection for 32,000 lakes, and facilitated unregulated development of oil and gas projects. Omnibus bills are designed to hide things; they are not designed to be read.

Historically, government bills in the United States have averaged about 3,000 words. The Patriot Act was about 90,000. The Affordable Health Care Bill was 314,000 words, on 2,700 pages. By contrast, the Canadian health care system was created in 1984 in an act 23 pages long.

There is no doubt complexity is used to hide things.

The November 2014 meeting of the G20 was in Brisbane, Australia, and many things could have been on the agenda. The world's top leaders could have focused on global poverty, which was getting worse, or the divide between the rich north and poor south, or the unending wars in the Middle East, or religious intolerance, or pollution. Instead, their final report of 21 points summarized what they discussed: economic growth, investment, and supporting trade.

What gives this small group of 20 people from rich nations the right to make decisions on global issues? Why wouldn't that be the responsibility of the United Nations?

Behind closed doors in Brisbane, the twenty people agreed they would grow their economies 2.1% by 2018, and they approved new financial rules to be enforced by the Financial Stability Board (FSB). The decisions seem innocuous, not worth mentioning, unless you read the details.

The FSB had been established at an earlier G20 meeting after the meltdown of 2007–2008, the financial crisis having created an opportunity to further entrench international bank power over nations. The Financial Stability Board is a not-for-profit organization under Swiss law, situated in the Bank for International Settlements in Basel. Their role is to regulate and supervise global financial policies. The Bank for International Settlements (the banker's bank mentioned in Chapter Five) and the International Monetary Fund accept the premise that banks can be "too big to fail," thumbing their noses at the fundamental basis of competitive enterprise theory.

At the Brisbane G20 conference, a resolution was approved changing the global rules of banking, so that money owed by one bank to another has a higher priority for repayment than money the banks hold on deposit for their customers. This means that if the bank where you keep your retirement funds also owes money to Goldman Sachs happens to get into trouble, they must pay Goldman Sachs before you!

The role of the state, which at one time balanced corporate power with worker welfare, has been co-opted to favour capital, the global corporate agenda, and the wealthy. Since Kennedy was killed, some historical researchers have begun referring to actions like his murder as being actions of the "deep state." Retired Republican staff worker, Mike Lofgren, refers to it as a shadow government: unelected and unaccountable. [124]

In the next chapter, I'll discuss how those changes were made and what they mean. Governments are no longer of, or for, or by the people. So, I'll look into the corporate state.

---

124 Lofgren, Michael. *The Deep State*. Penguin, 2016.

10.
The Corporate State

> There is nobody in this country who got rich on their own. Nobody. You built a factory out there—good for you. But I want to be clear. You moved your goods to market on roads the rest of us paid for. You hired workers the rest of us paid to educate. You were safe in your factory because of police forces and fire forces that the rest of us paid for … Keep a hunk of it. But part of the underlying social contract is you take a hunk of that and pay forward for the next kid who comes along.
> —Elizabeth Warren, US Senator, Massachusetts; CBS News interview; August, 2011

WARREN'S PLEA TO ENTREPRENEURS TO PAY THEIR SHARE OF taxes may succeed with some people, but it won't work with most corporations. They feel no guilt. They respect no social contract. And this is how things are.

Of the 100 largest economies in the world, 51 are corporations, 49 are nations. In this structure, corporate capitalism has the money to buy pro-corporate governments to get pro-corporate laws, making one global corporate-controlled playground. Economies that, at one time, were planned for people are now planned by corporations, for corporations.

David Harvey, mentioned earlier, published a short book entitled *A Brief History of Neoliberalism* in 2005. He's a professor of Anthropology at the City University of New York and writes wonderfully well. He traces the history of Western economics from the liberal Keynesianism of the seventies to the neo-liberal economics of Milton Friedman. The term neoliberal came into use in the 1930s in Europe to describe economics that mixed competitive theory with government planning. Then it morphed in meaning in the 1970s and 80s to mean economics that embraced free trade, privatization, deregulation, and austerity—the economics of Thatcher and Reagan. So, if you are confused about what neoliberal is, it's understandable.

Harvey's analysis is not only clear: it has two unique features. It's behavioural and Marxian.

Behavioural because the analysis focuses on what is done, as opposed to what is said. We have been told that free market competition is supposed to benefit everyone, but we have learned that it benefits the 1%. It's the behaviour—what gets done—not what's said that matters.

And, his analysis is Marxian because Harvey sees economics as Marx did, a struggle between workers and capital. As the rich, those with the capital, get richer and the rest of us get poorer, that's hard to argue with. Neoliberal theory postulates that individual freedoms are guaranteed by "the freedom of the market." That's now near gospel in the Western world. However, it's stated with no acknowledgement that this market freedom leads to business cycles, to unemployment, to wealth concentration, and to the elimination of competition.

Harvey summed up the meltdown of 2007. "The irrationality of the system right now is fairly clear. You have masses of capital, and masses of labor unemployed in the midst of a world that is full of social need. How stupid is that?"

His book begins by recounting the years from 1978 to 1980, and the changing economic policies in China. Deng Xiaoping was leader, as China's economy changed from a socialist economy to a socialist market economy, a new type of capitalism.

There are other types of capitalism: free market capitalism (the American model), state capitalism (the Egyptian and Arabic model), heroic capitalism (the name Mussolini used for his fascist capitalism), and welfare capitalism (the Scandinavian or Canadian style). And, occasionally, people have created their own forms: John Cadbury, founder of the chocolate business, was an English Quaker and from the time he started his company (1824) he had a strong commitment to workers' rights and fairness. This included respect for trade unions, providing housing, education, pensions, and sickness insurance for workers.

As China was changing to a socialist market form of capitalism in the East, Margaret Thatcher, Paul Volker, Ronald Reagan, and Milton Friedman were changing the nature of Western capitalism everywhere they could. They assumed that society would benefit most when entrepreneurial spirits were free; a romantic ideal based on free trade and free markets. Political and economic freedoms were equated. What they supposed was the best system for all, as we have seen, concentrated wealth and power in the hands of the few. Before that weakness became apparent, we had heard the new system called "neocon," or neoconservative or neoliberal. All these terms, it turns out, meant the same; as Harvey explained, it meant expanding upper-class power and wealth.

The state was increasingly being used to increase the power of corporations. For example, we were told that "liberalized" banking was good for us, but we've since learned that "liberalize" meant removing controls that, at one time, protected investors. It meant changing the system, which had worked safely for decades, into unregulated profiteering.

A small symptom of these changes was the emergence of the "payday loan," a near-banking product that emerged in the mid-1990s. The predators who sell these products do to poor people what the IMF does to poor nations: get them trapped in debt. Payday loans began with a court case in Minneapolis when the US Supreme Court overturned the US anti-usury law. (The ruling affected many states.) The door was opened to high-interest loans, or "usury," as it was once called, and payday loan stores started popping up in poor areas everywhere in the U.S, Canada, and Britain. Like many shady businesses, they define themselves as an "industry" in an attempt to gain some respectability.

Payday loans are an example of the way laws designed to protect individual people have been eroded. Laws protecting people were lost to corporate power. In the balance of this chapter, I will look broadly at compensation and globalization on the one hand, and the impact on specific people and nations, on the other.

Executive compensation

> The salary of the chief executive of a large corporation is not a market award for achievement. It is frequently in the nature of a warm personal gesture by the individual to himself.
> —John Kenneth Galbraith

Adam Smith wrote about how market competition over time would move towards being fair. If some people were making too much money, others would enter that profession, and the ensuing competition would drive those wages down. If too few were taking on jobs, wages would increase to attract people.

Today, with huge incomes at the top, there are questions that are seldom asked. "How much more should the 'boss' be paid?" And, "Are huge salaries at the top necessary?"

Let's start with "How much more should the 'boss' be paid?"

This is both an economic and an ethical question. How much is a person worth? What is a morally defendable income? If a person is a person, as Dr. Seuss stated, how much wage differential is justifiable? How much is needed to get the best results?

From the 1940s to the 1980s, the average CEO was paid about twenty times the wage of a worker. That ratio worked. It managed to attract capable people to top jobs and created steady economic growth in the economy. For over eighty years, the ratio of twenty to one worked.

Today, that ratio is closer to 296 to one.[125] Before noon on the second working day of a new year, the average CEO will have made as much as his average employee will earn in that year. I say *his* average employee because the probability of it being *her* is slight. Ethically, it's hard to justify paying one person the same amount as 20 others earn. It's impossible to justify compensation for one person to be equal to the annual earnings of 296 workers.

And a related question is, are larger salaries necessary or justifiable? Do larger salaries get better results? The corporate argument is that you have to pay for "talent" and that the "talent" to run a business is hard to come by. The market, they say, determines the prices. This doesn't stand up to scrutiny. Nothing fundamental has changed in management since we had the 20 to 1 ratio. In fact, we have more potential managers now due to of the dozens of business schools graduating thousands of talented young people. More people competing for the jobs should result in reducing wages.

While there is no common-sense explanation for huge wages, there is a historic one. It's summarized by Galbraith in the quote starting this section!

Executive compensation started to soar in the 1990s as the practice grew for publicly traded corporations to establish compensation committees. Corporate boards of directors wanted "objective" compensation policies to cover pay, bonuses, vacations, perks, and stock options. So, they established compensation committees of their boards, and board memberships overlapped. Some on the board of Corporation A sit on the compensation committee

---

125   Washington Brief 380, Economic Policy Institute, June 2014.

of boards B and C. Appreciation for doing this service results in mutually generous compensation policies.

Corporate marketing filled the remaining gap and reinforced the illusion that corporate leaders are a rare "breed" and "worth every penny." However, logic, and quite often the bad results of the rare breed, defy that.

The chart below shows the history of the relationship between the pay at the top, to the pay of workers. As you can see, the ratio of about twenty to one, that worked for decades, and possibly centuries before that, has long been lost.

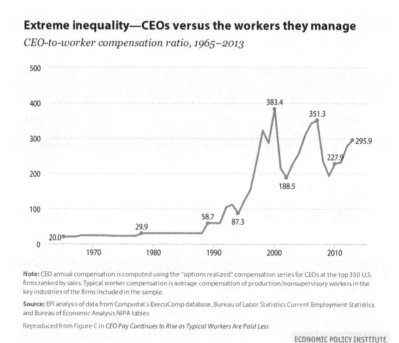

An example of how out of control the system had become occurred in 2013, when hedge fund billionaire Steven A. Cohen was paid $2.3 billion for his efforts.

This raises two questions: "Of what use is a hedge fund? and, "Are the labours of Cohen worth as much as 53,000 people?" The answers are: "Obviously, none," and, "No." What's worse, he had been convicted of insider trading and fined $1.2 billion. After he paid his fine, he was left with over a billion for pocket money.

A social science experiment shows how wrong the premise is that we are driven to be selfish. Two people are asked to decide how to split a sum of money. The proposer suggests a percentage split, and the other can accept or reject the offer. If it's accepted, the two will split the money. If it's rejected, both parties will get nothing. A 50/50 split is an easy decision, but is not always what is proposed. The proposer might ask, "Is 60/40 OK? How about 70/30?" The result of multiple tests of this experiment is that, more often than not, people prefer getting nothing to being treated unfairly. This experiment contradicts the neoconservative view that man is fundamentally selfish but confirms that we are fundamentally fair. More recent research at UCLA by psychology professor Paul Piff has shown that the rich are four times more likely to steal than the rest of us.

For over a decade, there has been a trend in executive compensation to have it "aligned" with corporate goals, and to pay "bonus" compensation accordingly. Does "aligned" income get the desired results? This question is loaded; it depends on what results you are looking for! Corporations exist, as the Disney Corporation memo said, to make money. Companies that were created to make things and serve people, get transformed into just another listing on the stock exchange. Compensation aligned to stock values moves business further from the "real" economy, and further from building traditional value—further from social usefulness, and further from providing useful employment, to becoming just another Wall Street listing.

The trend to pay corporate leaders with stock options focused them on financialization. It makes sense from a Wall Street point of view, but not from the traditional view of building sustainable enterprises. Shorter-term financial goals have replaced creating long-term sustainable value.

Executives were able to justify paying large salaries to themselves because of their belief that the market determines the value of everything. It was "God's work," as the Chairman of Goldman Sachs noted. The ethics were defined as meritocracy, because, "If I get it, I must be worth it."[126]

Escalating executive compensation, as Galbraith Sr. noted in the 1960s, was not market-driven. Compensation aligned with the stock market results in corporations caring less for people. It promotes money to trump everything.

Globalization and free trade

In 2013, to much trendy ado, Canada signed a free trade agreement with the European Union. There was almost no media coverage of the bigger story, which was that every time there is a trade agreement, the rights of corporations increase while the rights of people and nations decrease. These agreements are masked with the pleasant language of freeing trade, increasing opportunities, and creating jobs. They are presented as being so innocuous that we have been conditioned to accept them placidly.

---

126 McNamee, Stephen J., and Miller, Robert K., Jr. *The Meritocracy Myth*. Rowman & Littlefield, 2009.

We are told that they create jobs and there is some truth to that. They just don't say where the jobs are created. Nor do they say that the jobs created here are done at the cost of the jobs terminated there. Since China joined the World Trade Organization in 2001, thousands and thousands of jobs have been created in China at the expense of about 2.7 million American jobs. That's how free trade creates jobs.

Some folks in America blame the Chinese for "stealing our jobs," but the accusation is unfair. The jobs haven't been stolen—corporations have served them on a platter to China and to any other poor paying countries. Corporations have no national loyalty. It's certainly not the fault of the Chinese for accepting low-paying jobs; low pay is better than no pay at all. By moving jobs, corporations increase their profits, increase management bonuses, and as their actions make clear if we will only open our eyes and see it, corporations clarify that they have no responsibility to national welfare.

The effect of these changes has been studied by the Washington-based PEW Research Center, a nonpartisan research centre employing over a hundred people. PEW published an annual Global Attitude Survey, rating citizen satisfaction with their governments. Since 2005, the Chinese government has received the highest rating—over 80%—while western governments have received 30% or less. As jobs are shifting, the people being made poor in the West are slowly beginning to realize that they have more in common with Chinese workers than they had realized.

Analysis of the 1994 NAFTA agreement between Canada, the United States, and Mexico shows that it has destroyed more jobs than it created. That is net … there are fewer jobs in all of the three countries. And, in all countries, it has depressed wages, eroded social programs, worsened poverty, and decreased the power of all three nations to control their economies. It has, however, increased corporate profits.[127]

Free trade puts downward pressure on wages by making it easier for corporations to move work to lower wage areas. In itself, there is nothing wrong with that—it creates work for people who need it. The problem is, it leaves hardship behind, and the change is usually done with deceit, and without planning for the people displaced. The competitive market system was never intended to override the welfare of people or the rights of the nations.

In 2013, workers making cans in the Crown Metal Packing factory in Toronto went on strike. The workers had not had a pay increase for nine years, despite the fact that the workers had made their plant the most productive one in the company in North America. The year before the strike, the company had doubled profits and then demanded, not just pay cuts for existing workers, but that new workers would be paid 40% less.

The company, once known as Crown Cork and Seal, began in 1892 with the invention (and patent) of the bottle cap, a steel cap with a cork liner some of us remember. It required a bottle opener! Today, the company is an American multinational, making over $1 billion in annual profit. The CEO is paid almost $10,000,000 a year, and the company employs 23,000 employees in 149 factories in 40 countries, making cans for food and beverages.

---

[127] Centre for Policy Alternatives. http://www.policyalternatives.ca/sites/default/files/uploads/publications/National_Office_Pubs/lessons_from_nafta.pdf

After 22 months, the strike ended: the workers got a 30% pay cut and no increase in pensions. The people lost; they gave up because they needed to eat.

Corporations have power (staff, plans, organization) and deep pockets, and they use both to push their agendas. There is no equivalent people's power base—the system is unbalanced.

Venezuela took a small step to retain some balance. In 2010, they passed a law preventing outside funding for pro-corporate groups. This came back to haunt them when Obama declared the nation a threat to national security in 2015, and Trump, in May 2017, imposed his second round of sanctions on the country. People's rights have a cost.

Corporate rights seem to have no bounds. In February 2016, the nation of Colombia was sued by Tobie Mining, a Houston-based mining company, for $16.5 billion because the government was stopping the development of a gold mine that was threatening the Amazon rainforest. Profit has legal rights that may transcend the environment; it's still unsettled.

Trade unions have started to emerge in China, and when they get real power, that could be good news for both Chinese and Western workers. The All-China Federation has 134,000,000 members and at the moment has government support. If Chinese unions are successful in raising wages, it should lead to jobs reopening in the Western world. It is the kind of natural evolution that free markets are supposed to foster, at least in the long run. But, as Keynes said, "In the long run we are all dead!"

Austerity: an idea that keeps on failing

> The boom, not the slump, is the right time for austerity at the Treasury.
> —John Maynard Keynes, 1937

Austerity is an old idea. In an effort to save money to pay national debts, it's been tried in the United States in 1921, 1937, and 1946; in Argentina in 1952; Spain in 1979; and Portugal in the late 1970s and mid-1980s. In not one case did it work. It was supposed to generate growth, which would reduce debt.

In his 2013 book, *Austerity: the History of a Dangerous Idea*, Mark Blyth, a teacher of political economy in Rhode Island, examined the multiple times it has been tried and the multiple times it has failed. His book was published after the 2007 crisis and after the most recent impositions of austerity.

It's easy to see why austerity is believable. It fits some of our most cherished beliefs: live within your means; pay your debts; there is no "free lunch"; clean up your own mess; the nation has to cut back, just like a family would. (In Chapter Eight, I talked about why a comparison to family budgets is wrong.)

Now I'll look at what else is wrong with these arguments. In the 70s and 80s, the IMF and World Bank used "structural adjustment"—the early euphemism for austerity—to impoverish poor nations and in this century to impoverish richer nations. Over 100 countries have been victims of this economic attack. The dogma is that by reducing wages and reducing government spending, competitiveness would be restored, business would improve, and tax income would go up, thus making nations' debts easier to pay. It sounds convincing but it's dogma, not theory, and it has never worked.

The fact is that any attempt to tackle national debt by reducing wages will result in a reduction in demand, the economy will get worse, tax income will go down, and national debt can only go up.

To put national debt into perspective, in Chapter Five I discussed the 1970s' changes in government financing—from self-funding and paying interest to itself to borrowing from the banks, resulting in soaring debt. If a nation wanted to reduce its national debt, changing back to the old way of funding would do it.

It's not because nations lived beyond their means that debt grew: debt grew because of bad financing decisions.

Even without Mark Blyth's book, we should have known not to fall for the austerity arguments. Keynes had explained back in the 1930s why it wouldn't work. He also had explained what should be done. Boom times were the times for government cutbacks, recession was the time for stimulus, and stimulus would create growth. Somehow, Keynes' advice was forgotten or overlooked.

It wasn't just a memory lapse. It was abetted by a 2010 research paper written by two Harvard economists, Carmen M. Reinhart and Kenneth S. Rogoff, entitled "Growth in a Time of Debt," which purported to show that austerity was good policy. The World Bank jumped on the paper, and it became the new gospel.

Other economists also jumped on it, and they discovered that the study was wrong. The research was flawed. There was a coding error on a spreadsheet and a bias used in the way data was selected and so the study created incorrect results. By the time the study was found to be wrong, it had done a couple of years' worth of damage. Millions suffered, some severely, like those in the poorer parts of Europe and the working poor in America.

Why was bad policy embraced so readily? The answer is easy to see when you follow the money. Who benefits from austerity? "*Cui bono?*" as Cicero said. Let's look.

Austerity programs usually begin when indebted nations have trouble paying their bills. Of those bills, the ones cared about most are loan payments to banks. When a country cannot pay its bills, it appeals to the IMF and most of the time gets a new loan. Called "a bailout," the new money goes out immediately to the international banks to pay the old loans. Giving a country a bigger loan because it cannot pay a smaller one is as dumb as it sounds. The truth is, it's not the country being "bailed out," it's the international banks.

In order to pay the new loans, the nation is forced to sell off its assets, such as its telephone company or water facility, and that's a gift to people with money. It gives them a new place to invest, and usually, they buy in for a song. As we've seen, capitalism concentrates ownership. It leaves fewer places to invest. A fire sale of national assets is a dream come true.

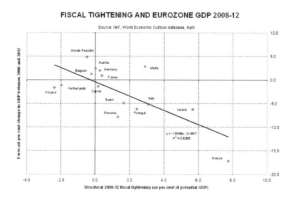

By June 2014, after seven years of austerity, nations that had been in trouble seven years earlier were still in trouble. Debts were higher, and there was no hope in sight. The IMF chart (above) shows the effect of fiscal tightening; "The more fiscal tightening, the more growth," we were told.

The opposite was true: Finland, France, and Germany did less tightening and suffered less damage. Portugal, Ireland, Italy, Greece, and Spain (countries derisively nicknamed PIIGS), did the most tightening, and suffered the most.

In the midst of the evidence that austerity policies were failing, the European Central Bank announced that, for the first time in history, they were going to pay people to borrow money: negative interest rates! This was stunning news.

I discussed monetarism in Chapter Eight: the theory of using money to control the economy. I noted that in 2003, Friedman had said monetarism had not worked. By 2014, European bankers must have forgotten his admission of failure when they announced they would pay money to borrowers and dropped loan rates to negative 0.1%. Paying people to borrow was supposed to make more money available and start a boom! It was another monetarist failure. They still had not understood that people borrow when they have use for the money, not because it's cheap. As bizarre as this new policy was, the European bankers lined up, like in a tug of war, to push on the rope of monetarist stimulus! It failed.

The austerity imposed on Germany at the end of World War I helped precipitate World War II. By 2012, the IMF acknowledged the failure of austerity and the consequent higher debt they had created. The IMF may have admitted it, but austerity policies continued. It's worth noting that austerity does have a purpose, it just isn't the purpose we are told. It couldn't reduce national debt, nor could it create employment, nor economic good times. But it made nations more indebted, thus more compliant, and it made the banks more money.

The forced sale of public assets created a global garage sale for the rich to pick up bargains, like beautiful Greek islands. Austerity is a highly successful privatization grab that does nothing to help the general public. (It's interesting to note that the Western press jumped on the austerity bandwagon but the *Guardian* newspaper, to its credit, never did.)

How high can the Dow Jones go?

The chart below shows the Dow Jones Industrial Average from 1900 to 2010. After the Great Depression of 1929 is the clear, albeit minuscule, bump above 1930. You need to look very closely to see it! The long-term pattern is clear, the rate of growth after about 1985 is not justifiable. The implosion in 2008 is huge, compared to the Depression.

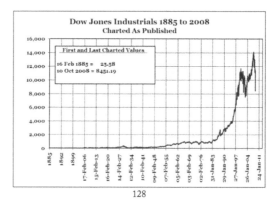

128

---

128   http://www.gold-eagle.com/article/dow-jones-industrials-40-declines-1885-2008

The questions we need to ask are, "Is this exponential growth real? Has the real economy grown so much? And, is such growth sustainable?"

The chart above covers about one-third of the history of capitalism, from the turn of the century in 1900, at the left, up through the sixties and seventies, when the Dow Jones average is flat, to today. The economy was very good during those years. Business was thriving, unemployment was low, and debt was not an issue. Money was found to fly man to the moon. Family incomes were going up. The value of shares on the stock market made sense. Then, for some reason, in the mid-eighties, share values began to surge to surreal numbers. Why?

Nothing mystical happened to cause this. It could have been the success of computer technology, but no. That resulted in an enthusiastic investment binge—a bit too enthusiastic—which resulted in the "dot-com bubble," which later burst.

Without a reasonable explanation for this unreal twenty-five-year surge, what should stocks be worth today? A straight-line projection from 1900 through the 1980s suggests the Dow should be at about $2,500, not $17,700 as it is now, as I write this. The chart of stocks on the Toronto Stock Exchange is similar.

A probable explanation is that the rise has been caused by the explosion of money and the financialization of the economy. Another is the possibility that dollars are overvalued by that much. No matter what the reason is, those factors don't foretell the future. The underlying "value" of shares (the value in terms of the "real economy"), remains as it always was: a straight-line projection from real history.

So far, in this chapter, I've looked at the effect of the corporate-controlled state as it affects the economy. Now I want to turn to how corporate power affected two nations: Haiti and Greece, both with populations of about ten million people.

Haiti, a country abused

> No matter how cynical you get, it's impossible to keep up.
> —Lily Tomlin

In the 1970s, world leaders promised to help the poor, and each of the countries participating promised to provide 0.75% of its gross domestic product to foreign aid. It was an honourable gesture, coordinated by the United Nations. Some thought this was to be payback for what the old world had stolen during the colonial years the century before. But it wasn't. It was simply charity, announced with fanfare, but without sincerity.

Thirty-five years later, we are further from that goal than ever. In 2012, Great Britain contributed 0.56%, Canada contributed 0.32%, and the United States 0.19%. The target of 0.75% had not been unreasonable—Scandinavians and a few other nations met or exceeded it. It was a matter of will, not wealth. The nations that could afford to do so most easily, didn't.

Haiti is a country that would have benefited from those plans but instead has been a victim of repeated mistreatment. A poor nation, and so close to us; only a two-hour plane ride south of Miami—it's in our backyard! It's the poorest country in the Americas. (It's about as large as Massachusetts, which has 7,000,000 people.) Haiti has 10,000,000 people, and 80% of those people live on less than $2 a day. Located on the west end of the island of Hispaniola, Haiti faces Cuba. On the east end is the Dominican Republic, where people pay hundreds of dollars a night to stay in five-star luxury resorts.

The Haitian people deserve better. When Columbus landed in 1492, he wrote of the Taino people who lived there:

> They traded with us and gave us everything they had, with good will ... they took great delight in pleasing us ... They are very gentle and without knowledge of what is evil; nor do they murder or steal ... Your Highness may believe that in all the world there can be no better people ... They love their neighbours as themselves, and they have the sweetest talk in the world, and are gentle and always laughing.[129]

The Spanish ruled the island for over one hundred years. European diseases killed Taino people by the thousands. They are all but gone today.

In 1625, the French replaced the Spanish, and imported thousands of African slaves who made Haiti France's richest colony. It was said that they generated 20% of France's wealth. Fairly rapidly, the 40,000 French were outnumbered by slaves and in 1791 two years after the French Revolution (and no doubt inspired by it) Haiti's slaves started their own brutal fight for freedom. Over 200,000 Haitian, French and British people died, but the people gained their freedom in 1804 in what was the first and is still the

---

129   Traboulay, David M. *Columbus and Las Casas: the conquest and Christianization of America,* 1492–1566. University Press of America, 1994.

only successful slave revolution in the world. Some nations were not pleased. One was the United States, which was still a slave-owning country.

In 1990, Jean-Bertrand Aristide, a popular Catholic priest and pro-democracy activist, became their first elected president. In 1991, the Haitian military overthrew him.

However, in 1994, with a United Nations operation tagged "Operation Uphold Democracy," the United States restored Aristide to power. There was one condition, as Aristide put it, and that was that he privatize, privatize, privatize. Twenty thousand troops stayed in the country, and the IMF came in with a $91 million loan, with conditions.

In 1995, Aristide shut down the army, saying they didn't need it, and used the money to start building schools. He increased the minimum wage to the equivalent of $1.60 US a day. It was becoming clear he was unsympathetic to corporate concerns. He talked about nationalizing the country's resources and asked France to consider returning some of the about $20 billion in gold that France had extorted. In 2000, the IMF added to the original $91 million debt, by lending more money and insisting that the minimum wage be dropped to the equivalent of 63 US cents a day and that the tariff on rice be dropped by 32%, which destroyed local rice farming. (In March 2010, ex-president Bill Clinton to his credit, apologized to the Haitian people for this decision.)

Over two days, January 31 and February 1, 2003, Canada hosted a meeting of the "Ottawa Initiative on Haiti." Representatives from Canada, the United States, France, the European Union, and El Salvador met. No Haitians were invited. The consensus of the meeting was that the earlier mission to uphold democracy be damned. "Aristide must go."[130] It took two years.

The following New Year's Eve, people gathered in Port Au Prince, the capital of Haiti to celebrate the nation's two-hundred-year anniversary of their declaration of independence. Luigi Einaudi, assistant secretary general of the Organization of American States was there. To a group in the lobby of the Montana Hotel, he declared, "The problem with Haiti is that the international community is so screwed up, they are letting Haitians run Haiti."[131]

Two months later, on February 29, 2004, the country was invaded again, and this time Aristide kidnapped and sent to Africa. The United Nations had created a stabilization mission, "Operation Secure Tomorrow,"[132] led by 2,000 United States Marines and supported by Canadian, French, and Chilean troops. Thirteen years later, the force is still there.[133] The newly appointed prime minister declared that they were open for business. The World Bank offered to rewrite the nation's mining legislation so all obstacles for foreign mining corporations would be removed—there was no need to leave it to the Haitians. Apparently, Haiti has "Gold in them thar hills!" There is also oil.

Aided and abetted by several nations, the corporate agenda trumped international law, democracy, and the history, will, and welfare of the Haitian people.

---

130 https://en.wikipedia.org/wiki/2004_Haitian_coup_d'%C3%A9tat
131 http://www.globalresearch.ca/haiti-coup-detat-secret-ottawa-meeting-to-overthrow-president-aristide-revealed/5363118
132 https://en.wikipedia.org/wiki/Operation_Secure_Tomorrow
133 http://www.nytimes.com/2004/02/29/international/americas/haitis-president-forced-out-marines-sent-to-keep.html

There was some black irony: six years after the first invasion (Operation Uphold Democracy), the second invasion of 2004 (for some reason nameless) overturned democracy. One thing was done right. The World Bank and International Monetary Fund cancelled US$1.2 billion of Haiti's debt in July 2009. About US$890 million of debt remains. The debt cancelled probably ensured oil and mineral rights for non-Haitians.

And then the Haitian people had more bad luck when, in January 2010, the deadliest earthquake ever in the Americas hit the country, just west of Port Au Prince. At seven on the Richter scale, it killed about 200,000 people, wrecked an estimated 250,000 homes, and collapsed 30,000 businesses.

Promises of aid poured in. USAID promised $651 million to support reconstruction. That's about $2,000 per displaced person, a very generous amount. The people had lived many to a house, so each family could pool their money and build as they saw fit—a solution that could have worked. But that wasn't the way it was done. Instead of letting the people build their own houses, it was decided to build 15,000 houses for them. At six to a house, they were short 35,000 houses. This target was then scaled back to 2,649 houses, while 300,000 people remained in tented slums. The international community awarded 1,490 contracts for reconstruction. Only 23 of those contracts were to Haitian companies.[134] The human disaster was used to make work for international corporations.

Reconstruction for family housing progressed slowly, but the new Occidental Royal Oasis Hotel in Port Au Prince opened

---

134 http://www.theguardian.com/global-development/datablog/2012/jan/12/haiti-earthquake-aid-money-data

quickly with the help of $2 million in aid money. A second hotel, a Marriott, has since been completed. It created 300 temporary jobs during construction, but only 200 ongoing jobs.

$300 million was spent to build a new 600-acre Caracol Industrial Park. It opened in 2013, under banners declaring that Haiti was "Open for business!" To build the park required displacing 366 families that had farmed the land for years. Not surprisingly, it created a food shortage. Fewer than 2,000 jobs have been created in the park and net pay for those jobs is under $2 a day.

Haiti remained under UN control for 13 years until April 2017, when they voted to end the occupation in October, later in the year. Haiti sits atop a pool of oil, a pool possibly larger than Venezuela's.[135] That may be behind many of the nation's problems.

Decades ago, the United Nations issued a report stating that $15 billion a year would end world hunger. It was possible then, and it's possible now. Today, it would cost only about $30 billion. I refer to "only" about $30 billion, because that isn't much, compared to the trillions of dollars that nations spend on arms, or the wages of corporate leaders getting bonuses of tens of millions of dollars. Eliminating hunger is not that expensive, it's just apparently, not that important.

Twenty-five years ago, the Canadian government unanimously passed a gutless bill to end child poverty within the country. Canada and the US are the twentieth and ninth wealthiest countries on earth; however, as the *Washington Post* reported in 2013 our two

---

135 http://www.worldoil.com/Haiti-could-have-larger-oil-reserves-than-Venezuela.html

countries stood twenty-second and twenty-ninth worst for child poverty out of a list of 30 nations.

The reason both countries have done poorly is not complex. The will just isn't strong enough. The lack of will is abetted by bad economic assumptions; such as insisting people work despite the fact that their jobs are moved offshore. It's self-evident that poverty should never exist in wealthy societies. In the West, it has always existed.

Why does poverty exist in wealthy countries?

When we allow corporations and the marketplace to control the agenda, only things that make money get done. There is little economic gain in ending poverty. The poor have no place at that table. They cannot afford to travel to international conferences. They cannot afford lobbyists. And most of the poor have a liability they share with most of the rest of us: we don't understand economics enough to realize what is wrong or what could be done.

We see the poor as a problem, not as people entitled to fully participation in society. It's a failure we have become increasingly insensitive to, but others have seen beyond.

People in southern nations have created the Global Call to Action Against Poverty (GCAP), challenging the structures and institutions that perpetuate poverty and inequality. Conceived in Maputo in Africa in 2005, and launched in Brazil, GCAP met in New York in 2015 and issued a declaration that pointed out the unsustainable development model we are living within.

Society remains obsessed with market growth, which drives inequality, the concentration of wealth, and climate change. GCAP members have not lost hope in their pursuit for meaningful and sustainable change.

But our bigger problem may be more subtle: what will happen if the poor, who have been ignored for decades, start to be seen, or even better, start to see themselves, as equals. Equals have rights; they may declare themselves to be worth more! They may even demand more. (In Chapter Twelve, I will take a look at Brazil, where a step in that direction turned out successfully.)

Greece, robbed in broad daylight!

During capitalism's implosion in 2007, not all nations suffered, and those that did, didn't all suffer to the same extent. The less financialized nations, or the nations with more restrictive financial legislation, did better. So did those nations that had, to use a term that's disappearing, a "middle class." Brazil, Peru, and Australia all did better, as did those beyond the Western system: China, India, Indonesia, and the Philippines.

But the Greeks were hung out to dry. The implosion of the Greek economy was reported initially, badly, judgmentally, and superficially, as their own fault.

All the PIIGS (Portugal, Ireland, Italy, Greece, and Spain) were in trouble. The acronym was cruel. How a country could be greedy and at fault because of an international currency collapse was not explained.

Instead of being given an explanation, we were told that Greece was in trouble due to two things: the Greeks were lazy, and the Greeks didn't pay their taxes.

Here's what we were not told. In 2006, Greek debt began to grow. In 2009, Goldman Sachs and J. P. Morgan Chase arranged to lend Greece money in a way that was hidden: it wouldn't show on their balance sheets. For this service, they were reportedly paid about $300 million. The secret loan was arranged in the form of a derivative. In 2010, the German news magazine *Der Spiegel* reported that these loans were disguised as "swaps." (The Greek government had lied about their finances, but Italy and France had done something similar.)

After the Greek economy imploded because they couldn't pay their debts, the IMF lent them more money. (How stupid is that?) The money was lent on the condition that they would have a massive sale of state-owned property.

The Greek people were being forced to pay for the folly and lies of Goldman Sachs, J. P. Morgan, and their political leaders, many of whom were corrupt! That, they knew, was wrong. They called a national strike. On May 5, 2010, an estimated 100,000 people marched through Athens. Train, plane, and ferry services shut down. Specifically, people were protesting proposed spending cuts and tax increases. They called their parliamentarians thieves. Three people died.

The first loan in 2010 was for €110 billion, and with it came the first round of austerity measures. Over 70,000 lots of state assets were auctioned off. The Emir of Qatar bought six islands. A Russian bought the island of Skorpios as a $100 million birthday present for his daughter. The Greek government was considering selling the train system, the water system, the electric grid, the government buildings, and the highways. The water utility was profitable, but the banks had no interest in Greeks retaining a profit centre. None!

It was true that many Greeks were not paying their taxes. But the Greeks not paying taxes were the rich! They were finding every excuse not to pay, thus depriving the government of revenue. This problem was made worse by recession: 25% of the stores in Athens went bankrupt, youth unemployment soared to over 50%. Now, after the worst has passed, 30% of the population live below the poverty level.

In May 2010, the IMF decided, because Greece was having trouble paying their loans (and this again is as stupid as it sounds), to lend them another €45 billion. When, as was inevitable, the Greeks needed more money, another loan was arranged. And in 2011, yet another €109 billion was loaned—It was probably the largest loan in history—on the condition of more austerity, followed then by yet another loan of €130 billion in 2012. Most of this loan, just like the others, went to European banks to pay off the earlier unpayable loans.

The media continued running stories about the problems caused by those lazy Greeks, while Greeks were working longer hours than the Germans, their chief accusers. Greeks were working 43.7 hours a week on average, compared to the Germans at 42.0 hours.

Sadly, the Germans had short memories. They had forgotten that after World War II ,50% of the German debt was forgiven, which included debt still outstanding from the First World War. Germany had the largest national debt failure of the twentieth century. At the end of the World War II, German debt was about four times their prewar GDP. (Hitler had run it up to 670%.) The

Greek debt in 2013 was only 175% of GDP, about one-third of what Germany had owed.

Instead of the sloppy reporting claiming Greece was being bailed out, the media should have said that the Greeks were being robbed and the international banks were being bailed out.

In Chapter Five, I mentioned Bob Chapman, the ex-Wall Street broker and his newsletter. In 2011, Chapman wrote about European banking:

> In Europe each time a new player is presented we find he is a Goldman Sachs' alumnus. Recent entries are Mario Monti "appointed" PM of Italy, Lucas Papademas "appointed" PM of Greece and Mario Dragahi "appointed" President of the European Central Bank. The banks blatantly control governments and agencies, presenting us with an oligarchy, which controls most of the nations on the planet. In America politicians are bought and paid for. In Europe there is a different mindset, a shared worldview of bureaucrats, technocrats, politicians and the elite bankers of world government and domination. What has happened in this process is that Goldman Sachs, JPMorgan Chase and other mega-banking has retained power for decades. They control all the players in the field, so the outcome is always in their favor. The bankers and others in turn are paid via billions of dollars in bonuses. Banks are now bank holding companies having become that to avoid failure as brokerage firms. That is the case in the US, UK and Europe.

To that, we can add Canada, where, until recently, the head of the Bank of Canada was Mark Carney (2008–2013), another Goldman Sachs alumnus. Since 2013, he has been governor of the Bank of England.

In the same way that the reparations at the end of the World War I punished average Germans for the mistakes made by their governments, the Germans were now insisting that average Greeks pay for decisions made by their government. Young people and average workers didn't cause the debt, nor did they have any say in the creation of the IMF, the Euro, the EU, or the rules that govern each of them.

Greece and its people were victims. Victims of bad politicians who paid for and accepted devious advice from Wall Street. They were victims of their own upper class, who preferred not to pay taxes. They were victims of the media, who turned misinformation into a lynching.

> On April 4, 2012, seventy-seven-year-old Greek pharmacist Dimitris Christoulas wrote, "I find no other solution for a dignified end before I start sifting through garbage to feed myself." Christoulas then shot himself in the head. The government had cut his pension as part of an austerity plan to pay foreign creditors. One in four workers also lost their jobs.[136]

---

136 http://www.gregpalast.com/the-vulture-chewing-argentinas-living-corpse/

In 2015, the Greek people elected the left-wing Syriza party, and 62% of the people voted for no more austerity. Yanis Varoufakis became finance minister. He's an economist who had taught in Essex and Cambridge in England, in Sydney, Australia, and at the University of Athens. He and his wife live on the island of Aegina, twenty miles south of Athens. He was recruited to become Finance Minister to try to salvage his nation from years of bad advice, immoral loans and unnecessary austerity, what he called "the most catastrophic failure in economic history!"

At the same time as he was negotiating on behalf of Greece, he ran a blog[137] as he still does, teaching anyone who will listen about the nonsense of austerity. He believed that one of the problems with capitalism is its inability to use technology for the benefit of everyone. He writes, like Keynes and Galbraith before him, in simple English, not economic jargon.

He believed that Greece had options better than laying off people and treating them as surplus, especially when wealth was still being created but disproportionally shared. In the end, he failed, his advice was ignored, and he quit the government. His prime minister felt Greece had no choice but to do what they were told, although he, too, knew it would fail. Possibly, he hoped it might buy time, but he was wrong, and Greece cannot, could not meet the terms of their current agreements. Their problems are worse now than when IMF aid began. Their last bailout loan was in July 2015, for €85 million and it all went to international banks. The Greeks got nothing but more debt.

---

137   https://www.yanisvaroufakis.eu/

Varoufakis has been compared to a "rock star" because of the popularity he has achieved explaining economics to the world. After he retired as Finance Minister of Greece, he began explaining to the world what is wrong with the European Union in addition to ongoing stories about what's immoral about the way the Greek people are being treated. His blog has a global following for his explanations of the failures of capitalism.[138]

The European Union was created after the Second World War with the Treaty of Rome in 1957, which was designed to create a common European market. That treaty was followed in 1992 by the Maastericht Treaty, signed in the Netherlands, which led to the creation of the common currency, the €uro. Today, it includes 28 states that have all surrendered control of their money to the European banks and surrendered their national sovereignty to European union laws, which are binding. Once a nation has given up control of its money, its foreign policy, its defense policy, and its trade policy, there is not much autonomy left. The agreement that makes European people voiceless against the power of private global banking.

(To put the ongoing Greek tragedy into perspective, Bloomberg reported in 2014 that the debt per person in Greece was about $38,444. Debt per person in the United States at the same time was $58,604: which nation should be considered in trouble?)

In January 2015, a half-dozen years after the first bout of austerity measures, Greek debt was 45% higher than when they began. The plan was never to save Greece. It was to protect the banks. The Leibniz Institute for Economic Research calculated that because

---

138   https://youtu.be/h54sVMXwJEs

of this crisis, the Germans benefited by income of over €100 billion in five years.[139]

And still the banks want more. Since 2016, Greeks must declare to the government all cash they have over €30,000 and all their jewellery over €15,000. It's easy to guess why: the banks want that next. This endless "loop of doom," as it's been called, would have been avoided if Greece had never given up control of its money.

The Greeks had other choices, but they weren't allowed to make them. They could have abandoned the €uro. It was a mistake to use a currency they didn't control. They could have learned from Argentina's experience decades earlier and simply said no. One purpose of this book is to raise awareness of our options, and the next section on Argentina is an example.

Lessons from Argentina

Adrián Salbuchi is a mid-sixties Argentinian political and economic analyst who writes about geo-economics from his nation's perspective. He is a good source. Let's look at what he has seen. In 1946, Juan Perón was elected President, and re-elected twice serving three terms before he was ousted in 1955 by a British-US coup. The coup came about, possibly because Perón made the mistake of paying off the national debt, or possibly because he wouldn't join the IMF. He had nationalized the central bank and taken a number of steps to reduce unemployment and improve the lot of the people by increasing income equality. (His very popular and powerful wife Evita, featured in the musical, *Don't Cry for Me*

---

139   http://www.socialeurope.eu/2015/08/how-the-german-government-saved-100bn-through-the-greek-crisis/

Argentina, was his political partner, a socially progressive supporter of labour rights and trade unions, who had a weakness for shoes.)

The Perón government paid off what debt they had. Argentina was the wealthiest country in Latin America, but once Perón was gone, Argentina joined the IMF, and debt began to grow. The country had a series of debt crises: in 1982, 1989, 2002–2005, 2010, 2014, and the last one is ongoing. In 2000, they took IMF money and cut spending as they were forced to do. Things got worse, which we know was inevitable. People started to doubt the safety of savings in their banks and wanted their money out.

By 2005, they were in the third year of depression and the middle class were lining up in soup kitchens. People rioted, directing their anger at the IMF. The government was overthrown, and the new government, rather than pay foreign debt, chose to go into default! They made payments, not to the banks, but to the unemployed. Economists predicted disaster! The government negotiated a settlement with the banks to pay 30% of their national debt. (The banks, in their language took a 60% haircut!) The country ended its old practice of pegging their peso to the American dollar and this had a huge positive impact. They had learned that if you don't control your currency, as was the case when their peso was pegged, you don't control your economy.

Three months after the peso was unpegged, the economy began to grow and grew at a phenomenal 63% over the next six years.[140]

---

140   http://www.cepr.net/index.php/op-eds-&-columns/op-eds-&-columns/why-greece-should-reject-the-euro

The lessons for the Greeks, and for the world, are not to trust the IMF—and to control your own money. Only then can you control your economy.

Despite their successes, Argentina's woes were not over. Vulture capitalists are now circling over their unpaid debts. They are hoping to grow fat on them. What are they?

Ventures and vultures

Some venture capitalists buy businesses, not always with their own money, but often with the money of the businesses they are buying. At one time, almost all venture investors took risks helping small businesses, and on occasion the profits were huge. Now many ventures are leveraged buyouts and I began to understand what they are, some months after I had done one.

I was running a business for the majority shareholders who wanted to retire. I had earned equity in the company as a result of five years' work, and with that equity and a bank loan, wrote an agreement to pay out the old shareholders. This buyout was small and amicable.

International buyouts are on a larger scale and usually not everyone is pleased. Find a vulnerable company, take control somehow, seize the cash, include the employees' pension money, and pay the organizers most if not all the cash available. The remaining business, now loaded with debt, is left on its own to survive. If it does survive, that's great. If not, so what? The "visionaries" got their money. To survive, the remaining company usually has to get huge wage concessions from employees, who are now victims of the deal.

Hostess Brands is an interesting example. (It used to be a client of mine.) It first went into bankruptcy in 2004, and remained there for five years. In 2009, Ripplewood Holdings, a private equity company, took them over. When Hostess came out of bankruptcy protection, they were in debt for $670 million dollars, almost 50% more than they owed when they went into bankruptcy. In January 2012, the company was taken back into bankruptcy protection, now owing close to a billion dollars. It's hard to make any profit with that much debt, harder still when the CEO gets paid $2.25 million a year for leading an insolvent organization. The company failed in 2013, and about 19,000 people were affected. The company left over $2 billion of its workers' pensions unfunded.

The remaining workers, who had made cupcakes and Twinkies at Hostess for years, saw their annual incomes drop from over $40,000 a year to $25,000. The wage cuts saved the company $110 million a year to pay bank loans and to pay the new investors, but it was not enough, and the company went under again. The pensions were gone. The management winding down the company asked the receiver for permission to pay the few managers who remained up to $1.7 million to close the business.

Venture capitalists are regularly heartless.

Vulture capitalists are worse! These are a new breed of "Wall Streeters" that prey on the poor. Elliott Management was founded by Paul Singer in 1977, and it specializes in "distressed debt." Singer is credited with being the inventor of "vulture funds."

Here's how they work.

In 1983, Peru was in trouble and defaulted on its loans. New terms for reduced payments with its creditors were agreed to and Peru moved on. The parties involved had agreed. Singer didn't! In 1996, he bought Peru's defaulted loans for $11.4 million. He then sued Peru for debt the world had forgiven and was awarded $58 million—over five times what he had paid. In 2008, he paid a little over $2 million to buy over $30 million of the Republic of Congo's debt. A British court awarded him more than $100 million, which the people of the Congo, many too poor to buy food, had to pay.

In 2014, the President of Argentina, Cristina Fernández, was serving her second term. Fernández took on the vultures. Argentina had negotiated a debt reduction with its creditors by as much as 70%. Nonetheless, the vultures bought the debt and sued. New York Judge Griesa ruled that 100% of the debt needed to be paid. The New York courts have no sane jurisdiction in Argentina but that didn't stop him. Suddenly, the debt Singer bought for $49 million was worth $220 million. Fernández has become an outspoken critic of this type of "financial terrorism," as she calls it. The lawsuit is at a standoff. Argentina's economy has done well. Brazil, Mexico, and France have supported Argentina's position.

One of the reasons Singer gets away with his vulture capitalist behaviour is because there is no bankruptcy court for nations. In September 2015, the United Nations took a big step to fix this, and 136 nations voted in favour of principles for debt restructure. Six nations voted against. You can probably guess who: Canada, Germany, Israel, Japan, the United Kingdom, and the United States. Even if the United Nations proposals gained universal support, world trade agreements could override them.

Meanwhile, in the Real Economy

During the 1990s, I became the chief executive of a manufacturing business. The company had strong technical ability and weak business skills. We embarked on changing the culture, upgrading skills, and investing in new equipment. The bank soon told me I owed more money than anyone in Ontario east of Toronto. Quite an accomplishment!

When you owe a lot of money, the bank treats you to receptions with other indebted people and serves you the finest wines and hors d'oeuvres. By 2000, we qualified for an award as "One of the 50 Best Managed Companies in Canada," co-sponsored by the Queens University School of Business and the global accounting firm Arthur Anderson. They too had a cocktail party for the 50 winners of the award.

Arthur Anderson was the accounting firm that had become famous partially for its involvement with Enron; *Fortune Magazine* had named Enron "America's most innovative company" for six consecutive years. Derivatives trading became a big part of Enron's business betting on energy developments, the weather, and newsprint. They had about 500 products on their books, with values that would not be known for many years. They opened *EnronOnline*, which, at its peak was trading $6 billion of commodities a day. Enron had strayed a long way from its core business and Arthur Anderson didn't seem to notice.

At the cocktail party, an Arthur Anderson partner was talking to a handful of us. This was a marketing event for him; he was one of the hosts. Instead of being a congenial host, he chose to brag. "Well, I have my BMW, I have my golf club membership, what more could I want in life?" He personified the shallow, arrogant culture that Arthur Anderson had become.

Enron went bankrupt a year later. The CEO, Ken Lay, was named the third worst CEO of all time. Bad judgement and bad accounting were blamed, and Arthur Andersen followed Enron into bankruptcy. I had seen why: their ethics were shabby. The

Enron bankruptcy, the largest bankruptcy in US history, was a preamble to the downpour of illegal corporate activity to come.

Anderson's "I've got my BMW!" partner was my second encounter with the "deal-making" mentality. Unfortunately, there were more to come.

A handful of "movers and shakers" were running a company making airbrakes for trains. They wanted to buy my company. Their business is interesting—it involves the technology that stops a train. Trains can be over a mile long, when one end's going up a mountain in snow and the other end can be going into a hot valley. Interesting engineering. But that didn't interest these movers and shakers as much as wheeling and dealing. Buying another business, with extra revenue to build their empire. They were out to convince us to join them, and over lunch gloated about how well they were doing and how well we could do if we joined them. "But," they advised, "put a good security system in your house because we fire a lot of people."

As the millennium dawned, Bill Clinton was in his last year as President, and Jean Chrétien (a politician who spoke neither official language) was prime minister of Canada. There was a minor recession in the United States; Canada had somehow avoided it. Neither Reagan's tax cuts nor Clinton's budget cuts had done much to stimulate the economy. The technology boom and Reagan's military spending helped, and people in North America were more or less as content as they had been back in the fifties and sixties.

By 2000, corporate tax had been reduced from about 39% to about 13% and, predictably, governments were up against the wall with debt. There is a correlation. The state had lost out to corporate greed as corporations began to pit nation against nation to pay even less tax.

> It is a well-known and very important fact that America's founding fathers did not like taxation without representation. It is a lesser known and equally important fact that they did not much like taxation with representation.
> —John Kenneth Galbraith

There have been many tax cuts in the last few decades for the rich. One that came early was the cut in capital gains tax. A capital gain is a profit on an asset. When a person sells property or stocks or bonds for a higher price than they paid, the gain is a capital gain. At one time, those gains were taxed at the same rate as the taxes paid on wages. Is that fair?

As I discussed in Chapter Eight, in the early 1940s, there had been a change to tax rates. It was a most deceptive move done with "smoke and mirrors." The capital gains tax appeared untouched, but the rate stayed the same. However, with the changed law, only half of the capital gains needed to be declared, so the rate was cut in half.

The rich argue that lower capital gains tax encourages them to invest and to create jobs. Both are simply silly comments. If you have lots of money, once you've bought the stuff you need, investing is about the only use for the rest of it! No extra incentive is needed. A savings account is one investment, but bigger returns usually come by buying shares. In that case, the government takes some of the risk away by allowing bad investments to be written off. Investing at triple the current capital gains tax rate would be better than leaving the money unused: the tax rate on capital gains has almost no effect on investment. And as I mentioned earlier, the silly argument that it is the investments of the rich that create jobs is almost never true. Reducing taxes on wage earners produces significantly more market demand than cutting taxes on the rich.

What now?

> The reason it is called the American Dream, is that you have to be asleep to believe it.
> —George Carlin

In the first three chapters of this book, I talked about the basics of economics: its basis; supply and demand; the economics of illegal drugs; and, foreign aid. In chapters four to nine, I reviewed the last five decades of economic evolution. That brought us from the middle of one century and into the start of another.

The basic requirements of a competitive free market, as once existed, no longer exist. The world of Samuelson has been shattered. By the year 2000, our social contract was in tatters. So, too, are the economic assumptions of Milton Friedman, as he confessed in 2003.

The state—the institution that, at one time, served the people—had steadily been co-opted to serve the corporations. In two decades, payday loan institutions, businesses that pretend to be banks and charge like loan sharks—sprang up like weeds across North America. Changes in laws in the US and Canada effectively allow interest of 500 to 1,000% to be charged to those foolish or desperate enough to be victim to these agencies.

If, as it's easy to predict, these loans remain unpaid, the banks bundle them and sell them to less scrupulous bill collectors. In allowing payday loans, our American and Canadian governments not only failed to protect their people, but made them fodder for predatory lending.

On his TV show, comedian John Oliver recently purchased almost $15,000,000 in bad medical debts for less than $60,000, and forgave them. What he did was an act in the long-standing tradition of a "debt jubilee"; he freed 9,000 people from their medical debts. In 2015, the Croatian government announced that it would do the same for 60,000 of its people.

Cutting aid to universities and colleges forced tuition up and young people into borrowing for student loans, which generated bank profits and created an indebted generation.

In the corporate-run state, corporations make tax avoidance an art. Oxfam America released a report in April 2016, which detailed:

> The 50 largest American companies received $27 in federal aid for every $1 they paid in taxes

> For every $1 they spent in lobbying, these companies received $130 in tax breaks and $4,000 in federal loans, loan guarantees, and bailouts

> Only five of the companies paid the regulated 35% tax on profits. The rest used more than 1,600 subsidiaries in tax havens to stash $1.4 trillion offshore

Oxfam reports that wealth has concentrated so that eight people have the same wealth as half of humanity; in 2010, it had been 388 people. If the trend to wealth concentration continues, the top 1% are on the verge of owning more than 99% of global wealth.

What were the effects of these changes? What happened when the economy tanked in 2007? Was financialization a factor? Were the proper actions taken? That's next.

11.
The 2000s: the system collapses

IN 1929, AFTER ALMOST A DECADE OF EVER-IMPROVING ECONOMIC times, the market imploded, and the Great Depression followed. The crash was a built-in systems failure and lasted for about a decade because of faulty economic assumptions. It need not have lasted so long.

As is always the case, the working class suffer most in depressions; they are victims and given no options.

The 1930s song "Brother Can You Spare a Dime?" summed up the despair:

> Once I built a tower up to the sun
> Brick and rivet and lime

Once I built a tower, now it's done
Brother, can you spare a dime?[141]

Only when stimulus spending finally happened, in part by plan, and in part by the emerging threat of war, were people able to get back to work.

Decades later, we went through this again at the start of the Great Recession in 2007, but the seeds were sown in the years in between.

In 1999, the Glass Steagall Act was repealed, a US law that, since 1933, had provided market stability by preventing banks from taking too many risks. That law separated banking for the people from banking for Wall Street. In 1999, the new bill with the trendy name, the Financial Services Modernization Act, ended that stability by allowing the merger of investment and traditional banks.

This led to the creation of financial supermarkets, and, as we were to learn, a self-serving concentration of financial power. These new entities developed high-risk, complex financial products full of undisclosed risk and conflicts of interest. The credit rating agencies were either baffled or bought. The unregulated market failed to rein in its own excesses.

Before the collapse, there had been at least one significant forewarning.

In the year 2000, 11,000 American property appraisers signed a petition. These were people who earned their living making judgements on the value of properties. Their petition asked both the

---

141   E. Y. Harburg, and Gorney, Jay. (1930). From the 1932 musical revue *Americana*.

government and their employers to stop appraisal fraud! Appraisers were being pressured into producing false appraisals: appraisals that were high, way too high, to justify mortgages that were also too high. The government was warned, but no-one took action.

Seven years later, the largest market failure since the Great Depression happened. Why did it happen? How did it happen, and what did the failure mean? Was it just because of appraisal fraud?

A few years before the appraisers' petition in the late 1990s, the number of subprime mortgage loans in the United States was growing rapidly. Subprime loans were loans to high-risk borrowers—not a new idea: student loans are subprime loans. ("Borrow now with no job and pay back when you get a job.") Subprime refers to the credit rating of the applicant. In return for lending on less than "prime" terms, the banks charge higher interest rates and may offer other less favourable terms.

As if that weren't risky enough, these dubious loans were then bundled and sold, so that the questionable loans would come off the banks' books! The bad loans became a "security." In 1994, subprime loans had been less than 5% of the market. By 2005, they were over 20%, and most were to new homeowners.

Moneylenders became creative and developed many different terms and types of loans to lure customers: payments could begin at a low interest, stay low for some years, then jump—an adjustable rate mortgage. Another included paying no principle for years—customers could pay just the interest until later, when principle would be added. Both were bad ideas. They assumed that people, who were not getting pay raises, would be able to pay more five or so years in the future. Foreclosures were inevitable.

These mortgages were easy to sell. They were called "sucker loans." Many well-intentioned people took them because of the economic assumptions they'd been raised with. And these assumptions were shared by many of those selling them: in a few years, the house would be worth more and in a few years the owner would be earning more. Both assumptions came from a different era. Both were no longer true. Wages did not go up, and property values began to decline. The most complex mortgages were being sold to the least sophisticated borrowers.

I became aware of these loans when our son-in-law and a few of his friends, all bright kids in their late-twenties, were being recruited to sell them. It was high-paying, easy money and many took the jobs. Fortunately, our son-in-law didn't. The new recruits were clean-cut, articulate young people who dressed like financial advisors and were taught to give a smooth sales pitch, which was designed to prey on the optimism of ordinary people.

These sucker loans were sometimes called "liars' loans" because borrowers were encouraged to lie on their applications. The liars were not just the clients, but also the sales reps who coached them and the banks that chose not to verify data.

While strange lending practices were changing the retail market, my company, Lofthouse Brass, qualified in 2000 as one of the fifty best-managed companies in Canada. Our major client was the Moen Faucet Company, and they had been a great business partner.

The United States housing market had been booming for years—it was a "bubble," as we learned later, which peaked about 2005–2006. But before that, we had made millions of Moen shower valves. These were primarily copper, made in Canada and shipped into the United States for US dollars. Our contract depended on trust, and every three months either of us could ask that price be renegotiated—usually because of change in either the price of copper or the value of the dollar.

Through the early 2000s, the prices for copper and currency swung a lot: copper went up, the Canadian dollar went down, and both drove our profits down. As a result, it was necessary to pay increased attention to the economy—especially currency and commodity prices, because they affected our cash. I had not yet taken up the task of understanding major issues in the economy, but these experiences were to help.

In 2001, a new US Government came to power when Bush Jr. became president. The decade-long housing boom was fading, and by March the US was moving into recession.

Predatory lending went viral for five years or so, and then the bubble burst. By the mid-2000s, these dubious mortgages started coming up for renewal and people couldn't afford them. Monthly mortgage payments jumped, while wages remained frozen. It resulted in a glut of foreclosures. Around July 2006, as more of these houses were put on the market, real estate values in the United States started to tumble. It was predictable!

In the end, it was the borrowers (i.e. the victims), who were blamed, not the lenders who created and cashed in on these schemes. The bright young mortgage salespeople became unemployed as the housing market imploded and the glut of foreclosures took the banks with it.

Before values peaked in July 2006, the economy was booming. Nonetheless, the US ran a $250 billion budget deficit, not something Keynes would have advised. Household debt was rising steadily. Many young couples had patterned themselves on the lives of their parents. The longer their parents had worked, the more and better things their parents had acquired. The new generation felt this was natural. However, they missed one important point: their wages, unlike their parents', were not going up. Believing they had the right to live the better life, young people used their credit cards to do so.

Greenspan's 2005 assertion that housing was not in a bubble was a comment that created a lot of suffering. He reinforced the long-held assumption that property values would always go up when he had to have known better. On *The News Hour* on September 18, 2007, Greenspan finally acceded. "We had a bubble in housing."

In the mid-1980s, just prior to the Soviet collapse, Kenneth Galbraith was in the USSR doing a comparative study of the Soviet and American economic systems with a leading Soviet economist. Neither of them anticipated the collapse of the USSR that was shortly to follow.

The collapse in the US in 2007 had been predictable for a number of reasons, but only a few economists had predicted it. Michael Hudson, whom I discussed in Chapter Six, did.

The collapse of bank liquidity was also predictable, because of the way money is created. That too was missed.

United States housing values peaked in July 2006, when the economy was growing, and stock prices were high. Despite that prosperity, the economy was vulnerable. Many Americans were becoming more pessimistic than optimistic. Bush was nearing the end of his presidency, and with his eight years of wars in Afghanistan and Iraq, his increased military spending, along with his tax cuts, resulted in the US dollar declining in value. National debt was higher than ever.

Banks had so many real estate loans, it was essential for real estate to hold its value for them to remain solvent.

The sucker loans of the previous five years had started coming up for renewal, as they would continue to do for a few years to come. But wages had not gone up. People couldn't afford the new terms and either sold their houses or were foreclosed on. As more houses were put up for sale, property values started to decline. As house prices went down, so did new house construction and new home sales. People were paying off, or defaulting on loans, and not taking out new ones.

Now the issue of how money is created became crucial.

When people take out loans, money is created out of thin air by the banks. For a $200,000 loan, they create $200,000. But, with interest, banks expect about $300,000 to be paid back. The extra money needs to come from new loans. It's like a pyramid scheme. But when no one is borrowing, and most are paying back, or defaulting, what happens? No new money is being created and old money is disappearing. The banks run out of money!

The economy: 2007–2008

At the time, we all heard that the banks were running out of money, but neither CNN nor the rest of the media explained why. How could banks run out of money? They have our savings in them! How could banks become "illiquid"? It wasn't discussed.

In February 2007, the Fed announced it would no longer buy subprime mortgages. In April, the first subprime mortgage lender filed for Chapter 11 bankruptcy. Another, American Mortgage, followed in August. Throughout that summer there were warnings about mortgage-backed securities from several ratings agencies.

Wall Street and the international financial markets were taking an ever-larger piece of the economic pie, but delivering no additional value. As I mentioned earlier in the book, at one time, way back in the 40s, financial services accounted for 4% of GDP. By 2007, they'd grown to 8%. Most people got no value from the billions of extra dollars that went to Wall Street. Some of those dollars were due to new products, such as the new "assets," which were just bundles of old assets lumped and repackaged: loans, for example, that were bundled and sold as a new product. These products were referred to as "secondary trading," since the assets already existed.

The financial markets were using bizarre new tools and new investments with ever more unknown, or in some cases, unknowable risk. Credit rating agencies weren't examining the risks as they used to, and they fraudulently gave these new products the highest credit ratings: "AAA." Demand for them soared.

As the banks became aware of their exposure to mortgages of dubious value, they started to pack them into bundles or tranches and sell them as Asset Backed Securities, or Collateralized Debt Obligations. They became "someone else's problem", and because of faulty credit ratings, people lined up to buy them.

It is hard to imagine, if you think about it, that our bank would take our mortgage and put it in a pile with hundreds of other mortgages and sell them off! Who would believe that this could be a "new" asset? It's baffling. Apparently, it also was confusing to the banks, because when foreclosures began, mortgage documents couldn't be found. Piles of mortgages had become undocumented piles of paper, an even shakier house of cards.

In August 2007, Lehman Brothers, a Wall Street investment bank, felt that subprime products were now too risky and closed their subprime lending division, hoping to avert a crisis. Although they were getting out of the subprime business, they were still stuck with dubious mortgages, declining in value. In the same month, BNP Paribas, the fourth-largest bank in France, announced it was suspending trading on three accounts because it could not confirm the value of US mortgage securities within them. No wonder: neither could the US banks!

In September, the Northern Rock Bank in England desperately needed money. It was the first bank in one hundred and fifty years to experience a bank run. Their business had depended on selling bundled mortgages, and suddenly there were no takers. Their customers became worried and wanted their savings out. If Lehman was the first shoe to fall, Northern Rock was the second. It was not just the North American markets that were vulnerable. It was banking in the entire Western world.

Strangely, the Dow Jones hit a record high in October 2007. It speaks volumes as to the disconnect between the real economy and the stock market. Two months later, the United States entered what is now referred to as the Great Recession.

As the year was ending, the Western world was in a liquidity crisis, which is fancy language for "out of money." In December, the largest monthly drop in US house prices ever put Wall Street and Washington up against the wall. The banks were technically insolvent. In January, the Bank of America took over Countrywide Financial. Another institution had failed.

> Then came Wall Street's implosion in 2008 and the ensuing global financial disaster. Nothing would be the same again.
> —Yanis Varoufakis[142]

The banks had run out money because of the way money is created. Bad management and trusting a system that cannot work created the massive failure. So why were the banks not allowed to fail? Lehman's acted responsibly, but too late, and eventually declared bankruptcy in 2008. It was the largest bankruptcy in US history. Why didn't the other banks follow?

The bubble has burst: now what?

> The banks were saved, not the economy.
> —Michael Hudson[143]

In February, Bush signed *The Economic Stimulus Act of 2008*. Ten pages that were supposed to prevent a recession by stimulating the economy. The stimulus was tax cuts, which can work, but tax cuts only work if the cuts are significant enough and only if people feel it's safe to spend. And if they work, they will work slowly. The estimated cost of the program was $152 billion. And the act wasn't enough. Five months later, in July, Bush signed another tax cut paper, and a then a third, in October. The fact that it took three kicks at the can suggests to me his economic advisors didn't have a clue about what was going on.

---

[142] Varoufakis, Yanis. *And the Weak Suffer What They Must? Europe's Crisis and America's Economic Future.* Nation Books, 2016.

[143] http://michael-hudson.com/2016/12/innocuous-proclaimations/

Liquidity, a term that refers to money and how quickly it can be moved, was a term that got talked about a lot. If there is lots of money around, things are liquid and can flow fast. If a bank or any business runs out of money they are illiquid. If a company runs out of money (and I've been involved in two that did), bankruptcy often follows. If a bank runs out of money, the bank may not be able to pay its bills, it won't be able to make loans, and worse it may not have the savings held in trust for their customers. When customers lose faith in their bank, a run on the bank usually follows.

In March 2008, Bear Stearns, an investment bank, was sold to J. P. Morgan Chase. Bear Stearns had been overexposed to bad mortgage risk. "Overexposed" is jargon for "insolvent." Tim Geithner, who at the time was president of the New York Federal Reserve, arranged the deal by providing J. P. Morgan with the $30 billion needed to buy Bear Stearns. Chief of the New York Fed during Republican years, Geithner became Secretary of the Treasury in Democratic years. (When it comes to money, the two parties usually see things alike.)

The sale of Bear Stearns was a forced sale, pennies on the dollar. Paul Volcker, ex-Fed chair, says the move was an action "at the very edge of the lawful and implied power of the Fed." This probably means it was illegal! The deal was arranged as if in an old boy's club, a backroom secret deal.

In July, when Bush signed the second of three acts, *The Housing and Economic Recovery Act of 2008*, it authorized lending $300 billion to provide 30-year fixed rate mortgages for people caught in the mortgage trap, on condition that lenders would write down the loans to 90 percent of the property's actual value.

Before the failures began, members of my family in Nashville had taken out a mortgage with Countrywide Financial. When it failed, Countrywide had been providing 20% of the nation's loans, and my family's mortgage was one of many sold to the Bank of America. My family members then lost their jobs in the recession that followed and applied for mortgage relief under Bush's Economic Recovery Act.

They were accepted and were going through the process of approval when they came home one day to find a foreclosure notice posted on their front door. Subsequently, they were evicted. Both actions—the foreclosure and the eviction, were illegal. As the result of a class action lawsuit, Bank of America withdrew the default claim from their credit record and paid them about $10,000, on condition they not publicize the settlement. The bank had acted illegally and in bad faith. Eventually, Bank of America sold the house at a loss. No one went to jail.

And Angelo Mozilo, the CEO who bankrupted Countrywide, walked away with hundreds of millions of dollars: $132 million in 2007 alone, a combination of wages, bonuses, and sweet stock options.[144]

While the Fed had intervened to save Bear Stearns in March 2008, in mid-September, they let Lehman Brothers fail. Lehman was the fourth-largest investment bank in the world and the largest bankruptcy in US history. All of its many bits and pieces were sold within a month.

---

144   http://www.rollingstone.com/politics/news/angelo-mozilo-former-countrywide-ceo-claims-he-doesnt-know-what-verified-income-is-20121228

That same month, Goldman Sachs and Morgan Stanley changed their status from investment banks to bank holding companies, making them eligible for state protection. That meant the government could bail them out. As an investment company, they hadn't been able to count on a bailout.

The third act, the *Emergency Economic Stabilization Act of 2008*, more commonly known as "the bailout," followed on October 3.

I felt overwhelmed at how fast change was happening and how little of it I understood. I understood free market economics: bailing out businesses was not part of the theory.

In time, we would learn that 80% of Americans had opposed bailing out the banks, but it was too late. The bill appeared to authorize $700 billion to buy things from the banks: things called troubled assets! (For us amateurs, troubled assets are bad debts!) The amount paid out appears to have grown to total in excess of $7.7 trillion dollars.[145]

Why were governments "bailing out" the banks? Why did the banks need money? That is not the way the system is supposed to work. What happened to "the steady hand of the market"? What happened to competition? The government seemed to abandon all free enterprise dogma!

If the $7.7 billion had been given to the American people, instead of to the banks, each person would have received about $25,000. With that money, people could have bought things, and the real economy would have recovered. The banks would have failed, but jobs would have been created. Another option would

---

145 http://www.bloomberg.com/news/2011-11-28/secret-fed-loans-undisclosed-to-congress-gave-banks-13-billion-in-income.html

have been to buy the banks: if that had been done, all interest paid to the banks would then have gone to the public.

The collapse was not only predictable but predicted and bet on. The 2015 book by Michael Lewis, *The Big Short: Inside the Doomsday Machine*, later made into a movie, tells the story of a few people who saw it coming and bet about $100,000 on it. They pocketed over $100 million.

A committee of the Senate looked into what happened[146] and reported that in January and February 2007, Goldman Sachs "rapidly sold off or wrote down the bulk of its existing subprime RMBS (residential mortgage-backed securities) and CDO inventory (collateralized debt obligations) and began building a short position that would allow it to profit from the decline of the mortgage market." So, Goldman Sachs had seen it coming while at the same time the Fed Chair Bernanke had been saying he saw no real problems. He and the Fed chose not to see, which left the rest the world to pay the losses while insiders reaped the gains. In September 2008, a year and a half after the insiders were safely out of the market, the Dow had it largest-ever daily collapse.

The collapse of markets was a "Western" phenomena: it wasn't shared by the non-capitalist countries or the countries known as the BRIC (Brazil, Russia, India, and China), which were unscathed. There are many economic systems that can work, and those countries less tied to the capitalist model escaped failure.

Some of these folks are trying to redefine the world's economic system with new institutions such as the New Development Bank

---

146 United States Senate, Permanent Subcommittee On Investigations. April 13, 2011.

(2014) and also the new Asian Infrastructure Investment Bank (AIIB), despite pressure from Washington not to do so. While the Asian Bank was being proposed by China, China did not insist on having a veto, such as the US does within the IMF and World Bank. In June 2015, fifty-seven countries created the AIIB. The United States and Canada were not among them.

The collapse of Western economies happened concurrently with the disappearance of the middle class and permanent jobs and also in the middle of an era of nonstop wars. At the peak of its power, the US had 15.3% of its population, almost fifty million people, living in poverty. Lots were children. Increased financialization made everyone more dependent on money, while, at the same time, pensions and family support were disappearing. We had been weaned away from simple things that once worked: home vegetable gardens, extended families, home baking, and belief in community.

Governments ignored corporate criminality and now worked against the people and, to the extent that we let it happen, we were all complicit!

The scale of intervention in 2008 was so enormously large and, by free market theory, so wrong, that it should have been the obituary for the free market. Competitive markets were history! Dead! The system should have been buried!

Instead, the bailout of capitalism in the US began under a Republican and finished under a Democrat. Which party it was made no difference. Tim Geithner, who began the bailout by saving Bear Stearns under Bush, as Chair of the New York Fed, finished it under Obama as Secretary of the Treasury. As I quoted Eric Kierans, in Chapter Four, "capital has no conscience." Nor, it appears do its masters.

In the turmoil of the bailouts. there was no explanation as to why the banks needed money. You have read about how and why in this book, but when it happened, the general public heard nothing about why, or how, the banks ran out of money. Perhaps it seemed like too stupid a question to ask! A downturn results in fewer new loans, and fewer new loans means less money is being created, and when not enough is being created, money disappears. The debt money system cannot survive downturns, and unregulated capitalism regularly has downturns. Therefore, a system of money created by debt is bound to fail repeatedly.

Hundreds of billions of dollars came out of nowhere and were put into the major Wall Street banks. And into Canadian banks as well. More billions bought and nationalized Fannie Mae and Freddie Mac, both US semi-private mortgage companies, which got $100 billion each. More billions ($13.4) bailed out General Motors and Chrysler, which had each gone bankrupt. And another huge amount—between $700 billion to some trillions of dollars—have been spent to buy "troubled assets" from banks moving their "bad debts" onto the backs of the public.

Things happened so quickly to save banks, auto companies, and insurance companies. Was there ever an opening left to ask, "Why not help the people?" As I mentioned earlier, if the amount of money given to the corporations, which was $25,000 per person, had been given to the people, it would have provided real stimulus. Instead, in the crisis, the government chose to save corporations—to save businesses owned by the richest people. Exactly the opposite policy that a competitive free market demands.

In February of 2009, Obama signed another act, this time for $831 billion: the American Recovery and Reinvestment Act. $237 billion was tax incentives for individuals, indirect stimulus. Most of the money went into more direct stimulus, as Keynes would have recommended. It was a better bill, but far from a good bill.

Canadian banks were not immune

> ...we have not had to put any taxpayers' money into our financial system in Canada, nor do I anticipate that we'll be obliged to do so.
> —Jim Flaherty, Minister of Finance

> It is true, we have the only banks in the western world that are not looking at bailouts or anything like that ... and we haven't got any TARP money.
> —Stephen Harper, Prime Minister

A large myth was circulated that the Canadian banks were not affected. In 2008, the Canadian government was led by Stephen Harper, leader of the Canadian version of the Tea Party called the Conservatives. His Minister of Finance was Jim Flaherty who represented the riding where I had my office. I met him several times, first when he was Minister of Finance in the Province of Ontario Government and later when he moved to federal politics. Over the years, we had the occasional lunch, he visited our factory, and I spoke at his Rotary Club. I got to know him well enough to see how his actions were driven by his belief in neoliberalism, not by any economic understanding.

In mid-October 2008, while financial institutions and markets around the world were crashing, Flaherty assured the public that this was no problem for Canada. He even announced that Canada would not run a government deficit. He was so over his head! Only a couple of short months later, he unveiled a budget with the highest deficit in Canadian history!

Flaherty later told the world in no uncertain terms, that, "In Canada, we did not suffer a single bank or federally regulated insurance company bailout or failure. Our country's financial institutions stood solid and steadfast, based on sound risk management and supported by a very effective regulatory and supervisory framework."[147]

Well, it turns out he was a little disingenuous. Canada's big banks were dipping deeply into the gravy bowl, to the tune of $114 billion. The US Federal Reserve provided $41 billion in short-term collateralized loans, while Canada's government-owned Mortgage and Housing Corporation provided $33 billion.

> Despite all the rhetoric about the stability of Canada's bank system, research into several key sources reveals Canada's big banks started receiving American and Canadian government help in September, 2008, and continued to draw on government help well into 2010. Between September, 2008, and the peak of government support in March, 2009, Canada's banks were the recipients of $114 billion in support from the U.S. Federal Reserve, the Bank of Canada and Canada Mortgage and Housing Corporation (CMHC).[148]

---

147   http://www.fin.gc.ca/n11/11-049-eng.asp
148   Macdonald, David. *The Big Bank Big Secret*. p. 10. Canadian Centre for Policy Alternatives, September 1, 2008.

"Ottawa pumped $75 billion into Canadian banks to take mortgages off their hands—a bailout anyway you cut it," as James Laxer, Professor of Political Science at York University, put it.[149] $75 billion amounts to about the same amount of dollars per person as the bailout in the US In addition, Canadian banks borrowed $33 billion from the US Fed. The Canadian government could have used the same amount of money to buy the Canadian banks: simply purchase the shares of the banks and all future profits would come to the people.

Canada's big banks are more like American banks than different. The CEO of each of Canada's big banks rank among the highest-paid CEOs in Canada, and as they waddled onto the 2008 and 2009 bailout gravy train, every bank CEO received a raise. For instance, Edmund Clark of TD Bank, saw his compensation jump from $11.1 million in 2008 to $15.2 million in 2009. Bank executives have to be laughing at us.

Canada's prime minister from 2006 to 2015 made the US Tea Party look moderate. Harper was a member of the Christian and Missionary Alliance, a Canadian evangelical cult that believes the free market is divinely inspired and that evolution is only a theory. That he was naïve about economics is not a surprise! But sadly for the country, so was his Minister of Finance. Fortunately, that government was replaced in 2015.

---

149 http://rabble.ca/blogs/bloggers/james-laxer/2009/12/stimulus-austerity-next-chapter-canadian-policy-making

What is quantitative easing?

In September 2013, the US press reported the Fed would continue with its bond purchase program, named Quantitative Easing 3, until the US economy was seen to be in recovery. There was no explanation that there could be no connection between the two events. The program, regularly called a "stimulus," stimulates nothing. Like Quantitative Easing 1 and 2, the private Federal Reserve banks were buying bad assets from the banks. In this way they provided the money to the banks that the banks had run out of. They took the banks' bad loans and made them a public liability. Quantitative easing meant adding to the national debt. The extra money dumped into the banks made the banks solvent and propped up the stock market, which then rose to new unjustifiable highs. Not surprisingly, it rose by an amount that equaled the sum of the "easing" dollars. Lots of new money was injected into the system, but none of that money went to create jobs or to create a recovery.

Government stimulus programs could have been used to improve schools, roads, harbours, cities, parks, and a host of things. Spend money to build stuff, and let people earn wages and have money to spend. That's stimulus! Tax rebates can also be stimulus: leave people more money to spend … it's not as direct nor as fast, but it is stimulus. Bailing out the banks is not. The United States government had provided some stimulus, in its February 2009 bill, but the Fed had not.

The Fed program of September 2013 bought $85 billion a month of bad debt from the banks and essentially the same was done by the Bank of England. Europe created €80 billion a month. In the end, over $4 trillion of bad American assets were bought. This was

11. The 2000s: the system collapses

an enormous fraud perpetrated on the American people because the debt went to them. The difference between the amount paid for bad loans and the reduced value of the property behind them, possibly $1 trillion, became an undeclared tax on the American people. The stock markets have done well in the recession because the so-called "stimulus" served them very well.

Quantitative easing is not badly named. Money spent to buy bank debt or bonds gives the banks quantities of cash to "ease" the problem they dug for themselves. The term was introduced by Bernanke in America, just a meaningless obfuscation (to use a Greenspan expression) but one that Greenspan would have been proud of. As he explained once:

> It's a — a language of purposeful obfuscation to avoid certain questions coming up, which you know you can't answer …
> —Alan Greenspan; CNBC interview; Sept. 17, 2007

Early in this book, I mentioned that it was only in the last couple of years that I began to understand the new language of economics. By the time quantitative easing came along, I had made real progress!

Alan Greenspan was a master of what American journalists referred to as "FedSpeak," a Greenspan variation of Orwellian "Newspeak." The Fed chairman had learned to be cautious because markets could turn on his comments. They would have turned even faster if he'd ever spoken honestly about what constituency he was serving—after all, he was an employee of the major private banks.

Obfuscation was his preferred strategy, as he once explained to a senator, "mumbling with great incoherence."[150]

The United States Federal Reserve, the Bank of Canada, the Bank of England, and the Eurozone have all done the same: bought bad debt from their private banks. Practically, Bernanke of the US Fed agreed to exchange the banks' bad debts for cash. The banks then bought government bonds with the cash. The banks got an asset backed by the government, an asset that earns interest to replace nearly worthless mortgages.

Bernanke said he would keep up quantitative easing until the unemployment rate went down. He didn't explain how this would work because he wasn't able to: there is no relation between the two. It may have been a delusional hope that if the banks got solvent people would borrow money and that would create jobs. That has never worked, did not work then, and isn't working now. However, as long as the unemployment rate stayed high, he could use that albeit fictitious excuse to keep giving public money to private banks.

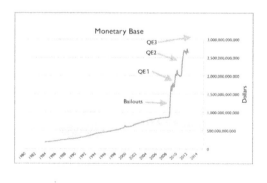

The chart below shows the impact of quantitative easing on the monetary base, the total amount of United States money. It's an unbelievable spike in the amount of money.

---

150   https://www.washingtonpost.com/archive/opinions/1991/01/24/mumbling-with-great-incoherence/60f7008a-9984-4c10-a87b-2b78da600e80/?utm_term=.7d9ba5311e9d

Making money available does not ensure that it will be borrowed, nor if it's borrowed, that it will be used to create employment. At the moment, corporations are sitting on billions of dollars in cash reserves, and many are using this money to buy back their own shares. The practice of companies buying back their own shares props up their share price and usually increases executive bonuses. Canadian banks were sitting on so much idle money that they were chastised by the governor of the Bank of Canada in 2012.[151] Having money available does not mean it will be lent, borrowed, or used.

If quantitative easing is a government program designed to stimulate the economy, as has been claimed, why would the government cut social spending at the same time? Spending on the unemployed, the poor, the elderly, and disabled creates demand and is humane policy. It's also a proven economic boost. Using public resources to buy overvalued assets from the banks is theft.

In summary, according to *The New York Times* [July 24, 2001]:

- the government authorized a bailout of $700,000,000,000 ($700 billion)
- the government eventually committed $12,200,000,000,000 ($12.2 trillion)

In 2010, the Dodd-Frank Wall Street Reform and Consumer Protection Act was signed by President Obama and authorized the United States Government Accountability Office to audit the Federal Reserve, and reported that there had been $16.1 trillion of

---

151   http://www.canadianbusiness.com/economy/dead-money/

secret loans made—a sum as large as the Gross Domestic Product of the country. According to competitive economic theory, none of that was justified!

These huge unauthorized expenditures were examples of what some refer to as the "deep state" at work, referring to unelected people making policy and directing action that elected politicians should be making. It's hard to argue against. The existence of a deep state is what we see when trade deals that usurp public policy are made in secret. Another example was convincing the public, or at least the media, that banks were "too big to fail." This fiction elevated the banks to near omnipotence, more powerful than government.

In 2013, *Time Magazine* had a headline story, "How Wall Street Won," detailing the myth of financial reform and the reality that the banks, which had failed almost everyone, emerged bigger and more powerful than before. The Fed had other options: they could have nationalized the banks! That would have put the control of money in the hands of the people.

The chart on the left, below, is from *Forbes Magazine* (December 2013), and shows what quantitative easing did: it inflated the stock market. You can see the rise of the stock market since the late eighties, the sharp dip from the crash of 2007 to 2009, and the bounce back since. In March 2013, *USA Today* published a story about the $16 trillion increase in value the bull market created—curiously, as I've noted, about the same number of dollars as the Fed created.

The chart on the right shows how workers fared over seven years of ongoing slump with no relief in sight. Quantitative easing did them no good.

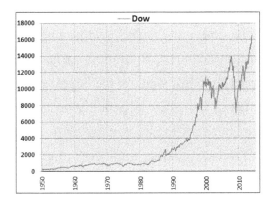

Dow Jones average

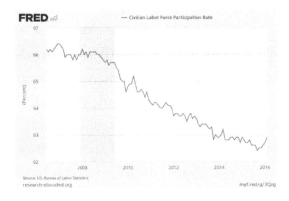

Percent of people working; over 66% on the left to 63%
Source: US Dept. of Labor Statistics

More economics events

> These people have made many rules that the rich may break but the poor may not. They take tithes from the poor and weak to support the rich who rule.
> —Sitting Bull, Sioux, about 1875

During the last two decades, economics changed to increasingly serve corporations, corporate leaders, and no one else. It reached a new low when the Walmart Corporation opened a department to help its employees apply for welfare: the largest corporation in the world was admitting they were depending on government handouts, rather than fair pay, for its employees to survive. Similarly, the McDonald's website advises employees to get two jobs if they cannot make ends meet with one job.

Research done at the Federal Institute of Technology University in Zurich, Switzerland, was released in September 2011 in a study entitled "The Network of Global Corporate Control," which looked at about 43,000 transnational companies. They learned these companies were interconnected by 147 companies as a "super-entity," which controlled 60% of the world's financial markets.[152] These companies are controlled by no more than a thousand people; one thousand people control 60% of the world's finance!

The New Scientist magazine reviewed the study. "When the team further untangled the web of ownership, it found much of it tracked back to a "super-entity" of 147 even more tightly knit companies—all of their ownership was held by other members of the super-entity that controlled 40 per cent of the total wealth in the network. In effect, less than 1 per cent of the companies were able to control 40 per cent of the entire network," says James Glattfelder, one of the study's authors. Most of the companies were financial

---

152 http://arxiv.org/PS_cache/arxiv/pdf/1107/1107.5728v2.pdf

institutions. The top 20 included Barclays Bank, JPMorgan Chase & Co., and the Goldman Sachs Group.[153]

There are many things that the free market does not do well: parks, libraries, art galleries, museums, border patrol, policing, land protection, endangered species protection, health care, universal pensions, and citizenship. There are things the competitive market should not do at all: prisons are the prime example. As I pointed out in Chapter Nine, a profit-based prison system has an incentive *not* to rehabilitate. In August 2016, the US Justice system announced they were phasing out use of private prisons because they were ineffective and not cheaper.

Declining work and declining wages are evidence of a system that is failing workers: the United States' median income of male workers is lower than forty years ago. Unemployment in Spain is over 25%.

The Social Security Act of 1935 provided old age security, and unemployment insurance. Seventy years later, in our more advanced, supposedly richer, capitalist society, we hear that pensions or social security are luxuries we can no longer afford. Payments that protected decency, that stabilized the economy, which we could afford a few decades ago, somehow are no longer affordable. That makes no sense.

At one time, we had a system that provided basic social security and it was run by the state: unemployment insurance, welfare, old age security, and public education. Every attempt is being made to disassemble every piece of this safety net. The rise of RRSPs in

---

153 http://www.newscientist.com/article/mg21228354.500-revealed--the-capitalist-network-that-runs-the-world.html#.VC6VI_ldV8E

Canada and 401(k)s in the US were steps to get rid of government pensions. Increasingly, people now face retirement without enough savings. Assumptions about giving people control and responsibility for their own retirement planning have failed. The result is a huge shift from a few decades ago when retirees by and large had no mortgage debt and safe, reliable, predictable pension incomes. Today, many need to work longer. Seniors are joining young college graduates as burger flippers. In the days of the old social contract, sometime before retirement, the average family would celebrate being totally debt free with a small ceremony: burning the paid-off mortgage. No longer.

This change has been studied by the Washington-based Economic Policy Institute, which published a report that reveals how 401(k)s have failed most American workers and how we have a retirement crisis that forces seniors to continue to work for more years or to live in poverty. They remind us that the first US Social Security check was issued in 1935—during the Great Depression at a time when the economy was as bad as it gets.

It makes no sense that North America continues to have people living in poverty, and that we have the greatest wealth inequality in the world. Changes in education funding in the US are creating class orientation, something the founding fathers sought to avoid. In rich areas in the US, $19,000 a year is spent on kids' educations. In poor areas, it's $7,400 a year. Health care is unaffordable to many: illness is the greatest cause of personal bankruptcy in the US All of these facts are out of sync with the myths about the success of free markets.

For the last dozen years, the Fed has continued its love affair with monetarism (keeping interest rates low to push on the rope of monetary stimuli). It has failed continually, fails still, has never worked, but those seem no reason to abandon it. Sadly, the low interest policy by the Fed results in almost no interest on the savings of older people—interest that seniors counted on for their retirement. Bad economics at the Fed is impoverishing our elderly for no useful purpose.

After the 2007 crisis, the G10 was expanded to the G20, and now includes the finance ministers of twenty of the more powerful economies in the world. Essentially, it's a super union for the world's largest banks. The G20 held their first meeting in 2008. They now meet annually and as you can guess, meet secretly as their parent group did since the mid-1970s.

An unintended consequence of the 2007 meltdown occurred in June 2013, when the Deutsche Bundesbank, Germany's central bank, announced it wanted its gold, which had been on deposit in the United States Federal Reserve vaults for over fifty years, returned.

Another consequence was Russia announcing in April 2014 that it was decoupling its trade from the US dollar and will buy and sell oil in rubles, gold, or local currencies.

These changes erode the value of the US dollar: interest rates and inflation will rise in the United States as a result. Both reflect the decline of American power.

China and Japan have followed Russia's lead in announcing that they intend to use their own currencies in their trades, as have Brazil and India. China has become Africa's largest trading partner and with it, a rise in the global use of China's currency, the renminbi, further displacing the US dollar. India is going to buy their oil from Iran in gold. Saudi Arabia is likely to stop using the dollar when trading with China.

In a generous move in 2015, China announced at a Sustainable Development conference organized by the United Nations that they will forgive debt owed to them by the least developed poor nations. In addition, they would contribute billions of dollars for aid.

In January 2016, folks with values different from those in the sustainable development crowd met at the World Economic Forum in Davos Switzerland, the meeting comedian John Stewart called "the money Oscars." There were about 2,500 attendees. Joe Biden was guest speaker. Ambrose Evans-Pritchard, Business Editor of the *Daily Telegraph*, reported on the discussions. The Davos folks were not concerned about the poor or about sustainable development but about global economies. Bank liquidity bothered them, as did the state of the European Union. The Davos folks don't relate to real people: concerns for the poor didn't make the agenda.

The North American media, like the folks who attend Davos, routinely equate capitalism with democracy and freedom. They don't report that without competition, the free market system is gone; nor do they seem to realize that democracy and freedom are gone when the wealthy have all the say, and the people have none. This power imbalance was confirmed in a 2014 Princeton study,[154] which revealed that wealthy people and the businesses they control have substantial impact on government policy, while individuals or mass-based interest groups have "little or no independent

---

154   https://scholar.princeton.edu/sites/default/files/mgilens/files/gilens_and_page_2014_-testing_theories_of_american_politics.doc.pdf

influence." The study continued, "the results provide substantial support for theories of Economic-Elite Domination and for theories of Biased Pluralism, but not for theories of Majoritarian Electoral Democracy or Majoritarian Pluralism."[155] In plain English, people power is gone!

When is competitive capitalism to be buried?

This isn't over yet. The most recent implosion of capitalism in 2007–2008 caused pain around the globe. When Greece got into trouble, so did the banks in Cyprus that had lent the Greeks a lot of money. Cyprus is a small island nation in the eastern Mediterranean, just south of Turkey, with a population of about a million people. It had become a large offshore banking centre, and their bank assets had grown to eight times the size of the economy. Cyprus banks lent Greece billions, but then the Cyprus banks ran out of money and closed for seven days. When the bail-*out* of their banks came, a bail-*in* was imposed on bank clients. People with more than $129,480 in their bank accounts lost a percentage of

---

155 https://scholar.princeton.edu/sites/default/files/mgilens/files/gilens_and_page_2014_-testing_theories_of_american_politics.doc.pdfhttp://www.princeton.edu/~mgilens/Gilens%20homepage%20materials/Gilens%20and%20Page/Gilens%20and%20Page%202014-Testing%20Theories%203-7-14.pdf

their bank deposits.[156] With the change in rules, savings were no longer safe in the bank—any bank—anywhere.

A small island such as Cyprus may not be that important, but that new banking precedent sure is! Money deposited in a bank is a loan from you to the bank—more accurately, it's an unsecured liability from the bank to you. The bank *owes* you the money, but because you are an unsecured creditor, and other banks are now secured creditors, the banks come before you in a crisis. With this new deal, other banks were paid in Cyprus before bank customers. This policy was endorsed by the International Monetary fund and also by *The Economist Magazine,* which even boasted they created the idea. The American Dodd-Frank act of 2011 made bail-ins legal in the US, putting ordinary savings at risk. On November 16, 2014, in Brisbane, Australia, the leaders of the G20 nations made bail-ins global policy.[157] We were not consulted. I don't believe they have the right to do so, but they took the power.

For all but the last decade or two of the prior two and one-half centuries since Adam Smith recognized the emerging market system, that system seemed to work; silently managing the business of the Western world with only slight tweaking. Smith didn't like the way the merchant class was rigging the system to their advantage in his era and wanted real competition, competition that worked for everyone. That was then. Now, when banks, auto companies, and insurance companies are "too big to fail," that system

---

156 http://www.forbes.com/sites/nathanlewis/2013/05/03/the-cyprus-bank-bail-in-is-another-crony-bankster-scam/#328918e72a87

157 https://www.imf.org/external/pubs/ft/sdn/2012/sdn1203.pdf

is dead. It failed in 1929, and again in 2007/2008. We wait for an official death notice.

Lincoln summed up thousands of years of mankind's evolving hope when he championed that "Government of the people, by the people, for the people shall not perish from the Earth." That hope seems long gone. Today the rules are made of, for, and by corporations. Elections, especially American elections, have become ceremonial rites or games of plutocracy: government by the rich for the rich. (Canada's multi-party system tempers this.) Citigroup in 2005 referred to it as a "plutonomy," an economy where growth is powered by and largely consumed by, the wealthy few. Consequently, wealth at the top continues to grow: at 20% in 2013, and the trend continues.

Since the 2007 economic collapse, there has been no fundamental change to fix it. Over 65 economics associations in over 30 countries have united and called for a rethink of the way economics is taught. It was bad economic practices and decades of bad economic teaching that allowed the crisis.[158] The Great Recession continues as a smouldering failure—the system behind it failed. The future is in limbo.

To sum up what's happened:

> Real competition, a necessity of the free enterprise system, is gone.

> The way money is created has failed.

---

158   http://www.isipe.net/open-letter/

The credit system serves the rich, not the average person, and is making things worse.

In the US, the world's largest economy, human rights have been eroded as corporations have been declared people.

The world is changing faster than ever, so fast that many call this the Exponential Age.

What can we do to regain rights for ordinary people? How do we restore opportunities, like those we had a few short decades ago? How do we give the next generation the opportunities we had? There are no easy answers.

But for the sake of the next generations, we need to try. We need to understand how big and how fundamental the problem is. Then we have to convince ourselves, and one another, that we have a horse in this race; we are not mere spectators. We need to find alternatives that are fair. To get to that system, somehow, we will have to take control away from the 1%.

In the next chapter, we will look at what else is possible.

12.
What will replace capitalism?

You have brains in your head.
You have feet in your shoes.
You can steer yourself
any direction you choose.
You're on your own. And you know what you know.
And YOU are the one who'll decide where to go.
—Dr. Seuss; *Oh, The Places You'll Go!*[159]

FROM 1776, THE YEAR *THE WEALTH OF NATIONS* WAS PUBLISHED, to the implosion of Western economies in 2008, two hundred and thirty-two years passed. That's a short time in the history of man.

---

159 Seuss Geisel, Theodor. *Oh, the Places You'll Go*. Random House Inc., 1990.

During that time, the market economy emerged, flourished magnificently, and failed.

Our hunter-gatherer ancestors of 12,000 years ago had an economy, albeit a simple one, which lasted thousands of years until their increasing population forced change.

In the past two hundred and thirty-two years, competitive capitalism organized Western society. People who today are in their seventies have lived through almost a third of it. They also have lived through all of the era of financialization, the last few decades when money came to dominate the real economy.

The system we are left with is not the only way an economy can work. This chapter provides examples of other choices. It is not meant as a guide as to what to do, but is about the wider scope of what can be done. Knowing there are choices may give us the confidence we need to take control.

Just to remind us: economics is not a science. In physics, for example, scientists have made discoveries that add one upon the other to create indisputable rules about how the universe works. Not so in economics. The failure of agreement as to know how to properly respond to the economic melt-downs of 1929 or 2007, and the conflicting theories economists proposed, attest to the failure of economics as a science. The fact that neither of the popular science magazines, *Scientific American*, nor *Discovery*, have an economist section seems to underscore that. The attempts to disguise economics as a science are like piggybacking a look-alike award onto the Nobel awards, which has provided confusion while providing kudos to bank-friendly economists: it's all fraud.

Some of us remember when capitalism was working: when there was a middle class, when there was an American Dream, and at that time the majority lived it. Those of us born in the middle class don't realize we were not just lucky, but we were economically essential for the American Dream to work. There were unions to protect the workers, and the middle class protected the economic system. As years passed, unions were increasingly demeaned and those considering joining them, discouraged from doing so. At the same time, corporations were organizing, creating their own type of unions, industry associations, boards of trade, and lobby groups.

The quote, "Workers of the world unite; you have nothing to lose but your chains!" is well known. It's from the handbook Marx and Engels wrote in German called the *Communist Manifesto*. The fear of aggressive union organization was seen as an immense threat by business. So it's ironic that businesses followed Marx's advice and organized themselves to fight his ideas. Marx could have urged, "corporations of the world unite ..."

In earlier chapters, I looked at how much economics changed, and how it increasingly controls our lives. If I have done my job, I have shown that economic theory is not impossible to understand.

The word economics comes from the Greek word "*oikonomia*" which means prudent household management. Smith's observations in 1776 about how communities had some self-directing order was emerging to become a set of rules controlling much of our lives.

We have seen that whatever else capitalism happened to be, it was flexible!

Capitalism was redefined to allow for freedom, security, and opportunity. It was changed over time and became somewhat self-correcting. It didn't always change for the good, nor was it divinely driven, nor has it helped us all equally. The Occupy Wall Street protestors of 2011 (the 99%) knew how wrong the system had become and set out to change it.

The economist John Weeks, wrote *The Economics of the 1%* in 2014. His book's lengthy subtitle, *How Mainstream Economics Serves the Rich, Obscures Reality and Distorts Policy*, explains how the myths of mainstream economics are used to serve the 1%. That's the economic system we now live in. Weeks is an American Professor Emeritus of Economics at the University of London. He explains that it's fake economics that dominate mainstream media. Fake economics he explains, is the triumph of nonsense over good sense. Fake economics assumes that being a consumer is the purpose of life; that government is by definition inefficient; and that taxes are contrary to the purpose of life. He shows that the economics of the 1% is economics where money dominates, and average people aren't relevant.

He explains that the system we know as capitalism is not an absolute doctrine: it's an "ism," a creed, a set of beliefs, and nowhere is it carved in stone. Weeks explains, "… you don't need to be an economist to understand the basic workings of the economy," but you do need to realize fake economics, nonsense, now guides governments, "… as if creationists had taken over the field of genetics, astrologers astronomy and alchemists chemistry."

As the definition of capitalism changed, assumptions about the nature of man have been changed. Our view of freedom has been directly affected. The emerging tendency has been to redefine man as a competitive animal, a brutish image that trumps the more traditional view of man as a fundamentally loving, caring creature. We cannot deny cruelty in our history, but people have a stronger bias to fairness and decency. It's part of our biology: our children wouldn't survive to become adults without it. Leaders who take "average" pay "walk the talk" of fairness.

It's also innate in Capuchin monkeys! Dutch professor Frans de Waal studies morality in animals and in the footnote below is a link to a video of one of his fairness experiments. It's delightful and worth a few minutes. It shows that even monkeys know what's fair and demand fairness.

Facebook exists because people need to share. As we separate into communities, often gated, and into jobs, without the personal interactions of the factory floor or lunchroom, people have found new ways to share their lives and to bond. Facebook, Twitter, cellphones, texting, and e-mail are now part of how we meet our need for social interaction.

As we consider the type of world we want, we could be relooking at the question of value: what's a person worth? The question, in this case, is economic, not philosophical. How much should one person earn compared to another? Dr. Seuss implied the answer, with his statement, "a person is a person"! To Seuss, we were equal! If that's so, then we should all be paid the same, but that doesn't match what we do.

When people are employed, it's common to say, "They've been hired," but it's more accurate to say that "They have rented their behaviour." Thus, the compensation question more accurately is, "How much is one set of behaviours worth, compared to another?" A study done by Bloomberg found that the CEO of J. C. Penny was paid 1,795 times the wage of an average department store worker. That makes no sense, because he cannot do 1,795 times more work. By contrast, Warren Buffet took home 25 times his average employee's wage. In the 1950s, the ratio between worker and boss was similar to Buffet's, a 20-to-1 ratio. That ratio worked in the business world for decades. By 1980, this ratio rose to 42-to-1, and then rose again by 2000 to 120-to-1. In 2014, the President of Walmart made more in one hour than his average employee (and he has 2.2 million of them) earns in a year.

José Mujica is the president of Uruguay, a country just south of Brazil and home to some three million people. Mujica lives on $1,250 a month. "I do fine with that amount; I have to do fine because there are many Uruguayans who live with much less." By law, he is paid $12,000 a month. However, he keeps only 10% and puts the rest into a fund supporting projects for the poor. He drives his old 1987 VW Beetle and lives in his wife's modest house rather than in the nation's expensive presidential residence. As we say in business, "he walks the talk." (There's a link to a *Guardian* newspaper article about him in the footnote.)

At one time, Mujica was a member of a guerrilla group fighting to end military government in the country. The group was notorious for bank robberies and for stealing food and giving their gains to the poor. Shot six times, he spent 14 years in prison. The country is not the poorest in the Americas, but it is poor, and he and his wife live and grow flowers on her small farm. He has been called "the world's poorest president." His government passed sweeping changes in marijuana legislation to take profit away from the drug traffickers. The state now has a role in the production and sale of the crop and drug abusers are given treatment, not put in jail. The presidential palace was made available to the homeless, and the global recession for their people was avoided due by higher public spending.

In the northwest of South America on the Pacific Ocean is Ecuador, another country that put people first. Rafael Correa, an economist with a master's degree from Belgium and a PhD from the University of Illinois (Joseph Stiglitz was one of his professors), was elected president in 2007. A democratic socialist, he speaks English, French, and Quechua and campaigned to create a "citizens' revolution" and use the resources of the nation for all of the people. He explained that Ecuador's national debt was illegitimate because it had been created by corrupt regimes. With the country's back to the wall, they defaulted on billions of dollars of debt and negotiated to have it reduced by more than 60%. He closed the United States military base in the country with the simple explanation that the United States could re-open it when Ecuador was allowed to have a base in Miami. On his re-election in 2013, he said, "In this revolution the citizens are in charge, not capital. This victory belongs to each of you. No one and nothing is stopping this revolution, my friends. We are making history." His government has cut the poverty rate by 27%, reduced unemployment by half, and increased spending on education, health care, and housing.

Ecuador and ten other countries formed ALBA, the Bolivarian Alliance for the Peoples of Our America, as an alternate economic alliance to the World Bank and the IMF. They aim to develop their own currency.

Milton Friedman, as I noted earlier was for several decades the high priest of capitalism. He later recanted. The man who popularized the monetarist agenda, created the theories used to justify the IMF and World Bank, and created fifty years of economic damage, ruining lives and nations, almost apologized. *The Financial Times*, in June 2003, quoted him: "The use of quantity of money as a target has not been a success," and Friedman added, "I'm not sure I would as of today push it as hard as I once did."

If Friedman was the high priest of capitalism, Alan Greenspan was a cardinal, and he too admitted he was wrong, as we saw in Chapter Eight. Before a Congressional committee in October 2008, in the most oblique apology I've ever heard, Greenspan admitted that he had found a "flaw in his model." Somehow, he seemed to imply, it had nothing to do with him!

John Kenneth Galbraith had the Galbraith Prize in Economics, an award created by the Canadian Progressive Economics Forum, named in his honour. In 2007, when the inaugural award was presented, his son James appropriately gave the first lecture. He told the story of the time in 1963 when President Kennedy and Prime Minister Pearson wanted to develop a civil aviation treaty between the two countries. Kennedy decided to appoint John Kenneth to represent the United States. Pearson, who lived with a twinkle in his eye, responded, "He's a good Canadian, I'll appoint him too!" And as James told the story, "Dad held hearings, negotiated with himself," and settled the issue to the satisfaction of both countries.

Towards the end of his speech, James had advice for both the economists present, and for people in the wider world. "It is time to get on with it. We need a replacement for neoclassical economics." He concluded that, above all else, a useful economic system needs to address full employment, climate change, and a sustainable quality of life. And added that they need to "… do so in a spirit of abiding liberalism, generosity of spirit, openness and fair play, combined always with humour and a touch of detachment. Those are my father's enduring traits and they should also be ours."

The wishful search for full employment

Somehow the mythical search for full employment stays alive, despite the cold, hard fact that North America has not had full employment since before 1900. New technologies, innovation, better machines, and efforts to eliminate work have all been responsible for reducing the work needed thus the size of the force. It seems likely that we can all live well without everyone having a job. The mythical search for full employment should be abandoned, and something creative put in its place.

It's not an easy prospect. Since losing the Vietnam War and the nearly simultaneous decision to withdraw from the Bretton Woods agreement, the United States has been in decline. Empires, such as the longest-lasting empire, the Portuguese, which lasted 584 years, or the Roman Empire, which lasted 503 years, often fail due to overreach. Now the time of the United States as an empire seems to be up. Its foreign policy is suspect, its debts are unpayable, the status of the dollar is less secure, financial criminality goes unpunished, and crime on the streets is increasing. It's decline, which could be dated to August 5, 2011, when the credit rating for the United States was downgraded, is the biggest historic factor of our time.

Stephen Covey was a business professor who wrote a bestselling self-help book, *The Seven Habits of Highly Effective People* in 1989. It sold equally well to business and non-business people alike. Habit Number Three was simple: understand! Take time to comprehend what's going on before you do anything.

It took me over two years of research to begin to understand what then became this book. We all need to begin by understanding what's going on before; only then can we face the uphill battle to get economics back to serving all the people. Many studies show that individuals, whether alone, or in organizations, have almost no impact on policy-making. More than 70% of American people want corporate power curtailed, yet it never happens. Unseen forces prevent it. That's the playing field we need to understand.

Covey also advised that if we want something done, we need to be pro-active. Simply do something! The world will not get better on its own. We need to take action, so let's look at examples of things people have done.

One simple step we can all take is to *disagree* when people say things you know are not correct. When they cite fake economics, at a minimum, simply disagree. We need to challenge what's incorrect—we need to offset the unchallenged messages from the corporate media. Disagreeing doesn't have to be aggressive; it can be polite. "I'm sorry, that's not the way I see it!" Just don't let fake economics go unchallenged.

People are taking action in many other ways: the Occupy Wall Street movement; the volunteers working for food banks; the musicians who create inspirational "Playing for Change" videos; the Green Parties, or Pay It Forward movements: all reinforce the right actions.

In the next few pages, I'll look at cooperatives, sympathetic national governments, and alternate economists. All expand our understanding of what can be done.

These ideas are possibly useful parts of the solution.

Getting control of the way money is created and controlled, as discussed in Chapter Five, is paramount. These other ideas could help.

Spain

Just an hour outside of Bilbao, a city in the Basque region in northern Spain, is the town of Mondragón. It was there that the Mondragon Corporation was founded in 1956. It's now the seventh largest corporation in Spain, employing over 80,000 people in a federation of worker co-operatives.

It all began in 1941, when a young Catholic priest, Father Arizmendiarrieta, was assigned to the town, which was suffering from unemployment, hunger, and poverty at the end of the Spanish Civil War (1936–1939). Before he became a priest, he'd had a role fighting against the fascists in the civil war and escaped a death sentence.

With the region's long tradition of cooperatives, Father Arizmendiarrieta saw the potential that co-ops might have to help the people and started a college in 1943 to teach how co-ops could transform communities. By 1956, they had established their first business, which made space heaters. Today, they have 256 manufacturing plants in 19 countries producing stoves, refrigerators, solar heaters, and other things. They run retail businesses throughout Spain and have branches in the south of France. This workers' cooperative federation has four divisions: finance, manufacturing, retail, and education. Most of their 80,000 employees live in Spain, and 85% of these people own the business. In bad times, the 85% of the workers who are owners decide what to do. Their norm is to share what work there is, and so share the incomes, which contrasts vividly with companies in much of the world, where layoffs and wage cuts are the norm.

The worker members hire and fire the directors and have an organizational rule that the top wage can be no higher than 6.5

times the pay of the lowest paid worker, a rule that mainstream business mythology would call disastrous! The co-op's success over almost sixty years suggests that 6.5 times may be the answer to the question of how much the top person is worth. Curiously, it's almost the same ratio that Plato wrote about, over two thousand years ago: the richest should be restricted in pay to five times the poorest.

Two benefits of co-operatives are that they do not have to earn profit and they do have to pay a dividend. Mondragon does earn profit and whatever profits they earn are spent in the community: 10% of profit is spent on education and socio/cultural activities and 10% on R&D to prepare for the future. Their website outlines their set of basic principles: one is a democratic workplace where labour is sovereign, and capital is subordinate. Profit is seen as the property of those who earn it.

In 2012, while the rest of Spain was suffering 25% unemployment, a broken banking system, and austerity measures, the co-op members were all working. It all began with the vision of a local priest.

Two additional Spanish successes are worthy of mention:

In January 2014, in the city of Burgos, the people were not pleased that the city was going to spend $11 million to redevelop a street in a working-class neighbourhood while, at the same time, people were facing cutbacks in education and health care. After a week of protests, the roadway project was abandoned, as were the planned layoffs of street cleaners and gardeners in Madrid.

And thirdly, the Platform of People Affected by Mortgages is a Spanish group that rallied and stopped 936 evictions and caused banks to renegotiate hundreds of planned repossessions.

It's a grassroots organization that has grown to 150 branches across Spain.

Iceland

Iceland is a nation that made the mistake of embracing neoliberalism, paid the price, saw the light, rejected it, and restored prosperity.

This North Atlantic island was once part of Denmark and in 1944 separated to become a republic. The word republic comes from Latin for a form of government where the power is with the people who elect their leaders who are to rule within the laws. Just over 300,000 people live in this small, cold country, which provides free universal health care and free education, including university. They see free education not as a naïve luxury, but as prudent investment.

Troubles began in 2003, when Prime Minister Davíð Oddsson followed global trends and privatized state-owned businesses, liberalized markets, and deregulated banks. He hoped to make Iceland a global financial centre and together with the privatized banks, had visions of the nation becoming a world leader in both financial services and investment banking. By 2007, the banks had made loans equivalent to nine times the size of the nation's economy. As the loans grew, so too, did national inequality.

In 2008, that came to a sudden halt. Three major banks failed—they owed nearly $100 billion US—and many of the banks' actions had been illegal. (Someone with a sense of humour put the country up for sale on eBay!) In 2009, the government proposed an IMF rescue that would bail out the banks and impose austerity on the people. In response, over 6,000 people took to the streets in Reykjavík the capital in what was called the Kitchenware Revolution. People banged pots and pans demanding that the government resign. The people won, got an election, and the new coalition government, led by Johanna Sigurdardotter, held a referendum on bailouts. 93% of the people rejected bailing out the banks! The previous government leader, Geir Haarde, was soon found guilty of negligence over his role in the country's 2008 financial collapse. He had said the country needed to pay $5 billion to the Dutch and UK governments, which had insured Icelandic bank deposits. This was debt that had been created by the failed banks and amounted to about $5,000 per Icelandic family! The people said no. Their three major banks failed. The people did better, and so did the economy. According to the International Monetary Fund, Iceland has rebounded after the 2008/2009 crisis and will soon surpass pre-crisis output levels, with strong performance in tourism and fisheries. Debt ratios are on a downward path, and balance sheets have been broadly restored.

It was easier for the people of Iceland to regain control of their economy than it was for the Greeks, due to the fact that Iceland never joined the European Union and as a result, retained control of its money. Countries using the €uro have lost that. As the president explained, "These were private banks, and we didn't pump money into them in order to keep them going; the state did not shoulder the responsibility of the failed private banks." Instead, he explained, "… we provided support for the poor … and four years later are enjoying progress and recovery."

The government put the welfare of people first. It jailed those convicted of insider trading, breach of trust, or market manipulation, and held government leaders responsible for negligence.

Oxfam reported in September 2013:

Iceland has used the social protection system to shelter more vulnerable groups during the crisis. Moreover, a trend towards increasing inequality was reversed during the crisis years of 2008 and 2009, and continued to drop in 2011 …

However, about 15 per cent of households still experience great difficulty in making ends meet. Various programs for the unemployed have been introduced, and existing ones strengthened, but there is disappointment over the lack of investment in new jobs. Despite this, unemployment has not become as big a problem as might have been expected given the size of the country's collapse and the severity of its economy's contraction. Iceland's unemployment rate in 2010 was 7 percent, but, by April, 2013, it had fallen to 6.6%, below the EU average …

The Icelandic economy has recovered after the worst economic crisis in the country's history. While much of Europe still battles with crisis, the economy of this island in the North Atlantic is growing—thanks to a currency decline, an export increase, a boom in tourism and the fishing industry and growing consumer confidence. The Icelandic way of dealing with the crisis could inspire alternatives to austerity in the EU.

The success of the government of Iceland shatters two myths: that you need to save the banks, and that you need to impose austerity. Even the International Monetary Fund said so:

Iceland's commitment to its program, a decision to push losses on to bondholders instead of taxpayers and the safeguarding of a welfare system that shielded the unemployed from penury helped propel the nation from collapse toward recovery ...

Cuba

The largest island in the Caribbean has had, for about five decades, a different economic system. Cuba is about the same size as Iceland, with about forty times the population: eleven million people living in a socialist economic system.

The capital, Havana, is just one hundred miles south of Key West Florida while Guantanamo, a small city with its infamous prison, is about 400 miles east on the south shore, closer to Haiti than Havana. The famous song *Guantanamara!* is a patriotic Cuban song about a woman who lived just south of where the United States has for decades leased 45 square miles for $4,085 a year for a naval station. Since 2002, that site has been used as an infamous illegal prison.

In the early 1950s, the country was run by the elite, with posh hotels and casinos for the rich while one-third of their people lived in poverty. Gambling and prostitution attracted tourists while poverty created social unrest and by 1959 there was a revolution, led by Fidel Castro, who became the leader of the country. He stayed in power so long he became the longest-serving leader in the world.

Shortly after coming to power in 1960, his government nationalized the phone company and reduced phone rates. Then they nationalized the refineries and the banks. In response, the US set up a boycott, so Cuba nationalized all US holdings. The boycott lasted over fifty years while the Cubans redistributed land from the large landowners and provided it to co-operatives for the poor. The legendary Che Guevara was in charge of this program. The logic was that it was the poor who had worked the land thus it was the poor who should benefit. Because of the US embargo, Cubans could buy neither new cars, nor replacement parts for the 1950s-era cars they kept running. Many of the wealthy who lost their holdings moved a hundred miles north and are members of the million-strong "Cuban mafia" in the greater Miami area.

Despite decades of embargo Cuba rates near the top of the *Happy Planet Index* published by The New Economics Foundation in Britain, which looks at economics "as if people and the planet matter." They sponsor this annual review of how people rate their well-being, including their life expectancy and ecological footprint. Costa Rica is consistently number one; Cuba and a few others are listed below;

Happy Planet Index	Rank	Score	Life Expectancy
Costa Rica	1	64	79.3
Cuba	12	56.2	79.1
Canada	65	43.6	81.0
United States	105	37.3	78.5
And lastly:			
Botswana	151	22	53.2

Cuba provides free education at every level and has the tenth highest literacy rate in the world. (Andorra is first, Canada is 30th, the United States 49th.) Cubans have developed sustainable agricultural practices that produce healthy crops without petroleum inputs. (Sustainable agriculture is the practice of farming without chemicals, pesticides, biotechnology, and Monsanto. Instead, it uses techniques to protect the environment, enrich the soil, treat animals with care, and provide healthy food.)

Cuba has one of the best health care systems in the world: people have a life expectancy about the same as North Americans. They graduate more than enough medical personnel to look after their own needs and send medical aid outside the country. Venezuela has been trading oil to Cuba for the services of about 30,000 medical personnel.

After he stepped down as leader at age 82 in 2008, Castro wrote a few articles on international affairs: one was on the tragedy of the earthquake on the neighbouring island of Haiti and how his people were able to send hundreds of doctors to help. When Hurricane Katrina hit New Orleans in 2006, the United States officially asked for international help, and the Cubans offered 1,586 doctors and 26 tons of medicine—which the Americans declined. Cubans had experienced their own hurricane when Category 4 Hurricane Michele hit the island in 2001, and they moved over half a million people to safety. That included about one-quarter of the population of Havana. Only 5 died. Over 1,000 died in New Orleans during Hurricane Katrina, a less dangerous Category 3 storm.

Now Cuba is creating a new economy, likely to be a form of socialism for the twenty-first century, Cubans are trying to keep the benefits of socialism in an increasingly capitalist world.

Many socialist nations, like those in the former Eastern Bloc, face the same challenges, as do the Chinese and Vietnamese, who are trying to transition to a mix of socialism and state capitalism.

Policies that serve people

The mantra of letting "open markets" control everything has included water, sewers, and electricity. Even though this routinely fails in these areas, the World Bank includes privatizing these essential services as standard procedure. Using their own figures, 34% of water and sewer privatizations failed between 2000 and 2014. Manila privatized water and prices increased by 500%. The World Bank lends money to private companies to "buy" these services in country after country. The country is told that they will get a cash infusion and then better service and efficiency as only the free market can provide. What they get is a cash infusion and huge increases in price, decreases in service, and the loss of profit forever.

On the other hand, the Netherlands closed eight prisons in 2009 because of a decreasing crime rate. In 2013, they announced that they were closing nineteen more. The country had a declining crime rate as a result of legalized prostitution, passing sane drug laws, and reducing income inequality. They further reduced their prison costs by offering convicts a choice to wear an electronic tag rather than go to jail. Offenders continue to live at home, go to work, and save the nation about $50,000 per convict per year. The main purpose of the system is rehabilitation. The proof that the system works is in their low rates of re-offending. Incarceration time is one-third that of North America.

The Bolsa Familia program, in Brazil, is a government social welfare program that gives money directly to the poor. Families who qualify must see that their children attend school, which is free. It's the largest cash transfer program for people anywhere in the world. (The Fed's Quantitative Easing program is larger, but it does nothing for the people!) The Bolsa program helps over twelve million families, 26% of the population. The *Economist* magazine had to report that it's a stunning success. Brazil also increased state pensions and research has shown that poverty is being reduced about 8% a year. And contrary to widely held assumptions, the poor are growing more independent, not more dependent, which is contrary to what neo-cons would expect.

General welfare didn't improve in Brazil because of the mythical hope that money would trickle down to those on the bottom. It improved because money rained directly on the poor, allowing them to improve themselves. Unfortunately, in 2016, a coup brought the rich back to power, and now the program may be in doubt.

Around the world, people are forcing change. The British Labour party has for a change elected a true labour leader! From 1997 to 2010, Britain's prime ministers—Tony Blair followed by Gordon Brown—had both abandoned their labour roots. Now Jeremy Corbyn leads the Labour Party. Elected in September 2015, he's a socialist, the kind of leader the party used to elect. We will see what develops.

In the US, the people in Ashville, North Carolina, have developed the Living Wage Program, designed to see that people are paid enough to live on. It's run by the Just Economics organization, formed in 2000, and at about the same time, Cambridge, Ontario, in Canada passed a living wage ordinance into their municipal code.

Alternatives to banks and money

We don't need banks or money as they are. It's possible to use credit unions and alternate currencies to avoid corporate banking. Only one of us withdrawing our money from the bank doesn't mean much, but if we all do, then we might get change.

Credit unions, and there are over 6,000 in the United States, are member-owned financial institutions designed to "serve people, not profit." Historically, credit union members have had a common bond: all teachers, neighbours, or people who work at the same place. They are democratically run financial cooperatives. If everyone used credit unions, we could eliminate private banks and keep their profits among us. We could avoid their crises and limit or shut down the system they use to concentrate wealth.

JAK Sweden (JAK stands for Land, Labor, Capital) is a unique credit union that lends like an Islamic bank—it doesn't charge interest. Their money comes from member savings, and those savings result in "savings points," which can be used when a loan is required.

Another, simple alternative: people can simply barter—trade your ten-speed bike for a patio grill.

We can use alternate forms of money, as I mentioned in Chapter Six. "Berkshares" is the alternate currency in the Berkshires region of Massachusetts. They have notes for 1, 5, 10, 20, and 50 Berkshares. *The New York Times* referred to them as a "great economic experiment."

During the Great Depression, "scrip" (paper money or tokens) emerged in the US and Europe with over 3,000 types in the US, which came about in response to banks closing and money becoming scarce. During the 1991 recession, "Ithaca Hours" emerged, printed with the motto, "In Ithaca We Trust," to save jobs in their home town.

The ten thousand inhabitants of Salt Spring Island, off Vancouver's Pacific coast, launched the Salt Spring Dollar in 2001, with a series of bills that are traded at par with the Canadian dollar. Each bill has a quotation from Einstein, "How I wish that somewhere there existed an island for those who are wise and of good will! In such a place even I would be an ardent patriot." The profits from the Salt Spring money are used for community projects.

Another variation on traditional banking are "micro-loan" banks. The concept was created by Mohammad Yunus, born in Bangladesh in 1940—the same year I was born in Toronto. He studied at Dhaka University and then got a PhD in Economic Development from Vanderbilt University in the US. From 1969 to 1972, he taught in MTSU in Murfreesboro. After Bangladesh won its war for independence, he returned home and was soon involved in poverty reduction programs. His research proved that among the poor, small loans to create or build up small businesses could make a huge difference in lifting people out of poverty, and founded the Grameen Bank. (Grameen comes from the Bengali word for rural.) For what he accomplished in addressing poverty with micro-credit, he won the Nobel Peace Prize, awarded in 2006. Micro-loan programs have been successful worldwide. The key to micro-loans is that the profits stay with the people.

Cyber currencies, such as Bitcoin attract speculators

Currently, cash transactions have been replaced by credit or debit cards. It's "digital money," and it can be transferred by smartphones and computers, by plastic cards or voice instructions. Governments like digital money because of the audit trail these transactions leave that allows increased visibility for taxation.

But the newest trend is to virtual currency or cyber currency or cryptocurrency.

Bitcoin was the first of what is now a proliferation of cryptocurrencies that have sprung up since 2009, when an anonymous Japanese person released bitcoin.

None of these cryptocurrencies are money; they are digital assets designed to be used as a medium of exchange you can swap for money, things, or services. They are designed to be secret (crypto—Greek for hidden or secret), using decentralized control in a public transaction database and something called blockchain technology: computer data, lists of fields, or files called blocks. There is no central computer; data is spread among the users.

To get involved in Bitcoin, you need a smart device a phone or computer onto which you put a virtual wallet into which you can save your virtual bitcoins. You can get bitcoins by buying them for money or by accepting them for payment or by mining them. When bitcoins were conceived, they were limited to a maximum of twenty-one million. Only about half have been released. The process of releasing more is done by confirming transactions, which is sort of an audit. That process is called mining and earns a small new bitcoin fee.

While seeming to offer a lot of promise, blockchain technology is not trusted yet. None of the cryptocurrencies have been perfected nor are they well understood. Goldman Sachs released a study of bitcoin in 2014 in which they concluded that "bitcoin likely can't work as a currency," which can limit its growth but that too, is not clear. That cryptocurrency prices can be as volatile as some have suggests they are just another commodity and vulnerable to price bubbles.

While becoming a popular curiosity, there is no consensus anywhere on where cryptocurrencies fit in investment planning.

My advice is that it's only sensible to invest in things you understand.

State-owned enterprises (SOE's)

We seldom hear of state-owned enterprises in the West. In part, it's because they are unfashionable and in part because the corporate media would prefer we never knew of them. In fact, they are a significant force on the global economic scene. China, the communist powerhouse, uses them, as does Taiwan. China seems to have copied its Taiwan neighbour, and now SOE production amounts to about 40% of China's output.

Singapore Airlines is a state-owned enterprise success story. It's 56% owned by the city/state of Singapore, an island country in the South China Sea. The country owns an investment company, which has major holdings in a variety of enterprises. Over 500 people manage their diverse holdings in financial services, telecommunications, life sciences, and energy.

Germany owns its railway company; the second largest transport company in the world, plus 11% of Airbus (the airplane manufacturer), and 20% of Volkswagen.

Britain's railways were nationalized in 1948, but privatized by the Conservatives in 1993. Rail management was renationalized after a train crash exposed the failures of the privately owned rail enterprise. Now the Labour Party, led by Jeremy Corbyn, is in favour of nationalization of the entire railway.

In the US, Fannie Mae, Freddie Mac, and the Post Office are government-owned, and Amtrak is partially government-owned. The Corporation for Public Broadcasting in the US provides funding for public radio, television, and other services. In Canada, the CBC and Radio Canada are publicly owned. The lesson is that state-owned enterprises can do a good job and the public can reap the benefits.

Go Green

> The pace of consumption, waste and environmental change has so stretched the planet's capacity that our contemporary lifestyle, unsustainable as it is, can only precipitate catastrophes, such as those which even now periodically occur in different areas of the world … we need to reflect on our accountability before those who will have to endure the dire consequences.
>
> —Pope Francis; May 2015

The capitalist system exploits resources, as we examined in Chapter Two. An obvious alternative to tolerating, or supporting this exploitation is to join the environmental movement.

Here's a short recap as to the economic reasons why.

If you own a copper mine, you make all the money you can possibly make when all the copper is sold; the faster, the better. There is no financial incentive to mine copper in an environmentally careful way, but there is every financial incentive to do it cheaply and fast. The earth's resources are finite, but greed is not. Unregulated competition and sound ecology are incompatible! Less than a century ago, steel mill air pollution was described as the smell of money. Now, fortunately, we know better about the true costs of pollution to our environment.

A symptom and symbol of our past and present failure is a floating garbage patch that fills an area in the Pacific Ocean the size of Texas, which American oceanographer Charles Moore discovered in 1997. It took him a week to sail through it. So too does the more *recently discovered* Pacific algae patch ecologists call the "blob."

In North America, about two million plastic water bottles are used every 5 minutes, and only a small percentage get recycled. There is no money to be made in providing, as we once did, free drinking fountains, but there are big profits with bottled water. The free market, again is the foe of the environment.

When he became Pope in 2013, the Argentinian Jesuit took the name Francis after the Italian Francis of Assisi, known for his care for animals and the environment. In May 2015, he released his second encyclical (a fancy name for a letter) to the people, entitled *Laudato Si: On Care for our Common Home*. The quotation above is from the encyclical, pointing out the dangers our economic system poses to life on earth.

The same message has come from 98-year-old Jacque Fresco, an American idealist visionary who teaches that we are part of nature, not in charge of it. Trained as an architect, in 1994 he established the nonprofit Venus Project to promote alternate ways for society to function. Venus is a small community in south-central Florida and visitors are welcome. Fresco wrote, with his associate Roxanne Meadows, *The Best That Money Can't Buy: Beyond Politics, Poverty and War*. They believe that science and technology should be used to create a secure and sustainable future for everyone, not just for the few. They are among the growing number of people and groups supporting sustainable development. It's a philosophy long shared by the First Nations people.

We are seeing more Green anti-corporate trends, such as the trend to small-scale farming and the 100-Mile Diet movement (a campaign to buy local produce) and the creation of "greenbelts" (protected farmlands around cities, where land planning, not the market, determines land use).

Climate change is a consequence of irresponsible, extensive market practices that create greenhouse gases. Corporate-funded "research" is used to delay regulation by creating confusion about whether or not climate change is real. Despite those tactics, we now are being forced to deal with it, which requires co-operation at all levels to undo the damage of decades of profit-seeking neglect and misdirection. We can only hope these measures will be successful in time.

To this end, more and more people are opposing the ethics of specific corporations like Monsanto and the pharmaceutical industry.

80% of antibiotics in the US are used in agriculture. Genetically modified foods, sold without warning labels in North America, are not allowed to be sold in Europe. As we become conscious of the exponential destruction we are doing to the planet, more people are "Going Green."

And despite what the critics say, green developments can work.

In Bali, the Ibuku team of design engineers are using sustainable Balinese designs—native craftsmen and modern engineering to create beautiful buildings. They build with the abundant native bamboo to create homes, school buildings, eco resorts, and even a small village.

In St. Paul, Minnesota, Compatible Technology is a non-profit organization that uses volunteer engineers to develop simple tools to help improve access to water and improve food production. They have designed low-cost coolers chilled by evaporation in India, low-cost water chlorination in Nicaragua, and peanut processing tools for Malawi, where three simple tools were developed to dig the nuts, remove the pods from the roots, and shell them ten times faster than previously.

A Toronto designer has developed an inexpensive pedal-powered washing machine that can do a load of laundry in about four minutes and is as easy as riding a bike!

The Green movement has many successes, and the more we become green, the more we escape OPEC and the fossil fuel economy.

Economic democracy

> Democracy is not just the right to vote, it is the right to live in dignity.
> —Naomi Klein

In the Western media, democracy is routinely equated with freedom and capitalism as an inseparable troika, but democracy is more than that. Democracy is a hard-won right to collective protection of, and for the common good. Economic democracy, if it existed, would oppose special rights or a privileged class. An active, politically powerful local workforce, if it existed, would never have consented to having local jobs moved offshore.

In the golden years of capitalism, democracy had more teeth, and if society is to work again, we need a society where money (especially money for political party financing) doesn't dominate. The multi-party system in Canada makes it more difficult for money to dominate than does the two-party system in the US. That's because with more parties there are more options than the simple two that dominate American politics, like green, socialist, Quebec regional, and more.

In this environment, a few people have managed to succeed in business and remain focused on their roots. Here are examples.

A century ago, the Greek Demoulas family started a food business in Lowell, Massachusetts, and when the Depression occurred, many of their customers were struggling. The Demoulas family, however, continued to provide both food and credit to them. The business has grown to 71 supermarkets in the New England area, and in its third generation, Arthur Demoulas continued to run the company with the same principles of the earlier generation. He used their stores to serve the many stakeholders, shareholders, workers, suppliers, and customers. He paid their workers better, kept prices lower, and gave managers more autonomy than other businesses did. In 2013, he gave customers another 4% discount, saying they needed the money more than the shareholders. Arthur's cousin tried to take control of the company, and this grew into a community dispute; employees and customers banded together to keep the leader they loved. The power of the people worked, and the rebellious cousin was forced to sell out.

On the other hand, Wall Street's capitalism assumes that business exists to serve shareholders and only shareholders. Stakeholder capitalism, like the Demoulas family business, is a rarely seen option. Because mainstream media is concentrated in corporate hands, real democracy is threatened by endless repetition of the message that corporate capitalism is our only option.

In this final chapter, I have looked at things nations have done differently: Iceland and Cuba, for example. I've looked at models for enterprises, co-ops, and credit unions, and state-owned enterprises that differ from corporations. I've looked at better forms of money, like Berkshares, and better community decisions such as mandating that people be paid living wages.

> We do better when we work together.
> —Wab Kinew; economist, journalist and contemporary Ojibway leader

One of my professors at university taught that the closer you come to contradiction, the closer you are to truth. So how much truth and how much contradiction is in our economic system?

Our economy:
- depends on competition, but eliminates it
- creates increasing inequality
- props up failed private enterprises with public money
- depends on banks to create money as debt
- creates money through loans but not enough money to pay the interest
- depends on the impossibility of exponential growth
- depends on endless consumption of limited resources
- creates national debts that are impossible to repay
- transfers money to the rich
- creates more food than is needed but leaves millions hungry
- creates empty houses and homeless people
- promotes rugged individualism as the path to collective security

In his 2007 speech (mentioned in Chapter Twelve), James Galbraith advised economists to develop a new paradigm in economics. However, as great as his advice was, I suggest the subject is too important to leave to economists. Why?

Almost forty years earlier, in 1968, James' dad John Kenneth, together with Paul Samuelson and another 1,200 economists, signed a document calling for the US Congress to introduce a system of income guarantees and supplements. It was a program designed to combat poverty and stimulate and protect the economy from repeated recessions. The program wasn't new, but was consistent with suggestions that had been made over centuries, by early Muslim leaders, by Napoleon, and by Thomas Paine. Such a program as Galbraith and the others suggested would make the decline in jobs a non-issue, but the idea went nowhere. It was neither widely understood nor widely embraced. That's why I believe it will take more than economists to come up with a plan that forces change: it will take enormous public pressure.

We need the vision that Galbraith, Sr. and the 1,200 economists and Galbraith, Jr. and thousands of other caring economists and they need to be joined by many more thousands of people.

Here are a few things I suggest that individuals can do to start.

1. Understand. Economics is not difficult: it is about the use of money and how it controls our lives, either to our advantage or disadvantage. Economics has been made to seem complex, but it doesn't need to be. If you understand economics, you will be less vulnerable.
2. Challenge "fake-economics" when you hear it: it's had a free ride for too long.
3. Get involved. Join a co-op or credit union or a "Green" organization: recycle, walk the talk.
4. Do not accept the media hype that international trade agreements are good for everyone. Learn about them; be prepared to fight them.
5. Support the public sector. It is not the public sector that has failed us. Education, social programs, pensions, and welfare can protect people and maintain decency.

6. Support making the banks public utilities. Support having the nation control its money.
7. Demand that plans that affect all of us be made in the open and for the long term. Corporate planning is secret and serves them not us. Worse, it puts their short-term bonuses first.
8. Realize that national debt is not a problem, only a bad, but changeable financing decision.

There are dangers involved in attempting to change the money system. On June 4, 1963, John F. Kennedy signed Executive Order No. 11110, allowing the government to issue currency without going through the Federal Reserve. He was killed five months later, and the order was revoked by Reagan.

Three writers on economics

> Unless someone like you cares a whole awful lot,
> Nothing is going to get better. It's not.
> —Dr. Seuss; *The Lorax*

Here are three writers—four, if you include Dr. Seuss—who care about justice and who have campaigned for change.

Ellen Hodgson Brown

Ellen Hodgson Brown is an attorney and expert on the Federal Reserve System. In 2007, she wrote *Web of Debt: The Shocking Truth about Our Money System and How We Can Break Free*. She describes how money is created in the United States (the stuff I discussed earlier in Chapter Six). She quotes former US presidents who were opposed to letting the private banks control the currency:

> If the American people ever allow private banks to control the issue of their currency, first by inflation, then by deflation, the banks and corporations that will grow up around [the banks] will deprive the people of all property until their children wake-up homeless on the continent their fathers conquered.
> —Thomas Jefferson

> If congress has the right under the Constitution to issue paper money, it was given them to be used by themselves, not to be delegated to individuals or corporations.
> —Andrew Jackson

> The Government should create, issue, and circulate all the currency and credits needed to satisfy the spending power of the Government and the buying power of consumers. By the adoption of these principles, the taxpayers will be saved immense sums of interest. Money will cease to be master and become the servant of humanity.
> —Abraham Lincoln

Ellen Hodgson Brown describes many examples of successful public banking introduced to North America by the Quakers in the colony of Pennsylvania. Today, only the state of North Dakota has a public bank, and it's because of that public bank that North Dakota escaped the fiscal problems of 2007/2008. North Dakota had the lowest unemployment rate and highest job growth in the country. How does having a state bank make that happen?

The bank was created by the North Dakota legislature in a law that directed all state taxes and fees be paid into the state bank. Then, with that money on deposit, the bank invests within the state, and the interest returns to the state. In other states, tax monies end up on Wall Street as does the interest earned on state debts. In 2008, when the "too big to fail" banks required a bailout, the Bank of North Dakota had record profits. Those profits came from investments in their own communities, money collected by the state and re-invested there. In 2014, the bank was more profitable than either Goldman Sachs or JPMorgan Chase.

Hodgson Brown has more examples of banking for the people.

Costa Rica has four public banks. That's four public banks out of twenty-nine, yet most Costa Ricans use the public banks because none have failed in 31 years. Private banks have come and gone. In 1948, Costa Rica was the poorest nation in the hemisphere, which resulted in civil war. Forty-four days after the revolution, Josë "Pepe" Figueres, a coffee farmer, democrat, and socialist came to power. He announced a plan to improve the nation by creating a state-owned bank that would finance enterprises owned by the public. The profits would be used for the people. The government also shut down their military. The nation went from desperate poverty, to become the wealthiest country in Central America.

They established more than 240 state-owned enterprises, guaranteed employment to the people, and profits from their enterprises went into infrastructure. With the lowest taxes in the region, they spend 30% of national income on health and education. They still have no army and have more teachers than police.

A steep drop in coffee prices in 1985 meant Costa Rican income went down, but the country chose to continue supporting social services and suspended payments to world banks. Because of that default, they became the first country in Central America to accept World Bank, IMF, and USAID assistance and the "structural adjustments" that came with it.

Local farmers were urged to change from producing traditional foods for their people and adopt an Agriculture of Change and grow exotic things for the North American market. This departure from self-sufficiency was supposed to increase exports and decrease the trade deficit. Many small farmers could not get financing for traditional crops and were forced off their land. Tax incentives were made available, but over 80% of the tax incentives went to five transnational corporations. Wages declined, poverty increased, infectious diseases increased, the trade deficit was increasing, and income distribution became more unequal. The program failed, and the deficit got worse, yet the World Bank declared Costa Rica an "economic success."

Predictably, social unrest grew. Ten thousand people took to the streets. Workers, students, and others joined together in the year 2000 to protest privatization of the state-owned power and telecommunications companies. Public utilities had served the public well and had great public support. After one person was killed and pictures of police beating students were shown on television, nearly half-a-million people marched nationwide. The students started a door to door campaign to teach people about economics, and the protests escalated until the government backed down.

Costa Ricans have underscored what the Rothschilds have understood for a couple of hundred years: whoever controls banking and money gets the benefits. (If you want to live on one of Costa Rica's tropical beaches, it's possible to get their excellent health care for 1/3 to 1/5 the cost in the United States.)

Ellen Hodgson Brown has just published a new book, entitled *The Public Bank Solution: From Austerity to Prosperity*.

George Monbiot

Monbiot is a British journalist, born in 1963, who writes for *The Guardian* on political economy and the environment. He published *The Age of Consent: A Manifesto for a New World Order* in 2003, and advocates a more democratic world, especially a more democratic United Nations. As it is, the few nations on the Security Council have all the power. He suggests the system be changed so that nations have votes in relation to their populations and that general assembly votes take precedence over the security council. He also suggests creating an International Clearing Union to prevent the accumulation of debt. This proposal was made by Keynes in 1944 at the Bretton Woods meeting. Without such an organization, Keynes felt the world would fall into self-perpetuating ever-increasing debt. His idea was rejected but, as we have seen, he was right. Debt has soared, and Monbiot has taken up Keynes' torch.

In an essay in July 2000, Monbiot dramatically wrote that "there is no Third World debt." His logic is straightforward: "Third World debt" began after millions of dollars of gold, silver, cotton, and spices were stolen from the colonies. If those things had been borrowed instead of pilfered, the interest alone would have bankrupted several European nations and the "Third World" would be rich. Instead, the poorest nations on earth have huge debts, which they are expected to pay to the rich nations! As I mentioned earlier, the "richest" nation, the United States, has debts so large they can never be repaid. Monbiot highlights the obvious injustice of expecting the poor, not the rich, to pay.

Pope Francis, in mid-2015, criticized the unjust social structures that create and sustain abundance on one hand and poverty on the other. He said that we can no longer trust the "… unseen forces and the invisible hand of the market" because capitalism has become "a new tyranny"! Francis is an Argentinian, and his theology for the people has roots in liberation theology defined in 1971 by Gustavo Gutiérrez, a Peruvian Dominican priest, who wrote *A Theology of Liberation*. (Shortly after that book came out, I was in Oxford for an Oxfam meeting and went to Blackwell's bookshop, where I skeptically wondered if they might have a copy. It was quite a bookshop: the bookseller asked, "What language would you prefer it in?")

Catherine Austin Fitts

I've met some interesting people, and Fitts is one. At one time, she was a Wall Street insider. After studying English and history, she then studied for an MBA in finance at the Wharton School in 1978. In the late 1980s, she was a Managing Director of Dillon, Read & Co., a Wall Street investment bank where she worked for eleven years. She was then recruited to become Assistant Secretary of Housing and a Commissioner at the United States Department of Housing and Urban Development (HUD) in the first Bush administration. HUD is a huge government corporation, with annual expenses in the tens of billions of dollars, 7,000 employees, over 80 offices in the US, and their mission is:

> ... to create strong, sustainable, inclusive communities and quality affordable homes for all. HUD is working to strengthen the housing market to bolster the economy and protect consumers; meet the need for quality affordable rental homes; utilize housing as a platform for improving quality of life; build inclusive and sustainable communities free from discrimination, and transform the way HUD does business.

Fitts believed in that mission. However, on joining the agency, she became aware that HUD had not been audited and, worse, appeared to have money missing and some divisions appeared to be losing money. At first, her efforts to raise the issue were stonewalled and eventually, as she kept trying, she was fired. When we met in the mid-1990s, she explained this to me, and it was almost déjà vu. In the late 1980s, I had heard the same thing: assets missing in the Redstone Arsenal in Alabama. (More details are in the Appendix.) By the early 1990s, she was reporting on missing millions in HUD. After Hurricane Katrina, HUD made the news again, unable to document expenses of $698.5 million.

Fitts developed software that looked at HUD investments by community and found a correlation between low government returns, high drug use, and high criminal returns. She found links between government agencies and illegal drugs. One of the communities she identified was in Los Angeles.

Michael Rupert had also documented government involvement in drug smuggling in L.A. I met him in Toronto in 2005. His mother was a cryptologist in WW II, and his father worked with the Air Force to help develop the Titan C3 spy satellite. When

Michael was 19, he applied to the LAPD for a job, and the Chief of Police took him aside and asked him to explain his "Q" security clearance. A "Q" security clearance is apparently a level above Top Secret, as Michael explained to me over lunch. He didn't know he had it, but his father explained that he got it because their whole household needed to be beyond suspicion. After Michael graduated from the police academy, he got a job with the LAPD and became a narcotics officer. By 1977, he was aware of the huge amount of money involved in drugs and the role the CIA was playing in smuggling them into New Orleans. Attempts were made to recruit him into the scheme, but instead, he became a whistleblower. He confirmed the same things that Fitt's research on drugs in L.A. had revealed. He had seen on the streets what she had discovered with data analysis.

A California journalist, Gary Webb, wrote a three-part series on the same story: the interrelationship of the CIA and the cocaine trafficking in L.A., which became a book, *Dark Alliance*, published in 1998. Fitts, Rupert, and Webb have all been labelled conspiracy theorists. More accurately, Gary Webb clarified, "It's not a conspiracy theory if it's fact." Webb died in 2004, reportedly a suicide after he shot himself twice, in the head.

When she left HUD, Fitts used her knowledge to develop what she called the Community Wizard software. It showed the high rates of HUD mortgage default in areas of heavy narcotics trafficking, including the areas in south central Los Angeles and how profits were being made from HUD defaults!

Ten years after Fitts was fired, the HUD Inspector General publicly confirmed the issue of the unaccounted billions that had gotten Fitts fired: $59 billion was unaccounted for. She was right.

12. What will replace capitalism?

Two years later, on September 10, 2001, Donald Rumsfeld revealed that up to $2.3 trillion was unaccounted for in the Defense Department. The next day was 9/11, and that story was gone from the news.

I met Catherine at her home in Hickory Valley, rural Tennessee and learned from her about what she called "the tapeworm economy." A tapeworm takes over the body it inhabits, and makes its host crave what's good for the tapeworm. In HUD she found that drugs were keeping people poor, keeping slums intact and slum investments profitable, all like the tapeworm. She also saw how the media was lying to convince average people to trust the stock market, which as an ex-Wall Street insider, she had learned to doubt. The tapeworm economy she described was like Wall Street in that it feeds itself first.

Where does she think people should invest? "Invest in friends and family, do that first, invest in your local community, invest in things you understand! Avoid the banks, use a credit union. Avoid Wall Street." And she should know. She had worked there

Recently, in 2017, professor Mark Skidmore, an economist from Michigan State University, heard her speak and as he heard her usual comments about missing trillions, thought she must be mistaken. That number was far too big. So he did the research. When it appeared she was right, he recruited a group of grad students to work with him and did detailed analysis to prove that there were unsupported entries 54 times larger than were authorized by

Congress.[160] Trillions were unaccounted for. It's evidence of the deep state's existence.

What I consider her greatest contribution to economics is not well-known. It's a tool she conceived for measuring economic progress: the Popsicle Index on community safety. Can you give a child money for a popsicle and let her walk to the store to buy it? In her community, when she was a child, like mine, it was ten. Very few American communities remain as safe: what we have accepted as progress has made our streets more dangerous.

What else can we do?

> Capitalism, free enterprise, the economy, currency, the market, are not forces of nature, we invented them. They are not immutable and we can change them.
> —David Suzuki; Co-Founder, David Suzuki Foundation; award-winning scientist, environmentalist, broadcaster

Capitalism has evolved and taken increasing control of our lives, from the time of Adam Smith through the Age of Enlightenment and then the scientific revolution. This evolution of capitalism began slowly, until the last thirty or forty years, when it began to change radically and faster and increasingly serving only the shareholders. In 2008, the basic foundation of the system—competition—was shattered. Nothing replaced it. We have allowed a failed system to limp along, serving only itself.

---

160 http://msutoday.msu.edu/news/2017/msu-scholars-find-21-trillion-in-unauthorized-government-spending-defense-department-to-conduct/

We need more widely based understanding and debate as to how to regain a system that serves most of the people as it once did. Our politicians need to understand that their roles have been usurped to serve trade and finance before the larger role they used to have serving liberty and justice.

Some people have started efforts to raise understanding. That's a start.

For example, the North American Occupy Wall Street movement raised these issues in 2011. They happened to be the same issues the French had raised in their revolution in 1789: the unfair concentration of wealth.

There isn't detailed data from 1789 to show how concentrated wealth was at that time, but the nobility and the clergy were what we now call "the 1%." Half of France's national revenue was spent on interest on its rising debt, which was partially due to money they spent to help fund the American Revolution. The French nobility did what the rich always do, they fought tax increases, leaving the nation's bills to the poor, unemployed, and starving peasants.

Was wealth more concentrated in France before their revolution than it is in the world today? It is hard to find facts, but the issues are similar.

Today, the clergy and nobility have been replaced by the high priests of finance, their compliant political agents, and the wealthy. Like Marie Antoinette and her peers at that time are the Bilderbergers of today, folks who grow increasingly rich and more detached from us. (At the moment, the concentration of wealth is somewhat greater in the United States than in Canada because Canada has more union members and thus a larger middle class.)

Adam Smith wrote about the form of capitalism he saw emerging and how it suited his times. It allowed the rich to prosper while creating opportunities for lots of others. Also, if some people got too rich, competition would encourage more people to move into that area. Now that system no longer works at the top; the system has failed.

Marx recognized that in its early years, capitalism would create both wealth and opportunity for most people, but he predicted in the end, it would implode. Keynes, too, saw that the system was not perfect and set out to manage the booms and recessions so most people would prosper.

In the late 1960s and the 1970s, J. K. Galbraith made us aware of the perils of corporate power, but that warning, as Eisenhower's warning before him, went ignored. Corporate and technocratic resources in both general businesses and military businesses were used to control attitudes and increasingly manipulate the economy.

I've reviewed simplistic economic assumptions from the time of Thatcher and Reagan, through the proliferation of so-called "think tanks," which together with the concentration of media, have stifled thought or popularized incorrect information. It took me almost two years of research to find writers on economics who made sense. There seem to be more of them now.

I have reviewed countries that have not bought into the corporate fictions. The Nordic countries, for example, have some of the world's strongest social support programs. They have less income differentiation, more equal education, and higher taxes to provide these benefits. Norway does an exemplary job of managing their more recent oil wealth by retaining ownership of 80% of petroleum production and roughly 85% of net revenues. Norway is a leader in climate protection and has built a fund from oil revenues that amounts to $664 billion to protect future social welfare benefits. It's all about making the right choices.

Canada hasn't made the right choices. It, too, is an oil-producing nation but mines tar sands, which are ancient oil-saturated sand pits. Mining tar sands leaves behind miles of polluted bogs, destroyed forests, and toxic wastewater. It's the dirtiest oil on earth and often uses about one unit of energy to produce three units of oil. As a result of allowing this, Canada reneged on its commitments to reduce greenhouse gases.

One major step Canadians can take to regain control of their economy is to have the Canadian government use its nation-owned bank to finance itself. The nation would borrow money from the Bank of Canada, and the interest would return to the people. That would be an immense step but be aware, the private banks will not embrace that willingly!

Scandinavians, like most Canadians, don't abhor taxes the way neocons believe everyone should. Some people see taxes as the price of living in a civil society. It's just the dues they pay. It's a big contrast to the Tea Party jargon in the US that says taxes are an attack on liberty.

We've seen there are many varieties of capitalism; mercantilism, laissez-faire capitalism, Keynesian capitalism, military capitalism, and corporate capitalism. Whether or not capitalism can be reworked again into something fair to most has yet to be determined. As it is, it continues concentrating wealth like never before. This trend is just a couple of decades old out of the more than two hundred years of this system. It's such recent history that some of us have lived through one-third of the years since Adam Smith first described it.

The options we face are two: redefine capitalism, once again, to fix its weaknesses, or find another system. Keynes tried to redefine it, and Galbraith, Sr. tried. Galbraith, Jr. is working on it. The process of redefining it needs to include a lot more people, ideally almost everyone in some open discussion that extends beyond the tunnel vision that Western media creates.

There are some changes underway: the city of Atlanta and 180 other communities in 35 countries have been reversing privatization of their water and sewage supplies. Atlanta's story began in 1999, when it entered a twenty-year contract for water and sewage with an American subsidiary of the French firm Suez. By 2003, they had had enough—service was worse, and prices were higher—so they took back the service.

In Canada, the city of Hamilton, Ontario, had a similar experience: they had signed a ten-year contract in 1994 to a newly formed company that was sold to a division of Enron, then to a German company. As the contract was coming up for renewal, the Canadian Union for Public Employees did an economic analysis of the impact of the contract and detailed a list of problems with the deal. The citizens formed Hamilton Water Watch, and in 2004, the city took back control. The city staff outperformed targets the private firm had not been able to meet in a decade.

Research done by the New Economic Foundation found that Londoners could save £328 per household, a savings of 25%, by undoing the 1990s privatization of their water supply.

And in 2009, Ireland was forced to take a loan for €85 billion from the International Monetary Fund and for that was forced to slash wages and pensions. Predictably, mortgage defaults reached all-time highs and then the government attempted to privatize water. The citizens had had enough and formed the Right2Water organization. Thousands protested.

Selling off water rights has been a standard part of neoliberal restructuring, but protests like the one in Ireland are getting louder. In a humourous misstatement of the situation, Irish Senator Martin Conway attempted to justify the government's position on selling the water system because, as he said, "… water doesn't just fall out of the sky." The fighting Irish have joined the Bolivians who fought Bechtel, and the people of Detroit, and Flint, Michigan, who are currently fighting for the right to water, as are other cities in the US. [161]

The world's not a level playing field. There are 7.3 billion individuals in 196 nations who are, as I discussed in Chapter Eleven, up against 147 super-entities controlled by about 1,000 people controlling 60% of the world's finances. These super-entities share a common, self-serving world view.

We outnumber them, but they are better organized! Our future should be up to us.

The last thoughts are with others;

> We shall require a substantially new manner of thinking if mankind is to survive.
> —Albert Einstein, 1954

---

161 https://www.thenation.com/article/detroit-is-ground-zero-in-the-new-fight-for-water-rights/

… all sectors of society need to join in an open discussion, … (that) will be crucial if we are to overcome the current global calamity.
—Margrit Kennedy, 2012

The attainment of a just society is the cherished hope of civilized man.
—Pierre E. Trudeau, 1968

Resist the war on terror… in failing to seek or find international consensus on what "terrorism" does and does not entail, we have simultaneously empowered governments across the world with new tools of political repression and left those governments entirely at liberty to decide who the "terrorists" are.
—Hayes, Ben. *Worried about the return of fascism? Six things a dissenter can do in 2016.* The Transnational Institute, January 2016.

Live as if you live for the day, farm as if you will live forever!
—Hans Wickholm, Swedish Calvary Officer (Retired), Deacon, farmer, family friend, 1974.

The old people must start talking and the young people must start listening.
—Thomas Banyacya, Hopi Tribe Elder, 1909–1999

Appendix

What a beautiful fix we are in now; peace has been declared.
—Napoleon Bonaparte; 1802

THIS APPENDIX IS ABOUT THE ECONOMICS OF THE MILITARY AND the way military enterprises have taken control of the national agenda. It also touches on how the line between economic warfare and traditional warfare has thinned. It ends with thanks to those who helped with the book.

Capitalism is often a very exploitive system. From the colonial period until today, it regularly recruits the military to its aid and the military machine has grown, taking an ever-larger percentage of our resources. This is truest in the US, where the military has become a power unto itself.

We've learned how corporations have been taking control of our lives, so we can easily see how the sector that is the military complex can and has done the same. What Eisenhower called "the military/industrial complex" in 1961, contemporary writers now call the American War Machine.

Eisenhower used the term "military-industrial complex" in his farewell address. Not all presidents choose to make a farewell address, but Eisenhower thought the issue of the growth in power of the military-industrial complex was important enough to warrant one. Here is part of his speech:

> In the councils of government, we must guard against the acquisition of unwarranted influence, whether sought or unsought, by the military-industrial complex. The potential for the disastrous rise of misplaced power exists and will persist. We must never let the weight of this combination endanger our liberties or democratic processes. We should take nothing for granted. Only an alert and knowledgeable citizenry can compel the proper meshing of the huge industrial and military machinery of defense with our peaceful methods and goals, so that security and liberty may prosper together.
> —Dwight D. Eisenhower; Jan. 17, 1961

At the end of World War II, Ike was not only the top American military officer, but he was also the top military officer in the Western world. He went on to be elected president twice and to serve for eight years. In making his final statement, he was admitting his own failure; he had not been able to control the war machine. He appealed to the people, "an alert and knowledgeable citizenry," to do what he was unable to do, take charge of the military. But it didn't happen.

This military market is huge, and the routine business practices of their market defy competitive norms. The global arms trade is almost $2 trillion a year; 2.2% of global GDP.[162] The US spends almost $6 billion, or about $5 billion a day.

The arms trade is not only huge, but it's beyond regulation. Since 1992, the Pentagon has not filed an audited annual report, as it is required to do by law! The practice of awarding contracts is now routinely done as "cost-plus" contracts, not competitive bidding; this opens the door for contractors to bill all they can get away with.

The reason I'm covering this subject in an appendix is that I don't want to confuse the understanding of general economics with the specifics of the military market. Military issues overlap with international politics, peace, and security, which can be emotional and patriotic and are not the subject of this book.

However, the role of the military is too significant a part of the economy to ignore. To put this into perspective, the United Nations has estimated that $44 billion[163] would end world hunger: that's nine days of global military spending. How did we get so misaligned?

Economics and the military

> The engineering of a series of provocations to justify military interventions is feasible and could be accomplished with the resources available.
> —Report to US Joint Chiefs of Staff, May, 1963[164]

---

162 http://data.worldbank.org/indicator/MS.MIL.XPND.GD.ZS
163 http://data.worldbank.org/indicator/MS.MIL.XPND.GD.ZS
164 Scott, Peter Dale. *The American Deep State: Big Money, Big Oil, and the Struggle for U.S. Democracy.* Rowman & Littlefield, 2014.p. 81.

The US Marine Smedley Butler was awarded more medals than anyone in United States Marine history. He was a hero. The Navy named a destroyer after him. He served in Cuba, China, Honduras, Mexico, and Haiti and retired in 1931. He had been raised among Quakers in Pennsylvania, become a high school quarterback, then dropped out of school, lied about his age, and enrolled in the Marines. His nickname was "the fighting Quaker." The first assignment of his 34-year career was in 1898 in Guantanamo Bay, fighting the Spanish. Of his 16 medals, five were for heroism, one for the time he was shot in the leg while rescuing a soldier in China. He rose to the rank of Major General, the highest rank in the Marine Corps.

In 1935, after retiring, he wrote a book, *War is a Racket*,[165] criticizing US foreign policy and especially the way the policy allowed business owners to prosper while soldiers were dying. In retirement, he became an aggressive campaigner against war profiteering, travelling the country and giving much of the money he earned speaking to the poor.

War is a Racket is written in simplistic, passionate prose describing who benefits and who suffers from war. It predated Eisenhower's warning about misused power by twenty-six years. The book sprang from an idea Smedley developed during WW I: a war fought with the noble purpose of being "the war to end all wars"! Butler thought wars should be to the benefit of everyone. Everyone should contribute equally: soldiers, financiers, steelmakers, and medics. Instead, he saw that "At least 21,000 new millionaires and

---

165 *War is a Racket* is available free online at http://www.ratical.org/ratville/CAH/warisaracket.html

billionaires were made in the United States during the first World War …" He said he knew this "because 21,000 people admitted their huge blood gains in their income tax returns." Profits soared in steel, copper, shipbuilding, and related industries. The costs for the war were passed on to all Americans, but the profits were concentrated in the hands of a few. That, Butler thought, was wrong.

After he retired from the Marines, he retired his uniform and never wore it again with one exception: his daughter's wedding. He died in 1940.

In 1969, John Kenneth Galbraith wrote a short book entitled *How to Control the Military*. It was two years after *The New Industrial State* was published, in which, as noted earlier he explained how corporations were taking over decision making and the dangers that came with it. In this shorter book, he raised the same points, but specifically about the military/industrial bureaucracy taking over foreign policy, which, like any corporate takeover, was self-serving; but in this case as he noted it was with deadly potential. War was their business.

The Vietnam War was in the fourteenth of its twenty years when Galbraith wrote this book, in the hope that the end of the war would be the opportunity to take control of the military/industrial bureaucratic machine. He was wrong: the United States troops withdrew from Vietnam in 1975, but military spending continued to grow.

The US military does the best marketing in the world. Using hand on heart patriotism, handsome uniforms, neat slogans—"Be all that you can be!"—and awesome fly-pasts, they create an overwhelmingly positive image.

It's an image so powerful that it obliterates the fact that they have not won any major campaign since the 1940s. Even then, it was one of 15 other countries that beat Germany. The corporate-bought media forget the wars lost by the West: Korea, Vietnam, the Bay of Pigs, Afghanistan, and Iraq. The media provide uncritical support for larger military budgets, new wars, and unwinnable objectives, like beating terror.

According to the United States government budget, nine divisions of the military (Army, Navy, etc.) had a budget for 2016 for $1.641.4 billion for recruiting and advertising. [166]The Canadian military spends far less, but in 2011 still spent $354 million and employed 661 people to promote their views.[167] Together, the two North American militaries spend about twice as much money promoting their view of the world than what McDonald's spends worldwide promoting its burgers.

The arithmetic for the arms industry is simple: the more bombs dropped, the more money made. That's not rocket science!

For the record, I've had some exposure to the military. My grandfather was a World War I veteran. He served as a stretcher bearer in the mud in France where he got what was called Trench Fever, which he suffered from for the rest of his life. His sons were military dispatch riders in Europe in WWII, and one of his daughters was recruited in Toronto to work in New York City, where Britain had established secret service headquarters. (No Americans could apply because the US was neutral at the time.) She signed Canada's Official Secrets act, lived a long life, and went to her grave

---

166   http://comptroller.defense.gov/Portals/45/Documents/defbudget/fy2016/fy2016_OM_Overview.pdf; p. 143

167   Engler, Yves. *A Propaganda System*. Fernwood Publishing, 2016.

without telling us what she had done there. (We deduced from the book, *A Man Called Intrepid*,[168] that she was involved in processing secret messages. She worked for William Stephenson (a.k.a. Intrepid), who was the model for M in the James Bond stories.)

I volunteered as a private in the Canadian Army's 32nd Signal Regiment and was trained on wireless and rifles. ("Aim here," said our Sergeant Major, pointing to the heart, and heard bullets zip overhead while on beach patrol.)

While in Kenya, I came face to face with the military. We had taken a safari (by plane) and were dropped at an isolated jungle landing strip with arrangements to be picked up in the afternoon a few days later. After a couple of days in the island town of Lamu on the Indian Ocean,[169] we arrived at the airstrip a bit early, threw our packs on a berm, and laid back in the shade to wait for the plane. Something stirred, I looked up to see the largest, most heavily armed soldier looming over me. He was on the top of the berm in camouflage clothing, bands of bullets, rifle ready, and looking around. "Jambo bwana!" He was Kenyan army, and they were on patrol for "rebels" in the area. He disappeared as quietly as he appeared.

Paul B. Farrell, who writes for *Market Watch*, was in the Marines in Korea. He then worked at Morgan Stanley as a Wall Street investment banker and became a behavioural economist and economic journalist. In 2013, he acknowledged the military economy this way:

---

168   Stevenson, William. *A Man Called Intrepid: The Incredible WWII Narrative of the Hero Whose Spy Network and Secret Diplomacy Changed the Course of History.* Lyons Press, 1976/2000.
169   Lamu is now a UNESCO World Heritage Site.

But most of all, wars are great for capitalists: Forbes' list of world billionaires skyrocketed from 322 in 2000 to 1,426 recently ... [yet] the adjusted household income of the rest of Americans flatlined the past generation. But still, life's great for capitalism and for 1,426 capitalists across America and worldwide, a tribute to the "disaster capitalism" doctrines of Nobel economist Milton Friedman and Ayn Rand's free-market capitalism dogma.[170]

There are plenty of examples of the overlap between war and banking. Here's a curious one: the Vietnam War started inching to an end, with talks in Paris, which became the Paris Peace Accords of 1973, although fighting continued until April 30, 1975. Then Saigon fell, and the last US Marines were evacuated by helicopter. Unlike the treaties to end the First and Second World Wars, this agreement did not require the aggressor to pay reparations.

However, eighteen years later, that tradition was revived! But with a twist! The Paris Club agreement was negotiated in secret, requiring the recently victorious and reunited Vietnam to recognize the debts of the old, defeated puppet government of South Vietnam. A group of private bankers, aided by the International Monetary Fund, arranged the deal. Unlike previous treaties, where the aggressor was fined, in this case, the victim, the newly freed and victorious nation of Vietnam, got to pay $145 million of debts rung up by the defeated, unwanted regime. [171]

---

170 Farrell, Paul B. *The Wall Street Journal.* Market Watch. *America needs a new war or capitalism dies.* April 17, 2013.
171 http://www.upi.com/Archives/1997/04/07/US-Vietnam-settle-debt-agreement/2966860385600/

More recently in November 2000, Saddam Hussein started selling Iraq's oil in €uros. It was Iraq's oil; it was under their sand. Hussein had nationalized it in the early 1970s. However, selling oil in other than US currency was an attack on the petrodollar, on the value of US currency, on the power of US banks. The US military responded three years later in March 2003, when it invaded the country, killed Hussein, and destroyed the nation. I will return to that, but the point it underscores is the link between money and war!

Indian Chief Dan George summed up how strange the world had become. I met him once in Lynn Valley Canyon in his native North Vancouver where he was filming a movie called *Shadow of the Hawk*. He was a ruggedly handsome elder of the Salish Coast nation and wrote *My Heart Soars*, in 1974:

> It is hard for me to understand a culture that spends more on wars and weapons to kill, than it does on education and welfare to help and develop.
> —Chief Dan George

In the next few pages, I'll look at military policy, NATO, and the economics of our more recent wars.

Military policy

In the 1970s, the foreign policy of Canada was peacekeeping. That policy had developed in the mid-1950s, when Canada's ambassador to the United Nations, Lester Pearson, suggested creating a UN peacekeeping force. Pearson had served, as my grandfather had, as a stretcher bearer in World War I and he returned home to become a federal politician. In 1957, Egypt nationalized the Suez Canal, and in response, Israel, with the aid of Britain and France invaded Egypt to get it back. Pearson conceived of a United Nations Emergency Force to prevent the situation from escalating and for this was awarded a Nobel Peace Prize. In 1963, Pearson became prime minister, and it was his passion that created Canada's role as a peacekeeper. The blue helmets of UN forces remain their symbol to this day.

Defense policy was explained to me in the mid-seventies by Major General Fred Carpenter: specifically, he explained why peacekeeping needed to be the Canadian military policy. It was simple logic: Canada shares the world's longest border with the most heavily armed nation on earth. Since the nineteenth century, the US has felt it is its Manifest Destiny to dominate the continent; thus, no nation on earth would risk attacking North America or Canada. If they did, the US would react. On the other hand, if the US were to attack Canada, there could be no defense; the US was too powerful.

The only possible defense that Canada might have, Major General Carpenter explained, was world opinion. The US would be reluctant to attack Canada if Canada was perceived globally as "the good guys." Thus, he said to protect ourselves, all our "military" expenses should be directed at peacekeeping or emergency aid. It made sense then, and it makes sense now. (Major General Carpenter confided to us [or possibly bragged] about the fact that his superior officer sent him for a brain scan to see if his opinions could be the consequence of a tumour!)

Twenty years later, in the early 1990s, Canada had a foreign policy review and released five papers for review. Judi Longfield, our local Member of Parliament, asked if I would read them and give her feedback. The five papers were entitled: *Overview; Diplomacy; Commerce; Development* (which held a special interest for me); and *Defense*. The first four papers were similar: written in a common style and all expressed typically Canadian values, such as fairness, and countries working together through the United Nations.

The paper on *Defense* was entirely different.

It differed in tone, differed in writing style, and differed in values. It had to have been written by a different group of folks. Given the differences, it could easily have been written in the Pentagon. It urged a closer military integration with the United States and showed no understanding that we were a different nation with a different culture and different values. Since that time, Canada's military role deteriorated to being an appendage of NATO. It was summed up by a recently retired Chief of Canadian Defense Command who said Canada's role was now killing "scumbags." Having read those policy review papers, I realized, in the 1990s, that Canada had lost control of its military. Military forces behind the scenes were out to control their policy, just as trade agreements were doing for non-military corporations.

United States military policy has been taken over by the American War Machine. How else can you explain that President Obama, the most powerful political leader in the world, spent eight years trying to fulfil a campaign promise to close the illegal, immoral prison at Guantanamo Bay? When Obama left office, there were still 40 prisoners there. The deep state prevailed.

Let's look at NATO for more detail.

NATO

In March 1948, a few years after the end of the Second World War, the Treaty of Brussels was signed to provide mutual defense for Belgium, the Netherlands, Luxembourg, France, and the United Kingdom. A year later, in 1949, the North Atlantic Treaty was signed in Washington, adding the United States, Canada, Portugal, Italy, Norway, Denmark, and Iceland to the original five and establishing NATO: the North Atlantic Treaty Organization.

The early agreements were prompted by fear of the Soviet Union, a cruel society still ruled by Stalin and the emerging Cold War. NATO was being created as a defensive organization; Russia was not identified as an enemy and even offered to join! As time would reveal, Russia was being set up as the new enemy, so their offer was summarily rejected and the "Cold War" simmered.

Today, NATO consists of 28 member states, all economically within the general framework of Western banking and capitalism but not all are on the North Atlantic. It has a democratic façade and has broadened its mandate well beyond the North Atlantic and has usurped national decisions about war and peace with the language of mutual defense. The most recent members added in 2009 were Albania and Croatia as part of the continuing steps to encircle Russia.

NATO has a quasi-parliament, the NATO Parliamentary Assembly, which has 257 delegates appointed from its 28 nations' members. The Assembly's role is stated on its website; it's "independent from NATO, the Assembly has no direct role of oversight over NATO policies." The real decision maker is the unelected North Atlantic Council, where the 28 members meet weekly as they have since 1954. Weekly!

It oversees NATO's military Supreme Allied Command in Brussels. Armies have Supreme Allied Commands; democratic organizations don't. This army reports to no country. I've pointed out several times in this book how corporations have used international treaties to change national laws in their favour. The military and military corporations have done the same most slyly by getting the military agenda moved beyond national control. Declaring war was, at one time, a gut-wrenching national process. Crazed leaders would not agonize about war, but democratic leaders would. Britain tried to appease Hitler at first, and the United States tried hard to avoid involvement in both the First and Second World Wars. Going to war used to be a tough decision. Hitler, Saddam Hussein, and George W. Bush didn't hesitate, or truly need a cause.

But with NATO, war now happens as a faceless bureaucratic routine. NATO took its first active military role in 1992, as a result of the breakup of Yugoslavia. The breakup was not accidental. The war that followed served the banks.

Yugoslavia 1999—a war that paid for itself

My parents visited Yugoslavia in the 1970s, years before the country broke up. It was a popular, affordable Mediterranean destination: welcoming people, plum brandy, good food, romantic towns, and lots of history. It was peaceful, stable, and prosperous. The nation had been created at the end of World War I when over 20 ethnic groups united in the area on the Adriatic Sea north of Greece and east of Italy.

Josip Tito ruled the country from 1945 until his death in 1980.[172] As a young man, he worked as a machinist, became a union member, and joined the Social Democratic Party. Prior to WW I, he worked for the Benz car company and was also a test driver for the Daimler Company. Then he served in the war, was wounded and captured. After the war, he became the leader of the emerging Communist Party, which took control in 1945. Under his leadership, the people acquired a decent standard of living, free education, and free health care: over 90% of the people were literate, and life expectancy was 72 years. Life was about as good as in North America, and in some ways better. The people had the right to jobs, and those jobs came with a one-month annual vacation. Their economy was a mixed market socialist economy, which had state-run enterprises, worker-run cooperatives, and "for profit" businesses. The nation, rather than be affiliated with NATO or Russia, was a non-aligned nation with no significant international debt. Tito was so revered by his people that his funeral in 1980 was the largest funeral for a statesman in recorded history.

In 1984, Reagan wrote a memo about changing the Yugoslav economy. The memo was secret, and the IMF approved loans to Yugoslavia with their usual terms of dismantling social services. What had been a healthy economy began a seven-year decline. By 1988, loans totalled $13.5 billion. Growth stopped, consumer prices went up 2,700%, and tens of thousands of people were laid off. In 1990, another "financial aid package" was delivered. Wages collapsed by 41%, and the banking system started to unravel.

---

172 http://topdocumentaryfilms.com/weight-chains/

Individual states began to declare independence, and civil war broke out.

In 1991, CIA agent Robert Baer landed by helicopter in Sarajevo. He's now a *Time Magazine* columnist and has written, in a yet-to-be-released book, about his role in the region. From Sarajevo, he moved to Slovenia, where he arrived with a few million dollars to fund organizations that would inflame hate in order to accelerate separation. "The aim of the propaganda was to divide the republics so they would break away from the motherland, Yugoslavia. We had to choose a scapegoat who would be blamed for everything. Someone who would be responsible for the war and violence. Serbia was chosen because in some ways it is a successor to Yugoslavia."[173]

NATO, using a new Orwellian term, started "humanitarian bombing" in March 1999. Seventy-eight days and 3,000 air attacks later, there were six nations instead of one and their collective debt had grown from what the IMF had said was a dangerously high $13.5 billion, to a wonderfully rewarding $184 billion dollars. The cost of the war was estimated at under $20 billion, a modest investment to provide Western banks the interest on about $184 billion in loans for years to come. The Yugoslav people were given no choice but to pay the interest.

The NATO "raids" were illegal, in violation of both the United Nations Charter and international law. However, the Security Council of the United Nations was a protagonist and provided a veil of legitimacy. The United Nations has 193 members, but the

---

173   From an interview in the British Serbian magazine; http://www.ebritic.com/?p=551270   http://awdnews.com/top-news/ex-cia-agent-we-got-millions-to-destroy-yugoslavia

power is in the Security Council. Five permanent members each have a veto: Russia, Britain, the United States, China, and France. They have control. Five, not 193 nations are united.

Despite the warnings of Butler, Eisenhower, and Galbraith

> They [the Marine corps] have a propaganda machine that is almost equal to Stalin's.
> —Harry S. Truman; Aug. 29, 1950

In 1997, the world was essentially at peace. It was so peaceful that Britain banned handguns and 121 countries signed a treaty banning landmines. There were no international wars. Tajikistan ended the only civil war in the world at that time. Nonetheless, a handful of Americans established a new think tank called The Project for a New American Century (PNAC). The "project" was as outrageous as its name: to have the United States dominate the world for the next one hundred years. The twenty-five founders included Dan Quayle, Jeb Bush, Dick Cheney, Donald Rumsfeld, Paul Wolfowitz, and Scooter Libby. Ten of the twenty-five founders became part of the second Bush administration.

Three years later, in September 2000, they released a paper entitled *Rebuilding America's Defenses: Strategy, Forces, and Resources for a New Century*, written for them by twenty-seven people, primarily from the military and military industrial complex. This ninety-page report called for the United States to increase its defense spending by $15 to $20 billion dollars annually, so it could fight "multiple wars at once."¹⁷⁴ They even listed the nations the United States should attack: North Korea, Iraq, Iran, Libya, and Syria. There was no explanation as to why and the tone was that no justification was required.

It was what Butler, Eisenhower, and Galbraith had all warned about: the military-corporate bureaucracy overreaching its role in defense and establishing national policy. The paper stated that the authors knew that the huge extra expenses would be a hard sell unless, as they foretold, there was "a Pearl Harbor like event." One year to the month after the release of the report, it happened: 9/11. The 342-page Patriot Act was passed, the huge increases in the military budgets were approved, and then PNAC faded away.

This self-appointed group met in secret and successfully got the multiple wars they sought: two to start Afghanistan and Iraq. But more significantly, they got billions of additional dollars poured into the American War Machine, which continues.

Iraq: pillaging a country

Since 1979, Iraq had been ruled by Saddam Hussein. He was ruthless, but he stabilized the country, ended both poverty and unemployment. The people got free health care, good education, and achieved the highest literary rate in the Middle East. He had never-ending battles and a reputation for killing anyone he saw as a threat. After his failed invasion of Kuwait in 1990, billions of dollars of reparations were charged against his country, a debt so

---

174   https://www.google.ca/webhp?gfe_rd=cr&ei=rAcuWNzyGcKC8QfPormoCQ#q=rebuilding+america's+defenses&*

large that the *Guardian* newspaper estimated it would take until 2125 to pay it off.

According to Paul O'Neil, who was G. W. Bush's Secretary of the Treasury, on January 20, 2001, Bush called his first National Security Council meeting, just days after becoming president, and he asked the Security Council to give him a reason to attack Iraq. From the beginning, he was planning war. Iraq was the second country on the Project for a New American Century's hit list. Eight months later was 9/11, and he had his reason. War followed.

Days after 9/11 on September 20, recently retired US Army Major General Wesley Clark visited the Pentagon, where he had served from 1966 to 2000. Clark was told by a serving general that the US was going to war against Iraq. This was top secret, and the two officers could see no reason for it. Congress knew nothing about it nor would Congress vote on it until over a year later—October 10, 2002. Even then, the war didn't begin until March 2003, but the decision, as Clark learned, had been made. In order to justify the war, Secretary of Defense Rumsfeld wrote a memo in November, asking his staff how to start a war with Iraq. He was one of the founders of the Project for A New American Century, so he was already committed. Rumsfeld came from a middle-class family, spent a couple of years in the Navy, and then went into politics. Somehow, he acquired a net worth of $15 million. Politics was apparently good for him, but Rumsfeld was not good for the military. In 2006, a number of generals demanded his resignation for his abysmal planning, and he resigned that November.

A few weeks after his mid-September Pentagon visit, General Clark was in the Pentagon again, the war on Afghanistan had started, the pending war against Iraq was confirmed, and then

Clark was told, "It's worse than that." A memo revealed that the US military was going to "take out" seven countries in five years: Iraq, Syria, Lebanon, Libya, Somalia, Sudan, and then Iran. (Clark's comments can be heard in an interview on YouTube.)[175] The Pentagon list of seven countries to be taken out was similar to that of The Project for a New American Century, with the additions of Lebanon, Somalia, and Sudan.

Since then, what's happened? Iraq was attacked. "Shock and awe," as Donald Rumsfeld said in 2003. Now, seventeen years after the PNAC list was created, Syria remains under attack: it's the only Mediterranean country with a state oil company and the only Arab country not indebted to the IMF. They have a country-owned National Bank.[176] Libya was attacked in 2011 (more below), and Iran has remained in the crosshairs.

Somalia has been a disaster since the 1980s, when its ten million people were the victim of IMF austerity policies. 50% of the population depended on cattle to survive in a nation that up until then provided all its own food. An IMF loan mandated that government veterinary services should be privatized. The nomadic cattlemen then had to have money to pay the vet and, predictably, cattle died, exports of meat plummeted, and so did Somalian food self-sufficiency. The world then sent food aid, which, as it usually does, destroyed the remaining local agricultural economy.

Sudan was a different story. Over forty million people lived in this third largest country in Africa, which has huge oil reserves, concentrated mainly in the south. Their major trading partner for

---

175   https://www.youtube.com/watch?v=SXS3vW47mOE
176   http://silentcrownews.com/wordpress/?p=5099

years has been China, which helped them develop their oil industry, becoming both a customer and an investor: China owns 40% of the Greater Nile Petroleum Operating Company. The West was not pleased, and in 2003, a conflict broke out in the western region called Darfur, which was used to divide the country. Even before the new country, now called South Sudan, was established, it applied to join the International Monetary Fund, and after South Sudan was officially created Conoco, Amoco, Chevron, and Phillips took control of the oil. Today, civil war continues, and a famine has resulted.

Lebanon, so far, is unscathed, the only country left unscathed on the target list. None of the countries targeted were members of the World Trade Organization, nor of the Bank for International Settlements.

Problems for Iraq did not end with the invasion of the country. In December 2005, the IMF provided a loan for $658 million on condition that subsidies to the people end and the market be given control. Overnight, the price of fuel increased nine-fold, the poverty rate rose by 30%, inflation skyrocketed, and food costs went up 20% a week. Some of the IMF money likely went to pay about $200 billion of old bank loans, dating back to the invasion of Kuwait. In 2015, the IMF provided another $833 million loan.

A decade before 9/11, Dick Cheney was Secretary of Defense for Bush Senior and he sub-contracted a study to Brown & Root (an American engineering company owned by Halliburton) on the subject of giving military contracts to private companies (no conflict of interest there!). That study somehow cost an unbelievable $8.5 million and was awarded the same year that Brown & Root got the contract to put out the hundreds of Desert Storm oil well fires. Cheney became Halliburton's CEO in 1995, and made millions from the company, some from selling oil well equipment to Hussein and more from the war contracts to destroy him.

Cheney personified the link between the War Machine and the financial markets.

KBR (a Halliburton subsidiary) got contracts worth $39.5 billion of the $138 billion in contracts awarded for Iraq and, as one critic[177] wrote, "for $40 billion, a single company may be willing to do a lot to keep a war alive. In the very least, it may not be eager to see it end." The Cheney family cashed in, and so did the Bush family. Ex-President Bush, Sr. was employed from 1998 to 2003 as senior advisor to Carlyle's Asia program, an investment firm involved in the arms industry whose clients included the Saudi Royals and the bin Laden families. Bush, Sr. was like Cheney, a link between war and crony capitalism.

In 2006, KBR was awarded another contract, this time for $385 million, by the Department of Homeland Security to build detention facilities for 6,700 people within the United States. Forbes reported in 2013 that Homeland Security had stocked 1.6 billion rounds of ammunition. For neither contract was there any explanation.

By late 2006, The Project for a New American Century had all but disappeared. It had wound down to a voice mailbox, and a few years later their websites were closed: mission accomplished!

G. W. Bush got the first $20 billion for the Iraq war approved by telling Congress that the war would largely "pay for itself." Payment

---

177   https://jonathanturley.org/2013/04/08/report-halliburton-subsidiary-received-39-5-billion-for-iraqi-war-alone/

would come from Iraqi oil revenues, estimated by Paul Wolfowitz at between $50–100 billion, and from the value of Iraqi assets that would be stolen. The reality is the price tag for the Iraqi War was about $11 trillion,[178] which the American people get to pay. The oil revenues and the value of assets "recovered" have gone to private industry and banks. Bush did not clarify what "paying for itself" meant but for some, he was right.

To make it pay for itself, there was a plan completed the month before the war began, a plan for the business takeover of Iraq. Baghdad fell in April, and in May 2003, Paul Bremer was appointed head of the Coalition Provisional Authority and ruled by decree. When he arrived, he didn't declare that the country was free of a monster or that the people could again have hope. He declared Iraq "open for business." The takeover plan called for massive privatization of Iraqi assets and included a year-long media campaign to convince the Iraqi people that this sell out was in their best interests.

Bremer created new laws. Order #39 privatized 200 Iraqi state companies in violation of regulations from the International Court of Justice. *The Economist* called it "a capitalist dream"! Order #81 was the Patent, Industrial Design, Undisclosed Information, Integrated Circuits and Plant Variety Law. It said in part that, "farmers shall be prohibited from re-using seeds of protected varieties or any variety mentioned in items 1 and 2 of paragraph (C) of Article 14 of this Chapter." The Iraqi government's historic national seed

---

178 The number comes from William K. Black, a former bank regulator. http://backbillblack.com/

bank vanished. Monsanto must have been pleased. War, as General Butler had said, is always about money.

Not only did many of Bremer's acts run counter to international law, but they were also in contravention of the US army Code of War.

After the war, the United States built the largest and most expensive embassy in the world in Baghdad: twenty-seven buildings on 104 acres, an area the size of Vatican City, to employ 15,000 people. It was a $750 million project, small change, given that almost $12 billion sent from the US American money simply disappeared.[179]

In a cabinet meeting, Vice President Dick Cheney once said that Reagan had proved that deficits don't matter. What did he mean? Did he mean that they don't matter in terms of getting elected, or that they didn't matter because the rich were getting richer, so who cared if the nation was getting poorer? It is possible he meant that they did not matter in his era (2007) because, despite the increasingly unpayable US government debts, the United States continued to prosper.

In the poorest countries, debts must be paid. The chart below shows the steady growth of debt in the United States compared to the gross domestic product. From the left, you see the declining residual debt from the Second World War, as it was steadily paid down until after Carter. Then economics changed. Today, the US debt is almost certainly unpayable.

---

179   https://www.theguardian.com/world/2007/feb/08/usa.iraq1

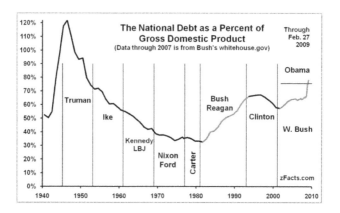

Despite the debt, the United States continues to expand its plans for global control. In 2006, it established its Africa Command (AFRICOM) in Stuttgart Germany to oversee operations in 53 African nations, an idea the Heritage Foundation proposed to them a few years earlier. One report was that AFRICOM was created to bring "peace, security, democracy, and economic growth" to Africans. AFRICOM's website more honestly states that it exists to "advance US national interests."

In 2012, the Pentagon awarded a contract for $80 million to Lockheed Martin to develop top secret "malware" and other computer-to-computer weapons that allow the military to take control of rockets, airplanes, or nuclear generators anywhere. In June 2013, *The Guardian* newspaper reported that Obama issued a top-secret order to have the Joint Chiefs of Staff draw up a list of cyber targets using new technologies, which will result in new war industry profits.[180]

---

180   Directive Twenty. http://www.theguardian.com/world/2013/jun/07/obama-china-targets-cyber-overseas

Since the 2003 invasion of Iraq, public perception of the military has been coloured by the use of "embedded" reporters, reporters who truly are no longer reporters because they have given up their journalistic freedom. They agree to have their reports censured in exchange for not being shot at. Not a courageous trade.

Canadian journalist Scott Taylor, the author of *Unembedded: Two Decades of Maverick War Reporting*,[181] explained this to me over dinner in a pub one night in Toronto. An "embedded reporter" is an oxymoron: the line between reporting and propaganda has been crossed.

The business of war is abetted by the psychopathic nature of capital as James Petras, Professor (Emeritus) of Sociology at Binghamton University, New York, whom I quoted earlier, sums up:

> The power and influence of the military-industrial complex in promoting serial wars has resulted in extraordinary rates of profit. According to a recent study by Morgan Stanley (cited in Barron's, 6/9/14, p. 19), shares in the major US arms manufacturers have risen 27,699% over the past fifty years versus 6,777% for the broader market. In the past three years alone, Raytheon has returned 124%, Northrup Grumman 114% and Lockheed Martin 149% to their investors.[182]

---

181 Taylor, Scott. *Two Decades of Maverick War Reporting*. Douglas & McIntyre, 2009.
182 http://www.globalresearch.ca/the-soaring-profits-of-the-military-industrial-complex-the-soaring-costs-of-military-casualties/5388393

Libya, 2011: protecting the dollar and stealing the oil

Libya is a country just west of Egypt and almost twice as big. It has only six million people compared to Egypt's ninety million. Under its sand is the largest proven reserve of oil in Africa, the ninth largest in the world. Muammar Gaddafi came to power in 1967, and over the decades, Libya's economy changed from one of the poorest countries to the wealthiest in Africa. Never short of confidence, his persona morphed from national hero to international pariah. He exploited the nation's oil and provided the people with free health care, free education, free electricity, and interest-free loans. The nation had no debt and $150 billion invested outside their country. Goldman Sachs had sold them $1.3 billion of options on currencies and stocks. China for many years had been a customer, an investor, and on some projects a partner.

In 2009, Gaddafi announced he intended to stop selling their oil in American dollars. Libya was attacked on March 19, 2011, when NATO (with United Nations Security Council approval) declared a "no-fly zone" over the country, a "humanitarian" intervention. This innocuous sounding declaration effectively declares war and disallows the nation the ability to defend itself. Over the next six months, NATO aircraft destroyed 640 targets, killed about 10,000 people, and injured 50,000. The war was over in six months, and British Defense Secretary Philip Hammond praised the departing troops as he welcomed business leaders from England and France. They arrived on what *The Guardian* referred to as their "spoils of war" tour. Hammond advised businesses to "pack their bags" for Libya, because there was more to be had.

The Libyan people, now "freed" from their dictator, no longer had a debt-free country but owed $5.3 billion to the international banking community. What had been Africa's richest country was turned into a "failed state," its economy in shambles, $39 billion in state assets were "frozen." Various militias were fighting for control, and oil production had all but stopped. NATO ruined the country, then left.

In September 2016, a bipartisan committee of the British House of Commons released a report that revealed that there had been no justification for the war, that it was not about protecting civilians but was about changing the regime, about economics, oil, and money, that it had ruined the nation, devastated the people, and made the world less safe.[183]

Today, the financialized corporate military industries use NATO as their agent of change, and the United Nations Security Council has been reduced to a rubber stamp. At one time, when the UN embarked on a military mission, they set up their own troops, the guys in the blue hats. Now it's NATO, the pro-Western, pro-business, non-government army that takes over, anywhere. It has experienced "mission creep" to become the self-proclaimed, almost global police force. Individual nations no longer declare war: NATO automatically does that for them.

The Ukraine: stealing a country's riches

Ukraine is a country in Eastern Europe—almost in Asia, east of Poland, Slovenia, Hungary, and Romania, and south of Moscow

---

183 http://www.salon.com/2016/09/16/u-k-parliament-report-details-how-natos-2011-war-in-libya-was-based-on-lies/

and Belarus—and it has been immersed in violence and war since 2014.

The steps to take over Ukraine began just after World War Two.

Although 43% of Europeans today believe it was the US that won the Second World War, the war was in its third year before the US even entered the war. It took the combined forces from nine nations to defeat Hitler. It was Russian troops that freed nearly half of Europe, and the USSR lost at least nine million soldiers. Casualties in the West were minute by comparison: Americans about four hundred thousand soldiers, the Brits the same. Canada lost forty thousand. In the peace accords, Germany was required to pay reparations: 50% to Russia, the balance to others. That split confirms how the victors perceived their contributions.

The war had devastated Ukraine. It had been part of and was returned to the Soviet Union, and it bloomed once again: their farmers made it the breadbasket for the region. It became an industrial leader, with a stable, planned economy. The people designed and made the Antonov aircraft, still the largest airplane in the world. The country has forty-five million people, mainly Ukrainian. A minority (17%) are Russian. Ukrainian and Russian are two of 18 languages spoken.

In 1991, the Soviet Union broke into a dozen separate countries, and Ukraine was one of them. Fifteen new countries emerged: Russia was one with a name we knew. Other names we have learned; Armenia, Belarus, Tajikistan, and Uzbekistan. As the old Soviet Union broke up, it provided opportunity for Western capitalism to expand into a handful of new nations and scoop up new businesses, usually for a song.

In 1994, the American-Ukrainian Advisory Committee (AUAC) was formed, and Henry Kissinger was a member. This private group, as Dr. Laurence Shoup describes, "suggested policies to the U.S. government, including U.S. training for Ukrainian militarily officers, promoting free enterprise and privatization programs in the Ukraine."[184] Behind the scenes, Western organizations, such as the National Endowment for Democracy, and the Centre for Private Enterprise, moved in to influence Ukrainian elections.

In 1998, the IMF made a first loan of $2.2 billion to the Ukraine with the usual conditions. One was selling government-owned shares in businesses, including grain elevators, and the price of bread rose overnight by 300%. Other conditions caused electricity to go up by 600%. Then subsidies on household natural gas ended and prices went up by 50%. This had to be galling to the people, since their country sits on 42 trillion cubic feet of shale gas, which the people believed belonged to them. (The estimate as to the size of the field comes from the United States Energy Information Administration, which tracks energy resources everywhere in the world.)

In November 2013, the *New York Times* reported that Chevron had signed a fifty-year deal with the Ukraine government to develop Ukrainian oil and gas. In 2014, the IMF approved another loan, this time for $17.1 billion, and this loan required cutting 24,000 government jobs, cutting pensions, raising taxes, and more privatization of assets. (With these billion-dollars loans, no real money changes hands. The IMF creates a loan out of thin air as

---

[184] Shoup, Laurence. *Wall Street's Think Tank: The Council on Foreign Relations and the Empire of Neoliberal Geopolitics, 1976-2014.* New York: Monthly Review Press, 2015.

a credit to Ukraine. Then the credit is transferred through the Ukraine to the banks to pay down existing debts. For doing such easy, risk-free business, the bankers pay themselves bonuses and the people of Ukraine face decades of higher taxes and lower incomes.) One clause of the IMF agreement says that Ukraine will cooperate to extend the use of biotechnologies. This allowed Monsanto to extend genetically modified crops into Europe, which for years had been prohibited.

The United States' involvement in Ukraine became most explicit in 2014, when CIA director John Brennan arrived in the country. He wasn't on vacation.

In 2014, the US passed a bill creating sanctions against Russian banking and energy and also to privatize Ukraine infrastructure, including electricity, oil, and gas. Bill number H.R. 5859—misnamed the Ukraine Freedom Support Act of 2014—is a bill attacking Russia and restarting the Cold War. It created new sanctions against Russia, provides money for propaganda and arms for Ukraine. Millions were authorized for use in supporting "democratic government"—newspeak for buying elections. The US would not take kindly to China or Russia providing influence on elections in America, as demonstrated by the uproar over claims Russia interfered with the US Election of 2016.

To keep it below the radar, the bill was introduced in the morning and rammed through the same night by the four people in the House.[185] In the same month, in Kiev, the Ukrainian Parliament

---

185 https://www.congress.gov/bill/113th-congress/house-bill/5859/actions

approved a plan to declare itself a military state and applied to join NATO. No doubt, the events were coordinated.

The interrelationship between banking/finance, trade, politics, and the military is unambiguous. It transcends national rights, individuals' rights and freedoms.

The economist Michael Hudson wrote, "Bear in mind that finance today is war by non-military means. The aim of getting a country in debt is to obtain its economic surplus, ending up with its property."[186] The steps are to lend a country money that the people will never see; it will go to the banks. However, the people will get to pay the interest and the debt. Then confuse them with economics as you steal their resources.

A handful of Ukrainians did well. According to *Forbes Magazine*, nine people became billionaires in the ten years following the phoney Ukraine orange revolution and rigged election. On December 10, 2008, the *Kyev Post* stated:

> It took some of America's robber barons many years to amass their enormous wealth. For example, John D. Rockefeller needed more than 30 years to become America's first billionaire. In contrast, Ukraine's (nine) billionaires achieved the same feat in less than half that time, thanks to the way privatizations were carried out from 1991 to 2004. As a result, billions of dollars in national wealth and potential state revenues were sold on the cheap to insiders.

---

186 https://www.rt.com/op-edge/170960-economy-imf-ukraine-oligarchs/

In 2015, Hudson published *Killing the Host, How Financial Parasites and Debt Destroy the Global Economy*,[187] about how Wall Street has become a parasite devouring Americans' savings, and how banks and corporations have taken over the role of government planning so that the system serves finance as opposed to, as it once did, serving the real economy. Wall Street is the tapeworm, as discussed in my last chapter.

There is a split evolving between Europeans and the agenda of international corporations. The corporations want Ukraine inside their tent as a member of NATO, to encircle the old Soviet Union in preparation for the next war. Europeans, on the other hand, with more vivid memories of World War II, are not so eager. The problem is that the farther we get from those memories, the more the risk of another European war increases.

In February 2014, the IMF approved a loan for $40 billion for "improving living standards for the Ukrainian people." It came with more of the usual conditions: lay off 10% of Ukraine's public employees, raise the retirement age, abolish old age benefits, and abolish payments to victims of the Chernobyl disaster.[188] It forced the country to allow a flexible exchange rate for their currency, which reduced the value of their money. With their money worth less, the value of their wages and savings went down; by two-thirds.

The new loan money would go to the banks to pay off part of past loans (they owe $140 billion) and to pay current interest. Despite what was claimed, nothing went to help the people. If it

---

187   Hudson, Michael. *Killing the Host, How Financial Parasites and Debt Destroy the Global Economy*. CounterPunch, 2015. https://store.counterpunch.org/product/killing-the-host-digital-book/
188   https://www.imf.org/external/np/sec/pr/2015/pr1550.htm

follows the usual pattern, $1–2 million will disappear. The living standards of Ukrainians have gone down, not up, as was repeatedly promised. What was once a stable, prosperous country has been described by the World Bank, in 2014, as a poor country.

Profiting from war: summary

> War against a foreign country only happens when the moneyed classes think they are going to profit from it.
> —George Orwell

> Military leaders benefit from mobilizations and war … promotions are more rapid and officers retire at higher pensions. Once one reaches the rank of major or lieutenant general, private and Pentagon consulting opportunities abound as do military/security corporate directorships in the "defense" industry. The financial rewards make the generals complicit in the propaganda of ever present "threats," whether "terrorist," Muslim, Russian, or Chinese.
> —Paul Craig Roberts; Economist; Assistant Secretary of the Treasury, 1981-1982[189]

During my life, I have "stumbled" onto things. In 1987, I was employed by an emerging telephone company, Palco Telecom, and I travelled to a number of our locations: one was in Huntsville Alabama, where the Redstone Arsenal sits on the edge of town. It's a military base and the home of NASA's Marshall Space

---

189   Roberts, Paul Craig. Interview, November, 2014.

Flight Center. Werner Von Braun, of Nazi rocket fame, worked there from the 1950s to the 1970s. In December 2014, NASA fired a rocket, preparing for manned flight beyond the moon using Huntsville resources.

Everyone in the town in the 1970s was aware that millions of dollars of assets were missing from the base! No one could tell me exactly how much, but they speculated it was anything from Jeeps, to money, to rockets. Sometime later, I learned that the Army, despite laws to the contrary, had not produced an audited financial report for years. Up until then, I had believed that the government obeyed the law.

In September 2001, as I discussed earlier, on the eve of 9/11, Donald Rumsfeld explained that $2.3 trillion was missing from the Department of Defense.

These issues and the timing of them have since the seventies interested me; there were economic, financial, and political ramifications. I've more recently had the opportunity to meet many of the researchers on the events of 9/11 (engineers, architects, chemists, economists, pilots, police, and military analysts).

There were two major conferences on the subject in Toronto: the first in May 2004, and again in 2011, when I was one of a dozen patrons at the 10-year anniversary of the event. Over four days, sixteen researchers from around the world presented their research to a jury of four people, who were asked to evaluate the events of what happened on 9/11, including the science such as engineering, economics, architecture, and microchemistry. Judge Ferdinando Imposimato, an Italian magistrate and honorary president of the Supreme Court of Italy, was one of the four judges and he wrote the final report on the jury's behalf. (In 2015, he was nominated as a candidate for the Italian presidential election.)

The panel of four concluded that there was enough evidence of a cover-up and possible criminality to warrant a proper investigation. Horrific crimes had been committed on 9/11, including the murder of almost three thousand people, aircraft hijackings, and three building collapses, yet none of the normal investigations for murder or hijacking or building failures were undertaken.[190] The panel concluded that this was justification enough for the International Criminal Court at The Hague to conduct an inquiry.

War and contemporary economics are easier to understand if you follow the money, even for the events of 9/11.

Only three months into his presidency, Eisenhower spoke to the American Society of Newspaper Editors about the reality of arms spending. "Every gun that is made, every warship launched, every rocket fired signifies, in the final sense, a theft from those who hunger and are not fed, those who are cold and are not clothed."

About 2.4% of global trade is the military/arms economy, which has now been called the "Permanent War Economy." Back in the 1990s, both Thatcher and Bush, Sr., talked of a Peace Dividend that would result from a reduction in military spending. That never happened. It is easy to see why.

One problem with the policy of the OPEC nations receiving American dollars for their oil is how to get the American dollars back to America. One way is investments: Wall Street bankers and brokers love it. Of the almost $70 billion of US overseas arms

---

190   http://torontohearings.org/ Also: see James Gourley's book listed in the bibliography following.

sales in 2011, over half—Apache and Black Hawk helicopters, for example—were sold to Saudi Arabia, which could then sell them, and do what they liked with the money such as fund militants. Whatever they do completes the loop: oil—currency—wars, and back.

Cui bono? Who benefits? Follow the money.

> The more a society drifts from truth, the more it will hate those who speak it.
> —George Orwell

Thanks
to those folks who helped with this book:

MARTY NORD, A VANDERBILT UNIVERSITY PROFESSOR AND BUSIness coach, encouraged me to try to understand current economics and that supported the research that became this book. Sadly, we have lost her.

My eyes were opened by Leila Williams, a strongly opinionated fan of her mythology of capitalism who showed me how essential this book was. Then there was Larry Logan and Richard Harville, two Republican friends who lost a party to vote for, and Blyth Brown, a Canadian Conservative who suffered the same fate. (Richard did the math on exponential interest in chapter 6).

And thanks to the dozen people who helped improve the chapter on money: Bob Brodie, Ed Lukow, Jim Harris, Bob Lewis, Jody Davis, Doug Swallow, Larry Logan, Richard Harville, and Ron Cooper in England. Thanks also to Bob Eady in Canada, and Rick and Aura Ferrando in Michigan.

Bob and Joanne Klassing provided early encouragement, as did Bill Nichols, who found the draft wordy. Thanks to Chris and Jenni for personal insights. And to Patout Burns from Vanderbilt University, who provided the most eloquent detail on the Catholic history of usury.

David Macdonald, the senior economist of the Canadian Centre for Policy Alternatives provided help for Chapter Five, and Jeannie Alexander and the folks at the No Exceptions Prison Collective in Tennessee helped with the cruel economics of incarceration.

Thanks, also, to my friend, the economist Michel Chossudovsky, who provided encouragement.

And to my patient supporting partner in life, Paula, who wonders why I find economics this important but knows the adverse way economics is shaping their lives.

> Remember, I'm pulling for you. We're all in this together!
> —Red Green, a.k.a. Steve Smith, Canadian comedian

Bibliography

Atwood, Margaret	*Payback: Debt and the Shadow Side of Wealth.* Toronto: House of Anansi Press, 2008.
Banerjee, Duffo	*Poor Economics: A Radical Rethinking of the Way to Fight Poverty*, New York, Public Affairs, 2011
Batra, Ravi	*Greenspan's Fraud: How Two Decades of His Policies Have Undermined the Global Economy.* New York: Palgrave McMillan, 2005.
Bowden, Charles	*Down By the River: Drugs, Money, Murder and Family.* Simon and Schuster, 2002
Brown, Ellen	*Web of Debt.* Baton Rouge: Third Millennium Press, 2007.
	The Public Bank Solution. Baton Rouge: Third Millennium Press, 2013.
Buchan, James	*The Authentic Adam Smith – His Live and Ideas,* New York, W. W. Norton, 2006

Chossudovsky, Michel	*The Globalization of Poverty*. Montreal: Global Research 2003.
	The Global Economic Crisis: The Great Depression of the XXI Century. Coauthored by Andrew Gavin Marshall. Montreal: Global Research 2010.
Davenport-Hines, Richard	*Universal Man: The Seven Lives of John Maynard Keynes*. London: William Collins, 2015.
Elon, Amos	*Founder: A Portrait of the First Rothschild and his Time*. New York: Viking Penguin, 1996.
Friedman, Milton	*Money Mischief: Episodes in Monetary History*. Orlando: Harcourt Brace, 1992.
Galbraith, James K.	*The Predator State*. New York: Free Press – Simon and Schuster, 2008.
	The Collapse of Monetarism and the Irrelevance of the New Monetary Consensus was the title of a speech given by James Galbraith at the 25th Milton Friedman Distinguished Lecture at Marietta College, Marietta Ohio, 2008.
	The End of Normal. New York: Simon and Schuster, 2014.
Galbraith, John Kenneth	*The Great Crash 1929*. Boston: Houghton Mifflin, 1954.
	The New Industrial State. Princeton: Princeton University Press, 1967.
	How to Control the Military. New York: Signet Books, 1969.

Economics and the Public Purpose. Boston: Houghton Mifflin. 1973.
Money: Whence it Came, Where it Went. Boston: Houghton Mifflin, 1975.
The Age of Uncertainty. Boston: Houghton Mifflin, 1977.
The Nature of Mass Poverty. Cambridge: Harvard University Press, 1979.
The Anatomy of Power. Boston: Houghton Mifflin, 1983.
The Voice of the Poor. Cambridge: Harvard University Press, 1983.
The Culture of Contentment. Boston: Houghton Mifflin, 1992.
A Short History of Financial Euphoria. New York: Whittle Books, 1994.
A Journey through Economic Time: A Firsthand View. Boston: Houghton Mifflin, 1994.
The Good Society: The Humane Agenda. Boston: Houghton Mifflin, 1996.
Name Dropping. Boston: Houghton Mifflin, 1999.
The Economics of Innocent Fraud, Truth for Our Time. Boston: Houghton Mifflin, 2004.

Goodhart, C.A.E. *The Basel Committee on Banking Supervision: A History of the Early Years.* Cambridge: Cambridge University Press, 2011.

Gourley, James (Ed)	*The 9/11 Toronto Report; International Hearings on The Events of September 11, 2001.* International Center for 9/11 Studies, 2012.
Greider, William	*Secrets of the Temple: How the Federal Reserve Runs the Country.* New York: Simon & Schuster, 1987.
Grey, Judge James P.	*Why Our Drug Laws Have Failed: A Judicial Indictment of the War on Drugs.* Philadelphia: Temple University Press, 2001
Griffin, G. Edward	*The Creature from Jekyll Island.* California: American Media, 1994.
Harvey, David	*A Brief History of Neo Liberalism.* Oxford: Oxford University Press, 2005. *The Enigma of Capital and the Crisis of Capitalism.* Oxford: Oxford University Press, 2010. *A Companion to Marx's Capital.* London: Verso, 2010. *Seventeen Contradictions and the End of Capitalism.* Oxford: Oxford University Press, 2014.
Heilbroner, Robert	*The Worldly Philosophers.* New York: Simon & Schuster, 1953.
Hellyer, Paul T.	*The Money Mafia: A World in Crisis.* Walterville: Trine Day, 2014
Herman, Arthur	*How the Scots Invented the Modern World: The True Story of How Western Europe's Poorest Nation Created our World & Everything in it.* New York: Random House, 2001.

Hopsicker, Daniel	*Barry and the Boys: The CIA, the Mob and America's Secret History*. Walterville: Trine Day, 2006.
Hudson, Michael	*Killing the Host: How Financial Parasites and Debt Destroy the Global Economy*. Germany: Islet Publishing, 2015.
Kennedy, Margrit	*Inflation and Free Money: Creating an Exchange Medium that Works for Everybody and Protects the Earth*. Okemos: Seva International, 1987.
Keynes, John Maynard	*Essays in Persuasion*. London, Macmillan and Co., 1931.
Kierans, Eric, with Stewart, Walter.	*Remembering*. Toronto: Stoddard Publishing, 2001.
Klein, Naomi	*The Shock Doctrine: the Rise of Disaster Capitalism*. New York: Metropolitan Books, 2007.
	This Changes Everything: Capitalism vs. the Climate. Toronto: Alfred A. Knopf, 2014.
Krehm, William	*A Power Unto Itself: The Bank of Canada – The Threat to Our Nation's Economy*. Toronto: Stoddard Publishing, 1993.
	Meltdown: Money, Debt and the Wealth of Nations. Toronto: Comer Publications, 1999.
Lancaster, John	*Whoops! Why Everyone Owed Everyone and No One Can Pay*. London: Penguin, 2010. Lancaster is a British journalist and this book is about the 2007 crisis from his London perspective.

Landes, David	*The Wealth and Poverty of Nations: Why Some are so Rich and Some so Poor.* New York: W. W. Norton, 1998. Among his observations: the invention of bifocals was one of the most significant inventions for the betterment of mankind; they doubled the lifetime contribution of craftsmen.
LaPavitas, Costas	*Profiting Without Producing: How Finance Exploits Us All.* London: Verso, 2013.
Lebor, Adam	*Tower of Basel: The Shadowy History of the Secret Bank that Runs the World.* New York: PublicAffairs, 2013.
Livesey, Bruce.	*Thieves of Bay Street: How Banks, Brokerages, and the Wealthy Steal Billions from Canadians.* Toronto: Vintage, 2012.
Lofgren, Mike	*The Deep State.* New York: Penguin Books, 2016.
Madrick, Jeff.	*Seven Bad Ideas: How Mainstream Economists Have Damaged America and the World.* New York: Alfred A. Knopf, 2014.
Mayer, Martin	*The Fate of the Dollar.* New York Times Books 1980.
Morris, Charles R.	*The Tycoons: How Andrew Carnegie, John C. Rockefeller, Jay Gould and J. P. Morgan Invented the American Economy.* New York: Times Books, 2005.
Palast, Greg	*The Best Democracy Money Can Buy.* New York: A Plume Book – Penguin, 2003.

	Armed Madhouse; From Baghdad to New Orleans – Sordid Secrets and Strange Tales of a White House Gone Wild. New York: Dutton, 2006.
	Democracy and Regulation: How the Public Govern Essential Services. With Oppenheim and MacGregor. London: Pluto Press, 2008.
	Vultures Picnic. New York, Dutton, Penguin Books, 2011.
Perkins, John	*Confessions of an Economic Hit Man.* Oakland: Berrett-Koehler Publishers, 2004.
Prins, Nomi	*All the Presidents' Bankers: The Hidden Alliances the Drive American Power.* New York: Nation Books, 2014.
Rifkin, Jeremy	*The End of Work: The Decline of the Global Labor Force and the Dawn of the Post-Market Era.* New York: G. P. Putnam's Sons, 1995.
Roberts, Paul Craig	*The Failure of Laissez Faire Capitalism.* Atlanta: Clarity Press, 2013.
Samuelson, Paul	*Economics: An Introductory Analysis.* Sixth Edition. New York: McGraw Hill, 1964.
Scott, Peter Dale	*The American Deep State.* Maryland: Rowman & Littlefield, 2015.
Smith, Adam.	*An Inquiry into The Nature and Causes of The Wealth of Nations.* Washington, Regency Publishing edition, 1998.
Smith, Adam [George J. W. Goodman]	*Paper Money.* New York: Summit Books, 1981.

	The Roaring '80s. New York: Summit Books, 1988.
Stanford, Jim	*Economics for Everyone: A Short Guide to the Economics of Capitalism*. Ottawa: Fernwood Publishing, 2008.
Stewart, Walter	*Towers of Gold, Feet of Clay: The Canadian Banks*. Toronto: Collins, 1982.
	Bank Heist: How our Financial Giants Are Costing You Money. Toronto: Harper Perennial Canada, 1997.
Stiglitz, Joseph E.	*Globalization and its Discontents*. New York: W. W. Norton, 2002.
Varoufakis, Yanis	*And the Weak Suffer What They Must? Europe's Crisis and America's Economic Future*. New York: Nation Books, 2016.
Weeks, John	*Economics of the 1%: How Mainstream Economics Serves the Rich, Obscures Reality and Distorts Policy*. New York: Anthem Press, 2014.
	Weeks is an American economist, Professor Emeritus University of London. He uses the term "fakeconomics."

Note: an index is available on a free pdf version of this file on the Insidersmemoir.com web site. I can be reached at aninsidersmemoir@gmail.com.

Gordon Bryant Brown

INTERESTING OPPORTUNITIES WIDENED BRYANT'S KNOWLEDGE OF economics. He worked in corporate and private business and was involved with a few business turnarounds. He was owner and chief executive officer of one of Canada's "50 Best-Managed Businesses." He was asked to teach business management in Kenya, which taught him about Third World poverty, and he was asked to advise the Canadian Government on marijuana legislation, which taught him about money laundering.

He also served as a director of a Chamber of Commerce, a founding director of a YMCA/YWCA, vice chairman of Oxfam Canada, and on the board of two credit unions. He served on the Public Library Board and Art Gallery Boards in London, Ontario. He is married, with grown children, and splits his time between Ontario, Tennessee, and the Florida Keys.

Written for the next generation

"There is so much wuv in the world!" Taylor O'Malley, great-granddaughter, when she was 7.

"You're teaching me!!!" Jaden LaRocque, grandson, when he was 6.

CPSIA information can be obtained
at www.ICGtesting.com
Printed in the USA
LVHW01s0310070618
579880LV00004B/7/P